Work, Labour, and Professions in the Roman World

Impact of Empire

ROMAN EMPIRE, C. 200 B.C.–A.D. 476

VOLUME 23

The titles published in this series are listed at *brill.com/imem*

Work, Labour, and Professions in the Roman World

Edited by

Koenraad Verboven
Christian Laes

TUTA SUB AEGIDE PALLAS · 1683 ·

BRILL

LEIDEN | BOSTON

Cover illustration: 'Altar of Atimetus and Epaphra. 18th century drawing showing two scenes from Atimetus' professional life depicted on the sides of the altar. Left: retail scene with market stall. Right: manufacturing scene in the workshop. Drawing ascribed to Vicenzo Dolcibene. British Museum (AN1047418001)

Library of Congress Cataloging-in-Publication Data

Names: Verboven, Koenraad, editor of compilation. | Laes, Christian, editor of compilation.
Title: Work, labour, and professions in the Roman world / edited by Koenraad Verboven, Christian Laes.
Other titles: Work, labor, and professions in the Roman world
Description: Leiden ; Boston : Brill, 2016. | Series: Impact of empire : Roman Empire, c. 200 B.C.–A.D. 476, ISSN 1572-0500 ; volume 23 | Includes bibliographical references and indexes.
Identifiers: LCCN 2016035591 | ISBN 9789004331655 (hardback : acid-free paper) | ISBN 9789004331686 (e-book)
Subjects: LCSH: Labor—Rome—History. | Working class—Rome—History. | Professions—Rome—History. | Human capital—Rome—History. | Slavery—Rome—History. | Rome—Economic conditions. | Rome—Social conditions. | Rome—History—Republic, 265–30 B.C. | Rome—History—Empire, 30 B.C.–476 A.D.
Classification: LCC HD4844 .W67 2016 | DDC 331.10937—dc23
LC record available at https://lccn.loc.gov/2016035591

Typeface for the Latin, Greek, and Cyrillic scripts: "Brill". See and download: brill.com/brill-typeface.

ISSN 1572-0500
ISBN 978-90-04-33165-5 (hardback)
ISBN 978-90-04-33168-6 (e-book)

This book is printed on acid-free paper and produced in a sustainable manner.

Contents

Preface

This is the second book of the research programme 'Factors of Production in the Roman World', initiated in 2009 by the Roman Society Research Centre, our joint research group at the University of Ghent and the Flemish Free University of Brussels. In 2012, the programme was taken over by the international research network 'Structure and Determinants of Economic Performance in the Roman World', funded by the Flanders Research Foundation (FWO Vlaanderen). The first volume in the programme, *Ownership and Exploitation of Land and Natural Resources in the Roman World*, was published by Oxford University Press in 2015. The third, on *Capital, Investment and Innovation in the Roman World*, is currently in preparation.

The aim of our programme is to unravel the driving forces behind the long-term development of Roman economic performance. We study the Romans' approach to land, natural resources, labour and capital; their modes of exploitation, management and organisation of natural, human, financial and man-made resources, as well as how they thought about these issues. We ask what the logic was behind the choices they made, and how this affected economic outcomes. As information on production factors in the Roman world derives from historical and archaeological sources in the widest possible sense, the programme is inevitably multidisciplinary, involving the work of specialists in various fields—historians, archaeologists, and scholars from other disciplines. It is also explicitly comparative since only in this way can we meaningfully relate different or similar outcomes (performance) to different or similar structures. Both orientations call for a broader theoretical framework to facilitate a mutually fruitful communication between disciplines. In line with the *Cambridge Economic History of the Greco-Roman World* (2007) we have adopted a neo-institutionalist frame. We assume that institutions ('the rules of the game'—formal laws and regulations, as well as informal conventions and customs) determine transaction costs and thereby lay out the incentive structure of society upon which people act. While institutions determine the shape and form of a society's organisational units, however, they are themselves determined by the value systems, mentalities and world views prevalent in that society. The advantage of this approach, in our view, is that it makes the work of cultural, social and economic historians/archaeologists relevant to each other, thus enabling a more realistic account of the past in which 'the economic' is not separated for analytical purposes from the rest of society, without denying the presence of price-setting markets and therefore the validity of key concepts from neoclassical economics. It allows us also to focus on the specifically Roman institutional set-up, which may have been conducive to growth in ways that might not fit the European experience since c. 1700.

Measured by the quantity, the quality, and the variety of its material production the economic success of the Roman Empire, was unparalleled (with the possible exception of Song China) until the early modern period. Favourable natural conditions, capital accumulation, technology and political stability greatly contributed to this success, but ultimately economic performance depended on the empire's ability to mobilize, train and direct human efforts. This book sets out to study the various ways in which this was realized, how these processes were regulated, and how they shaped society.

After an introductory chapter ('Work, Labour, Profession. What's in a Name') we open with two chapters that study the role of (semi-)dependent labour. **Arjan Zuiderhoek** studies the persistence of pre-Roman dependence relations in Asia Minor. He argues that this persistence was not the cause for the under-development of labour markets (as argued by Finley), but rather a response to it. **Cameron Hawkins** uses the theory of the firm to analyse the role of slaves and freedmen in Roman urban workshops during the Principate, arguing very similarly that labour markets for skilled labour were tight, forcing entrepreneurs to invest in slaves rather than rely on free wage labourers.

The following chapters move attention to wage labour and its relation to dependent and coerced labour. **Seth Bernard** shows how the Roman building sector relied on a mix of labour regimes. Contractors hired independent craftsmen who worked with their slave assistants and apprentices. The huge need for unskilled and lowly skilled labour was filled by free wage workers. Standing staffs for maintenance and repairs were made up of slaves, who also provided skilled labour. Corvée and penal labour was used for routine maintenance. **Claire Holleran** argues that although slavery and patronage distorted the Roman labour market, the possibilities of finding free salaried workers were effective enough to preclude structural labour shortages. Social networks and *collegia* pooled and conveyed information regarding the character and skills of workers. Day labourers commonly congregated in particular areas like *fora* or quays. Trust relations could grow as day labourers were rehired. **Miriam Groen-Vallinga** and **Laurens Tacoma** study the underlying structure of Diocletian's Prices Edict, which, they argue, reflects the structure of the Roman labour market. Except for skill levels—which typically doubled remuneration—the Edict shows little differentiation. The absence of differentiation based on legal status confirms, according to the authors, that slave and free labour were each other's substitutes. The diversity of 'urban' professions compared to the generic concept of 'rural workers', reflects a much greater division of labour in urban than in rural contexts. Wage levels for unskilled labour were insufficient to feed a family, implying that women and children as well had to work—a situation best described by the model of the 'adaptive family economy'.

After this we move on to how material working conditions reflected and affected social relations between workers. **Elizabeth Murphy** studies different types of pottery workshops to establish the organisation of labour. She advocates the use of the 'workgroup' as the main analytical unit, rather than the (material) 'workshop'. Workgroups were part of larger communities with workers being neighbours, family and friends. Religious rituals were performed inside or close to workplaces. Housing units were often adjacent to workplaces and in some cases work spaces were even used as burial places for infants and still-borns. Murphy concludes that labour organisation cannot be understood in isolation of the social organisation of the communities to which the workers belonged. **Miko Flohr** asks how the 'communicative landscape' of *tabernae*, domestic workshops and production halls affected the formation of occupational social identities. While communication was strong in the household based groups (the *tabernae* and domestic workshops), production halls favoured fragmented communication in smaller clusters. The staffs of large work halls were predominantly composed of adult men, with a rigid and extensive division of labour that led to deskilling of parts of the workgroup. In domestic workshops and work halls the production process remained invisible to the final consumers of the products. This adversely affected the formation of a social identity based on occupational criteria. Conversely, open *tabernae* were closely connected with public spaces and provided a platform to affirm and negotiate occupational identities.

The next chapters discuss the role of occupationally defined associations. **Koenraad Verboven** argues that *collegia* served to structure urban populations and to connect the middle- and upper segments of the working population (the *plebs media*) with the civic elites and public institutions. Roman guilds were never formally part of public administrations, but their importance for public life—by assisting the supply of food, realising building project, levying taxes, and so forth—gave guild elites leverage. Top magistrates of *collegia* were often economically close to civic elites and usually sided with them to quell social unrest. Interestingly, the most important Roman guilds received recognition directly from the imperial level, which gave them privileges and protected these against violation from local and provincial authorities. **Jinyu Liu** analyses Roman *collegia* as trust networks that created social capital for the members. However, she warns against seeing this as necessarily beneficial for economic development. Like medieval guilds, *collegia* fostered particularized trust among their members, possibly at the expense of non-members. Liu also warns against overestimating the importance of professional *collegia* to the Roman economy. Informal networks based on family, friendship and patronage also provided reputation based sanctions. Apprenticeships, she argues, played a major role in structuring relations between craftsmen families, but contrary to medieval guilds *collegia* did not play a significant role in organising these.

Sarah Bond goes on to study the status and work relations of workers in imperial mints in Late Antiquity—an archetypical example of state-controlled bound labour. She shows how the system replaced the slave based mint organisation of the early Principate. Although it tied the workers to their jobs and 'technically stigmatized' them, the system also endowed them with social prestige and privileges—a strategy adopted more generally for the professional *corpora* of workers servicing the state and the army. Mint workers formed singular closed communities closely connected to the imperial state

We end with two chapters on the role of 'work' and professions as creators of social status. **Nicolas Tran** argues that the value systems of Roman elites and common people were not incompatible. Both groups shared the positive view that craftsmen, like intellectual professionals, were 'masters of an art'. Professional skills endowed them with the elevated status of *docti*. The social status of established *artifices* was apparent and confirmed by the fact that they were surrounded by apprentices (*discipuli*). **Catharina Lis** and **Hugo Soly** close the volume with a comparative chapter on ancient and medieval appreciations of work. They challenge the commonplace that Greco-Roman culture scorned labour, while Christian medieval culture valued it. Ancient elites stressed 'independence' from the need to work as a prerequisite for their leading public roles and the education required for these. However, they appreciated diligence as a moral virtue, considered idleness a vice, and admired craftsmanship. Thus there was no ideological obstacle for workmen and merchants to pride themselves on their professional skills and success, and openly to affirm their professional identity. In medieval culture, on the other hand, the church emphasized work as a necessity imposed by God. Consequently, to work (hard) was a divine duty, but it was never a source of virtue. Craftsmanship was valued only insofar as it was used to glorify God. Merchants had to be content with modest profits and could redeem their soul only by donating to the poor and to the church. As a result occupational awareness was low and contributed little to the construction of workers' public social identities.

As may be clear from this short survey of chapters—and in line with our broader research programme as explained above—most of the authors in this book draw on models and concepts from the social sciences and find inspiration in the work of labour historians of other periods. We hope that by taking this approach our book will not only increase understanding of social and economic developments in the Roman Empire, but will help also to bridge the gap with the labour history of other pre-industrial societies, and thereby integrate ancient economic history in global economic history. We hope and believe that this will contribute to a greater insight into the causes and consequences of economic growth in pre-industrial societies generally, and ultimately lead to a better understanding of the reasons behind development and prosperity in our own society.

To conclude this preface, it is our great pleasure to thank our editorial assistants Kasey Reed and Luka Tjampens for helping to prepare this manuscript, and the Flanders Research Foundation (FWO-Vlaanderen) for financing the collaborative efforts that made this book possible.

Abbreviations of Ancient Sources

Ancient literary sources, authors and their work have been abbreviated as in the *Oxford Classical Dictionary* (4th ed.) (also available at http://classics.oxfordre.com/staticfiles/images/ORECLA/OCD.ABBREVIATIONS.pdf (accessed 21 May 2016)). Authors and works not mentioned in the *OCD*, have been abbreviated according to the *Oxford Latin Dictionary* (http://www.oxfordscholarlyeditions.com/page/abbreviations) or Liddel and Scott's *A Greek-English Lexicon* (http://perseus.uchicago.edu/cgi-bin/philologic/navigate.pl?LSJ.0 (accessed 21 May 2016)).

Corpora and specialised publications of Greek inscriptions are abbreviated following 'CLAROS. Concordancia de Inscripciones griegas', http://www.dge.filol.csic.es/claros/cnc/2cnc.htm (accessed 21 May 2016). For publications of Latin inscriptions we have used the abbreviations of the 'Epigraphik-Datenbank Clauss / Slaby', http://db.edcs.eu/' (accessed 21 May 2016).

Publications of papyri and ostraca are abbreviated as in the 'Checklist of Greek, Latin, Demotic and Coptic Papyri, Ostraca and Tablets', http://library.duke.edu/rubenstein/scriptorium/papyrus/texts/clist.html (accessed 21 May 2016).

Greek words in the text have been transliterated (following the system of the Chicago Manual of Style) to increase readability. In the footnotes and tables, we have preserved the Greek.

About the Authors

Seth G. Bernard
is assistant professor of Classics at the University of Toronto. His research focuses broadly on the socioeconomic and urban history of Rome and Italy, and his current book project looks at how Rome's labour supply met the demands of large-scale public construction during the Republican period.

Sarah Bond
is assistant professor of Classics at the University of Iowa (United States). She received her PhD from the University of North Carolina at Chapel Hill in 2011. Her various articles and scholarly publications focus on perceptions of worker-bodies, the period of Late Antiquity, and the disconnect between Roman literature and law. Her book *Trade and Taboo. Disreputable Professions in the Roman Mediterranean* is due to appear in 2016 with University of Michigan Press.

Miko Flohr
is researcher and lecturer in Ancient History at Leiden University. He works on urban economic life in Roman Italy, and has published the monograph *The World of the Fullo: Work, Economy, and Society in Roman Italy* (Oxford University Press, 2013) and co-edited volumes on Roman craftsmen and traders and on the economy of Pompeii.

Miriam J. Groen-Vallinga
is a PhD student in Ancient History at Leiden University. Her thesis on the Roman urban labour market is part of the larger research project 'Moving Romans', funded by the Dutch National Research Organisation (NWO).

Cameron Hawkins
is assistant professor of History at Queensborough Community College, of the City University of New York. His published work, which focuses on the economic history of the Roman world, includes a recent monograph entitled *Roman Artisans and the Urban Economy* (Cambridge University Press, 2016).

Claire Holleran
is senior lecturer in Classics and Ancient History at the University of Exeter. She is the author of *Shopping in Ancient Rome: the Retail Trade in the Late Republic and the Principate* (Oxford University Press, 2012), and numerous articles on the social and economic history of Rome and the Roman world.

Christian Laes
is professor of Latin and Ancient History at the University of Antwerp and adjunct Professor at the University of Tampere. He has published five monographs, among which *Children in the Roman Empire: outsiders within* (Cambridge University Press, 2011), and over seventy international contributions on socio-cultural history of Roman and Late Antiquity.

Catharina Lis
is professor emeritus of Social History at the Free University of Brussels ('Vrije Universiteit Brussel'), and currently guest professor at the University of Antwerp. She has published extensively on the social history of pre-industrial Europe, including (with Hugo Soly) *Worthy Efforts: Attitudes to Work and Workers in Pre-Industrial Europe* (Brill, 2012).

Jinyu Liu
PhD (2004), Columbia University, is Shanghai "1000 Plan" Professor at Shanghai Normal University, and associate professor of Classical Studies at DePauw University. She has published a monograph, *Collegia Centonariorum the Guilds of Textile Dealers in the Roman West* (Brill 2009) and several articles on Roman *collegia*. She has also published on Latin Epigraphy, and Classical Reception in China.

Elizabeth A. Murphy
PhD (2014), Joukowsky Institute for Archaeology and the Ancient World, Brown University, is visiting assistant professor at the Institute for the Study of the Ancient World, New York University. Her research focuses on the archaeology of Roman workshops and craft production.

Hugo Soly
is professor emeritus of Early Modern History at the Free University of Brussels ('Vrije Universiteit Brussel'), and currently guest professor at the University of Antwerp. He has published extensively on the social and economic history of pre-industrial Europe, including (with Catharina Lis) *Worthy Efforts: Attitudes to Work and Workers in Pre-Industrial Europe* (Brill, 2012).

Laurens E. Tacoma
is lecturer in Ancient History at Leiden University. He has written about Roman social mobility, demography, economy and labour, local elites and urbanisation, and migration. He recently published *Moving Romans. Migration to Rome in the Principate* (Oxford University Press, 2016).

Nicolas Tran
is professor of Roman History at the University of Poitiers and currently member of the Institut Universitaire de France (2012–2017). He has published extensively on Roman epigraphy, *collegia* and professions, including a recent book *Dominus tabernae: le statut de travail des artisans et des commerçants de l'Occident romain* (Ecole Française de Rome, 2013).

Koenraad Verboven
is professor of Ancient History at Ghent University. He published extensively on social and economic history, including recently (as editor with Paul Erdkamp and Arjan Zuiderhoek) *Ownership and Exploitation of Land and Natural Resources in the Roman World* (Oxford University Press, 2015) and (as editor with Paul Erdkamp) *Structure and Performance in the Roman Economy. Models, Methods and Case Studies* (Collection Latomus, 2015).

Arjan Zuiderhoek
is associate professor of Ancient History at Ghent University. He has published on the social, political and economic history of cities in the Roman east (primarily Asia Minor), and has just completed a book on *The Ancient City*, due to appear with Cambridge University Press in 2016.

CHAPTER 1

Work, Labour, Professions. What's in a Name?

Koenraad Verboven and Christian Laes

The Concept and Terminology of Work in Roman Society

> The study of labour in Roman antiquity is beset by intractable problems in the empirical record: what evidence survives is typically vague, unrepresentative, or ideologically coloured.[1]

This quote by Kyle Harper confronts us head-on with one of the most basic methodological problems in the field of ancient labour history: the elitist bias of ancient literary sources is so pronounced that we can only dimly hear the voices or visualise the practices of the vast majority of the population who had to work for their daily bread. The 'honourable society' from which these texts emanate and the prejudices they reflect severely distort our views on the practice and experience of Roman workers. Ancient literary sources mostly offer only approximate terms and value judgements on people performing jobs.[2] How should we then define and delineate what constitutes the subject of this book? What is the difference between 'work' and 'labour'? At what point and why does 'work' become a 'profession'?

The concepts 'work', 'labour' and 'professions' are hard to translate in ancient Greek or Latin. Classicists have invested a lot of effort discussing what meanings the ancients attached to 'work', and studying the various Greek and Latin terms used for it.[3] *Ponos, mochthos* and *labor*, for instance, connoted effort, suffering, and harsh labour. *Ergon, opus*, and *industria*, on the other hand, were more neutral terms that could refer to human activity in the broadest sense of the word—building structures, art creations, enterprises, zeal, etc. *Opus* usually referred to work performed in the service of another person, but

1 Harper (2008: 97). See now also Marcone (2016a) for an edited volume of over 800 pages, dealing with various aspects of labour in the Roman world, from ideology to labour activities and typology of work.

2 Laes (2011: 148–152).

3 Vanhaegendoren (2007) is an examplary study for this approach. See also De Nardis (2016a).

 | DOI 10.1163/9789004331686_002

operae supposed a free will and a desire to serve.[4] In legal texts *operae* denoted working days; an *operarius* was a labourer who is paid for his daily work, even though the contract could cover a longer period.[5] *Athlos* was often connected with the rewards of athletes or soldiers. Lexicographic and semantic studies have helped to decode ancient texts, but the plethora of nuances they show rather illustrate the rich vocabulary available to talk about 'work', than unveil clear-cut concepts in ancient thinking about the topic.

Scholars have also looked at key texts that seem to reveal Roman concepts of labour. By far the most famous of these is Cicero's discussion in the *De Officiis* ('On Duties'), inspired by Posidonius, on respectable and unrespectable (*sordidi*) pursuits of profit (*quaestus*).[6] The latter include first of all occupations that incur ill-will, such as the occupations of tax gatherers and usurers. Hired workmen (*mercennarii*) who are paid for their efforts rather than their skills are not to be held in high esteem either; their wages are rewards for voluntary slavery. Craftsmen (*opifices*) are also unrespectable since 'no workshop can have anything fit for a freeborn about it'. Retailers need to lie in order to make a profit. Most vulgar of all, though, in Cicero's eyes, are livelihoods that cater to sensual pleasures: fishmongers, butchers, cooks, poulterers, fishermen, perfumers, dancers and all others who provide 'low' entertainment. The text continues with slightly more acceptable areas of work. Medicine, architecture and teaching constitute trades that are beneficial to society and require a certain intelligence on the part their practitioners. There is however one important restriction: such occupations are appropriate only for those whose social position they become. Finally, in the last paragraph, the preconceptions of the aristocracy become very clear. Wholesale trade, involving imports from overseas, is not as vulgar as retail. Not only is it useful to society, it also allows a person to reinvest his profit in agriculture, the most respectable activity of all and the most becoming to a free man.

Like most other ancient literary texts this passage in the *De Officiis* reflects the opinions of just a small section of society that often did not even abide by its own rules. Aristocrats did not represent themselves as businessmen,

4 LS s. v. *opera*: Service, pains, exertion, work, labour; *opus* was used mostly to denote work as a mechanical activity, as in the case of animals, slaves, and soldiers.

5 The fundamental text on the term *labor* is Cic., *Tusc.* 2.15.35: *Interest aliquid inter laborem et dolorem.* (…) *Labor est functio quaedam vel animi vel corporis gravioris operis et muneris, dolor autem motus asper in corpore alienus a sensibus.*

6 Cic., *Off.* 1.150–151. Cf. Finley (1999: 41–43); Nicolet (1988: 168–182). In a similar vein (also based on Posidonius) see Sen., *Ep.* 88.21–22.

landowners or wholesalers, even though in practice they often were.[7] The rhetorical and philosophical authority of Cicero caused his views to be regarded as typical and significant for 'the' ancient discourse on labour.[8] It is not hard, however, to find other appreciations of paid work—as shown by Lis and Soly in this volume[9]—as well as ambiguities and contradictions on what constituted work, labour, or professions. In Artemidorus' 'Book of Dreams', unemployment is a major concern for urban dwellers: no less than 21 dreams are about impending *scholē, apraxia* or *apragia*.[10] Some patently productive and important efforts by workers were not acknowledged as constituting 'jobs'. While agriculture, for instance, was the basis for all ancient societies farming was not considered a profession. Hence, in Egyptian census documents, some farmers declared themselves *atechnos* (without a trade), *idiotēs* (unskilled) or even *argos* (not working the ground, living without labour).[11] Ancient aristocrats never considered cultic duties or political office-holding as 'their job', even when it consumed much of their time and brought handsome rewards, as in the case of provincial governments or high military posts. The value of training and technical skills was acknowledged in the discourse of slave values and prices,[12] but in the eyes of elite authors, slaves did not have a job; they merely did what their masters ordered them to do.[13] Nevertheless, professional activity was used to indicate a slave's position in the hierarchy of his *familia* and slaves and freedmen set up inscriptions identifying themselves as 'professionals'. Epigraphy reveals a wide-spread culture of occupational pride among slaves and freedpersons as well as among freeborn non-elite, as shown in the contributions by Tran and Lis and Soly.[14]

7 See Veyne (1976: 118–128); Verboven (2004).
8 See Laes (2011: 149–151).
9 See also Lis and Soly (2012: 54–98). Merola (2016).
10 Pleket (1988); Pomeroy (1991); Parkin (2006).
11 Huebner (2013: 26).
12 Laes (2008: 242) on the term *artificium*. On the reality of skill premiums see De Nardis (2016b); see also the contributions by Hawkins, Holleran, Bernard, Groen-Vallinga and Tacoma in this volume.
13 A dissociation between the body of a slave and the work he performs occurs in legal thought concerning the letting of services of a slave to a third party. In that case one distinguishes between the slave owner, who has a right to his body, and the person who wields power on the slave in order to profit from his work. See Thomas (2002).
14 Joshel (1992); Scholten (2003); Cristofori (2016).

The Terminology of Work in Academic Discourse

While classicists have spent a lot of effort on analysing ancient discourse there has been surprisingly little reflection on what grounds concepts such as 'work', 'labour', or 'professions' cover in present-day academic debates and how this relates to ancient realities. Although extensively used terms such as 'work', 'labour', and 'professions' remain fuzzy concepts that resonate differently in various languages. This is more problematic than the ambiguities and contradictions in ancient sources because how *we* (rather than the ancients) fill these words with meaning reflects the way we tailor the questions we ask, the data we select, the analytical models we apply and inevitably the conclusions we draw. What are *we* talking about when we speak of 'work', 'labour', or 'professions'?

The easiest term to pin down is 'profession'. The Oxford English Dictionary describes it as an 'occupation in which a professed knowledge of some subject, field, or science is applied; a vocation or career, especially one that involves prolonged training and a formal qualification.' In common usage the concept has a social ring to it, indicating how professional expertise creates a specific social identity and bestows status on its practitioners.[15] It expresses how occupations requiring training or special skills create categories of workers who are difficult to replace.[16] There is no comparable word in ancient Greek or Latin—although sometimes *ars, technē,* or *artificium* come close (see Tran in this volume). But the principle that workers acquire a social identity and status from the profession they exercise is clearly visible in our sources.[17] The possession of specific skills and expertise enhanced the social status of the workers and distinguished them from workers performing unskilled or lowly skilled occupations.[18] Occupational *collegia* testify to the 'professional' aspect of many ancient occupations (as argued by Verboven in this volume).

15 *OED Online. Oxford English Dictionary. The Definitive Record of the English Language.* Oxford, 2007, http://www.oed.com/view/Entry/152052 (accessed 17 May 2016); a more specific definition is used in sociology, which stresses licensing and various forms of control (in collaboration with governmental authorities) over the goods and services provided; cf. Abbott (2001; 2005); Tilly and Tilly (1998: 26–30).

16 Note the related concept of 'vocation', expressing the personal nature of a worker's occupation and how this contributes to his personal identity; the German word 'Beruf' and the Dutch 'beroep' for the English 'profession' literally mean 'vocation'.

17 See Joshel (1992); for a survey (with a special focus on Italian historiography) Salvaterra (2006); Cristofori (2016).

18 Tran and Lis and Soly in this volume; note, however, that the level of expertise could be low and that even low-skilled jobs could create social identities, especially in the case of slaves and freedmen; see Joshel (1992).

The line between 'work' and 'labour', however, is harder to draw. 'Labour' calls to mind strenuous efforts and hierarchy, 'work' is a more general and slippery term, but there is no fixed boundary between them. In Hannah Arendt's philosophy 'labour' indicates the burdensome efforts necessary for man as an *animal laborans* to survive, while 'work' refers to the creative action of *homo faber*. Necessity and constraint make labour. Possibilities make work.[19] This distinction between the passive *animal laborans* and the active *homo faber* resonates well with the opposition between dependent workers performing executive tasks, and workers who thanks to their skills and creativity enjoyed greater independence, even when formally under the authority of others. Professionals 'work', they do not 'labour'.

These reflections, however, do not bring us much further in defining 'work'. The paid services of a barber constitute 'work', but a man shaving in the morning is not 'at work'. Having sex is not 'work'—except for prostitutes—but how should we conceptualise the livelihood of courtesans who are financially supported for the enjoyment they provide? A farmer ploughing his field or harvesting his vegetables is 'working', but the same cannot be said (or at least not in the same sense) of the retired professional tending to the carrots in his urban garden.[20] How can we deal with these ambiguities?

Lis and Soly argue that the concept of 'work' hinges on 'socially recognized needs'. There is no consensus on what constitutes such needs, nor is the social valorisation of efforts fixed. Hence there can be no intercultural consensus on what constitutes 'work'. The valorisation of (worthy) efforts as 'work' and of workers for the results of their work is subject to change and negotiation.[21]

Chris and Charles Tilly propose a social definition in which 'work' refers to 'any human effort adding use value to goods and services'—that is, when the efforts contribute (at least in principle) to the performance or enjoyment of activities carried on by other persons as their producers. Doing sports for fun, however strenuous the training, is not 'work'. Doing sports for fans to enjoy is 'work', however badly it may be paid. Remuneration is not the defining characteristic. Labour markets became the dominant way to mobilise labour only in modern society. Throughout history and even today in most places in the

19 Arendt (1998). In Arendt's view, pre-capitalist society cherished the ideal of *homo faber*, whose *vita activa* was on a higher level than that of the *animal laborans*. Modern *homo economicus* is a developed form of the *animal laborans*: by subordinating workers to the exigencies of mass production, capitalism undermined the existence of *homo faber*.

20 Abbott (2005: 307–309) on the difficulties in conceptualising 'work'.

21 Lis and Soly (2012: 1–3 (and *passim*)).

world, the Tillys observe, the bulk of all work takes place outside the market, in households or in large organizations.[22]

Studying the history of 'work', therefore, implies studying the various ways in which societies conceptualise efforts as 'work', and how they mobilise labour power and organise co-operation between workers; which institutions regulate this cooperation, and how this affects social organisation and economic performance.

Work Mobilisation Systems in the Roman World: A Variety of Labour Statuses

Supervision and regulation impose constraints on workers, but no master controls the muscles and thoughts of his slaves. From a biological perspective, all work efforts are voluntary regardless of whether they are performed by an independent worker aiming for profit or by a slave fearing the whip. Setting labour in motion implies moving the minds of humans.[23] So, why do people work? Why do they value the results of their efforts more than the leisure they forfeit? Workers aim to satisfy personal needs or wants: the pleasure or necessity of consumption, avoidance of pain and harm, care for loved ones, maintaining social status, satisfying intellectual curiosity or an artistic drive. But such internal motivations have to be materialised in an institutional and organisational set-up that is beyond the worker's control. Personal preferences inspire the choices we make. Institutional and organisational constraints and incentives guide the decisions we take. Understanding labour, therefore, requires understanding the institutions that make up the work mobilisation system—or in the terms of economics handbooks the 'labour allocation system'—in a society.

Charles and Chris Tilly distinguish three classes of work incentives: compensation, coercion and commitment. 'Coercion consists of threats to inflict harm, compensation the offer of contingent rewards, commitment the invocation of solidarity'.[24] Compensation includes wages, profits and all forms of utilities acquired by a worker in return for his efforts. Coercion includes physical force and psychological threats. Commitment rests on workers identifying themselves in relation to others, perceiving their interests as their own.

---

22 Tilly and Tilly (1998: 22–23); Linden and Lucassen (1999: 9–10) for a discussion.

23 Cf. above n. 13 on the dissociation between the body and labour activity of slaves, which made them more than just *instrumenta vocalia*.

24 Tilly and Tilly (1998: 72–75); Linden and Lucassen (2001).

Labour may be allocated through markets, when workers 'sell' or 'hire out' their labour power, but there are no pure markets in history. Real labour markets (as opposed to their abstract models) are driven by comprehensive incentive systems that link rewards, compulsion and commitment in various ways. Hierarchies (firms, public administrations, guilds, ...), and networks (of family, freedmen, friends, patrons, clients, *collegiati*, ...) cut through and provide alternatives to market incentives.[25] The dominant work incentive system today is that of the labour market. Compensation consists primarily of profits and wages, coercion comes from labour contracts or the threat of unemployment, and commitment to the firm is a part of the ideal corporate culture (and as such a target of HR-management). In pre-industrial economies labour markets (insofar as they existed) seldom occupied a central or dominant place in society. Where households were the prime production units, commitments were kinship and family based. Chattel slavery mobilised work through coercion in the form of physical and psychological violence. Workshops as social units organised towards the production of items intended for the market[26] relied mostly on incentives derived from household, family and (in the Roman case) slave/freedmen obligations.

While European labour history has traditionally focused on remunerated labour—wage levels, contracts, supervision, guilds etc.—Greek and Roman labour history has long been dominated by a focus on slavery. Free workers have been approached mainly as peasants, marginal (day) labourers or freed slaves. It was never denied that free peasants were ubiquitous, but small freeholders were thought to have become tenants as they were outcompeted in the late Republic by slave-run rural estates. The competition from slaves was thought to have reduced wages to bare-subsistence minima and to have prevented the development of a free labour market.[27] Workshops run by autonomous craftsmen were

25 Van Bavel, De Moor, and van Zanden (2009: 11): historical factor markets have nearly always been embedded in 'political, social, and cultural arrangements' based on voluntary personalised exchanges (gift-exchange, reciprocity) or coercion. Networks and hierarchies enclose, replace and supplement factor markets.

26 See the contribution by Murphy to this volume.

27 Cf. Frank (1927: 326): 'most of the work in the household, in the shops and factories, and on the farms, at least in and near Rome, was performed by slaves and ex-slaves.' Similarly Rostovtzeff (1957: 191 (and *passim*)); De Robertis (1963: 101–181) (contra Nörr (1965)); Mossé (1966: *passim*); De Martino (1979: 165–174, 263–293); Hopkins (1978: 108–111). See Marcone (2016b) for an overview of traditional scholarly views on Roman labour.

the dominant production units, but they would have been operated mostly by slaves and freedmen.[28]

Closely linked to this focus on slavery is the emphasis already discussed that classicists have placed on ideology. Greek and Roman elite authors are dismissive of remunerated labour, which they tend to associate with slavery. Until quite recently scholars generalised this view as representative for Greco-Roman society as a whole, even though other appreciations are easily found in ancient sources (see above).

Both emphases (slavery and ideology) have faded somewhat the past 20-odd years. Slaves represented only between ten and twenty percent of the population empire-wide. Many were domestic servants rather than productive workers.[29] The bulk of the labour force in the Roman world consisted of free workers. The research focus has shifted towards free labour and the role played by markets as incentive structures and price setters (see the contributions by Groen-Vallinga and Tacoma, and Holleran). The collected essays on *Non-Slave Labour in the Greco-Roman World*, edited by Peter Garnsey in 1980, were a mile-stone in this reorientation.[30] In the same year, Peter Brunt published a seminal article in the *Journal of Roman Studies* in which he argued that public works at Rome depended on free wage labour—a thesis now generally accepted for the whole empire (see the contribution by Bernard).[31] In his monograph on *Lohnarbeit im klassischen Altertum* (1989) Mrozek showed that wages and labour conditions for salaried workers in the Roman Empire were not so bad in historical perspective and that the presumed competition between slave and free workers is not documented in the sources for the Principate.[32] Scheidel recently confirmed this by means of a long term comparative study of real wages from 1800 BC to AD 1300.[33]

Reliance on wage labour was not limited to large urban projects. Production on rural estates and market oriented farms also depended on the availability

28 Rostovtzeff (1957: 104); in contrast Finley (1999: 65, 74) stresses the quantitative importance of free independent craftsmen … but mainly to argue the small scale of craft production.

29 McKeown (2007: 97–140); Scheidel (2011) for a discussion (estimates between 9–14%) and a short bibliographical essay (309–310).

30 Garnsey (1980); originally presented and discussed at the 1978 'Seventh International Economic History Congress (Edinburgh); followed up by Garnsey (1981) (on independent freedmen).

31 Brunt (1980); a follow up on Brunt (1966), which stressed the importance to 'the mob' of occasional free labour.

32 Mrozek (1989: 119–120).

33 Scheidel (2010; 2014); see also Allen (2009).

of free wage labour. Free peasants—especially from the poorest families—provided the bulk of this labour force, but townsmen as well hired out their labour during harvest time. In some regions and provinces even a landless 'rural proletariat' may have existed.[34] Entrepreneurs, such as the 'Mactar harvester', stepped in to organise and let out bands of rural labourers needed for harvesting.[35] Rathbone showed that the third century AD estate of Appianus in Egypt used both short term hired labour and free workers employed under long term labour contracts.[36] This was no doubt the 'dominant mode of production' on large estates also in other provinces where the stock of slaves was small, as in Africa.[37] Erdkamp introduced the concept of 'externalization of labour costs' to argue the potential of peasant households for the structural development of rural and urban labour markets. Peasant households typically have surplus labour. This is partly because of the inevitably seasonal nature of most agricultural activities, and the division of labour inside the household, but partly also because peasant families have little or no access to production factors outside the family farm. Hence they can (and will) hire out their labour on the market cheaply because their subsistence costs are born by the family farm.[38]

Even mining and quarrying, the epitome of slave and convict labour in the minds of many modern scholars, often relied on free wage labour. Two labour contracts preserved in one of the Dacian gold mines show that (unskilled) wage labour was used to operate the mines.[39] Most of the work-force of the quarries in the eastern desert of Egypt were salaried, despite the difficult conditions and the hard work. The workers lived at the site without their families. Every month a group travelled to the Nile to buy supplies. The workers of an alabaster quarry in the second century AD even went on strike when a new group of (convict?) workers was brought in.[40]

The renewed attention for free workers stimulated also a renewed interest in occupational *collegia*. Since the late 19th century scholars have downplayed the economic significance of *collegia*. Today, they are seen as moral communities where workers (particularly craftsmen) enjoyed respect for their

34 Erdkamp (1999; 2005: 80–86) (who does not believe in a wide spread rural proletariat).

35 CIL VIII 11824; Stone (1998: 106). See also Cato *Agr.* 144; Suet., *Vesp.* 1.4; and Holleran in this volume.

36 Rathbone (1991).

37 Whittaker (1978; 1980).

38 Erdkamp (1999; 2015); Carlsen (2016).

39 CIL III p. 948.10; p. 949.11; Hirt (2010: 232–234, 270–274).

40 Hirt (2010: 206–214); PSI 7.822 for the strike. See also Fezzi (2016).

expertise and where professional identities were forged and linked to moral values. Inevitably, occupational *collegia* provided a framework to defend professional interests and to organize co-operation between free workers. (see the contributions by Verboven and Liu in this volume)

Another rapidly growing field of interest in ancient labour history is that of technical skills.[41] We are far away today from the old idea that technological innovations in antiquity were rare and spread only slowly and irregularly. Archaeology has shown that Roman production and transport technology was more advanced and widespread than in any previous economic system. The level and spread it reached was not matched in Europe until the early modern period. What made this possible? Richard Saller argued that investment in schooling was low and unorganised.[42] But this is hard to reconcile with the importance attached to skills in epigraphic, papyrological and literary evidence. Clearly, apprenticeships were intimately bound up with the 'workshop mode of production'. Tran shows in this volume how skilled artisans were also respected *magistri* working with *discipuli* as their assistants and passing on their know-how to apprentices.[43]

The importance of wage labour, professional associations and training, however, must not blind us to the limitations of market based narratives. Markets were an important *aspect* of the Roman work incentive structure. But this incentive structure cannot be reduced to market dynamics. Wages and workshops provide only a partial answer to how the Roman Empire succeeded in mobilising and organizing the intellectual and physical work efforts needed to achieve the performance level it attained.

Rome was an agrarian empire. The bulk of its rural workers were subsistence farmers. Peasants toiled to grow their own food and to pay taxes and rents. If they had to pay these in money they had to sell part of their crops on the market. But the price they received was not what mobilised the work efforts of a peasant household. The family's well-being, ensuring its survival, in some cases even attaining or preserving its prosperity—those were the driving forces of household labour. It was self-evident that women and children worked together with their husbands and fathers to achieve this. As most other

41 White (1984); Greene (2000); Wilson (2002); Schneider (2007); Oleson (2008); Marcone (2016c).

42 Saller (2012).

43 On apprenticeships see also the contributions to this volume by Hawkins, Bernard and Liu; Freu (2011; 2016); De Nardis (2016b).

pre-industrial societies, the concept of 'child labour' let alone its problematization did not exist.[44]

The importance ascribed by 19th and 20th century scholars to slavery as the single most important mechanism to mobilise labour in the Roman world has rightly been abandoned. But one cannot deny the importance of slavery in many parts of the empire, most of all in its heartland Italy where the stock of slaves was probably double that in the rest of the empire—15–25% of the population, half of whom in cities. Roman society in Italy was exceptional because it was not just a society with many slaves, but a society based on a slave economy.[45] While slavery played an important part in providing the market with the labour resources it needed, the incentives for slaves to provide the labour required were not market incentives.[46] Positive rewards certainly played their part. In the case of care intensive tasks a master could allow his slave to share in the profits by granting him a *peculium* or use psychological incentives, like the prospect of manumission. But because a slave could not leave his master for another or sell his services to an outsider without his master's consent, such rewards only dimly reflected labour market wages. In most other circumstances slave labour would be mobilised through coercion and manipulation. The 'rewards' gained by chain gang slaves were limited to not being whipped, locked up, or disposed of. Ideally (from the master's point of view) a slave was socialised to embrace the interests of the *familia* as his own, thereby generating commitment based incentives. In the case of house-born slaves (*vernae*) this may often have worked.

Distinctions between free persons and slaves were not always clear-cut.[47] Freeborn children might be sold into a contract by their parents, which in practice reduced them to slaves. Adult free persons as well sometimes sold themselves 'voluntarily' (and temporarily) into slavery. We don't know the extent of this phenomenon, but it was common enough for jurists to discuss its legal implications.[48] In some provinces traditional forms of semi-dependent labour continued to be used until deep into imperial times. (see Zuiderhoek in this volume) Coercion in these systems was no less real than in formal slavery, but the workers could not be sold or replaced to enhance efficiency. They did not constitute 'capital' that could be used as collateral or turned into cash.

44 Laes (2008; 2011: 148–152, 206–210); Porena (2016). See d'Aloja (2016) on labour of women.

45 Scheidel (2005a; 2008; 2011: 288–289); Jongman (2003); Verboven (2012b).

46 Unless of course their master allowed them to hire themselves out as they saw fit, in exchange for a part of their income.

47 Herrmann-Otto (2005).

48 See Ramin and Veyne (1981); Silver (2011).

Curiously, although debts were a recurrent problem throughout Roman history, we hear little about debt-bondage. Varro claimed that in his day (first century BC) debt-bondsmen (*obaerarii*) were still numerous in Illyricum, Asia and Egypt, but apart from an elusive moralizing reference by Columella, the issue remains absent from our sources afterwards.[49] Many scholars nevertheless believe that large landowners continued to rely on their heavily indebted tenants to find the low-cost seasonal workers they needed. There seems little doubt that rent arrears and other debts (loans to replace tools, buy animals, seed, and so forth) were an effective instrument to tie tenants to their land and may thus have foreshadowed conditions in Late Antiquity when the mobility of tenants was legally limited. While such debts may not have been the formal ground for imposing rural labour, they clearly increased the land-owners bargaining position.[50]

Corvée labour does not appear to have been a central institution to the Roman economy, but it was a common fiscal strategy and a way to mobilise the labour needed for the upkeep of dykes (in Egypt), and probably roads and public infrastructure.[51]

Convict labour was not as wide-spread in the Roman Empire as in Han China and as we already saw wage labour was also used for some of the most typical convict labour types, but convict labour was a reality nevertheless. Convicts were not just set to work in mines and quarries. Minor offences were punished by putting the offenders at work on *opera publica*—maintenance and repair of roads, dykes, and various public constructions.[52]

Last but not least, the army provided a major contribution to the Roman work force both in terms of muscle and know-how needed to build roads, bridges, ports, aqueducts, to dig canals and realise numerous other public projects. Without military muscle and brain power much of the public capital goods that boosted economic performance would never have been realised. Although wages and extra benefits (housing, food, clothing) were no doubt incentives to enlist as a soldier, the hierarchical command structure, the long duration of service (25 years), the impossibility to leave or refuse to obey

49 Varro, *Rust.* 1.17.2; Columella, *Rust.* 1.3.12.

50 Finley (1976); De Martino (1979: 269–271); Neeve (1984: *passim*); Lo Cascio (2009); Kehoe (2007: 148–155), but see also *ibid.*, 106–108 for practical limitations on the land-owner's bargaining power).

51 *Dig.* 50.4.1; Millar (1983); Sirks (1989).

52 Millar (1984); Groen-Vallinga and Tacoma (2015).

orders, underscore the extent of coercion and commitment demanded from the troops.[53]

This mixed incentive structure for labour—free independent and wage labour, slave labour, traditional arrangements of semi-dependent labour, debt-bondage, corvée labour, convict labour, military duties—should remind us that while the incentive structure that made Roman economic performance possible accommodated markets and while it seems that markets played a much greater role in the Roman Empire than, for instance, in Han China, the market as an exchange system was not nearly as dominant as it would become in modern times. While markets stimulated performance, the work mobilisation systems they rested upon, only partially relied on labour markets.

The Economics and Sociology of Work in Ancient History

Until recently, ancient labour historians have shown little explicit interest in social science theories. Nevertheless, different models have been influential in shaping the field.

One of the first explicitly to advocate the use of social science models was Moses Finley. His 'orders and status' model was tributary to Max Weber according to whom mentalities, norms, and values (usually enshrined in religious beliefs), either stimulated or blocked economic developments. According to Weber, the rational organisation of free wage labour based on explicit contracts developed only in early modern Europe, where they were supported by Judaeo-Christian beliefs (especially protestant ethic).[54] Finley, in turn, argued that concerns for social status prevented the development of labour markets in Greek and Roman society. Because the ancients failed to distinguish between labour-power (an abstract notion) and the worker providing labour services, labour contracts were perceived as instruments to subject a worker to his employer, and free wage-labourers were assimilated to slaves. The dominant forms to mobilize labour-power, according to Finley, were based on compulsion 'by force of arms or by force of law and custom'. Dependent workers included everyone who 'was bound ... by some pre-condition, birth in a class of dependents or debt or capture or any other situation which, by law

53 Wierschowski (1984); Erdkamp (2002); Verboven (2007c).

54 Weber (1922: 7; 1925).

or custom, automatically removed some measure of his freedom of choice and action, usually for a long term or for life.'[55]

Most ancient economic historians no longer accept Finley's 'status and orders' model. Cultural beliefs play an important part in how labour is organised, divided, and allocated in a society,[56] but Weber's cultural determinism is largely abandoned by social scientists today. Chris and Charles Tilly recognize three still relevant 'clusters of theories' that have been important also in ancient labour history: Marxist theory, neo-classical or rational action theory, and institutionalism or structuralism.[57]

Marxist theory has been most influential in the study of Roman slavery. For a long time, Marxist inspired ancient historians stuck to the orthodox view that the Roman economy was characterised by a pre-capitalist 'slave mode of production' that was itself opposed to the development of a capitalist free market economy.[58] This view changed in the 1970s when a number of neo-Marxist scholars (mostly Italians) explored the interrelation between slavery, technological development, and competitive markets—thereby blurring the traditional divide between rent-seeking slave-owning aristocrats and capitalist market-oriented entrepreneurs.[59] Slavery was revalued as the institution 'par excellence' that enabled the growth of commodity markets in the ancient economy. This view has gained wide acceptance in scholarship today. Neo-Marxist scholarship thus made a valuable contribution to ancient labour history. However, it faces a number of limitations. First of all, it has little to say on independent labour by urban craftsmen or rural small-holders. More importantly, 'class struggle' is not a very helpful concept to understand the relations between workers and employers in the small to medium-sized workshops that characterised ancient urban economies, operated by a single craftsman with the help of household members, apprentices, and one or two trusted (semi-) skilled slaves. (see Hawkins in this volume).

The pre-Finleyan Meyer-Rostovtzeff historiography implicitly favoured the neo-classical model. Most of these scholars, however, disregarded possible

55 Finley (1999: 65–71, and *passim*) (citation on p. 69); the problematic association between wage-labour and slavery was noted by many others see Lis and Soly (2012: 54–98); Verboven (2014); for a psychological analysis see Vernant (1956).

56 See, for instance North (2005: 23–80); Greif (1994); Hofstede (2001). See also below the contribution by Lis and Soly.

57 Tilly and Tilly (1998: 5–20).

58 Štaerman (1969; 1975). Among western historians see mainly De Ste. Croix (1981), on which see also the excellent reviews by Crook (1983) and Konstan (1986). See also below the contribution by Zuiderhoek on Marxist analysis as 'undersocialized'.

59 Capogrossi Colognesi, Giardina, and Schiavone (1978); Kolendo (1980); Carandini (1979).

labour markets. Thus, Rostovtzeff argued that 'industry' in the Roman economy essentially consisted of small workshops run by independent craftsmen (mostly freedmen) assisted by their sons and a few slaves, and production halls operated by slave or (in Late Antiquity) forced labour.[60] This view was still prevalent in the 1980s when Hopkins advocated the explicit use of neo-classical and Keynesian models. Hopkins downplayed the role of a labour market in his *Conquerors and Slaves*,[61] but stressed the increased division of labour resulting from the fact that free peasants ('the bulk of the labour force') had to sell part of their crops to meet rent and tax obligations, and tax income from non-militarized provinces was redirected towards heavily militarized (mainly frontier) provinces, where it created a military market.[62] The most elaborate neo-classical approach to Roman labour, however, has recently been put forward by Peter Temin. He argues not only that hired free labour 'was the rule, not the exception' in most parts of the empire, but that there existed a well-functioning unified labour market that equalized wages empire-wide. Slaves entered the same labour market as free workers under largely the same conditions. Because care-intensive tasks were routinely entrusted to slaves, Roman slavery was characterised by positive incentives, including monetary rewards and the prospect of manumission. Consequently the cost structure of slavery resembled that of free wage workers.[63] Temin's argument for a unified labour market is not convincing,[64] but his exercise does highlight the complex relation between ancient slave and wage labour (a topic addressed by Hawkins and Bernard in this book).

Since the publication of the *Cambridge Economic History of the Greco-Roman World* (2007) New Institutional Economics has been highly influential.[65] It studies the 'efficiency characteristics' of institutions, i.e. how they reduce transaction costs and affect economic performance—for instance how institutions such as slavery, labour contracts, apprenticeship practices, etc. structure the allocation of work and how this affects economic performance, quantitatively (how many people work, how long they work) and qualitatively (for instance which schooling or training they have). This approach to ancient labour history

60 Rostovtzeff (1957: 3, 36 and *passim*); cf. also Mossé (1966: 28), but commonly shared by the authors cited above in n. 27.

61 Hopkins (1978: 108–111).

62 Hopkins (1980) (104 for the role of the peasants).

63 Temin (2004 (516 for the quote); 2013: 114–138).

64 See the reviews by Bang (2013) and Erdkamp (2014).

65 See also Scheidel (2012a); Bang (2009).

is particularly visible in Scheidel's work on slavery and wage labour,[66] Kehoe's work on tenancy and rural labour,[67] and Hawkins' on urban craftsmen—as exemplified by his contribution to this volume.[68]

The past few years, network theory has rapidly been gaining ground. Social networks structure human agency, monitor social norms, and facilitate collective action.[69] How social capital is distributed and which social norms are fostered, profoundly affect how labour is allocated.[70] Social capital can include norms of generalised trust that facilitate hiring unrelated and previously unknown workers. But norms of trust can also be particularistic and networks can be closed formally (for instance by establishing formal voluntary associations (*collegia*, guilds)) or informally (for instance through shared cultural or ethnic identities, religious beliefs, locality, or genealogy ((extended) families)).[71] Thus, social networks play an important role in labour markets, matching employers and employees.[72] In the case of particularistic networks, desirable jobs and contracts are allocated primarily to network insiders. Insofar as the market plays a part in these allocation processes it is a closed market.[73]

Not much work has been done so far on the role of social networks in the allocation of labour in the ancient economy. Roman society was highly clientelistic. Particularistic norms of patronage and instrumental friendship (*amicitia*) were culturally cherished and promoted. We would expect, therefore, that labour allocation predominantly bypassed markets or passed through closed markets. Verboven argued that networks based on *amicitia* and patronage were the prime providers of business representatives.[74] Broekaert studied the role of *collegia* to provide the same function.[75] Holleran in this volume refers to the effects of patronage and neighbourhood networks on the Roman job market. However, particularistic social capital also improves the bargaining position and status of workers. Verboven (in this volume) argues that professional associations (guilds) empowered workers in Roman towns. Liu, on the other

66 Scheidel (2005a; 2008; 2010; 2012b; 2014).

67 Kehoe (2007; 2012).

68 See also Hawkins (2006; 2012; 2016).

69 Ogilvie (2011: 427).

70 Cf. Castiglione, Deth, and Wolleb (2008).

71 Putnam (1997; 2000); on the antisocial effects of particularized trust networks see Warren (2008: 135–138).

72 Tilly and Tilly (1998: 190–194); Sabatini (2009).

73 Cf. Van Bavel, De Moor, and van Zanden (2009: 13–14).

74 Verboven (2002).

75 Broekaert (2011).

hand, points to the potentially antisocial effects of social capital controlled by guild members.

Comparative Perspectives

Labour history has long been a popular topic in European social history, but there are very few links or cross-overs with the history of labour in Greco-Roman or non-European societies. Since the late 1990s European labour historians and global historians have become aware of this, but while significant progress has been made to compare the structure of early modern European labour regimes to those in non-European pre-industrial states—such as Japan, India, China, etc.—ancient labour history has received only scant attention.[76]

While ancient labour historians revalued the importance of wage labour since the 1980s, European and global labour historians have taken an opposite course as they realised that the definitions and models used to analyse European labour cannot be applied cross-culturally and may have been overstretched even for pre-industrial Europa itself. Linden and Lucassen note that the analytical core of European labour history, free wage labour, became dominant only in modern societies. If we want to study labour history from a global cross-cultural perspective, they argue, we need more varied schemata. They propose a classification scheme that embraces a wide variety of possible labour relations, ranging from unremunerated forced labour (by slaves or convicts) to free salaried labour on integrated markets. The basic distinctions they propose are between paid and unpaid work and between heteronomous and autonomous work. The latter is organised by the household without supervision from outside, the former is supervised by outsiders to the household. Regulation by public authorities is considered as a form of indirect supervision.[77]

In global perspective, free wage labour is not the most common solution to the problem of labour allocation. Throughout history most work has been organised in households or work-units run by households, such as farms or workshops. Co-operation between households in most historical cultures was structured along family or community lines, based on reciprocity or authority exercised, for instance, by village elders or tribal chiefs. In early states and more complex societies coerced labour (for instance on plantations, or public

76 Cf. the Global Labour History project of the International Institute for Social History in Amsterdam: http://socialhistory.org/nl/onderzoek/global-labour-history (accessed 17 May 2016); for a few major recent exceptions see Ehmer and Lis (2009); Lis and Soly (2012).

77 Linden and Lucassen (1999; 2001).

projects) has been much more pervasive than wage labour or hired services from independent free workers.

Van Bavel, De Moor and van Zanden argue that the early rise of labour markets in late medieval Western Europe was one of the most significant early signs of the economic development that would lead to European modernity. In their view, factor markets improved the allocation, and therefore the efficient use, of production factors by making labour, land, and capital more mobile. This development, however, was not unilinear and was geographically uneven throughout Europe and the world.[78] Elsewhere in the world, Tokugawa Japan saw a similar development from the 17th century onwards.[79] By the same time labour markets were on the rise also in China, where guilds had already by the 16th century, under the Ming emperors, begun to challenge the age-old reliance on coerced labour.[80] In most other parts of the world, however, (Ottoman Empire, India, Africa,...) labour markets remained small and fragile.[81]

Van Bavel and his colleagues identified different development paths and competing sets of institutions to re-allocate labour, land and capital from low- to high-productive activities. In their view, the efficiency of labour markets compared to alternative systems depends on relative transaction costs. Because coerced labour requires high costs to control and motivate workers, it usually only competes well with free labour if wage levels or transaction costs for wage labour are high, for instance because labour scarcity increases search and bargaining cost.

How did the Roman Empire compare to these early-modern examples? Theoretically, the persistence of slavery as a central institution in the Italian economy after the wars of conquest might suggest that free labour markets were thin (making free labour scarce, hence costly). But this view disregards the positive incentives characteristic of Roman slavery—such as the wide use of *peculia* and flexible arrangements for manumission—that reduced the monitoring and enforcement costs for slave labour. As argued by Hawkins in this volume, slavery/freedmanship competed well with free wage labour or hired services in the case of skilled or care-intensive work, but in the case

---

78 Van Bavel, De Moor, and van Zanden (2009: 9–10); an introduction to the special issue of *Continuity and Change* 24 (2009) on 'Factor Markets in Global Economic History'; see also Van Bavel (2014); Van Bavel, Campopiano, and Dijkman (2014).

79 Saito (2009).

80 Allen *et al.* (2011); Pomeranz (2000: 80–91, 165) (who sees a more developed China and Japan, resembling Europe rather than the Ottoman Empire, India or South-East Asia); Moll-Murata (2008: 217–218).

81 Van Bavel, De Moor, and van Zanden (2009: 16–17).

of lowly skilled jobs slaves were usually no match for wage labourers, whose remuneration hovered only slightly above subsistence.[82] Overall the Roman labour market for low-skilled work seems relatively well developed, while at least in some provinces (such as Egypt) contract labour was common even for medium-skilled jobs.

A lot more research is needed to understand how the history of work and labour in the Roman world compares to that of other historical societies, how the allocation/mobilisation of work was structured, and how this affected economic performance. We hope that this book, by the way it was conceived and how it is organised, with its distinctive comparative and theoretical focus, will help to bring ancient labour history to the heart of current debates in comparative and global economic history.

---

82 With the obvious exception of domestic services, where other factors come into play. On wage levels and inequality see Scheidel and Friesen (2009); Scheidel (2010; 2014); Allen (2009).

CHAPTER 2

Sorting Out Labour in the Roman Provinces: Some Reflections on Labour and Institutions in Asia Minor

Arjan Zuiderhoek

I

The Roman Empire confronts us with a plethora of labour-statuses. This is true of its core areas, but even more so of its provinces, particularly in the east, where the institutional legacy of sophisticated pre-Roman and pre-Hellenistic social formations further complicates the picture. Asia Minor is a case in point. Scattered evidence, literary, but mostly epigraphic, suggests a considerable variety of categories of both (semi-)dependent and free workers, ranging, in agriculture, from slaves to serf-like native peasant populations, people in debt-bondage, slave and freedman agents on elite estates, free agricultural labourers, and free tenant-farmers, and in an urban context, from bought slaves to house-bred servants (*threptoi*), various types of freedmen, free wage workers, the free self-employed, and so on.[1] On the present state of the evidence, it is difficult to say anything definite about the relative prominence of these various categories.

Such complex assortments of statuses naturally render difficult any effort to arrive at a general model of work or labour relations in the Roman world. Existing approaches, which generally touch on labour as part of a broader evaluation of the ancient economy, employ two different tactics in dealing with this complexity.[2] The first of these tactics consists of minimising the importance of complex status differentiations for overall economic outcomes—no matter whether such outcomes are framed in terms of economic performance (growth) or in terms of exploitation (surplus extraction, predation). This is a tactic we might call 'undersocialization.'[3] It is typical of models of the ancient

1 For references and discussion, see below.

2 For a more detailed version of the argument presented in the rest of this section, see Zuiderhoek (2013).

3 I borrow the terms 'undersocialization' and 'oversocialization' from Ian Morris's introduction to the 1999 updated edition of Finley's *Ancient economy*, where he uses them to characterize

 | DOI 10.1163/9789004331686_003

economy based on either the market or on class. Peter Temin, for instance, has argued, framing his analysis in explicitly neo-classical economic terms, that the Roman Empire in fact had a unified and integrated labour market. Slaves and free workers were part of the same labour market, not just because they often performed the same jobs interchangeably, but also because Roman slaves, with their *peculium* or working capital that they could manage and amass, and with which they might eventually buy their freedom, were in fact a kind of long-term employees.[4] To provide another example, in his Marxist analysis of Greco-Roman society, G.E.M. de Ste. Croix argued that chattel slaves, various categories of serfs (among which he included tenant-farmers), debt-bondsmen and other types of agricultural workers in fact constituted one single exploited class, which produced the agrarian surplus that constituted the basis of the wealth of the ancient landowning propertied class.[5]

Both of these approaches can be criticized on their own terms. For instance, Temin's conceptualisation of slavery as a long-term labour contract sits uneasily with the fact that, in antiquity, slaves were considered property and were dealt with as such, both in law and in practice. Translated into neo-classical terms, slaves were capital goods, valuable assets requiring considerable investment, and over which owners exercised full property rights. Regarding slaves as pseudo-employees means ignoring the extra-economic power the owner exercised over the person of the slave. As for de Ste. Croix, even to Marxists, his model of class struggle must look decidedly one-sided, consisting mostly of the exploitation visited by the propertied class upon their dependent labourers. The most important problem with these models, however, is that they tend, in a surprisingly similar way, to minimize or (partially) ignore the great diversity and socio-political complexity characteristic of the Greek and Roman labour situation, which is why I have dubbed them 'undersocialized.'

It was of course precisely against generalisations of this kind, both those of (an earlier generation of) market-oriented scholars as well as those of orthodox Marxists, that Moses Finley formulated his status-based model of the ancient economy. The accumulation of wealth in antiquity, Finley argued, was not an end in itself, but served, and was constrained by, the accumulation of status. The complex Greek and Roman status structures in fact provided the key to ancient underdevelopment and lack of economic growth, since they

---

different categories of critical responses to Finley's work on the ancient economy. They derive ultimately from Granovetter's famous discussion of the embeddedness of economic action, see Granovetter (1985).

4 Temin (2004) and (2012).

5 de Ste. Croix (1981).

were predicated on, and reinforced, an unproductive mentality. In line with his overall model, Finley suggested that, when analysing ancient labour, we should take into account 'a spectrum of statuses with the free citizen at one end and the slave at the other, and with a considerable number of shades of dependence in between.'[6] Different categories of labourers and types of work were judged in moral terms rather than in terms of their (marginal) productivity. Trade and manufacture were unbecoming of the free citizen, as was working for another person to gain one's livelihood. Elite wealth remained concentrated in land, while trade, retail and manufacturing work was carried out by the poorest, socially most marginalised groups: slaves, freedmen and foreigners (*metoikoi, peregrini*). Wage-labour remained a peripheral phenomenon, and a proper labour market, in the modern sense, never developed.

Unlike the market and Marxist models, Finley's status-based approach allows us to take proper account of the social, legal and political complexities of the ancient labour situation. At the same time, however, precisely because his status-model is so sensitive to specific social context, one runs the risk, whilst using it, of not seeing the forest for the trees, that is, of losing sight of the broader patterns of labour relations of precisely the kind which scholars employing class and market models emphasize. In other words, just as one might accuse those using the market and class models of undersocialization, so one can indeed accuse Finley of employing the tactic of oversocializing the ancient economy. And, as Ian Morris has pointed out in his introduction to the 1999 edition of *The Ancient Economy*, many of Finley's critics have indeed done so (though without using the term). Finley, it is argued, took the moralising statements in elite-produced literary sources too much at face value, and in recent decades scholars have produced a mountain of mainly epigraphic, papyrological, numismatic and archaeological evidence suggesting that the Roman economy was considerably more complex and dynamic than Finley imagined it to be.[7] Yet, despite the claims of those favouring simple market models, much of this complexity and dynamism still refuses to look recognisably 'modern' in any Western European or North American sense. In the new, more dynamic Roman economy that recent studies have presented us with, it seems perhaps even more difficult to make sense of the great variety of labour statuses that we find in the sources.

6 Finley (1981: 98; 1999: 67–68).

7 See Scheidel, Morris, and Saller (2007), a massive 'interim report.' See also Scheidel (2012a) for more thematic discussions.

II

For Finley, the ancient status structure acted as a brake on economic development. The prevailing acquisitive mentality among the wealthiest sectors of society created an institutional framework and incentive structure that left little room for innovation and productive investment but rather favoured the maximisation of social prestige. Hemmed in by institutional and status constraints, large-scale integrated and interconnected product and factor markets, including, as we saw, a market for labour, simply did not develop. In this context, it is interesting to note that economic historians of early modern Europe have consistently found that increased commercialisation of the economy went hand in hand with a strong *decrease* in the variety of different labour statuses. The example of the Dutch economy during the later sixteenth and seventeenth centuries, often considered to be the most advanced economy of early modern Europe in commercial terms, is paradigmatic: around the middle of the seventeenth century, easily more than half of the entire labour force was engaged in wage-labour, in both urban and rural settings.[8] This suggests that the wide variety of labour statuses which we find in the Roman world might indeed reflect a poorly integrated or fragmented labour market.

Contrary to Finley, however, I would argue that we should interpret the diversity of labour statuses not so much as a cause of, but rather, at least in part, as a *response to* a lack of labour market integration. The Roman Empire was vast, much larger than many later European states. Information, including information on prices, the quality of goods and the competence and trustworthiness of people one might possibly employ or do business with, travelled slowly and its reliability was often difficult to assess. Also, despite its vast and complex legal system, the Roman state offered its subjects surprisingly little actual assistance in enforcing contracts.[9] In addition, given the absence of institutionalized forms of professional schooling accessible to a fairly broad section of the non-elite population, skilled labour was scarce and expertise was mostly gained in private settings such as households or workshops.[10] This ensured that human capital was subject to strict forms of extra-economic control, since, given its scarcity, private individuals, groups or institutions that had invested in the attainment of expertise by others or had bought individuals with such expertise had a strong incentive to restrict the mobility of the skilled labour thus created or obtained.

8 De Vries (1994: 39); De Vries and Van der Woude (1997); Van Bavel (2007).

9 Terpstra (2013).

10 See Hawkins in this volume.

All these circumstances did not favour the development of an empire-wide free labour market. They do suggest something else, however. Recent scholarship on Roman manufacture and trade has indicated that to reduce risk, uncertainty and high transaction costs, Roman artisans and entrepreneurs often made use of informal social network-type institutions and organisations.[11] In similar vein, I would argue that to make sense of the great variety of labour statuses in the Roman world, and to understand how and why this variety might in fact have constituted a response to an underdeveloped labour market, we should analyse the various labour statuses in their institutional and organisational context. Within a given institution or organisation, the use of individuals with different labour statuses for different tasks might well have provided a way to reduce transaction costs in the employment of labour, given a situation of fragmented and underdeveloped labour markets, in order to increase overall efficiency. I should add the caveat here that 'efficiency' might mean a facilitation of processes of production and distribution to increase income or profit, but that it might equally well imply a facilitation of exploitation, i.e. predation or rent-seeking. As critics of the 'naive' application of institutional economic theory in economic history have justifiably argued, there is no intrinsic reason why institutions, even apparently 'successful'—that is, historically long-lasting- ones, should always have served to increase economic efficiency.[12] Their 'success' in terms of societal prominence or longevity might equally well be due to the way they facilitated exploitation, to the benefit of their members or stakeholders.[13]

III

In an attempt to put the various categories of labourers in their socio-economic context and see whether some kind of rationale can be found for the great diversity of statuses among workers, I shall briefly examine some institutional/organisational frameworks and the place of labour within them. I focus on Roman Asia Minor. I have deliberately opted for an eastern provincial region, since in the east, unlike in the west, the Romans were confronted with the already existing status-structures of an advanced urban civilisation (itself a compound of Greek and indigenous elements), structures which, in due course, were partially adapted to, and partly blended with, the principles

11 Broekaert (2011; 2012c); Hawkins (2012); Terpstra (2013).

12 Ogilvie (2007).

13 Bang (2009).

of social hierarchy introduced by the Romans themselves. The resulting social complexity proves a particular challenge for simplified, single-variable class, market or status models, and I would suggest that an institutional approach serves us better here. I will briefly discuss two institutional/organisational frameworks, i.e. the household (*oikos/familia*) and the city, though others can easily be thought of (the village, the temple, the workshop, the *collegium*, the *phulē* etc.). I start with the household.

To be able to operate as economic units, households required continuous access to labour power. This labour was needed for the production and distribution of goods and services, both for internal consumption and for the market. Households of course came in a variety of shapes and sizes, from small farming families and urban-based households of manufacturers, traders or service providers to the *oikoi* of the local civic elites, who owned estates in the territory of their own city and perhaps in the territories of other cities as well, to the extensive *familiae* of the equestrian and senatorial elites, who might own large properties in various provinces, to, ultimately, the emperor, who was the head of the largest household in the empire, as well as its biggest landowner. Despite the huge differences in size and complexity between these various types of households, all households required continuous access to what we might call a core labour supply, for those tasks without which the household was unable to function or even survive. Beyond the labour supplied by direct family members (siblings, wives, children) it is noteworthy that, throughout the Roman world, households did not turn to wage labour for this core supply, buying labour power in exchange for a wage, but almost universally opted for forms of dependent or semi-dependent labour. Local and regional conditions however determined which varieties of this type of labour were preferred, as can be illustrated from the Asia Minor material.

In the urban context, slaves of various categories constituted a significant part of the core labour force employed by households. This is clear not only from vague, general statements such as the casual reference to (household) slaves (*oiketai*) by Dio Chrysostom when describing the urban masses attracted by the court sessions in Apamea Celaenae,[14] or Galen's famous throwaway remark that in his native Pergamum, besides 40,000 (adult male) citizens, there were 80,000 'wives and slaves'[15] (even if the latter number is rhetorically inflated), but particularly from funerary epigraphy; inscriptions often refer to *douloi* or *sōmata* belonging to households, who might even start their own slave-family in the context of their master's household, as did Commodus,

14 Dio Chrys., *Or.* 35.15.

15 Gal., *De cognoscendis curandisque animi morbis* 9 (5.49 ed. Kühn).

doulos of L. Calpurnius (?) Proculus, who erected a monument for himself, his wife and son.[16] Interestingly, mixed marriages between slaves and free individuals, either freeborn or manumitted, are attested quite frequently. For instance, Nestor son of Herennios, citizen of Savatra, erected a grave monument for his wife Pola, who has no patronymikon and was therefore presumably a slave.[17] At Atlandy (Laodicea), the *doulos* Epaphroditos married his mistress Pardalas, as is clear from the inscription belonging to the grave monument for their son, Phosporos.[18]

Freedmen (*apeleutheroi*) are also quite commonly attested, mostly in urban settings, a further indication for the widespread existence of slavery in the cities.[19] Again funerary epigraphy is our most informative source. It is very clear from this material that strong bonds and close, lifelong ties generally continued to exist between the freedmen and their former masters, since many inscriptions mentioning freedmen actually refer to them as having the right to be buried with their former master, now patron, and his family in the same tomb.[20]

A specific category of household slaves, to be differentiated from the *douloi*, are the *threptoi. Threptos* was a term, employed widely throughout the Roman east, for an individual raised by others than his or her natural parents. *Threptoi* were often 'adopted' at an early age, but they never became official members of the households of their nurturers in a legal sense. They could have a variety of social positions, and free *threptoi* are certainly attested. The majority of *threptoi*, however, seem to have fulfilled servile functions in their nurturers' households, and the term is often used interchangeably with other terms used for, or associated with, slavery, which has led scholars to conclude that most *threptoi* were in fact, or had at some point in their life been, slaves. *Threptoi*, then, were a common type of household slave, and their presence is widely attested throughout Roman Asia Minor. Many *threptoi* will have been abandoned infants (a common form of family limitation), or children sold by their natural parents. Unless freeborn status could be proved, these categories of children could be enslaved by their nurturers. Thus, the child became a servant

16 *MAMA* I 41.

17 *MAMA* VIII 244.

18 *MAMA* I 295; Golubcova (1992: 88–90) for further examples and discussion. See also Martin (2003) for a perceptive analysis of the many different roles that slaves could play within family structures in Roman Asia Minor.

19 E.g. *IGR* III 800–802.

20 E.g. *IGR* IV 1475 = *I.Smyrna* 228 + II(2) p. 371 = McCabe, *Smyrna* 818; *IGR* IV 510; *SEG* II 578; Golubcova (1992: 95–101).

in the household of its nurturers.[21] What the precise tasks of *threptoi* were is difficult to ascertain, since the evidence for their existence mostly consists of funerary inscriptions, but we have no reason to assume that their work differed much from that of other categories of household slaves. What the evidence *does* reveal, however, is a discourse signifying strong bonds of mutual affection between *threptoi* and their nurturers/masters. We have numerous inscriptions where *threptoi* are commemorated in the most affectionate terms by their masters/foster-parents/nurturers, or, in the case of manumitted *threptoi*, patrons. Epithets like *teimiōtatos* (most valued), *philtatos* (most loved), *aeimnēstos* (unforgettable), *potheinotatos* (most strongly missed), *glukutatos* (sweetest), *chrēstos* (honest), *haploustatos* (most frank), *pistos* (faithful) and so on abound. *Threptoi* themselves also commemorated their masters/foster-parents, often in equally glowing terms, using terms like *asunkritos* (incomparable) or *agathos* (good).[22] Frequently, *threptoi* are commemorated alongside biological sons and daughters, and often they were admitted to the family tomb.[23] *Threptoi* were also often manumitted. Some scholars have noted that *threptoi* are somewhat more frequently attested in the cities and villages of central and eastern Asia Minor (but including Lydia), and less often in the cities of the westernmost parts of the peninsula and the islands. One explanation for this might be the presence of more robust and developed slave markets in the great cities of the west (e.g. Pergamum, Ephesus, Miletus, Smyrna), which would allow households to purchase slaves at any given age, whenever they wanted or needed them.[24]

For the exploitation of the household's landed properties, if any, in the case of small farming households use would of course be made of immediate family members in addition to any *threptoi* or *douloi*, if present. The management of larger estates in Asia Minor, i.e. those belonging to urban elites, knights and senators, was mostly in the hands of slave or freedman overseers. Slave or freedman *epitropoi* (*vilici/procuratores*) and *pragmateutai* (*actores*) are widely attested epigraphically for elite estates.[25] An unusually

21 Cameron (1939); Nani (1943–1944); Golubcova (1992: 90–94); Ricl (2009); Dry (2013).

22 Ricl (2009: 105).

23 Martin (2003: 225); Destephen (2010: 142–143).

24 Golubcova (1992: 122).

25 Broughton (1938: 663–676) for numerous examples; Mitchell (1993: ch. 10). As Carlsen (1995: 15–16) points out, the Greek term *epitropos* could be used to denote a *vilicus* or slave-bailiff (this is how Cicero renders *epitropos* in his Latin translation of Xenophon's *Oeconomicus*, see Columella, *Rust.* 11.1.5; Xen., *Oec.* 12.2) but during the imperial period is also used for *procurator*. Another term for *vilicus* was *oikonomos*. See Schäfer (1998: 10–11)

informative dossier of inscriptions from the region around the city of Kibyra in south-western Asia Minor, on the border between Lycia, Caria, Phrygia and Pisidia, provides important clues as to the actual administration of such large estates, and also to possible changes in administrative practices over time.[26] According to Thomas Corsten's reconstruction, several of the texts refer to a large estate that, around the middle of the second century, belonged to a certain L. Marcius Celer M. Calpurnius Longus, who was consul ca. AD 148 and lived in Attaleia (modern Antalya) in Pamphylia. Longus had his estate administered by a freedman *epitropos* (*vilicus/procurator*), and also rented large parts of the estate out to (his own) freedmen, as *misthōtai* or *conductores* (in fact, the *epitropos* L. Calpurnius Salvius played a double role, because he is also attested as *misthōtes*).[27] The *misthōtai*, in turn, may have sub-let plots of land to local farmers, but the inscriptions do not mention this. There are also some references to an *oikonomos* or steward (*vilicus*) of the estate, who may have been a slave. It is unclear what the precise relationship was between the *oikonomos* and the *epitropos*.

Then, according to Corsten, at some unknown point in time, the estate probably changed hands and became the possession of the senatorial *familia* of the Ummidii, who seem to have owned it from about AD 200 until well into the third century. The Ummidii employed a slightly more complex form of estate administration. In charge of the estate as a whole was an *epitropos*. The estate was divided into three domains, each of which was in turn administered by a *pragmateutes* or *actor*. The *epitropos* and the *pragmateutai* all were slaves of the Ummidii; unlike their predecessors, the Calpurnii, the Ummidii did not employ freedmen in administrative functions.[28] Nor did they rent out their estate to their freedmen. Instead, the domains were let to *misthōtai* or *conductores* who belonged to the free, indigenous population of the region, and who in turn sublet the land in plots to tenant-farmers (*coloni*) belonging to this same indigenous population. Here we find strong parallels with the

---

on the looseness of Greek terminology for 'administrators' or 'managers', and for further references.

26 Corsten (2005) with an epigraphic appendix containing all the relevant documents.

27 Corsten (2005: 17–18).

28 Corsten (2005: 11–12) refers to the *epitropoi* mentioned in the inscriptions concerning the estate-personnel of the Ummidii as *procuratores*, but he also (persuasively) argues that they were slaves, since they have only single names (i.e. no father's names are given). Presumably, therefore, the *epitropoi* of the Ummidii were *vilici* rather than *procuratores* (the term *epitropos* in imperial times could mean both, seen n. 25 above), since as formal legal representatives of their principals, *procuratores* could never be slaves, see e.g. Schäfer (1998: 22–23).

management of imperial estates in North Africa.[29] The *coloni* appear to have held the land in perpetual leasehold, since the inscriptions show that many of them had been present on the land for at least three generations. Although some of them bear Greek or Latin names, none can be shown to have held Roman citizenship before the *Constitutio Antoniniana*, and very few were citizens of Kibyra. Corsten argues that all this suggests a strong continuity of presence on the land: the forefathers of the *coloni* on the Ummidii estate may well already have been cultivating this land in pre-Roman times. The new Roman owners then simply took them over as a workforce after the provincialisation of the region. Given the well attested presence of indigenous semi-dependent rural workforces in many areas of Asia Minor during the Hellenistic and (early) imperial periods, this seems a very likely scenario.[30]

Widespread references in epigraphic material from all over Asia Minor to slave or freedmen *pragmateutai, epitropoi* and *oikonomoi* as well as to *misthōtai* and local tenancy suggests that the administrative situation attested for the Calpurnii/Ummidii estate was fairly representative of conditions in Asia Minor more broadly. Agricultural slavery in the sense of chattel slave workforces as known from the *latifundia* of Republican Italy is nowhere attested clearly. Slaves were certainly present on estates, but generally in management functions, as we saw, or as household helps in and around the central villa, as is suggested by a passage of Aristides,[31] who refers to landlords of estates in Mysia neighbouring his own lands as arming their *oiketai* and *misthōtai*, that is, their slaves and lease-holders, where *oiketai* refers to household slaves. Of course *coloni* might have employed their own slaves to assist them, but we have little evidence of this.

Households in Asia Minor no doubt also employed some free wage-labour, but, if the parallel with the rest of the Roman world can be trusted, probably mostly on a casual or temporary basis. In an urban setting this might entail, for instance, the hiring of a contractor and his workforce to build or repair an urban residence, in a rural setting we could refer to the hiring of temporary labour at harvest time, mostly supplied by local farmers or residents from nearby towns who sought some additional income. In the case of the Appianus estate in Roman Egypt, Dominic Rathbone has been able to show the presence of long-term skilled salaried employees as well as casual wage-labourers, but it is doubtful whether we can simply extrapolate from this for the rest of the

29 Kehoe (1988).

30 Schuler (1998: 198–215).

31 Arist. 50.105–108 (Keil) (= 346 Jebb page).

Roman world.[32] Varro, in a discussion of extra labour that could be hired during the busiest periods on the estate (the vintage, the haying season), refers to the hiring of free men, but also to *obaerarii*, that is, those working off a debt through their labour, 'of whom there are many still in Asia, in Egypt, and in Illyricum', he says.[33] This might suggests that in Asia Minor as well as in the other regions mentioned, debt-bondsmen may have been at least as common a type of labourer as free wage-workers.

At first sight, then, households in Asia Minor seem to have made use of a rather confusing jumble of individuals in various status positions to cover their labour needs. In several respects (i.e. burial of freedmen and slaves together with masters/patrons and their kin, use of slaves and freedmen as estate managers, only casual employment of free wage labour) their behaviour conforms to what we find elsewhere in the Roman world, whereas in others, it seems more regionally determined (*threptoi, obaerarii*), but this does not lessen the confusion. The fact that to us, as ancient historians, some of these various labour statuses seem very familiar simply because we encounter them so often in our sources does not make them any less idiosyncratic when looked at from a comparative perspective, from the perspective, say, of an early modern historian used to the commercialised labour markets of seventeenth-century Holland. When, however, we assume a context of thin and fragmented labour markets, slow circulation and endemic uncertainty concerning the trustworthiness of information and individuals, a context, moreover, in which skilled labour in particular was scarce and difficult to come by, the strategies adopted by households in Asia Minor to supply their labour needs begin to make sense, and the impression of needless complexity disappears.

First, it is noteworthy that for household tasks, many of which would have required a certain amount of skill, households generally made use of labourers who had strong ties of legal, social and emotional dependence to the household: slaves, freedmen, and house-bred servants (*threptoi*). This is fully conversant with a situation in which skilled labour is scarce and costly, and reliable information on the trustworthiness of outside individuals is difficult to come by. The market for wage labour was insufficiently developed for households to employ wage workers at low risk and low transaction costs for the tasks performed by slaves, freedmen or *threptoi*. For this reason, households ensured that those with skills, or those whose skills they had developed, were tied as closely to the household as possible, and could be fully controlled.

32 Rathbone (1991).

33 Varro, *Rust.* 1.17.2–3.

Second, as elsewhere in the Roman world, elite households made use of slaves and freedmen to manage their landed estates. This of course is fully in line with recent scholarship on the use of slaves and freedmen as agents in other economic sectors such as trade and finance, and this scholarship indeed suggests some of the reasons behind a similar employment of dependents in agricultural administration.[34] The *epitropoi, oikonomoi* and *pragmateutai* were no doubt skilled individuals with previous management experience. Scarcity of skilled labour and the costliness of human capital again provided households with a strong incentive to maximise social and legal control over such workers, hence their servile or freedman status. They are also likely to have belonged to their master's or patron's household for a long time already. Not only would this have enabled the master or patron to select for aptitude, but also bonds of loyalty and trust would have developed that were of absolute necessity for this type of absentee landlordism. Furthermore, slaves and freedmen of course had few alternative sources of support beyond their master or patron, and could therefore also be expected to display loyalty and diligence.

Third, there is the relationship between the household and those who did the actual agricultural work on the estates. Unlike Republican *latifundia* owners, landlords in Asia Minor do not seem to have employed chattel slaves. There may have been practical reasons for this, given that the agronomists suggest that for far-away, less intensively exploited estates, tenants were a better option,[35] and indeed we often encounter tenants in provincial settings. Yet there may have been an element of path dependence here as well: indigenous semi-dependent peasant populations had been an important source of labour in Asia Minor already during the Hellenistic period, and the new Roman landowners had few incentives to radically alter such existing structures by shifting to a slave mode of exploitation. It should be noted, in this context, that the *coloni* on the Calpurnii/Ummidii estate in the Kibyratis could reach a certain level of wealth, that is, they were not subsistence peasants. This is signified by the fact that many of them were able to make small cash contributions to public subscription schemes, and that some of them managed to become *misthōtai*.[36] Nonetheless, their social and legal position, as far as this can be ascertained, suggests fairly limited bargaining powers: none were Roman citizens and only very few apparently were even citizens of the polis in whose territory the estate was located. This suggests that landlords potentially had some considerable extra-economic control over these individuals.

---

34 See above n. 11; see also Hawkins in this volume.

35 E.g. Columella, *Rust.* 1.7.6–7.

36 Corsten (2005: 13–17).

Hints in the evidence from other parts of Asia Minor similarly suggest that rural populations, although legally free, were not always completely independent, as is indicated, for instance, by an inscription from Hierapolis recording a contribution by an unknown local benefactor to rebuilding the city's theatre.[37] In addition to a sum of money he also contributed 'the aid of his own agricultural workers' (*tōn idiōn agroikōn*), which at least suggests a position of semi-dependency for these workers. Again, such circumstances can be associated with a situation in which rural labour markets remained fairly underdeveloped and households therefore made use, if not of slaves, then at least of the labour of populations over whom they could exercise a considerable level of control. And if indeed in Asia Minor debt bondage was a fairly common source of additional labour for elite estates during peak periods, as Varro suggests, then a similar analysis can of course be applied to this category of workers.

We now turn to the second institutional/organisational framework to be discussed in this paper, namely cities. My discussion will be somewhat briefer here, given that there is some theoretical overlap with what has already been said regarding households. Urban communities acted as important 'buyers' and employers of labour in their own right and are therefore an important type of institution to consider in this context. For a great number of public tasks, cities relied on public slaves (*dēmosioi*), whose presence is widely attested in Asia Minor. Numbers could be impressive: an inscription from Kibyra mentions 107 public slaves who had been sold illegally, but were recovered for the city.[38] From the correspondence between Pliny the Younger and Trajan we learn that public slaves might be employed as prison guards, a highly responsible position, but that they were also often used for dirtier, more labour intensive jobs such as cleaning sewers, paving streets and work in the public baths, in short, all those tasks necessary for the proper and continued functioning of the urban infrastructure.[39] In addition, we find public slaves in secretarial functions, as archivists, as staff members in a gymnasium, as *oikonomoi* (treasurers, bursars) of the polis, and so on.[40] Again, these are fairly respectable and responsible jobs, some of which were essential to the administration of civic public life. It is interesting to note that cities, to supply their core labour needs, and to secure the performance of jobs that were essential to the smooth running of civic life, and which, in the case of administrative functions, also required a considerable level of skill, made use of dependent labour.

---

37 *IGR* IV 808 = *IAlt.Hierap.* 4.

38 *IKibyra* 41.

39 Plin., *Ep.* 10.19, 20, 31, 32.

40 Golubcova (1992: 85–87); Weiss (2004: esp. 50–59) on οἰκονόμοι τῆς πόλεως.

In addition, some of these jobs (prison guard, *oikonomos* of the city) were of a kind that required the community to place a considerable level of trust in the persons who performed them.

To some extent, of course, the use of public slaves by Greco-Roman urban communities was path dependent, i.e. the result of the particular socio-political development of ancient cities. In the Greek polis and Roman *civitas*, the annual rotation of magisterial offices was meant to ensure that power did not come to rest with a certain individual or group for a sustained period of time. For this reason, ancient cities never developed actual professional bureaucracies. Those tasks that did need doing continuously, but were either too humiliating or required a level of technical skill or know-how that could not be expected from an amateur magistrate, were entrusted to public slaves, who had no social status and could be fully controlled by the city, and therefore, despite the permanent character of their assignments, could accumulate no socio-political power.

However, the fact that cities in Roman Asia Minor and elsewhere even under the more settled conditions of the empire still chose to have many core tasks performed by dependent labourers again testifies to the underdeveloped nature of labour markets, and to the scarcity of skilled labour, which, once obtained, needed to be tied as firmly as possible to the institution employing it. Slavery was an obvious choice. Public slaves, moreover, as slaves of the community were totally dependent on that community for any position that they might hold; they had no outside source of social power. This provided them with the incentive to be loyal, diligent and, if only for fear of punishment, trustworthy, and it meant that one could entrust them with responsible public tasks. In all this, cities were very much in the same position, and guided by the same incentives, as households. The fact that slaves could become *oikonomoi tēs poleōs* is particularly noteworthy in this respect: the position resembles that of a slave or freedman overseer of a household or estate, who was also often called *oikonomos* (see above). It has been suggested tentatively that in the east the Roman practice of employing slaves or freedmen in such positions within households (with the *familia Caesaris* as most evident example) could have inspired Greek poleis to replace the Hellenistic magistracy of *tamias* (treasurer) with public slave *oikonomoi*.[41]

With regard to free wage-labour, cities also behaved very much in the same way as households, in that they often employed wage labourers on a temporary basis, for specific tasks. In the case of urban communities, that task was often public construction. In Asia Minor, as far as the scarce evidence allows us to

41 Weiss (2004: 57–58).

reconstruct, public building projects were managed by public overseers and public architects, who gave out the work to groups of free workmen, who contracted to carry out part of the construction project. This at least is clear from scraps of evidence such as an inscription from Miletus, in which the workmen who had contracted to build part of the theatre in that city ask the oracle of Apollo at Didyma whether they should continue with the work or seek some other employment elsewhere—perhaps they had gotten into a conflict with the city?[42] The text suggests that the workers were mobile and might move to another city to seek similar temporary employment on a project there.

We find little evidence in Asia Minor for more permanent salaried posts in the cities, such as, for instance, those attested for the assistants of the *duoviri* and the *aediles* in the *lex Ursonensis* from Spain.[43] What we do find, as in other cities, are references to doctors, philosophers and orators in civic employ, highly skilled professionals who received a *honorarium* from the city, and often had immunity from liturgies and civic services, which we might perhaps interpret as yet another strategy to tie skilled labour to its place of employment, this time through a positive incentive, a sort of 'skills premium', rather than force.[44]

To conclude, in Roman Asia Minor (and probably in many other parts of the empire) neither institutional traditions (path dependence) nor market conditions favoured the employment, by cities, of a permanent workforce of skilled and unskilled wage-labourers to carry out core public tasks. Instead cities as institutions made use of individuals in various status positions to carry out those tasks that were beyond the scope of their magistrates but were nonetheless vital to the upkeep of civic infrastructure and the smooth running of civic life, responding as best as they could to the incentive structures generated by the institutional environment of which they themselves formed a part.

IV

In this essay, I have tried to argue that the great variety of labour statuses that we find in our source material for the Roman world does not suggest the existence of a unified, integrated labour market in the empire, but should rather be interpreted as a response to a situation of fragmented, underdeveloped labour markets, endemic uncertainty, scarcity of skilled labour and high trans-

42 Buckler (1923: 34–36); Broughton (1938: 837–838).

43 *CIL* II 5439,62.

44 Jones (1940: 184–185, with n. 56).

action costs. I have also suggested, using evidence from Roman Asia Minor as an initial case study, that an institutional-economic focus, that is, a focus on the institutional/organisational frameworks within which Roman labour functioned, might be a productive way to analyse precisely *how* the great variety of labour statuses in the Roman world in fact constituted a response to such (partial) labour market failure. Inevitably, within the confines of a short essay, my discussion has been somewhat brief. Much more can no doubt be done with the evidence, from Asia Minor and from other regions, but that would require a larger study. For now, however, I want to conclude with a few remarks on what I think are some of the general benefits of an institutional approach to Roman labour, both to stimulate discussion and as pointers to further research.

First, as I hope the above discussion has made clear, an institutional approach does not require one to downplay the importance of or even partially ignore the attested variation of labour statuses, as scholars developing Marxist class-based approaches or neo-classical market analyses often do. On the contrary, in an institutional analysis, the variation as such becomes the focus of analysis.

Second, an institutional approach also frees us from the endless and, on present evidence, irresolvable debate regarding the question whether the Roman Empire was a 'slave economy' or a 'slave society', or (a minority position) a society mainly based on wage-labour. Once one adopts an institutional approach, this debate is rendered pointless because attention shifts from the (unanswerable) questions of the relative quantitative or qualitative dominance of various types of labour to the ways in which institutions and organisations strategically employed individuals in various status positions to fulfil their labour needs, responding to the incentive structures created by the wider institutional environment. From the standpoint of comparative economic history, this seems a much more fruitful type of analysis.

This brings me to my third and final point, which is the obvious but important one that an institutional approach to Roman labour might potentially allow us to determine in what ways, if any, the ostensibly complex Roman status structure in fact contributed to the empire's economic performance. Finley's status model was built on the assumption that the ancient status structure presented a hindrance to economic development and growth. Institutional analysis might allow us to forge meaningful connections between structure and performance and discover ways in which Romans managed to employ labour and other production factors in such ways as to increase productivity. Demonstrating such productivity gains was not the aim of this essay, and it is certainly a very difficult thing to do, but that should not deter us from trying.

CHAPTER 3

Contracts, Coercion, and the Boundaries of the Roman Artisanal Firm

Cameron Hawkins

The funerary altar of the knife-maker Lucius Cornelius Atimetus provides one of our few direct glimpses into the dynamics of a Roman artisanal workshop. When Atimetus commissioned the altar in the middle of the first century AD, both on behalf of himself and on behalf of his former slave, Epaphra, he had it decorated with two reliefs. In one, Atimetus and another man—either Epaphra, or perhaps a client—stand beside a cabinet in which a small collection of the workshop's products is on display. In the other, Atimetus and Epaphra are hard at work in the smithy. On the left side of this relief, a seated Atimetus holds a work-in-progress on the anvil with his left hand, and a small hammer in his right; across from him stands Epaphra, poised to deliver a strong blow to the piece in a spot to be indicated by a tap from Atimetus' own hammer.[1]

Together, these reliefs evoke an image of an artisanal enterprise in which a proprietor relied heavily on the labour of a slave, who in this case ultimately earned his freedom. That image of a small slave-based firm finds enough echoes in other categories of evidence to suggest that it was a widespread feature of Rome's artisan economy. Several other funerary inscriptions from Rome, for example, suggest that skilled artisans began their careers as slaves in workshops belonging to other craftsmen, as did the wheelwright Marcus Sergius Eutychus,[2] even if they too ultimately earned their freedom. Equally instructive is a letter written in the late second century AD by a shopkeeper or artisan who may have worked in one of the Greek cities of Asia Minor. In the letter, preserved for posterity by the Roman lawyer Q. Cervidius Scaevola,[3]

1 Rome, Vatican Museums, Galleria Lapidaria, inv. 9277. Full discussion and bibliography can be found in Zimmer (1982: 180–182). For further discussion, see Clarke (2003: 121–123); and Kampen (1981: 97–98). The precise identities of the men depicted in the first panel are disputed: Zimmer prefers to interpret them as Atimetus and Epaphra; Clarke and Kampen, on the other hand, prefer to read the scene as a depiction of Atimetus making a sale to one of his clients. See also the contribution by Flohr in this volume (with a drawing of the reliefs).

2 *CIL* VI 9215.

3 *Dig.* 20.1.34.1.

 | DOI 10.1163/9789004331686_004

the author pledged security in exchange for a loan; that security consisted not only of his shop, but also of the slaves who presumably worked within it.

In one sense, it is hardly surprising that artisans who lived and worked in a slave society relied extensively on the labour of enslaved workers. If nothing else, slaveholding itself was inherently satisfying in a world in which 'owning slaves always served to express *potestas* in a society highly sensitive to gradations of status, esteem, and authority'.[4] Yet, in another sense, the decision to acquire slave workers was not one that Roman artisans could undertake lightly, since the product markets in which they earned their livelihoods were affected strongly enough by seasonal and uncertain patterns of demand that it would have been risky for entrepreneurs to maintain costly assets—human or otherwise—if those assets were likely to be underemployed for extended periods of time.[5] This was true even in a large and metropolitan consumer market like that of Rome itself, where seasonality and uncertainty ensured that demand for the products and services of most artisans was neither consistent nor entirely predictable during any given year. For those producers who made day-to-day goods and small luxuries, or who provided services for the average urban resident, uncertainty was mostly a product of agricultural variability: by driving up food prices, a bad harvest could depress the overall consumption of non-agricultural products among the bulk of the urban populace.[6] For those who manufactured quality goods for the high-end segments of the market, on the other hand, uncertainty was largely a result of a tendency on the part of wealthy clients to order products that were at least partly customized to their own tastes; from the point of view of individual artisans, these kinds of purchases were always unpredictable.[7] Seasonal patterns of consumption only added to these complications. In low-end markets, the purchasing power of many consumers varied over the year not just in response to cyclical changes in the price of grain (which tended to be low immediately after the harvest, and much higher near the end of the next growing season),[8] but also in response to seasonal changes in the availability of certain kinds of work. Building work, for instance, took place between the beginning of April and the beginning of

4 Bradley (1994: 10–30); the quotation itself can be found on p. 30.

5 I offer a more detailed discussion of this point in Hawkins (2012).

6 Erdkamp (2005: 143–167) offers an excellent overview of grain markets in preindustrial contexts.

7 Good overviews of demand in upper segments of the market in the early modern context can be found in Schwarz (1992: 31–73 and 103–123), and in Sonenscher (1989: 99–173). For more detail on bespoke consumption in the Roman world, see Hawkins (2012: 186).

8 Erdkamp (2005: 147–155).

November, while the summer sailing season generated considerable employment for the labourers who unloaded ships at Ostia and Portus, as well as the bargemen, animal handlers, and porters who moved goods from these harbours to Rome itself.[9] Finally, demand in low-end and high-end markets alike was affected by seasonal patterns of travel and migration that produced fluctuations throughout the year in the number of consumers resident in the city: seasonal changes in wages stimulated complex inter-sectoral flows of labour between city and countryside at different points in the agricultural calendar, while wealthy visitors and residents moved between Rome and their primary residences or country estates in response both to the rhythms of political life and to seasonal outbreaks of diseases like malaria.[10]

In what follows, I explore the considerations that may have prompted artisans to acquire enslaved workers, in spite of the risks that this entailed in an environment characterized by seasonal and uncertain demand. I do so by drawing not only upon recent research that focuses on the social and economic contexts of wage labour and slavery in the Roman world,[11] but also upon theoretical scholarship that treats the firm as a particular kind of economic organization designed, among other things, to smooth problems that can arise during the course of economic exchange. In the process, I offer two main arguments. First, because artisans were embedded in labour markets that were relatively tight, they had incentives to recruit small but permanent workforces—or, in other words, to expand the boundaries of their firms—in order to secure reliable access to at least some skilled labour. This was true even if there were a danger that members of those workforces would be underemployed for some of the year, and even if they hedged their bets by continuing to make some use of the spot market. Second, they preferred to staff those permanent workforces by acquiring slaves rather than by hiring workers on long-term contracts. In the tight labour market conditions that motivated them to recruit small permanent workforces in the first place, Roman artisans found it difficult to enforce long-term labour contracts with hired workers, especially since they

9 The *locus classicus* for the seasonality of the building trades is Frontin., *Aq.* 2.123. For further details, see Brunt (1980: 93) and Martin (1989: 73). Cf. Anderson (1997: 145–151). On the rhythm of the sailing season and its impact on work in Rome's maritime and riverine harbours, see Aldrete and Mattingly (1999: 192–204).

10 For further discussion of the economic impact of seasonal patterns of travel and migration (in both ancient and early modern contexts), see Hawkins (2013).

11 See Scheidel (2012b) for an overview of the state of this debate, which ultimately hinges on our ability to assess both the relative costs and relative productivity of hired versus slave labour.

could not rely on relational contracts based upon reputation and social sanctions to help them do so. By contrast, the coercive authority that they exercised as slaveholders ensured that they had no such fears when they staffed their enterprises with slaves.

Artisanal Firms: Theoretical and Comparative Perspectives

Since very little of our surviving evidence reflects the outlooks of Roman artisans themselves, two heuristics—one theoretical, and one comparative—offer the best starting point for any discussion of their business strategies. In this section, I suggest that both the theory of the firm and the experiences of artisan employers in the early modern context provide some sense of the factors that may have encouraged some Roman artisans to assemble small permanent workforces, many of which consisted primarily of slaves. As we shall see, these heuristics suggest that the critical variables responsible for the decisions Roman artisans made concerning employment were the character of the labour market in which they worked, and the extent to which informal institutions or norms permitted them to enforce agreements by employing personal reputations and social sanctions to create strong relational contracts.

I begin with the theory of the firm. For heuristic purposes, a firm can be defined as 'an integrated and durable organization of people and other assets, acting tacitly or otherwise as a "legal person", set up for the purpose of producing goods or services, with the capacity to sell or hire them to customers, and with associated and recognized corporate legal entitlements and liabilities.'[12] This definition is, by design, broad enough to apply to organizations in a range of different historical contexts—including those in the Roman world, in which an entrepreneur could stand at the head of a firm consisting not only of slaves or other dependants in his power (that is, members of his *familia*), but also of other individuals who had assumed obligations to him under contract. Yet, at the same time, by emphasizing that firms are organized primarily in order to produce goods or services for exchange, the definition remains specific enough to differentiate a firm from other kinds of organizations that might otherwise seem similar (such as a household not organized for the production and sale of specific goods or services).[13]

By treating Roman artisanal enterprises as firms in this sense, we can formulate a framework for studying the business decisions of Roman entrepreneurs

12 Hodgson (1999: 235–241, and esp. 238).

13 Cf. Hodgson (1999: 235 n. 13).

by drawing upon a rich theoretical and empirical literature devoted to the problem of economic organization. This is a potentially rewarding approach precisely because much of this literature seeks to explain why entrepreneurs choose to organize or integrate some of the transactions necessary for the production of a good or service within firms in the first place, especially when they can choose instead to coordinate those transactions by engaging in a series of repeated contractual exchanges with other independent actors.[14] Broadly speaking, efforts to address this problem generally posit that entrepreneurs decide whether or not to organize a given transaction within a firm by grappling with trade-offs in two dimensions. The first is a trade-off in the realm of production costs. Put rather simply, entrepreneurs who choose to coordinate transactions within an integrated firm can sometimes realize economies of scale in the process by reducing their overall per-unit production costs. Integration, however, comes at a price, since among other things it means that entrepreneurs who do expand the size of their firms convert what would otherwise be variable costs into fixed costs: while entrepreneurs who opt for disintegrated production strategies typically contract with and pay specialists only as and when necessary, those who choose instead to coordinate production within a firm must generally bear increased fixed costs in the form of regular wages for employees, ongoing maintenance for specialized equipment, and rent for larger workspaces.

Entrepreneurs who contemplate integration also face a second trade-off, which unfolds in the realm of transaction costs. These are generally conceptualized as both the direct costs and the opportunity costs that arise because individuals must devote time, energy, and resources to certain specific processes in order to smooth exchange. They include the costs of activities such as locating and vetting potential economic partners, negotiating agreements in the face of potential uncertainties, and—potentially most importantly—enforcing the terms of any resulting contracts.[15] From this perspective, the firm can be conceptualized as a governance structure that permits entrepreneurs to mitigate their overall transaction costs. Entrepreneurs who do choose to integrate certain kinds of transaction within their firms incur a cluster of internal transaction costs in the process: some of these arise because large and complex organizations can be less responsive than individuals or smaller firms to

14 Coase (1937) remains the classic study on transaction costs and the firm. For good overviews of recent developments in various branches of the theory of the firm (with emphasis on questions concerning boundaries), see Gibbons (2005) and Zenger, Felin and Bigelow (2011).

15 Acheson (2002) offers a useful introduction to transaction costs.

sudden changes in market conditions, while others reflect an entrepreneur's need to create internal incentive structures to replace the high-powered market incentives that motivate independent actors to find new ways of improving quality or reducing prices. At the same time, however, the entrepreneur can potentially rely on his or her own authority within the firm to reduce or eliminate some of the more severe transaction costs that can otherwise make coordinating production through market-based contractual exchange difficult or impossible, especially when potential contractual partners are difficult to locate, or contracts are difficult to enforce. Crucially, the magnitude of individual transaction costs, whether of those internal to the firm or of those arising in the course of contractual exchange, depends heavily on the broader institutional and social environment in which an entrepreneur works, which among other things determines the efficacy of legal mechanisms for contract enforcement. In particular, recent literature has emphasized the important role played by informal organizations and norms in economic life. These strongly affect the extent to which entrepreneurs can mitigate both internal and external transaction costs by taking advantage of relational contracts—that is, agreements and understandings embedded in relationships of trust, which individuals enforce through social sanctions based on reputation rather than through legal mechanisms.[16]

Comparative evidence complements this theoretical framework by providing some sense of how these considerations could play out in economic environments characterized by the kind of seasonal and uncertain demand that was typical in the product markets of the Roman world. In the cities of early modern Europe, in which urban producers were forced to contend with comparable market forces, the fixed costs associated with integration tended to discourage artisans from expanding their firms. Artisans who catered to the high-quality bespoke trade found integration particularly risky, since there was a very good chance that their workers would be underemployed for much of the year. This was the case not just because it was difficult for artisans to produce for stock when so much work was custom-made, but also because the manufacture of many of the products sold in these segments—lavish furniture, coaches, gold and silver plate—drew on the services of specialists whose skills were not always necessary for every piece. Yet even within individual workshops in these trades, or within workshops in industries in which divisions of labour were less apparent, artisans still faced risks if they expanded their firms and strove for regular output: a sudden change in consumer

16 On relational contracts, especially as they relate to the theory of the firm, see Gibbons (2005: 236–238) and Baker, Gibbons, and Murphy (2002); cf. Hawkins (2012: 176–177).

purchasing power or in consumer preferences could leave them with excess stock, which they might find not only expensive to store, but also difficult to sell in time to generate the cash necessary to pay their employees and to make payments to the suppliers from whom they purchased goods and services on credit. For these reasons, many urban producers therefore favoured production strategies in which they sought to minimize their ongoing fixed expenses, while nevertheless attempting to retain the flexibility to produce small batches of goods in response to prevailing levels of demand. In practice, this meant that most operated firms consisting at most of only one or two apprentices or journeymen employed on long-term contracts; when confronted by demand that exceed the capacities of their own firms, they either tendered out subcontracts to other artisans, or—if they wished to reserve a greater share of the profit for themselves—they secured additional manpower by recruiting additional workers on the spot market, whether by the day, by the week, or even by the job.[17]

Importantly, artisan employers in the early modern context could rely on the spot market in order to adapt their workforces to changes in market demand only to the extent that workers with the requisite skills were available when needed (that is, if the market in skilled labour were relatively well-stocked).[18] When this was not the case, transaction costs in the spot market could be high enough that artisan employers ran the risk of not being able to secure the short-term help necessary in order to benefit from favourable conditions of demand. Permanent labour agreements offered one potential solution to this problem, since employers who selectively offered a small number of permanent contracts could ensure reliable access to at least some of the labour that they were likely to require during high season—provided, that is, that they could not only configure these contracts in a way that minimized the fixed costs they incurred by taking on a regular employee, but also ensure that their employees honoured their agreements. Employers could potentially minimize the fixed costs of permanent employment agreements by taking advantage of the fact that they were likely to be less risk-averse than their employees. More specifically, in an economy in which employment and income were both seasonal and somewhat unpredictable, an employer could offer an employee a permanent contract which featured a somewhat lower wage than what the employee could expect to earn on the spot market under ideal conditions, but

17 For overviews of the risks artisans faced in the early modern context, and of the production strategies they adopted in response to those risks, see Farr (2000: 52–56), Sonenscher (1989: 130–173 and esp. 135–138), and Schwarz (1992: 31–33 and 117–123).

18 Cf. Grantham (1994: 15–16).

which compensated him for a relatively low wage by guaranteeing a regular and steady income over the course of the year.[19] Yet, at the same time, an employer could find that such a contract was difficult to enforce, since it created scope for opportunism on the part of the employee. Because a permanent contract of this sort eliminated fluctuations in an employee's income by smoothing that income over time, there were inevitably periods of elevated demand any given year in which an employee could increase his short-term gain by reneging on the contract in order to enter the spot market. An employer's ability to craft a permanent or long-term labour contract was thus contingent upon his ability to find some way to structure incentives in a way designed to ensure that an employee stood to lose more than he gained by breaking his agreement. In practice, employers were therefore most likely to employ permanent labour contracts of this sort when they could rely on relational contracts backed by reliable reputation mechanisms in order to sanction employees who violated their agreements, and could therefore amplify the social costs incurred by a defaulter by persuading other employers not to offer him work in the future.[20]

Slaves, Labour Markets, and Reputations: Roman Artisans and Their Firms

By drawing attention to the importance of both labour market conditions and informal institutions or norms, the theoretical and comparative heuristics discussed above provide the outline of a potential explanation for efforts on the part of artisans to create small and permanent workforces consisting of slaves. On the one hand, they suggest that the character of labour markets in the Roman world may have given artisans some incentive to expand the boundaries of their firms: if labour markets were tight and transaction costs in the spot market correspondingly high, then artisans may have sought to lessen their dependence on the spot market by permanently recruiting some of the workers that they could anticipate employing when conditions were good. On the

19 Assuming that he had a concave utility function, a risk-averse employee derived more utility from a steady income than he did from a fluctuating income, even if his income in the former case was somewhat lower than in the latter. Discussions of the relevant theory can be found in Mukherjee and Ray (1995) and in Ray (1998: 515–522). Both of these pieces focus on agricultural employment in developing economies. For comparable wage payment schemes in early modern craft production, see Stedman Jones (1984: 33–34), and Sonenscher (1989: 190).

20 Ray (1998: 519–521).

other hand, these heuristics also indicate that those artisans who did choose to experiment with some level of integration were likely to take two specific considerations into account when assessing the relative merits of hired versus servile labour: first, the magnitude of the fixed costs that they stood to incur in either case; second, the extent to which they could be confident in enforcing long-term labour contracts. In the remainder of this paper, I develop this explanation in more detail, first by examining the nature of the labour market, and then by considering both the costs and the incentive problems generated by permanent labour contracts and by slavery, respectively. As we shall see, the skilled segments of the labour market in the Roman world were relatively tight, because skilled labour was scarce—scarce enough, perhaps, that artisans could not always rely on the spot market in order to recruit help in periods of elevated demand, and were instead willing to tolerate some degree of integration to ensure that they had at least some skilled help available when conditions were good. At the same time, many must have found that slaveholding was preferable to hiring workers on long-term contracts. This was true not because slaveholding offered any particular advantage over permanent labour contracts in the realm of fixed costs—skilled slaves were valuable, and their labour was accordingly expensive. Rather, artisans opted for slaveholding primarily because they found it difficult to rely on relational contracts in order to enforce agreements with permanent workers, and instead preferred the security offered to them by the coercive authority that they exercised over their slaves.

Apprenticeship, Opportunity Costs, and Tight Labour Markets

I begin by noting that not all artisan employers depended as heavily on skilled help as did others. In industries in which part of the production process could be broken down into relatively simple tasks, artisans could meet some of their needs for additional labour by recruiting unskilled workers who could quickly acquire necessary skills on the job. In these circumstances, transaction costs on the spot market were presumably low, especially in large cities like Rome, where unskilled segments of the labour market were undoubtedly overstocked, and artisans could readily hire workers on an as-needed basis. Miko Flohr, for instance, has stressed that the remains of large fulleries point to a system of task organization in this industry in which several of the individual stages required very little training;[21] the proprietors of such establishments could therefore presumably recruit short-term help with little effort, and had no need to create permanent and integrated workforces. Even the production

---

21 See Flohr (2011b), along with his contribution to this volume.

of low-end manufactured goods like footwear could be partly rationalized in a way that made it possible for artisans to recruit unskilled workers who were willing to learn specific tasks quickly or who had acquired some familiarity with materials and processes through learning-by-doing.[22]

Skilled help, however, remained critical for many artisans. While this was true especially of those who produced goods for the high-end segments of the market, even a smith like Lucius Cornelius Atimetus required skilled assistance in order to increase his output in response to high demand. As I have already noted, his funerary altar seems to depict him sitting at his anvil as his freedman Epaphra works as a striker. Crucially, a good striker needed to have essentially the same knowledge of the process as the smith with whom he worked, particularly if they were to work efficiently together as a team.[23] For artisans in this position, tight labour markets meant that it could be difficult to recruit qualified help as necessary on the spot market: in these circumstances transaction costs were likely to have been high, and artisans would not have been able to count on locating qualified workers on short notice, particularly during times of the year when general conditions of demand in urban product markets were strong.[24]

High wage premiums for skilled workers offer one indication that the market for skilled labour was indeed potentially tight enough to complicate artisans' efforts to recruit workers on an as-needed basis and to encourage them to contemplate integration as an alternative. At the beginning of the fourth century AD, for instance, Diocletian's edict established maximum wages for skilled workers that were at least twice as high as those for common labourers (see Groen-Vallinga and Tacouma in this volume). While the relationship of those putative maximums to actual wage rates is far from clear, as is their relationship to wages in the first and second centuries AD, the twofold skill premium established by the edict is consistent with some of our evidence for real wages in Roman Egypt during the early imperial period. In his recent study of prices and wages in Egypt, Dominic Rathbone suggests that skilled workers could command a premium somewhere on the order of two to three times the wages earned by unskilled workers, especially in urban contexts.[25] The same pattern is evoked in isolated references in our Italian evidence to the effects of dedicated training on the value of slaves: Columella suggests that a slave who had been trained as a skilled vinedresser may have been worth six to eight thousand

22 For the clearest example of this in the ancient world, see Xen., *Cyr.* 8.2.5.

23 So Watson (2000: 33–34), albeit with reference to more recent periods.

24 Hawkins (2013: 346–351).

25 Rathbone (2009, esp. 314–321).

sesterces in the first century AD[26]—perhaps two to four times as much as an unskilled adult slave—and the jurist Paul assumed that a slaveholder who trained a slave in a skill like smithing or carpentry could double that slave's market value.[27] Judging from the comparative data compiled recently by Jan Luiten van Zanden, the skill premiums visible in these sources therefore fall into the upper range of what was typical in north-western Europe during the late medieval and early modern periods.[28] In that sense, they seem consistent with Richard Saller's conclusion that inhabitants of the Roman Empire did not invest as heavily in human capital as did individuals in later historical periods, and were less likely to acquire specialized skills through professional training.[29]

That conclusion is only reinforced by what we can infer about the opportunity costs of apprenticeship. Ancient historians have tended to overlook these costs, which were probably high enough relative to household income in antiquity that they discouraged most household heads from arranging formal training for their sons.[30] These costs can be difficult to assess, largely because the surviving apprenticeship contracts from Roman Egypt show that there was considerable variety in the terms of apprenticeship agreements: the lengths of the recorded apprenticeships in these documents range between half a year and six years; in some cases instructors were willing to shoulder some of an apprentice's living expenses, while in others these remained the responsibility of the apprentice's parents or guardians; and some apprentices received wages or stipends in exchange for their labour, especially during late stages of their training.[31] That said, several of the surviving documents suggest that the parents or guardians of an apprentice with no previous training often retained the responsibility for paying for much of an apprentice's upkeep during the early

---

26 Columella, *Rust.* 3.3.8.

27 *Dig.* 17.1.26.8. On the typical costs of slaves in the first and second centuries AD, see Scheidel (2005b: 2–8), who notes that 2000 sesterces can be considered an approximate value of an unskilled, adult slave. By way of contrast, Fogel (1989: 68) notes that skill premiums for blacksmiths and carpenters in the antebellum south were roughly 55% and 45%, respectively.

28 Van Zanden (2009, esp. 126–131). But see Bernard's contribution in this volume, which suggests that skill premiums in the construction sector were only slightly higher than in pre-modern Europe and well in line with or lower than comparative figures for other periods and cultures.

29 See, most recently, Saller (2012, esp. 75–77 and 82–85).

30 On the opportunity costs of apprenticeship from a comparative perspective, see Minns and Wallis (2013: 344); see also the contribution by Liu, below.

31 Bergamasco (1995) offers a comprehensive overview of the existing documents. See also Freu (2011); Laes (2011: 191–195); Bradley (1991: 103–124), and Westermann (1914).

years of an agreement. They also indicate that the work of the apprentice generally went unremunerated during this period. This was clearly the case when a resident of Oxyrhynchus named Ischyrion arranged a five-year apprenticeship for a minor in his charge, Thoonis, in the workshop of the weaver Heraklas. Although Heraklas agreed to provide Thoonis with a new tunic during each year of the contract, Ischyrion otherwise remained responsible for the boy's living expenses throughout the contract's five-year term. Likewise, Heraklas agreed to pay wages to Thoonis only during the final two years and five months of the apprenticeship, and even those wages seem to have been below the going rate for a semi-skilled worker.[32] In these circumstances, Ischyrion may have incurred opportunity costs on the level of roughly 100 *drachmai* per year for the first half of the contract, which represented the income that Thoonis could have generated on behalf of his household by undertaking unskilled work for pay.[33]

In practical terms, opportunity costs on this scale were high enough relative to typical household incomes that they operated to constrict the supply of skilled workers in the Roman world, simply because most household heads could not afford to seek apprenticeships for children in their care.[34] Walter Scheidel's recent estimates for real earnings in early economies suggest that most men who worked as unskilled labourers in Roman Egypt would have been unable to generate sufficient income on their own to maintain their families at even a bare-bones subsistence level, let alone in conditions of relative comfort;[35] for that reason alone, they had strong incentives to maximize the present value of the labour of their children, rather than to make the costly investments necessary to provide them with apprenticeships. Furthermore, if Walter Scheidel and Steven Friesen are correct in their estimate that almost 85% of the population of the Roman Empire hovered below, at, or just above subsistence level, then the overwhelming majority of household heads in the ancient world would have found it equally difficult to secure specialized training

32 *P. Oxy.* IV 725; Thoonis' wages were 12 *drachmai* per month during the last five months of his third year as an apprentice, 16 *drachmai* per month in the fourth year, and 24 *drachmai* per month in his final year. These wages were significantly lower than the monthly wages earned by skilled workers at the imperial quarry of Mons Claudianus (see below).

33 Here, I follow Scheidel's estimate for the income than an adolescent male could generate on behalf of his family in any given year. See Scheidel (2010b: 433–435).

34 For a contrary view, see Saller (2012: 76–77). Cf. his comments in Saller (2007: 109), in which he expresses more strongly the claim that the investment made by parents or children in these contracts was minimal.

35 Scheidel (2010b: 427–436).

for their sons.[36] Moreover, those who could afford to pay for such training probably did so with an eye to establishing their sons as independent producers rather than as wage workers.

The Relative Costs of Labour: Slaves and Permanent Employees

Tight markets for skilled labour therefore potentially gave artisans some incentive to expand the boundaries of their firms in order to lessen their dependence on the spot market, especially when artisans felt confident that they would attract sufficient customers to offset additional fixed costs, or when they had the resources necessary to shelter themselves from the potential consequences of a bad spell of business. Those who did expand their firms would have made decisions about how to do so based on the balance of production costs and transaction costs generated by the two main paths to integration—slaveholding, and the employment of hired workers on long-term or permanent contracts. The poor state of our evidence for wages and prices complicates any effort to compare the fixed costs incurred by artisans who opted for one or the other of these two paths. That said, crude estimates of the magnitude of those costs can be extracted both from the limited price and wage data preserved in Egyptian papyri of the second and third centuries AD, and from Cato the Elder's notorious discussion of slave rations. Rough though they may be, these estimates indicate that the fixed costs artisans incurred when they relied on slave labour were comparable to those they incurred when they hired workers on long-term contracts. In that sense, they suggest that any preference artisans exhibited for slaves over long-term hired labourers was driven instead by differences in the transaction costs associated with the employment of these two different kinds of workers.

The costs artisans incurred when they relied on slave labour can be modelled by taking into account not only the direct costs necessary to feed and house a servile worker, but also several additional explicit and implicit costs that arose from the value a slave possessed as a capital asset. On the explicit side of the ledger, these included both depreciation costs reflecting the decline in a slave's market price as he or she aged, and costs reflecting the reality that some slaves either escaped from their masters or succumbed to illness; on the implicit side, they included the opportunity costs of capital, which reflect the value to an artisan of the alternative uses to which the money he or she used to purchase a slave could be put.[37] Our fixed data points in this model

36 Scheidel and Friesen (2009, esp. 84–85).

37 Although the Romans themselves would not have engaged in this kind of calculation, they did understand that the value of a slave depreciated over time, and that the capital

are, first, Cato's recommendation that slaveholders provide their slaves rations worth roughly 400 kg to 700 kg of wheat per year, and second, known prices for slaves in the Egyptian papyri, which suggest that the market value of an unskilled adult slave, measured in real terms, was probably on the order of 4500 kg of wheat-equivalent. If we assume that a skilled slave had a market value equivalent to two to three times that of an unskilled slave, then we can estimate that artisans in Roman Egypt who relied on the labour of skilled slaves faced real annual costs of approximately 2400 kg of wheat per slave.[38]

Although it is more difficult to offer an estimate for the wages that artisans in Roman Egypt would have been compelled to pay in order to retain skilled workers on annual contracts, there is some reason to believe that those wages would have been more or less comparable to the annual costs of slave labour. In the third century AD, urban shipwrights working on a day-to-day basis in the Fayum were paid at a rate of eight *drachmai* per day, which amounted to roughly 11.7 kg of wheat equivalent;[39] if other skilled workers were paid at the same rate, and if they were able to secure constant work, then they would have earned the equivalent of roughly 4200 kg of wheat-equivalent per year. Given the seasonal and uncertain demand that characterized urban product markets, however, most skilled workers were unlikely to have found employment on such a consistent basis. For that reason, it is perhaps better to assume that they were only able to secure enough work to remain employed for between half and two-thirds of any given year, and that artisans hoping to retain skilled hands on long-term contracts would have therefore found it necessary to offer annual wages on the order of 2100 to 2800 kg of wheat equivalent per year.

---

used to purchase slaves did have alternative uses. The calculation therefore has some value in allowing us to compare the costs of slave versus free labour. For more discussion about the difficulties Roman slaveholders faced from an accounting perspective when reckoning the value of their slaves, see Minaud (2005: 143–149).

38 I have based this calculation on the method employed by Whitman 1997: 54–55, using the following values: market value of a skilled slave, 11250 kg wheat-equivalent; annual opportunity cost of capital, 6%; annual depreciation, 6%; annual risk of flight or death, 3%. On the probable market value of unskilled slaves in Roman Egypt, see Scheidel (2005b: 5). I have calculated the risk of mortality at 1.4% per year between the ages of 15 and 30 on the basis of the level 3 Female model life table in Saller (1994: 24), and I have arbitrarily assigned roughly the same value for the risk of flight. For direct maintenance costs, I have used the high value proposed by Cato, *Agr.* 56–59 (see Scheidel (2005b: 13)), which seems the most appropriate to apply in the case of slaves who performed a considerable amount of physical labour over the course of a year.

39 *P. Flor.* I 69. This assumes a putative price of 18 *drachmai* per *artaba* of wheat; see Scheidel (2002b: 103).

The payment *entolai* from Mons Claudianus offer some support for this view by indicating that smiths and stonemasons who were employed at the imperial quarry were paid at a monthly rate of 47 *drachmai* plus an *artaba* (30 kg) of wheat, which represented an effective annual wage of roughly 2400 kg of wheat-equivalent.[40] The quarries at Mons Claudianus were hardly in an urban environment, but to the extent that the Roman state needed to ensure that its skilled workers did not seek more lucrative opportunities elsewhere, the wages it offered were probably on par with what those workers could have earned in an urban market.

Although we lack reliable data for wages and prices in other regions of the Roman Empire, our best guesses for slave prices, wheat prices, and wages in Roman Italy suggest that artisans in this context too found the costs of slave labour comparable to those necessary to hire skilled workers on long-term contracts. In his treatise on estate management, Columella estimated that a skilled slave—more precisely, a vinedresser—possessed a market value between 6000 and 8000 sesterces during the first century AD. At putative wheat prices of roughly 6 sesterces per *modius* (itself equivalent to roughly 6.8 kg of wheat), the midpoint of this price range represented roughly 7900 kg of wheat-equivalent, which would imply that slaveholding artisans at Rome incurred real annual costs of about 1900 kg of wheat equivalent per slave.[41] Although we are almost wholly in the dark where skilled wage rates in Italy are concerned, Cato suggests that the rate for skilled labour in the second century BC was roughly 8 sesterces per day. Naturally, there is no guarantee that skilled wage rates in the early imperial period were comparable, but on the basis of some stray references that may refer to unskilled wage rates on the order of 3 sesterces and 4 sesterces in the first centuries BC and AD, respectively, it seems acceptable to take Cato's figure as a reasonable estimate.[42] At that rate, a fully-employed skilled worker in Italy would have earned some 3300 kg of

40 On the pay grades for craftsmen at Mons Claudianus, see Cuvigny 1996, along with the comments of Rathbone (2009: 312–313).

41 Columella, *Rust.* 3.3.8–9; wheat prices in central Italy may have ranged between 4 sesterces and 8 sesterces per *modius*, but see Rathbone (2009: 307–308) for the difficulties involved in assessing those figures.

42 The references in question are Cicero's remark that unskilled workers in Rome may have been able to earn 3 sesterces per day in the 70s BC (*QRosc.* 28), and a stray graffito from Pompeii indicating that a wage paid to a day labourer may have consisted of a denarius (4 sesterces) plus bread rations (*CIL* IV 6877). Both pieces of evidence are subject to problems of interpretation; for more detail, see Scheidel (2010b: 444 (with n. 56) and 445).

wheat per year, while those who were more realistically employed for half to two thirds of the year would have earned between 1650 and 2200 kg.[43]

Reputations, Coercion, and Transaction Costs

Although artisans who sought to expand their firms may have found that it was difficult to formulate a preference for either slaveholding or long-term employment contracts on the basis of fixed costs alone,[44] they were more likely to notice profound differences between the two labour management choices on the level of transaction costs. More specifically, while many would have been unable to rely on strong relational contracts in order to secure long-term labour agreements, the coercive authority they exercised over their slaves obviated some of these problems. From that perspective, many must have felt that slaveholding offered a preferable route to integration than did the recruitment of employees on a long-term basis.

When artisans sought to hire permanent workers, they found that their ability to create strong relational contracts was limited not just because the services of skilled workers were in high enough demand that defaulters could find other employment after reneging on their agreements, but also because employers could not necessarily rely on reputation-based sanctions in order to increase the costs of default to the point that these could reliably prevent an employee from reneging in the first place. As I have argued elsewhere, professional associations (*collegia*) in the ancient world did in fact function as private-order enforcement networks that supported relational contracting among artisans in two critical ways: first, many featured mechanisms designed to help members resolve disputes among themselves internally, and to disseminate vital information about the personal reputations of the disputants to other members in the process; second, because association members enjoyed access to a wide range of important community goods, such as the ability to accumulate social capital by participating in their *collegium*'s internal social and political life, they could impose costly sanctions on known defaulters by

43 At this level, the putative income of a skilled worker in Rome compared favourably with the income of a soldier serving in the urban cohorts, who earned between 1350 and 1500 sesterces (1530 and 1700 kg wheat-equivalent) for most of the first century AD (Rathbone (2007: 161)). This provides some reassurance that the income I have proposed here for skilled wage-earners is at least in the right range.

44 While this was true in the short term, over a time horizon of several years it was possible for artisans to reduce the costs of slave labour by manumitting slaves in exchange for *operae* (see below).

restricting access to those goods.[45] Crucially, however, artisans could really only benefit from these aspects of associational life when they transacted with partners who belonged to their association, most of whom were probably proprietors in their own right rather than wage workers.[46] In that sense, while artisans could use the relational contracts that were facilitated by these networks in order to secure transactions with subcontractors, they could not necessarily do the same with employees: not only did they lack the ability to punish defaulting employees by threatening their access to community goods, in the absence of organized reputation mechanisms they were also dependent on gossip to transmit information about defaulters' reputations. Artisans could perhaps rely on gossip to punish defaulters in small urban communities, in which proprietors working in a given trade interacted with one another on a regular basis, but gossip alone was unlikely to have been particularly effective in a large city like Rome, where some industries supported hundreds of independent employers.[47]

Without the ability to rely on relational contracts backed by strong, private-order enforcement networks, artisans would have been especially vulnerable to enforcement problems when they relied on tacit or semi-formal agreements grounded in trust in order to govern their relationships with their employees. One can imagine, for example, that some artisan employers essentially relied on a patron-client relationship to structure their transactions with their employees. In this kind of situation, a patron may have provided material support to his client throughout the year—especially when product markets were slow and work correspondingly difficult to come by—in the expectation that his client would reciprocate by making himself available to work when demand picked up, and ideally at below-market rates.[48] Alternatively, one can

45 Hawkins (2012).

46 There is no evidence that artisans were required to be proprietors in order to join *collegia*, but in most cases the bulk of the membership of any given association probably consisted of independent artisans. See e.g. Garnsey (1998c) and Martin (1989: 65–68). This was undoubtedly a consequence of the fact that many *collegia* charged a substantial fee for the privilege of membership.

47 The *collegium fabrum tignariorum* (builders' association) in Ostia consisted of roughly 350 members in the late first century AD; in the late second century, on the other hand, the builders' association in Rome consisted of more than 1300. See Royden (1988: 27 and 127); on the size of *collegia* see also the paper of Verboven in this volume.

48 Ath. 6.274 c–e offers an interesting parallel when he notes that Mucius Scaevola, Aelius Tubero, and Rutilius Rufus all expected to purchase commodities from their clients at prices well below market value. Artisans were arguably able to secure comparable discounts from those whom they regarded as their clients when hiring their labour.

also imagine an employer who engaged a skilled worker on a monthly contract with a specified wage, in the expectation that the worker would tacitly consent to its regular renewal.[49] In neither case could an artisan credibly threaten to impose sanctions on an employee who decided to end the relationship in the hope of profiting from more lucrative opportunities in a period of elevated demand. More importantly, unless he and his employee belonged to the same professional association, then in neither case could he necessarily impose costly social sanctions, nor even reliably damage the employee's reputation in a way that would prevent someone else from hiring him in the future.

Yet even artisans who made use of formal and specific long-term contracts were vulnerable to certain kinds of opportunism that could be difficult to prevent unless an employer could take advantage of strong reputation mechanisms and the relational contracts that they supported. While an employer could use a formal and specific contract to specify and enforce certain aspects of an employment relationship with relative ease—in particular, the duration of the contract—employer and employee were likely to leave other aspects of an agreement unspecified. Generally speaking, because partners to a transaction are often unable to predict all of the eventualities that can arise over the course of a long-term agreement (let alone agree on mutual responsibilities in the event that those eventualities come to pass), they often make no attempt to do so and instead produce 'imperfect' contracts in an effort to preserve their flexibility to adapt to contingencies. As a result, many aspects of a given contractual relationship are unspecified and difficult for a court to enforce. Instead, they remain open to constant interpretation, negotiation, and renegotiation by the parties to the agreement. That process of interpretation and negotiation is constrained by those terms that the parties do specify concretely, but one party can still take advantage of another by adhering to the specified terms of an agreement even if new developments render the specified terms contrary to the agreement's original spirit, especially when the other party cannot rely on non-legal means like reputation penalties to amplify the costs of intransigence.[50]

Employment contracts in particular tend to exhibit this kind of tension between contractual flexibility and contractual enforcement. On the

49 Ulpian implies that tacit contract renewals were not uncommon between landlords and their tenants (*Dig.* 19.2.14; for detailed discussion, see Pichonnaz (2002)). Theoretically, labour contracts could have been renewed in the same way, provided that they were formed under the rubric of *locatio-conductio* (du Plessis (2012: 17–18)).

50 Klein (1996) presents the basic theory behind this idea, along with some empirical case studies. Cf. Gibbons (2005: 236–238).

one hand, employment contracts allow for a degree of flexibility by their very nature: unlike a subcontractor, an employee typically grants his or her employer a sphere of authority (or, in Herbert Simon's words, a 'zone of acceptance'), which permits the employer to make decisions about both the nature of the work to which an employee will be assigned, and the pace and timing of that work. In theory, an employer therefore has some flexibility to respond to changes in the economic environment by redirecting his or her employee's labour in response to new circumstances without necessarily renegotiating the terms of the relationship at every step. On the other hand, the zone of acceptance an employee cedes to an employer is seldom unlimited, but is instead understood by both parties to encompass a set of general terms, even if those remain implicit. Conflict and contractual hold-ups can therefore emerge when circumstances make it necessary or desirable for one party to reinterpret the extent of a given zone of acceptance.[51]

In an environment characterized by seasonal and uncertain demand, a wide zone of acceptance was clearly optimal from the point of view of Roman artisans, since it gave them the ability to respond to changing market conditions by adjusting both the tasks they assigned to hired workers and the effort those workers expended. For one thing, artisan employers undoubtedly stood to benefit by redefining the scope of an employee's responsibility during periods of relatively low output in the workshop, when skilled but underemployed workers could potentially be put to work on necessary but relatively unskilled tasks—routine maintenance, cleaning, and so on—that they normally may have considered to be beneath them. Additionally, and more pressingly, artisans in the Roman world were undoubtedly interested in enhancing output in periods of intense activity by altering the contours of the working day in ways designed to extract more effort from employees, whether by reducing or eliminating periods of rest, or by sustaining activity in the workshop by lamplight well into the night. In the early modern period, it was not uncommon for artisans to keep their employees working by candlelight when they faced impending deadlines and heavy workloads (even though doing so could provoke conflict),[52] and there are some signs in our evidence that Roman artisans too probably sought to lengthen working days under comparable pressures. The wife of the poor craftsman in Apuleius' *Metamorphoses*, for example, complains that she is compelled to work late into the evening spinning wool at home in order to earn extra income for the household,[53] and the jurist Alfenus

51 For the classic study in this genre, see Simon (1951).

52 See e.g. Sonenscher (1989: 164, 202, and 235); Reith (2003: 127–128).

53 Apul., *Met.* 9.5.

makes passing mention of a case in which a shopkeeper kept his premises open after dark, only to find it necessary to chase down a passer-by who snatched away the lamp he had suspended over his counter.[54]

Employers in the Roman world could certainly negotiate for wide zones of acceptance, which they could then articulate explicitly in a formal contract, but skilled workers probably had sufficient bargaining power to refuse such terms (or, alternatively, to charge a steep premium for them).[55] On the one hand, employers could attempt to negotiate extensive control over an employee's time, as seems to be implied in the jurist Paul's abbreviated remark that workers sometimes hired out their services both by day and by night.[56] On the other, they could also attempt to secure extensive control over the kinds of tasks to which an employee could be assigned: one of the Dacian mining contracts, for instance, records an explicit agreement on the part of what was probably an unskilled worker to perform whatever work his employer cared to impose upon him.[57] Judging from Petronius' fictional portrayal of the odd-job man Corax, however, workers who agreed to such terms found them burdensome and in a certain sense degrading, since they could be thought to blur the boundary between slave and free: subjected by his employers to extraordinary demands on his time and energy, Corax protests about those demands in a scene in which he implies that there were limits to what employers could expect from freeborn workers, even if they were forced by circumstances to accept undesirable jobs.[58] That sentiment is echoed, albeit indirectly, in the comments of the Roman jurists, who distinguished between the services of free men and those of slaves by emphasizing that the latter could expect their masters to exercise heavy control over their time.[59] Skilled workers, however, almost certainly had sufficient leverage in negotiations that they did not need to accept such terms, except in exceptional circumstances. That point is underscored by the agreement of a weaver in Roman Egypt named Harmiusis to bind himself to a man named Heron for two years during the middle of the first century AD. Although Harmiusis entered into a *paramonē*-style contract with

54 *Dig.* 9.2.52.1.

55 Cf. Brunt (1980: 99–100).

56 Paul., *Sent.* 2.18.1.

57 CIL III p. 949 XI (*quidquid opus erit*).

58 Petron., *Sat.* 117.

59 So Alfenus, who refers to 'services of free men', or *liberas operas* (*Dig.* 38.1.26.pr), which entail breaks throughout the day (unlike, it is implied, the services of slaves). See below for more on the kinds of control that employers exercised over the time of their employees. Scheidel (2002a) offers a discussion of the extent to which Roman workers may have assimilated wage labour to slavery in certain respects.

Heron, and agreed to do whatever Heron ordered, the fact that he received nothing but a basic food and clothing allowance in return for his promise suggests that he found himself in an exceptionally weak bargaining position. The most probable explanation in this case is that Harmiusis had been compelled by some unfortunate circumstance to indebt himself heavily to Heron, and that he had agreed to accept a *paramonē* contract in exchange for the loan.[60]

Artisan employers who were unable to negotiate wide zones of acceptance with skilled employees found themselves constrained by specific expectations that governed both the daily pace and the nature of an employee's work. While we cannot draw firm conclusions about the nature of those expectations, some of our sources do offer hints about kinds of limits they imposed both on the working day and on the nature of the tasks that an employer could assign to a skilled hired worker. In the context of a discussion about what a patron could expect from a former slave whom he had manumitted in exchange for a promise to provide labour services (*operae libertorum*), the jurist Alfenus alluded briefly to the contours of a typical working day: in his view, patrons were to let their freedmen rest at noon, and to allow them other short breaks during the day so that they could take care of their health and wellbeing.[61] Neratius echoed the latter point, and stated more explicitly that it applied not just to freedmen, but to anyone engaged in providing services.[62] Alongside other scattered *testimonia*, these pieces of evidence therefore point to a recognized working day which was bounded by sunrise and sunset, but which also included regular periods of rest.[63] Likewise, Alfenus also broached the question of what tasks a patron could assign to a skilled freedman who owed him *operae*, and who normally would have been expected to discharge them by performing skilled work.[64] At issue was the question of whether or not a patron could call upon such a freedman to render him services of a general or non-specific nature. Alfenus was of the opinion that he could, but what matters most in this context is that the answer to this question was not clear-cut; instead, some of Alfenus' contemporaries must have held the view that a former slave discharging his obligations to his patron could expect the scope of those obligations to be circumscribed when he possessed specific craft skills. If so, then it seems

60 *P. Mich.* v 355; this is the suggestion made by the text's editors. On *paramone* agreements in general see the classic study, Westermann (1948).

61 *Dig.* 38.1.26.pr.

62 *Dig.* 38.1.50.1.

63 For further discussion of the rhythms of the working day, see Laurence (2007: 154–166, and esp. 159–161).

64 *Dig.* 38.1.26.pr.

plausible to conclude that hired workers, both freed and freeborn, would have expected no less.

Given these expectations, artisans must have found it necessary to negotiate with their permanent employees when they sought to respond to changes demand by temporarily broadening the scope of their employees' tasks, or by asking them to work extra hours. It was precisely in the context of this process that they exposed themselves to potentially costly opportunistic behaviour, especially when they were unable to ground those negotiations in strong relational contracts backed by organized reputation mechanisms. Because Roman *collegia* lacked the institutional authority of early modern guilds, which were capable of creating and enforcing industry-wide regulations concerning overtime and wages, Roman artisans could only bargain with employees on an ad-hoc basis.[65] Employees may have been willing to grant their employers a certain degree of forbearance by agreeing to exceed the parameters of their formal contracts, perhaps in the expectation that they would be offered the kinds of gratuities that Seneca took pride in awarding to workers in his service.[66] That kind of forbearance, however, required trust on the part of the employee, since the employer himself was under no compulsion to deliver such gratuities. While some employees undoubtedly were willing to offer that level of trust, the absence of strong reputation mechanisms capable of securing it may have persuaded many that it was better to demand more concrete concessions from their employers. Here, employers found themselves at a decided disadvantage: because employee effort was difficult for the courts to assess and verify, an employee could opportunistically hold up production in an effort to secure a higher pay-out simply by putting less energy into his work, all without breaking the formal terms of his contract. From the perspective of an employer, this was a particularly pressing and costly problem, especially when general conditions of demand were strong and wages were high. More importantly, without the ability to use strong reputation mechanisms to sanction such an employee, there was little that an employer could do to avoid it.[67]

On the other hand, artisans who chose instead to expand their firms by acquiring slave labour were able to avoid many of these complications. At the most basic level, and precisely because masters enjoyed strong and coercive property rights over their slaves, artisans who turned to slavery in order to

65 Sonenscher (1989: 202–203 and 235) discusses some good examples of guild legislation designed to regulate working hours.

66 Sen., *Ben.* 6.17.1.

67 Comparable problems are discussed from a theoretical point of view in Baker, Gibbons, and Murphy (2002: 58–67).

avoid the transaction cost problems that afflicted the market in skilled labour were able to circumvent one of the main sources of those costs—namely, the ability of hired workers to renege on their agreements outright by withdrawing their labour from their employers.[68] Although slaves could and sometimes did attempt to break free of the power of their owners by running away, most would have found escape a difficult enough proposition that it was an option of last resort;[69] for that reason alone, artisans who acquired and trained slaves of their own found it much easier than those who hired help to secure reliable and long-term access to the labour of skilled workers.

Just as importantly, artisan slaveholders were able to leverage the coercive authority that they held over their slaves in ways that permitted them to secure compliance from slaves more easily than they could from hired workers, even when they placed heavy demands on their slaves' time, or assigned to them tasks that hired workers would have been reluctant to perform.[70] For one thing, because the nature of the master-slave relationship permitted masters to engage liberally in socially-sanctioned violence against their human property,[71] artisans could depend more heavily on physical punishment as a tool for extracting effort when they relied on the labour of their own slaves than they could when they relied on the labour of hired hands. Under the influence of a widespread belief that corrective punishment could facilitate learning, artisans did use physical punishment to correct freeborn apprentices who performed unsatisfactory work, but beyond that their formal ability to discipline hired workers in this way was limited.[72] By contrast, artisans—like other slaveholders—faced few limitations on their ability to punish their own slaves. Apuleius provides a sense of the harsh treatment that some may have inflicted upon their slaves in his fictional depiction of life in a combined mill and bakery, in which he evokes an image of slaves who were not just sickly

68 For an extensive analysis of turnover costs as they pertained to slavery in North America, see Hanes (1996). For an application of the concept to the ancient world, see Scheidel (2008).

69 Bradley (1994: 117–128).

70 On the tools masters had at their disposal for controlling their slaves, see Scheidel (2008: 107–115), and, more broadly, Bradley (1987).

71 For a general discussion of slavery as a relationship of violence and domination, see Patterson (1982: 1–14). Bradley (1987: 113–137) discusses these issues in a specifically Roman context.

72 On violence as an aspect of the instructor-apprentice relationship in comparative perspective, see Lancy (2012: 118). The *locus classicus* in our Roman evidence is Julian's report about the shoemaker who blinded an apprentice in one eye by striking him with his last (*Dig.* 9.2.5.3).

and half-starved, but also heavily scarred from the repeated blows of their master.[73] Even if most artisan slaveholders did not treat their slaves as severely as did the baker in Apuleius' novel, the fact that many worked closely alongside their slaves on the shop floor meant that they were in a position to monitor their slaves closely and to dispense punishment as they saw fit.

At the same time, artisans were also able to take advantage of the powerlessness of their slaves by using rewards in order to secure their obedience and compliance. In many cases they probably did so by offering their slaves material inducements, which could include extra rations, holiday time, or even the privilege of holding some property in a *peculium*—a separate account that belonged *de iure* to the master, but which was treated for practical purposes as the property of the slave himself.[74] Artisan slaveholders were also able to make credible and effective use of the prospect of manumission as a tool for motivating desired behaviours from slaves, primarily because they were able to retain a high degree of control over the labour of slaves whom they set free. Formally, that control derived from their legal right to demand that freed slaves promise to provide a stipulated number of days' worth of work—the so-called *operae libertorum*—in exchange for their freedom. Thanks to that right, artisans were able to demand several hundred *operae* as the price of a slave's freedom, to call upon those *operae* as and when necessary over a period of several years, and to expect a freedman to assume responsibility for most of his own living expenses. Informally, artisans—like other slaveholders—often continued to wield enough leverage over their freedmen that they could potentially expect those freedmen to comply willingly with their demands, even if they frequently elected to stretch the working day beyond the bounds of what was customary from the perspective of hired workers.[75]

Thanks to the rights that they exercised over their slaves as property, and to their ability to leverage their authority in order to coerce compliance from their slaves, artisans who relied on slave labour enjoyed extensive control not just over the kinds of work to which they could assign those slaves, but also over the timing and pace of their slaves' work during periods when the workshop was particularly busy.[76] For that reason, they were able avoid the kinds

73 Apul., *Met.* 9.12.

74 On rewards of this kind, see e.g. Bradley (1987: 40–45 and 108–110).

75 I provide a more detailed discussion of manumission in exchange for *operae* in Hawkins (2016: 130–191) and in Hawkins (forthcoming), along with a discussion of the kinds of leverage that artisans could exercise over their freedmen.

76 Cf. Wright (2006: 122), who makes the point that one of the main advantages of slavery from the perspective of plantation owners in the antebellum South was their ability to

of transactional difficulties that made it difficult for them to adapt long-term labour contracts to some of the challenges presented by seasonal and uncertain demand, while simultaneously making use of slave labour in ways that may have mitigated some of its costs. In the first place, because slaveholding artisans were able to use the labour of their slaves in any way they saw fit, they could extract work of at least some value from those slaves even during lulls in demand that would have left skilled workers who had been hired on long-term contracts underemployed. Within the workshop itself, for example, artisans could assign their slaves to a range of menial tasks that were often delegated to junior apprentices in other historical contexts: these tasks could include cleaning and maintaining the shop and its equipment; making deliveries to clients or fetching raw materials or intermediate goods from suppliers; and perhaps even visiting clients to request outstanding payments for prior orders.[77] Conceivably, however, artisans could also redirect the work of underemployed slaves to various kinds of domestic service, in much the same way that householders in the medieval context tended to employ their servants both in domestic work and in production for the market as circumstances warranted.[78]

Second, slaveholding artisans faced few constraints on their ability to demand long hours from their slaves, whether in response to seasonal peaks in demand, or in response to unexpected windfall orders. Columella leaves little doubt that slaveholding aristocrats were willing to demand long days from their slaves in agricultural contexts: among other things, he advised slaveholders to keep their slaves at work by lamplight well into the night or in the pre-dawn hours if necessary, during which time they could finish manufacturing stakes and withies for the vineyard if nothing else.[79] It is easy to imagine that workshop-based artisans likewise kept their slaves employed late at night or in the early morning hours during busy periods of the year, when multiple deadlines demanded their attention. Even artisans who performed much of their work on site rather than in their own premises seem to have been sensitive to the fact that their authority as slaveholders permitted them to demand more work from slaves than they could from free, hired workers. The Hippocratic author Aretaeus, for example, reports a curious story about an artisan who worked in

---

'override the preferences and family responsibilities of their slaves, assigning them to any tasks in any season of the year.'

77 For discussions and examples of the tasks normally assigned to apprentices, see Lancy (2012: 117), Singleton (1989: 18–19), Lane (1996: 76–77), and the autobiography of the cabinet-maker T.R. Dennis, in Burnett (1974: 347–355).

78 Goldberg (2000: 61–62).

79 Columella, *Rust.* 11.2.12.

the construction trade as a specialist in interior woodwork.[80] Aretaeus' interest in the story was provoked by the artisan's unfortunate habit of losing his senses whenever he left the worksite, but what is more interesting from our perspective is what the story says about the rhythms and pace of work in an artisanal enterprise staffed by slaves. According to Aretaeus, the woodworker himself enjoyed considerable freedom of movement during the day, and took breaks to visit the agora, to run errands, and even just to visit the baths. During these breaks, however, he seems to have left his slaves behind at the worksite, presumably because he expected them to continue the work while he himself was absent.

I opened this chapter by positing that seasonal and uncertain demand made it risky for artisans to expand the boundaries of their firms, let alone to do so by acquiring slaves. Yet the flexibility with which artisans could deploy the labour of their slaves—a flexibility grounded ultimately in the coercive authority and property rights that they exercised over those slaves—suggests that this position must be modified, at least in part. Slaveholding did impose costs on artisans that could be problematic if product market conditions were particularly unfavourable in any given year. For artisans who had the resources and wherewithal to buffer themselves against those costs, however, there were some advantages to be gained by permanently integrating at least small numbers of skilled slaves into their enterprises, even if they continued to rely on the spot market for additional help. Those advantages were chiefly the product of an economy in which intensive human capital was expensive from the perspective of most free household heads, many of whom consequently could not afford apprenticeships for their sons, and in which skilled labour was therefore both scarce and costly. Acting alongside professional associations that united proprietors, but not necessarily their employees, in organizations capable of supporting strong reputation mechanisms, the scarcity and cost of skilled labour ensured that transaction costs in the skilled segments of the labour market remained high for artisan employers, whether they sought to recruit short-term help or permanent employees. Artisans who expanded the boundaries of their firms by acquiring slaves therefore lessened their dependence on both spot and permanent labour markets that did not necessarily meet their needs. This was true not simply because owning slaves permitted them to avoid some the transaction costs that plagued those markets, but also because the strong and coercive property rights that they enjoyed as slaveholders gave them considerable leeway to adapt the ways in which they exploited their human property to the fluctuations of their product markets.

80 Aret., *SD* 1.6.6.

CHAPTER 4

Workers in the Roman Imperial Building Industry

Seth G. Bernard

In celebration of the opening of the Colosseum in AD 80, Martial begins his *Liber Spectaculorum* by comparing the new amphitheatre to the buildings of other, earlier societies:

> Let barbarous Memphis stop talking about the miracle of the pyramids; Assyrian labour is not to vaunt Babylon, and the soft Ionians are not to garner praise for Trivia's temple; let the altar of many horns say nothing about Delos, and do not let the Carians lavish extravagant praise on the Mausoleum suspended in empty air and exalt it to the stars. All labour yields to Caesar's amphitheatre: Fame will tell of one work instead of them all.[1]

Martial calls these monuments *labor*, and the Latin word stands by metonymy for the great effort that went into their creation. If architecture is the human capital expended upon it, the poet declares, imperial Roman architecture now surpasses all.

It is hard to argue with this opinion: Roman emperors and provincial elites invested considerable capital in building projects across the entire empire. The architecture that resulted was characteristically monumental and durable, and therefore its creation was labour intensive. In general, construction played a significant role within any pre-modern economy as it represented one of the greatest single concentrations of labour, and it output a highly valuable product. Not by coincidence, builders are the workers whose wages are most

* Ancient texts cited from the Loeb Classical Library edition unless noted. Matthew Karp and Ben Russell read and commented on drafts. Janet DeLaine kindly shared her forthcoming work on the Pantheon.

1 Mart., *Spect.* 1: *Barbara pyramidum sileat miracula Memphis, / Assyrius iactet nec Babylona labor, / nec Triuiae templo molles laudentur Iones; / dissimulet Delon cornibus ara frequens / aere nec uacuo pendentia Mausolea / laudibus immodicis Cares in astra ferant. / Omnis Caesareo cedit labor Amphitheatro, / unum pro cunctis fama loquetur opus.* Text and trans. Coleman (2006) with slight modification.

 | DOI 10.1163/9789004331686_005

frequently preserved from the medieval period onwards.[2] The slenderness of wage-data in the Roman world notwithstanding, there remains evidence to suggest that building labour and builders themselves were no less essential to the urban economies of the Roman Empire.

From the viewpoint of labour, Roman public architecture could be deemed a comparative success. This chapter asks why. What organizational structures allowed Rome's labour supply to meet demand for monumental architecture? How efficiently was human effort mobilized around the Mediterranean? One obvious ingredient was a large labour supply, and ancient sources recognized that large-scale buildings result from 'so many hands' at work.[3] Output of imperial architecture was also shaped by the utility of building labour and the institutions of the Roman world, and scholarship since the nineteenth century has focused in particular on the role of slaves and the related question of a worker's personal status.[4] Finley felt that slavery vitiated the presence of a labour market and rendered wages conventional; the ancient workforce was virtually market-less and characterized by heavy interference from the Roman state.[5] In the past decade, however, the Finleyan model has given way to a focus on institutions and performance, and there is more room in the current debate to consider market forces. Temin recently argues for the existence of an integrated labour market across the Empire. He holds that slave labour itself was incentivized by the comparative openness of Roman slavery and the frequency of manumission; under such conditions, slaves might consider their servitude term-bound, similar to a long-term contract.[6] Temin's insistence that we situate Roman slavery within the wider context of the Roman labour market is valuable, and there is some evidence of competition between free

2 Goldthwaite (1980); Phelps Brown and Hopkins (1981); Allen (2001); Özmucur and Pamuk (2002); Van Zanden (2009); some caveats in Dyer (1989: 220–222).

3 Diod. Sic., 1.31.8–9 *polucheiria*; Stat., *Silv.* 4.3.49 *quantae ... manus*.

4 Choisy (1873: 187); Kühn (1910); more recently Rainer (1990).

5 Finley (1999: 23, 212 n. 19) calls evidence for Roman wages 'skimpy.' Goldthwaite (1980: 120) summarizes the broader historical context: 'In ancient Rome, nothing was easier than tapping the resource of labour, but the expansion of the market economy that is so central to the development of the West changed all that by redefining the basic terms of social organization ... By the thirteenth and fourteenth centuries neither slaves nor serfs—or even prisoners—were prominent in construction work; the European builder could hardly avoid the marketplace for labour.'

6 Temin (2013: 115); anticipated by Hopkins (1978: 126) thinking specifically of skilled slave labour.

and servile workers.[7] However, recent work has also emphasized the strong economic dependency that continued to bind freed Roman slaves to their ex-masters, particularly in urban settings.[8] We still might ask whether Roman slaves or even many freedmen ever possessed sufficient personal or professional mobility to respond to market forces. Temin's most valuable point may be that ancient historians have long set their expectations too high: a worker capable of changing jobs at will to meet fluctuating demand was not a reality until the nineteenth century.[9] Instead, nominal wages in Western preindustrial economies were 'sticky' and slow to react to shifting commodity prices.

This being the case, it is important that recent research on Roman wages has demonstrated that the price of free labour reacted in broad outlines to market pressures.[10] Urban and many rural free workers in the Roman world could expect compensation, often in cash, and a skilled labourer earned more than his unskilled peers. If these conditions are not immediately surprising, we must bear in mind that they were not the case throughout antiquity.[11] Admittedly, the Roman evidence for wages is thin (see below), and the question of how expansive or how integrated individual markets for labour were is elusive. One case, however, is suggestive: Cuvigny demonstrates remarkable similarity between the nominal wage structure of quarrymen at Mons Claudianus and miners in Dacia at about the same time.[12] Important for our present concerns, the former were granite-workers whose product adorned the monuments of imperial Rome.

The Organization of Building Labour

As a productive activity, Roman building had several distinctive traits. For one, it was seasonal: construction took place during the drier summer months when concrete walls and foundations would set rapidly and evenly.[13]

---

7 See Harris (2011: 46) on *IEphesos* XI 1a 17–19. I agree with his view that this sort of evidence says more about the lowness of manual labour than it does about the high status of slaves.

8 Mouritsen (2001b: 19): 'Manumission can be seen as a more refined form of exploiting un-free labour in a developed urban economy, and as such it was clearly not a sign of humanity or an expression of any inherent decency in the slave system.'

9 Temin (2004; 2013: Ch. 6).

10 Allen (2009); Rathbone (2009); Scheidel (2009; 2010).

11 For example, see the absence of a skill premium in fifth-century Athens below in Table 4.3.

12 Cuvigny (1996); the real wage may not have been so even, Rathbone (2009: 315–316).

13 Front., *Aq.* 123.2; confirmation in the construction 'journal' from the Baths of Trajan discussed below at n. 63.

Furthermore, all monumental construction relied on a considerable diversity of skillsets. A growing body of cost-analysis studies of archaeologically excavated monuments can shed further light on the compositional balance of such large workforces. Such analyses start by reconstructing a building's original dimensions, then they apply standard work rates to volumetric quantifications of various building materials needed for the project. Rather than representing precise costs, the resulting figures represent models of required labour for a project in man-days or man-hours, and this facilitates historical comparison. In her now-classic study of the Baths of Caracalla, DeLaine first applied such methodology to Roman architecture. Since the 1960s, Pre-Columbian archaeologists have employed a similar approach; recent studies analyse Bronze Age, Byzantine, and Islamic architecture.[14] Across all cultures, one observable constant is the high component cost of material transport and processing, sometimes well above a monument's on-site construction costs. This translates into high demand for unskilled labour: nearly 27% of the minimum construction workers and quarrymen needed for the Baths of Caracalla were low- or unskilled.[15] 41% of total labour required to build a monumental building at the Mayan city of Copan (AD 715) went into the low-skilled task of transporting materials; 77% of all work on Çanlı Kilise, an eleventh-century masonry church in Anatolia, was low-skilled.[16] DeLaine's study also demonstrates how demand varied greatly over a project's course: at the Baths of Caracalla, unskilled labour was needed initially for transport and to clear the site, while the building's final phases were given over to skilled masons carving architectural ornament.[17]

Slave Labour

Because building labourers could be idle for long stretches of time owing to the season or to uneven work schedules, maintaining a permanent dependent workforce of unskilled labour was impractical.[18] While slavery was a component of urban construction labour, especially where this form of labour was available, slaves were more likely to be skilled. The *columbarium* of the Statilii Tauri, a wealthy family with attachments to public construction at Rome, included several slave builders, as well as freedmen who were probably skilled ex-slaves retained in the family's economic circle.[19] In densely built-up areas, repair and upkeep provided more consistent work than *ex novo* construction,

14 Erasmus (1965); Abrams (1994); Fitzsimmons (2007); Pickett (forthcoming).

15 DeLaine (1997: 196–197).

16 Abrams (1994: 133); Pickett (forthcoming).

17 DeLaine (1997: 196–197, 201–202); also Shirley (2001: 141).

18 Similarly, Epstein (2008) on Classical Athens.

19 Martin (1989: 64); Anderson (1997: 78).

and this explains why the best attestations of large slave gangs operating in Roman construction relate to rebuilding and maintenance.[20]

Unskilled Casual Labour

Brunt famously suggested that Rome's building industry used casual wage-labour from the city's underemployed poor to meet the uneven but sometimes high demand for unskilled labour.[21] He pointed to a passage of Suetonius' biography of Vespasian in which the emperor remunerated a *mechanicus* for the invention of a more efficient crane for lifting columns, but declined to use the crane so that he 'be allowed to feed the plebs'.[22] Following this, some have gone so far as to ascribe to the Roman state a populist economic policy aimed at raising employment by putting urban populations to work on building projects. We should be chary about attributing proto-Keynesian economics to this world of (*neg*)*otium* where instability of employment was often a basic condition of life.[23] Public works formed part of an emperor's *indulgentia*, and imperial funds often paid for aqueducts, roads, and harbours that local communities could not themselves afford. That these were major endeavours meant that mass employment was a natural by-product, whether or not this was the emperor's overt aim.[24]

Prices were likely higher at Rome, and Brunt's scenario therefore requires both high wages and high unemployment among Rome's large population. Because migration was the primary way that ancient cities maintained high populations, this indicates something akin to the Harris-Todaro model, where workers' decisions to migrate from rural areas to an urban centre is not motivated purely by wage differential, but by expected wage differential (*wage* × *probability of employment*). Thus, migration remains strong even if a proportion of migrants do not find employment, and this produces a distinct mix of high wages and unemployment.[25] Rome's *annona* system was less likely to have incentivized movement to the capital as has sometimes been suggested, since new arrivals to the city may not have been eligible for the grain dole's

20 Crassus retained 500 architects and builders to repair and resell houses, Plut., *Crass.* 2.4; two *familiae publicae* maintained Rome's aqueducts, Front., *Aq.* 119, 124 with epigraphic evidence discussed by Bruun (1991).

21 Brunt (1980); Skydsgaard (1983) relates this to agricultural production.

22 Suet., *Vesp.* 18.

23 The comments of Goldthwaite (1980: 297) are germane.

24 Bodei Giglioni (1974); Lo Cascio (2007: 632–633) remains charitable to the idea of state intervention.

25 Harris and Todaro (1970). I thank Peter Temin for bringing this to my attention.

benefits.[26] This is all a reminder that Brunt's thesis implies a specific hierarchic relationship between Rome and its hinterland that was only reproducible at major regional centres that received significant centripetal migration.[27] A stable, underemployed urban population was less possible in smaller cities, or within networks of cities with little differentiation in priority and consequently less migratory pull. These lower-rank settlements might instead have drawn unskilled free labour *ad hoc* from the surrounding countryside without ever forming the stable non-agricultural workforce that supported the urban labour market of Rome.[28]

Forced Labour

There were other means of raising unskilled labour for a construction project, and not all free labourers were remunerated.[29] State corvées for public works date back to archaic Rome, and the practice persisted to some extent well into the Empire. Corvées had little bearing on the building industry at Rome itself during the Empire, but there is evidence to suggest their role outside the capital.[30] Spanish town charters from Urso and Irni record nearly identical provisions permitting local magistrates to requisition labourers of a certain age along with draught animals for the upkeep of local fortifications (*munitiones*).[31] Corvée was limited to five days of work each year, and the same term appears regularly in the institutionalized *penthēmeros* corvée for dyke-maintenance in Egypt.[32] In this case, five days of forced labour may have been broadly traditional. This was hardly an arduous requirement when compared, for example, to the month's labour owed annually by adult males in Han China.[33] In North Africa, several inscriptions attest to the use of civilian labour for public works

26 Bernard (2016).

27 E.g. at Jerusalem after the conclusion of construction for Herod's Temple, Joseph., *BJ* 20.219.

28 Erdkamp (1999) on surplus labour from seasonal and structural underemployment in Roman agriculture.

29 Brunt (1980: 82); Duncan-Jones (1990: 174–175); Garnsey (1998b). Note that compulsory labour does not necessarily exclude compensation, as e.g. when Pope Hadrian I paid conscripted workers to repair Rome's walls (*Liber Pontificalis* 97.52).

30 Brunt (1980: 82) downplays their prevalence.

31 Crawford (1996: no. 25, §98); Crawford and González (1986: §83). The largely repetitive clause in both charters suggests a more widespread phenomenon.

32 The *penthēmeros* is attested in a corpus of papyri discussed by Sijpestein (1964); dependents or hired-labour could be substituted for the personal obligation.

33 Loewe (1968: 75).

in the third century AD.[34] Evidence in Italy for civic labour taxes picks up in the fourth and fifth century.[35]

In all these cases, building-type was key: utilitarian public structures like fortifications or ports, whose maintenance was deemed a public necessity, could draw upon citizen labour as a form of taxation.[36] Road maintenance fell into this category: in many Italian towns, streets and drains were a public duty and remained so through the Carolingian period.[37] Compulsory labour for wall-building is commonplace from classical Greece well into medieval Europe, nor is this attachment by any means restricted to the Western world.[38]

To some extent, Roman construction drew labour from those condemned to public work (*damnatio ad opus publicum*) or to imperial mines and quarries (*damnatio in metallum*).[39] Roman penal labour relied on a system of criminal law that was closely related to social status. For this reason, *damnatio* was often applied to socially-marginal groups, and this distinguished it from corvée labour, which was normally bound to citizenship.[40] *Damnatio in metallum* was barely preferable to capital punishment, and *damnati* in mines and quarries faced quasi-life sentences working under brutal conditions. Imperial stone quarries are a frequent destination for Christian martyrs or war-captives, although it is worth noting that none of the almost 900 *ostraka* thus

34 *ILS* 5590, a covered market in Auzia; *ILAlg* 2.1.3598 a cistern at Tiddis; three examples of fortification walls in Mauretania: *ILS* 6887–6889.

35 Ward-Perkins (1984: 35–36). The complex reasons for this upturn are beyond this paper's scope but include a thinning urban labour supply, a decline in the availability of slave labour, and increasing pressures on civic budgets.

36 *Cod. Iust.*, 8.11.7 transmits a fourth-century law specifically permitting corvées for walls, ports, and aqueducts; see also the list of building types at Cic., *Off.* 2.60: *illae impensae meliores*.

37 Street maintenance: Cato, *Agr.* 2.; Plin., *Ep.* 10.31.2; Suet., *Cal.* 27; medieval Italian references in Ward-Perkins (1984: 133–134).

38 *Pandemei* wall construction: Thuc., 1.90.3, 5.82.6; Diod. Sic., 11.40.1, 12.47.4; medieval examples in Goldthwaite (1980: 122); Chinese imperial wall corvées: Barbieri-Low (2007: 212–227).

39 Millar (1984); Tacoma and Groen-Vallinga (2015); on *damnatio in metallum* see Hirt (2010: 222–225).

40 Tacoma and Groen-Vallinga (2015). I do note some overlap between civic corvée and *damnati ad opus publicum*: Plin., *Ep.* 10.31 relates *damnati* performing *munitiones viarum et vicorum*. Compare this with a group called *viasei et vicanei* in the *Lex agraria* (Crawford 1996: no. 2, ll. 11–12), presumably landholders exempted from other taxes but retaining road-maintenance duties near their estates.

far published from the imperial granite quarries of Mons Claudianus explicitly records convict labour, despite an otherwise high level of bureaucratic detail.[41]

By contrast, *damnati ad opus publicum* normally served a term-sentence. Their employment in maintaining local public works seems implied by a letter of Trajan to Pliny in which the emperor advises Pliny that *damnati* who had shirked punishment and were acting illegally as public slaves, but who were old and whose verdict was given more than a decade prior, could be put to work in local municipalities cleaning baths and sewers, or labouring on roads and streets 'as they were accustomed to do'.[42] In rare circumstances, *damnati* may have offered a source of labour for large imperial projects such as when Nero ordered that courts convict criminals *ad opus publicum* to raise labour for a canal from Lake Avernus to Ostia.[43]

Within the larger category of unremunerated free labour, military labour was vital to the Empire's frontier cities.[44] Soldiers possessed a wide array of skills and not only built military structures, but also baths, basilicas, and amphitheatres. Some military engineers went on to careers as civil architects, Vitruvius being the most famous example.

Contractual Labour and Building Contracts

Building patrons, emperor or elite citizen, are known from hundreds of dedicatory inscriptions. While the language of such inscriptions is often direct (e.g. *aedem fecit*), the patron was not normally involved in building himself, even if one enthusiastic patron of an amphitheatre at Tivoli commemorates his contribution of 200 days' labour to the project.[45] Instead, most records imply a contractual obligation between patron and contractor (*redemptor*). Censorial and aedilician building contracts are well-enough attested in Republican Rome. The major innovation of imperial Rome was the development of *curatores operum publicorum* to oversee state construction; normally, these were individuals of higher status.[46] Outside the capital, different parties guided

41 Hirt (2010: 224) discusses martyrs and war-captives at quarries; Bülow-Jacobsen (2009: 2) on the absence of *damnati* at Mons Claudianus.

42 Plin., *Ep.* 10.31.2.

43 Suet., *Ner.* 31.3; I do not share the pessimism of Millar (1984: 133) that Nero's orders were never carried out, although he seems correct to stress that this was an unusual means of raising labour.

44 MacMullen (1959); for the wide range of specialization attested among the legions, see Veg., *Mil.* 2.11.

45 *ILS* 5630.

46 Vitellius held the office; Vespasian entrusted the repair of the Capitoline to equestrians; Kolb (1993).

construction's initial steps as was customary by region. In the East, for example, work was overseen by high-ranking supervisors (*epimeletai* or *epistatai*) in collaboration with the provincial procurators.[47]

Redemptores of all status, including at least one slave, took up building contracts.[48] Some but not all found the practice moderately lucrative.[49] At Rome, select families of *redemptores operum publicorum* span several generations, and a few may have fostered political connections.[50] Q. Haterius Tychichus, whose tomb was decorated with reliefs depicting a tread-wheel crane and several Flavian monuments including the Colosseum and the Arch of Titus, perhaps descended from a freedman of the *consul ordinarius* Q. Haterius Antonius of AD 53.[51]

Building contracts normally fell under the rubric of *locatio conductio operis*.[52] The party taking on a contract (*conductor*) stood to fulfil a set task (*opus*) within a specified period at a set price (*merces*). The set price, often paid in instalments upon approval, shielded the lessor (*locator*) from the risk of future added costs. This has two important implications:

1. *Redemptores* used subsidiary *locationes operum* to hire builders (*fabri*) and *locationes rerum* (the letting of things, instead of works) to obtain equipment or slaves. Subcontracting promoted the creation of smaller building 'firms' (DeLaine's term). These are, unfortunately, not well attested, although DeLaine plausibly suggests that members of Rome's large *collegium fabrum tignariorum* may have owned or operated such firms.[53] Admittedly, the relationship of these Empire-wide *collegia fabrum* to the building trade has been questioned;

47 Full discussion in Barresi (2003: 20–51). The triangular relationship between emperor, civic *epimeletai*, and provincial procurator is well-represented by a recently published letter from Hadrian to Aphrodisias (*SEG* L 1096).

48 Martin (1989: 54–59); Anderson (1997: 95–112). *Ingenui redemptores* and freedmen are numerous. A slave purchases a contract for work on Cicero's brother's estate, Cic., *Quint.* 3.1.3.

49 Note, however, that *Cod. Iust.*, 8.10.12.9 refers to provisions for a contractor who was a pauper.

50 Martin (1989: 57) on the Coccei who appear as both *redemptor* and *architectus* under Augustus and again in relation to building under Hadrian.

51 Coarelli (1979).

52 Martin (1989); Taylor (2003: 14–18); Du Plessis (2012: 74–81); Bernard (2013: 113–114).

53 DeLaine (1997: 204; 2000: 121) draws a connection between collegial *decuriae* and several sources' use of *decuria* to describe individual work gangs (of ten?). Symm., *Relat.* 14 suggests that *collegia fabrum* held an advantage in obtaining building contracts.

however, a professional attachment to building seems in many cases desirable.[54] *Collegia* of *fabri tignuarii* (carpenters, builders) are attested empire-wide; one such group at Rome proudly displays their carpentry tools on their altar.[55] At Arles, an *architectus* used his membership to stake a claim for excellence in building crafts: his sarcophagus boasts of his *ars summa* for which his fellow *artifices* named him *magister* of his *collegium*.[56]

Different building tasks called for different modes of organizing workmen. Work could be arranged for a duration of time: daily wages are well-attested, either as direct labour or as the basis for longer-term contracts (see the section on wages below). Otherwise, rate work was appropriate for builders like brick masons who worked with materials readily divisible by piece or unit. An intriguing inscription from Laodicea in Asia Minor corresponds different groups of building workers with three differently sized linear measures. This may pertain to a rate-based pay scale, and there does appear to be coordination between the skill-level of the specializations named and the length of the measures.[57] It was also possible to define work by contracting out a whole structure to individual work gangs building discrete segments. Subtle differences in the finished product—staircases, formwork, or putlog hole spacing—can help reconstruct the pattern by which work was divided up in complex or outsized structures.[58] This composite reality, however, is entirely hidden in most building inscriptions, which instead record wholesale contracts let for single and sometimes astronomical sums, such as the two million sesterces for the Baths of Neptune at Ostia.[59] Such amounts were not drawn from thin air. The figure for the Baths of Neptune seems to have been predictive, because the inscription records Antoninus Pius' supplement of an unspecified amount (*pecunia adiecta*) to Hadrian's initial two million sesterces in order to complete the building's ornament.

---

54 Cf. Plin., *Ep.* 10.33. Martin (1989: 65–68) and Kolb (2008: 105) are sceptical; Verboven in this volume is more optimistic. Liu (2009: 114–115) suggests that the *utilitas publica* of *collegia fabrum* may have differed from region to region.

55 *CIL* VI 30982.

56 *CIL* XII 722.

57 *MAMA* XI 254; the inscription has no internal evidence for dating and no archaeological provenance: the editors suggest that the text may relate to local enforcement in the wake of the Diocletianic Price Edict, but since the Price Edict does not refer to rate work for these classes of builders, this is by no means certain.

58 Lancaster (2002) provides an exemplary study of the Colosseum's work arrangement; Booms (2007) differentiates Ostian work gangs by their putlog-hole signatures.

59 *ILS* 334.

2. Predictive, wholesale price information may imply that the contract process encouraged estimates of a project's cost from its outset. Vitruvius advises architects that arithmetic is important for reckoning building costs.[60] Aulus Gellius' description of a visit of some builders to M. Cornelius Fronto is enlightening, even if it comes from a private context:[61]

> We found him lying on a Greek couch … by his side stood several builders, who had been summoned to construct some new baths and were exhibiting different plans for baths, drawn on little pieces of parchment. When he had selected one plan and specimen of their work, he inquired what the expense would be of completing that entire project. And when the architect had said that it would probably require about three hundred thousand sesterces, one of Fronto's friends said, 'And another fifty thousand, more or less.'

The joke was for a client to expect an architect's calculations to be low, but estimation was an assumed part of the bidding process. Considering how significantly labour figured into total cost in the form of wages or maintenance for slaves, might estimates have included more than just material costs, and did Romans form and apply standard labour rates? There is no direct evidence, but it is not impossible. Simple, spatial tabulations sufficed for less sophisticated structures, but it is hard to imagine that more complex architecture did not promote further extrapolation.[62] It is also suggestive that at least some Roman builders generated records of daily progress: recent excavations at the Baths of Trajan on the Oppian in Rome have revealed a series of consecutive calendar dates painted by masons directly onto the structure's brickwork over the course of the building season.[63] Since the Republic, a unit measurement of labour input in days (*operae*) existed.[64]

---

60 Vitr., *De arch.* 1.1.4; see Taylor (2003: 17) on such calculations in Roman and Byzantine architecture.

61 Gell., *NA* 19.10.1–4: *Offendimus eum cubantem in scimpodio Graeciensi … Adsistebant fabri aedium complures, balneis novis moliendis adhibiti, ostendebantque depictas in membranulis varias species balnearum. Ex quibus cum elegisset unam formam speciemque operis, interrogavit quantus esset pecuniae sumptus ad id totum opus absolvendum. Cumque architectus dixisset necessaria videri esse sestertia ferme trecenta, unus ex amicis Frontonis: 'Et praeterpropter,' inquit, 'alia quinquaginta.'*

62 Roads may have been priced by foot; see Duncan-Jones (1982: 124–125); Cato, *Agr.* 14.3 tallies a small structure's cost by counting roof-tiles.

63 Volpe (2002); Volpe and Rossi (2012).

64 *Dig.* 38.1.3.1 *operae sunt diurnum officium*. Harris (2007: 528) for the Republican origin.

While the lessor was chiefly interested in setting the lowest possible contract price, the *redemptor* needed a firmer idea of potential expenditures to maximize net income. Accordingly, we should look foremost to building contractors themselves as organizers of labour even for public works, and evidence of direct state interest is thin.[65]

Specialization and Skilled Labour

Adam Smith begins *The Wealth of Nations* by discussing the division of labour, which he considered the 'greatest improvement in the productive powers of labour.'[66] Importantly, efficiency in *per capita* output is achieved, as his famous example of the pin factory illustrates, by vertical specialization, rather than by horizontal diversity of occupation present in most complex societies. To be sure, the Roman building industry saw horizontal specialization: Harald von Petrikovit's catalogue of occupations identifies 192 different titles from Rome itself, 22% relating directly to building; there seems to have been no less diversity outside the capital.[67] Compare the 1527 census of Rome, which displays greater total diversity, but shows less attachment to building trades (11%, N = 228).[68] Problematically, there is overlap in the Roman evidence, as in the case of *marmorarii*, who could place marble into a building, quarry blocks, or deal in the marble trade.[69] *Architectus* itself is notoriously difficult to define.[70]

Archaeology, instead, affords better evidence of workshop-level division of labour, and the potential development of vertical specialization is worth considering. The massive imperial production of regularly-sized bricks presumes levels of coordination, even if brickstamps primarily shed light on brickyard owners and operators, rather than the workforce itself.[71] To some extent, the marble trade also achieved economies of scale and semi-industrialization: already by the Augustan period monuments at Rome employed standard-module column sizes.[72] This had repercussions for the entire supply chain; as

65 Hadrian's organization of Rome's building force 'in the appearance of a legion' is presented as exceptional, Aur. Vict., *Caes.* 14.5. Pliny (*Ep.* 10.40–41) seems to have had a better idea than Trajan of the availability and skill of builders in his province.

66 Smith (1793: 5).

67 Von Petrikovits (1981); see Kolb (2008: 103–104) for the Western provinces.

68 Figures derived from Lee (2006).

69 Frezouls (1995: 39).

70 Eck (1997).

71 On business managers in the brick industry, Aubert (1994: 217–244).

72 Column sizes: Zink (2008: 59).

provincial quarries transitioned from quarrying-to-order to continuous production, efficiency ramped up considerably. The stockpile of marble blocks imported from provincial quarries to Ostia outpaced the needs of the emperors and continued to serve demand after the end of the Empire.[73] An interesting if ambiguous case of the effects of this new scale of production comes from ancient Simmithus, where marble workshops were at some date installed into a large building nearby to the city's famous coloured-marble quarries. The spatial distribution of partly-worked artefacts inside the workshops suggests to Wilson that this was a sort of marble manufactory with apparent vertical specialization of production.[74] However, the archaeological data are not so clear: during the peak of imperial quarrying, the building functioned instead as a residential structure, perhaps for *damnati* working at the quarries. Marble workshops were only installed in the fourth century, towards the very end of Simmithus' productive lifetime as a quarry-town.[75]

Close study of architectural ornament yields some evidence for vertical division of labour, but organizational practice more often differed from site to site. Marble carvers working on a large and highly-ornate building could be divided into teams assigned to zones of a monument.[76] Alternatively, masons might specialize in producing particular elements for multiple sites; 'ateliers' producing Corinthian capitals were maybe five or six men strong.[77] Material dictated such arrangements: at Ostia's Forum Baths, Attic masons produced capitals in Pentelic marble, while Asiatic masons worked in Proconnesian marble.[78]

The process by which workers acquired their skill remains elusive. Building training has always been hands-on as much as theoretical; Vitruvius makes it clear that Roman builders in his day were disinclined to transmit their knowledge in written form.[79] Predictably, builders appear in our evidence for apprenticeship.[80] Crassus has little trouble acquiring five hundred slave architects and builders. The *Digest* preserves a case in which a *faber* purchases and

73 Greenhalgh (2009: 111–119) on the post-Classical use of stockpiled marble including Ostia. Fant (2001) argues that much of the Ostian material was faulty or damaged.

74 Wilson (2008: 409).

75 Mackensen (2005: 100–101, 111–114) dates the establishment of marble workshops to ca. AD 335–340. I thank Ben Russell for this observation.

76 As was the case with the Basilica Paulli at Rome, see Lipps (2011: 173–179).

77 Freyberger (1990) on Rome, where at least three workshops produced capitals for particular classes of monuments; Rohmann (1998) suggests the size of a workshop active at the Pergamon Trajaneum.

78 Freyberger (1990: 135).

79 Vitr., *De arch.* 7.pr.18.

80 Bergamasco (1995: 105–106).

trains a slave, then sells him at double the cost.[81] Only in the later Empire do we see public investment in educating builders. Severus Alexander instituted salaries and lecture facilities for several professions including architects and engineers; similar legislation appears under Constantine. The Price Edict records a maximum wage for an *architectus magister*.[82] Cuomo argues that these measures reflect the changing role of architecture and its practitioners in Late Antiquity, rather than anxiety over a dwindling skilled labour supply.[83]

Technology and Innovation

Specialization is intimately bound up with the topic of technological innovation, and particularly the 'industrialization' that several detect in Roman construction. A longstanding systematic approach to Roman architecture, best exemplified by Lugli, presumes a series of technological discontinuities over time as one technique 'supplants' another.[84] Lancaster's recent overview of Roman building technology reads as a continuous narrative of diffusion and change.[85] Wilson compares the rapid completion of grand imperial buildings to the slower timespan required for Gothic cathedrals: the productivity of Roman architecture was not solely due to large workforces or more financial resources, but also relied on the innovation of more efficient building techniques.[86] We must note that innovations in Roman construction only rarely sought to replace human labour, and there are only a few exceptional examples in the building trade of the sort of mechanization that may have had a deleterious effect on wages during the Industrial Revolution.[87] However, some building innovations during the Empire such as serial masonry may

81 *Dig.* 17.1.26.8.

82 SHA, *Alex. Sev.* 44.4; *Cod. Theod.*, 13.4.1; *Edictum de Pretiis*, 7.74; Donderer (1996: 59–60). See below the contribution by Groen-Vallinga and Tacoma.

83 Cuomo (2007: Ch. 5).

84 Lugli (1957).

85 Lancaster (2008); the older view of stagnant Roman technology seems in this respect refuted.

86 Wilson (2006: 230).

87 For the effects of mechanization on wages, see Samuelson (1989), drawing on Ricardo's observations for the early stages of the Industrial Revolution. Some Roman exceptions include lifting engines and advanced transport vehicles, (see Bernard (2013)), and late antique marble saws (see Seigne (2006)). This is not to deny any mechanization in the Roman world, as see Wilson (2002a).

have effectively increased workers' *per capita* output and are therefore worth considering.

The greatest Roman contribution to building technology was concrete and its related techniques, which begin in the second century BC and evolve constantly through the High Empire.[88] This includes mortared-aggregate (*opus caementicium*), as well as serial wall-facings in brick (*latericium*) or tessellated stone (*reticulatum*). Facing techniques have attracted attention for their improvements in efficiency, and Brunt supported his thesis of casual employment for building by supposing that such techniques deskilled the industry *in toto*.[89] This requires some modification. While brick and reticulate required less skill than carving intricate stone ornament, Roman builders never abandoned the latter. Ideally, Roman architecture combined concrete vaulted construction with traditional post-and-lintel stonemasonry. As an illustration, consider an iconic concrete building like the Pantheon where only a tenth of minimum total cost went into building the colonnaded porch. However, the porch was the building's display side, and its post-and-lintel construction depended on highly skilled masons to shape columns and marble ornament.[90] Rather than deskilling or multiplying output by phasing out skilled labour, concrete and its related technologies allowed for the rapid scaling up of structures that still frequently presented themselves as cut-stone and required skilled stonemasonry.

It is impossible to disentangle the early development of concrete from the context of slavery: the technique formed in second-century BC Campania where requisite natural resources ('pozzolana') met a burgeoning slave-based villa economy. Some related innovations such as the appearance of Punic-derived waterproof plaster flooring technology in Latium seem directly related to the movement of slaves.[91] This leads us to challenge the idea that slaves contributed little more than their labour to building projects. Some historians of the Colonial Americas promote an analogous phenomenon: West African slaves were vital to the increased efficiency of early American rice cultivation because they brought with them an indigenous knowledge of cultivars and

---

88 Lancaster (2005).

89 Brunt (1980: 93); Coarelli (1977), Torelli (1980), and Rakob (1983) focus on slavery and the development of *opus reticulatum*.

90 DeLaine (2015) suggests that nearly 85% of the porch's total minimum labour-cost went to shaping stone and marble, perhaps occupying a team of 50–60 masons for a period of two years.

91 Gaggiotti (1988).

planting techniques.[92] Similarly, Central Italy after the Hannibalic War saw slaves with local knowledge moved to an area of intensive capital investment, producing an environment conducive to technological innovation.

Even into the Empire, technological development was never far away from the milieu of slavery. MacDonald emphasizes the inventiveness and plasticity of vaulted concrete architecture at Rome following the Neronian fire of AD 64.[93] Around the same time, Nero's tutor Seneca composed an imaginary debate with the philosopher Posidonius over technology's role in human advancement. Posidonius held that philosophy's search for human betterment supported invention; Seneca instead promoted the importance of experiential knowledge and cleverness (*sagacitas*) over wisdom (*sapientia*). Thus, he saw the inventor as craftsman, not thinker, and this had important social implications. Building technologies illustrated his point:

> We know that certain devices have come to light only within our own memory—such as the use of windows which admit the clear light through transparent tiles, and such as the vaulted baths with pipes let into their walls for the purpose of diffusing the heat... Why need I mention the marble with which our temples and private houses are resplendent? Or the rounded and polished masses of stone by means of which we erect colonnades and buildings roomy enough for nations?... All this sort of thing has been devised by the lowest grade of slaves. Wisdom's seat is higher; she trains not the hands, but is the mistress of our minds.[94]

Seneca is most interested in improvements to comfort or style, not to the efficiency of production. But it is worth stressing that Seneca would see nothing contradictory about attributing *sagacitas* and innovation to slaves. This would have confounded Adam Smith, who felt that slaves had no self-interest 'but to labour as little as possible' and could be motivated only by violence.[95] Of course, Smith's frame of reference was not Roman slavery, and Seneca reminds

---

92 Wood (1974); Carney (1998).

93 MacDonald (1982: 1).

94 Sen., *Ep.* 90.25–26: *Quaedam nostra demum prodisse memoria scimus, ut speculariorum usum perlucente testa clarum transmittentium lumen, ut suspensuras balneorum et inpressos parietibus tubos, per quos circumfunderetur calor... Quid loquar marmora, quibus templa, quibus domus fulgent? Quid lapideas moles in rotundum ac leve formatas, quibus porticus et capacia populorum tecta suscipimus?... Vilissimorum mancipiorum ista commenta sunt; sapientia altius sedet nec manus edocet, animorum magistra est.*

95 Smith (1793: 385); see Vivenza (2013: 31) for the general Roman evaluation of slave labour not conforming to modern economic thought.

us that, in the Roman building industry at least, slaves often served in more highly skilled capacities. This also encourages Temin's view that Romans somehow incentivized slave labour, particularly skilled slave labour. Otherwise, we might also stress the potential role of the contractor, the *redemptor* or *manceps* who may not have occupied a much higher social rank in Seneca's eyes than *vilissimi mancipii*. Vitruvius tells the story of the *redemptor* Paconius, who devised a novel way of dragging a large statue base by setting its ends into a pair of wooden wheels.[96] Unable to pull the load in a straight line, his machine cost more than it was worth, but even if innovation did not in this case guarantee success, the depiction of contractor, and not theoretician, as inventor is plain.

Reflections of a Labour Market: Wages and Mobility

If wage evidence were fuller, we might better gauge the extent and performance of a labour market as reflected by the movement of wages or the mobility of workers themselves. Still, some evidence is worth considering:

Wages

Only two moments in the entirety of the Empire allow anything approaching a series of builders' wages. Since we often have wheat prices for the respective periods, I translate nominal wages into litres of wheat, not as an actual consumption basket, but as an index of real wages to facilitate cross-cultural comparison. A 'skilled' wage represents that of a specialized labourer, not of a foreman or engineer.

1. Roman Egypt, as so often otherwise, provides several figures. Drexhage catalogues over two dozen attestations of builders' wages, thirteen of which record a *per diem* (Table 4.1). Problematically, we cannot always tell when a worker is specialized and, if so, to what degree. These wages are higher than for a common labourer, and this fact, along with the specification *oikodomos* or *tektōn*, implies skill-based differentiation, but *SB* XIV 11958 col. I l. 8 records undifferentiated workers (*ergatai*) receiving the same daily rate as *tektones*.

Like other prices from Roman Egypt, skilled builders' wages divide into two 'bands' of stability, before and after the Antonine Plague.[97] Wilson demonstrates a downturn in building inscriptions across the Mediterranean in the decades after AD 165, which he connects with the plague's effect on demand

96 Vitr., *De arch.* 10.2.13–14.

97 Scheidel (2002b).

TABLE 4.1 *Daily building wages from Roman Egypt*

Date (AD)	Location	Corpus number	Wage, *per diem* unless noted
ca. 100	Oxyrynchus?	*P. Oxy.* XVIII 2190	2 drachma
117	Oxyrynchus	*SB* XIV 11958 col. I	1 dr. (3 times)
2nd century	Tebtynis	*SB* VI 9494	2 dr.
2nd century	Upper Egypt	*O. Berl.* 71	1 dr. 2 ob.
2nd century	Upper Egypt	*O. Bodl.* II 1755	1 dr. 1 ob.
2nd century	Upper Egypt	*O. Stras.* 701 col. I	1 dr. 3 ob.
246	Euhemeria	*SB* VI 9406.2	24 dr. for 6 days plus bread
ca. 250	Theadelphia	*SB* VI 9409.5	24 dr. for 6 days
255	Theadelphia	*SB* VI 9409.1	8 dr. for 2 days
253 or 256	Theadelphia	*SB* VI 9408.2	20 dr. for 5 days
265	Hermopolis	*SB* X 10299	4 dr.

for public architecture.[98] The epidemic also interrupted the supply of brick and marble to imperial construction sites.[99] Daily wages rise from a mean 1.5 Egyptian drachma in the second century to a consistent 4 drachma in the third. The regular 4 drachma wage for similar work in the Fayyum and at Hermopolis further south is suggestive.[100] Egyptian wheat cost a mean of 9.2 drachma per *artaba* (= 38.8 litres) in the second century, and ca. 18 drachma per *artaba* in the third.[101] Mean daily wheat wages for Egyptian builders are 6.32 litres for the second century, and 8.62 for the third. It is worth noting that a skilled builder who found full annual employment at these rates could afford just above the cost of Scheidel's 'respectability basket' of consumption

98 Wilson (2011: fig. 7.1). I take this as roughly correspondent with the labour supply since the plague was, after all, a demographic phenomenon.

99 Duncan-Jones 1996. We want to know more about the plague's impact on the workforce at Rome itself, where 2,000 people died daily (Dio Cass., 73.14.3).

100 This begs the question of how much wages reflected changes in commodity prices across the geographical extent of the market. In the second century, nominal wages from Upper Egypt are somewhat lower, and Duncan-Jones (1990: 144) notes that general wheat prices were lower there as well.

101 Second century follows Cuvigny (1996: 141); third following Rathbone (1997).

requirements. By his calculations, an unskilled worker's income only sufficed to pay for 70–90% of the same basket.[102]

The Egyptian evidence mostly attests to private construction.[103] For public comparanda, the wages of stone-cutters at the imperial quarries of Mons Claudianus conform to a monthly pay scale of 28/37/47 Egyptian drachma in the second century; remarkably, pay may have been calculated annually.[104] For a thirty-day month, the daily basis was 0.93/1.23/1.57 drachma. The top of the pay scale is close to the mean wage in papyri of the same time, revealing similarity between private and imperial wages for broadly similar work. This produces a wheat wage scale of 3.92/5.19/6.62 litres per day. Cuvigny calculates an average unskilled worker salary at the same date of 25 drachma per month, 3.39 litres of wheat per day.[105]

Cuvigny reckons that the best paid quarrymen's annual wages at Mons Claudianus sufficed to feed five adults; calculated on an annual basis, the monthly pay of 47 dr. easily met the cost of a 'respectability' consumption basket as calculated by Scheidel. Considering how close the wage of workers at Mons Claudianus was to the rest of Egypt, the longer term contract may represent the state's attempt to draw skilled workers to an otherwise unappealing part of the Empire, what economists call a compensating wage differential. It is also worth observing that refuse deposits at Mons Claudianus suggest that workers there had easy access to imported luxury foodstuffs; it is unknown, though we might speculate, whether the importation of such foodstuffs was owed to the encouragement of the state.[106] Mons Claudianus attracted quarrymen from Syene, Thebes, but also as far as Alexandria, where there was always demand for builders and stonecutters. For this reason, I suspect that daily wages in the Egyptian capital were not excessively different from those at Mons Claudianus.

2. Diocletian's Price Edict of AD 301 gives the following maxima for builders' wages and those of related workers in denarii (Table 4.2).

---

102 Full employment here taken as a 250 day year. Scheidel (2010: 434), who offers a slightly modified version of Allen (2009), puts the cost in drachmas for a 'respectability' consumption basket at a mean 354 dr. in the second century and 838 dr. in the third. A skilled builder appears to have had the potential in 250 days of work to earn 375 dr. (106% respectability basket) in the second century and 1000 dr. (119%) in the third.

103 *SB* XIV 11958 records wages for work on a temple; for what it's worth, these are the lowest recorded.

104 Cuvigny (1996), who finds this regular payscale in a large number of *entolae*.

105 Cuvigny (1996: 141) calculates this general unskilled wage from twenty-two papyri around Egypt.

106 Van der Veen (1998).

TABLE 4.2 *Maximum building worker wages in Diocletian's Price Edict*

Worker	Wage in *denarii per diem*
Lapidarius structor (Stonemason)	50 + *pastus*
Faber intestinarius (Joiner)	50
Faber tignarius (Woodworker)	50
Calcis Coctor (Lime burner)	50
Marmorarius (Marble-worker)	60
Musaearius (Mosaicist)	60
Tessellarius (Tesserae maker)	50
Pictor parietarius (Wall painter, plasterer)	75
Pictor imaginarius (Picture painter)	150
Carpentarius (Cartwright)	50
Faber ferrarius (Iron worker)	50
Architectus magister (Master architect)	100 (monthly per student)

Skilled builders make a minimum twice the daily wage of an unskilled worker, commonly earning maxima wages of 25 denarii plus maintenance (*pastus diurnus*, ca. 11.1 denarii).[107] The 2:1 cash wage ratio is so common in the Price Edict as to be formulaic.[108] In this case, the skill premium, which represents the percentage of an unskilled wage paid in addition to a skilled worker, was 100%, or twice the unskilled wage. If we consider that both workers received the same *pastus*, we might add the value of kind payment to cash, as Robert Allen recently does. Adding the value of *pastus* as 11.1 denarii to all wages, the skill premium falls slightly to 69% for skilled workers earning 50 denarii (61 to 36 denarii), and 97% for those earning 60 denarii (71 to 36 denarii). The Price Edict lists wheat at 100 *denarii* per *kastrensis modius* (1 *k.m.* = ca. 13 litres wheat), making the builder's maximum daily wheat wage equivalent to 0.61 *k.m.*[109] Including *pastus*, the stonemason's maximum wage in the Price Edict was 7.94 litres daily, with select building craftsmen wage set at a maxima of 9.23 litres, and the picture painter earning a maximum of 20.94 litres. We cannot settle here the problematic question of the relationship of these maxima to actual wages earned. I do note, however, that the 8.62 litres/day

107 Maintenance cost follows Allen (2009: 330).

108 See Tacoma and Groen-Vallinga in this volume; Rathbone (2009: 314).

109 Conversion follows Duncan-Jones (1976).

wage from third century Egypt stands favourably in the middle of the Price Edict's range of maxima for roughly similar work.

We may compare these figures to some historical data from antiquity and the Middle Ages in the Mediterranean and Middle East (Table 4.3).

TABLE 4.3 *Comparison of wheat wages and skill premia for builders*

Period and date	Wheat wage (litres)	Skill premium (% above unskilled wage)
Athens, 408/7 BC	7.2–8.7	0%
Epidaurus, 329/8 BC[a]	10.9–26.0	(30)–100%
Ptolemaic Egypt, 210–183 BC[b]	4.3–6.5	133–233%
Roman Egypt, second century AD	3.39–6.62	16–95%
Roman Egypt, third century AD	8.62	150%
Roman Empire, AD 301[c]	7.94–9.23 (6.5–7.8 excluding *pastus*)	68–97% (100–140% excluding *pastus*)
Eastern Byzantine Empire, 500–550[d]	14.4	410%
Egypt, ca. AD 700[e]	9.3–10.4	60–80%
Baghdad AD 760s[f]	3.6–5.3	133–250%
Cairo, AD 1199[g]	14.4–31.5	60–250%

a For wages in Athens and Epidaurus, see Loomis (1998: 99, 120).
b Builders' wages are scarce in Maresch (1995). *BGU* VI 1290 records wages for *oikodomoi* with a *kulein lithous* (stone transporter?) earning 20 dr./day and *paidaria* earning 6–10 dr.
c Excluding the wall-painter (9.75 liters / 200 premium without *pastus*) and the picture-painter (19.5 liters /500 premium without *pastus*).
d Jones (1964: 858, 1358, n. 82). The Byzantine Emperor Anastasius (AD 491–518) pays skilled builders an inflated 4 *karats* (Zach. Myt., *Chron.* 7.6). Elsewhere in the empire in the sixth century, a skilled stonecutter earns 1 *karat* a day, ideally 14.4 litres wheat (*V. Dan. Scet.* 9); a worker on a cistern (AD 516–524) earns 5 *folles*, 2.9 liters wheat, per day (Joh. Mosch., 34). The last price aligns with unskilled wages in Scheidel (2010b). 1 *karat* seems high, and the premium higher still.
e Morrisson and Cheynet (2002: table 18), annual wages for carpenter and caulker in *P. Lond.* XIV 1910 compared to that of *misthios*; wheat price is harder to obtain, but I use a late-sixth century Egyptian figure from *ibid.* table 5. As the skill premium seems low, the annual contract term should be considered as well.
f Ashtor (1969: 64) considers these low and suggests they were accompanied by state subsidies; *contra* Scheidel 2010: 450.
g Goitein (1967: 95–99); Ashtor (1969: 224) finds skill premia in Fatamid Egypt ranging from 33% to 133%, with 50% being regular. Scheidel (2010: 451–452) notes comparatively high unskilled wages for this period.

This may be complemented with data, particularly for skill premia, from medieval to modern Europe: prior to the Black Plague, premia of 100 or even 200 were not uncommon, but from 1450 until the First World War, the skill premium for builders settles with remarkable stability around 50.[110]

While the Roman data are insufficient to make any nuanced or far-reaching conclusions, as best we can tell, Roman skilled builders' wages in Egypt and in the Price Edict were not unusually high when compared to wages in antiquity and beyond. The skill premia are somewhat higher than much of Europe in the early-modern period, and this may reflect some comparative thinness to the market for skilled builders, as Hawkins discusses elsewhere in this volume. However, it should also be noted that the wages collected here for builders show skill premia that were by no means unusual when compared to antiquity and the medieval period.[111] Meanwhile, demand for building labour in the Roman world was undoubtedly high, and in modern labour markets a low wage matched with high demand might conceal other forms of employment incentives such as occupational stability. In this context, it is again worth emphasizing the potential appearance of non-cash incentives to workers at Mons Claudianus.

Mobility

Market pressure for builders in the cities of the empire ought to have moved workers towards higher wages. Roman evidence produces a mixed picture: recruitment was not strictly local but also not necessarily dependent on the free mobility of the workman. Architects like Cossutius or Hermodorus of Salamis seem to have changed location freely already by the Republic. Later, the emperor could send *architecti* or *libratores* to assist in provincial buildings

110 Dyer (1989: 215) on medieval England; Phelps Brown and Hopkins (1959: 27–28); Van Zanden (2009: 129) starts at 1300. Rathbone (2009: 314) sees twofold and threefold premia as more widely exhibited in Roman wages, putting the Roman wage structure in line with medieval evidence.

111 Further work on the relative cost of skilled labour, building and otherwise, in the Roman world, is needed. Hawkins (above) points to the argument of Saller (2012) that certain demographic constraints, particularly higher mortality rates in cities, discouraged Roman investment in human capital by comparison to early-modern European economies. Perhaps, but note that Lo Cascio (2016) now raises significant concerns about the assumption of higher urban death rates, while the Roman world's mortality regime does not seem to have been broadly different from other pre-transitional Western economies (see Scheidel 2007). Thus, the degree to which demographic factors, particularly mortality, constrained Rome's skilled labour market in comparison to those other economies remains to be tested.

or to settle contract disputes.[112] The army moved engineers and architects around.[113] The famous inscription of Nonius Datus records how an engineer with the *Legio III Augusta* was recalled by the provincial governor to Saldae in Mauretania Caesariensis in AD 152 to oversee the channelling of an aqueduct. Nonius had drafted plans several years prior but was called away to work in Lambaesis in the neighbouring province of Africa. In his absence, the construction project went wrong; apparently, Nonius was the only capable engineer in both adjacent provinces.[114]

Demand's pull on lower-level builders is harder to recover. Rome itself attracted craftsmen from across the Empire. The appearance of 'Roman' building techniques in the provinces suggests that Italian builders themselves travelled, if not necessarily freely. A close connection with Agrippa, for example, may have helped Herod obtain skilled labourers for *opus reticulatum* walls and *pozzolana* harbour moles in Judea.[115]

Performance and Status

At the outset of this chapter, I suggested that the success of Rome's building industry has previously been framed as a question of status. To the contrary, what emerges is that the categories of free and slave are not particularly useful for thinking about the structure of the Roman building industry as a whole. Overlap was considerable at all points; moreover, our sources were largely indifferent. Consider several architects employed by Cicero and his acquaintances (Table 4.4).[116] Nomenclature is suggestive in cases such as Vettius Cyrus, very likely a freedman, but Cicero rarely bothers to clarify. His lack of interest in naming a building worker's personal status suggests that the issue was immaterial to him as it probably was to most Roman employers, nor was there any concern that an individual's status affected the quality or output of his

112 Pliny frequently makes such requests: *Ep.* 10.17b, 10.39, 10.41, 10.61.

113 E.g. *ILS* 2034, 2082; further examples in Mitchell (1983: 338–339).

114 *ILS* 5795.

115 Netzer (1990).

116 Martin (1989: 50–51). Freedmen predominate Donderer's epigraphic catalogue, but since this evidence is largely funerary, the status of the practicing *architectus* remains indeterminable without knowing age of manumission.

TABLE 4.4 *The personal status of Cicero's architects*

Name	Citation	Personal status
Vettius Cyrus	*Att.* 2.3.2; *Q.fr.* 2.2.2; *Mil.* 46	unspecified
Vettius Chrysippus	*Att.* 2.4.7, 14.9.1, 13.29.1, *Fam.* 7.14.1	freedman
Cluatius	*Att.* 12.18.1, 12.36.2	unspecified
Corumbus	*Att.* 14.3.1	slave
Numisius	*Q.fr.* 2.2.1	unspecified
Rufius	*Fam.* 7.20.1	unspecified

labour.[117] Cicero elsewhere equated hired labour to slavery,[118] and his indifference probably says more about the low status of all manual labourers than it does about the high standing of servile builders.

Fuller wage evidence might afford stronger conclusions. What little we do have leads us to question why builders' wages in Egypt or in the Price Edict were historically unexceptional, despite obviously high demand. Perhaps an answer rests in apparently high rates of urbanization, at least by pre-modern standards, in many parts of the Roman world.[119] As Aelius Aristides put it, there were never more cities, and all of them were adorned.[120] Rome itself was immense, and while we know nothing of wages in the imperial capital, we know that the city's architecture required massive work crews. DeLaine estimates that 15–24% of Severan Rome's wage-earners may have found work on construction projects.[121] This is impressive, but the figure is still somewhat lower than the 30% of wage-earners in construction in seventeenth-century Rome.[122] However, the Severan city was roughly an order of magnitude more populous than Baroque Rome: a workforce that may appear unexceptional in relative terms was enormous in absolute terms, and this may have made imperial Rome's free labour supply seem elastic. In the seventeenth-century record

117 This applies to skilled labour; there are complaints over the inferiority of chattel slave labour, e.g. Plin., *HN* 18.36 (vii).

118 Cic., *Off.* 1.150.

119 Morley (2011); Wilson (2011).

120 Arist. *Or.* 26.93 (ed. Oliver (1953)).

121 DeLaine (1997: 201).

122 Metzger Habel (2013: 2).

of the Roman building industry, we find contractors complaining about difficulties retaining both skilled and unskilled builders during periods of high demand.[123] There are no extant parallels from antiquity for such complaints. In this case, the success of the capital's construction industry may not have been owed to the absence of a labour market, but precisely to its pressures, which ultimately did little to benefit the earning power of the city's free workers.

Outside of Rome, the aspect to emphasize is constant variety. Different labour systems were proportionally available in the cities of the Empire, just as certain buildings or building techniques utilized different organizational structures. Walls were appropriate for corvée; large cities counted on casual free labour; frontier towns employed soldiers, etc. Above all, flexibility was key, and this highlights the institutional importance of *locatio conductio* and the Empire's policy of farming out state obligations to private contractors. It is truly remarkable that, allowing for a degree of regional variation, Roman architecture was relatively homogeneous across the Empire—it remained (and remains) recognizably Roman. No other pre-modern Western culture achieved similar homogeneity across such an extensive geographical space. Considering the diverse forms of labour on which Roman building depended, that fact becomes all the more impressive.

123 Metzger Habel (2013: 97–98). Holleran in this volume notes the lack of Roman complaints about labour scarcity: what she attributes to efficient recruitment, I might attribute to urbanism rates.

CHAPTER 5

Getting a Job: Finding Work in the City of Rome

Claire Holleran

It was long held that there was no labour market in Rome, with the freeborn population viewed as an idle one. Carcopino, for example, described the recipients of the grain distributions as 'idlers, chronically out of work and well satisfied to be so', while Louis talked of a 'proletariat', able to 'live in idleness'.[1] This idleness was supposedly facilitated by two key institutions: the grain distributions, which fed the population at the expense of the state, and slavery, which enabled the freeborn to live a life of leisure while work was undertaken by slaves and ex-slaves. Thus while the existence of wage work in Rome (and in the Roman world in general) was recognised, it was viewed as a marginal activity, spasmodic and casual in nature.[2] Yet the free inhabitants of Rome could not live off public munificence alone.[3] While the grain distributions were relatively generous, adequately meeting the calorific requirements of more than a single adult male, the amount distributed was not enough to feed a family, and diets still had to be supplemented with other food.[4] Moreover, they were based on status rather than need and were open only to a subset of adult male citizens; the number of recipients was apparently reduced from 320,000 to 150,000 by Caesar, and fixed at just over 200,000 by Augustus in 2 BC.[5] Furthermore, while slaves and freedmen may dominate the record of occupational inscriptions from Rome, this should be viewed primarily as a consequence of the particular 'epigraphic habit' of this group, rather than forming an accurate reflection of the profile of the urban workforce.[6] Indeed, Augustus' failed attempt to

1 Carcopino (1941: 194); Louis (1927: 2).

2 Most famously, see Finley (1999: 73; 185–186). For the opposite view, see now Temin (2004; 2013: 114–138). Also Brunt (1980: 100) who denies that the hiring of free labour was of 'secondary importance in imperial times'

3 See, for example, Le Gall (1971).

4 Garnsey (1998a: 236).

5 Caesar: Suet., *Iul.* 41.3; Dio Cass., 43.21.4. Augustus: *Mon. Anc.* 15; Suet., *Aug.* 40.2; Dio Cass., 55.10.1.

6 Joshel (1992: 46–49).

 | DOI 10.1163/9789004331686_006

reorganise the grain distribution process in order to reduce disruption clearly presupposes that the recipients worked for a living.[7]

In reality, the vast majority of the freeborn inhabitants of Rome had to work to support themselves, regardless of the grain distributions and the presence of slaves in the city, and there is much to suggest that there was a functioning labour market in Rome. In the most basic terms, a labour market is characterised by the buying and selling of labour. Workers offer their labour to employers in exchange for rewards, primarily wages or salary, which differ depending on the roles undertaken.[8] For a labour market to function effectively, workers must be free to change their location and their occupation, and should be paid relative to their skills.[9] With these criteria in mind, is it legitimate to speak of a labour market in Rome? Were workers free to move between occupations and were they paid for their labour, commensurate with their skills?

Although much of the population may have been relatively static, there was certainly some movement of people within the Roman Empire, and the city of Rome in particular was a centre of migration.[10] Free workers were also able to move between occupations, since there were no hereditary limitations or restrictions imposed by guilds or the state, at least not until late antiquity.[11] Although clearly intended to be humorous, we might think, for instance, of the Pompeian graffito about a person who had worked as an innkeeper, a 'clay worker', a dealer in salted fish, a baker, a farmer, a maker of bronze trinkets, a retailer, and a dealer in jugs.[12] To identify the presence of a labour market, however, we also need to identify exchange between employers and workers,

---

7 Suet., *Aug.* 40.2; See also Tac., *Hist.* 1.86 for misery caused by a flood in Rome in AD 69; the people of the city faced famine not only because of a lack of supplies, but also because of a lack of employment.

8 Other potential rewards include power and status. See, for example, Kalleberg and Sorensen (1979: 351).

9 See Temin (2013: 115) for the fulfilment of these two conditions as key to a functioning labour market.

10 For mobility in general, see e.g. Scheidel (2004; 2007: 50). For migration to Rome, see e.g. Holleran (2011: 159–160), with further refs.

11 In general, see Jones (1964: 1050–1051); see also 699–700 (bakers); 702 (pork butchers); 861 (urban craftsmen); 594–595 (civil servants); 835 (workers in state factories); 838 (miners) all with further references.

12 *CIL* IV 10150: [*cum*] *de*[*d*]*uxisti octies tibi superat ut* (*h*)*abeas sedecies coponium fecisti cretaria fecisti salsamentaria fecisti pistorium fecisti agricola fuisti aere minutaria fecisti propola fuisti laguncularia nunc facis si cummu*(*m*) *linx<s>e<e>ris, consummaris omnia*: Peña and McCallum (2009: 63). The joke would surely only work if changing occupations were possible.

with workers being paid for their labour relative to their skills. Anecdotal evidence drawn from ancient literature indicates that the hiring of labour was relatively commonplace in the Roman world, with hired workers known as *mercennarii*—a term which derives from *merces* (pay or wage) and thus clearly implies payment—and *operarii*.[13] In literary and legal sources, hired workers appear primarily as agricultural labours, but they are also mentioned in a more urban context, as domestic workers, porters, muleteers, in construction, in a bakery, and in a variety of miscellaneous tasks.[14]

Perhaps the most telling piece of evidence for a Roman labour market, however, is the catalogue of daily wages in Diocletian's Price Edict.[15] The listing of different wages for a wide variety of different tasks, ranging from skilled work such as cabinet-making (50 denarii a day, with maintenance) to unskilled work such as farm labouring (25 denarii a day, with maintenance), rather presupposes a market for labour.[16] Labour here is classified as a commodity like any other, and wages are adjusted to reflect the different levels of skill required for particular tasks. These are maximum prices, so do not necessarily signify an integrated labour market across the Roman world, but the presence of wages within the price edict certainly points to the importance of hired labour.[17] Some contracts of employment between free workers and employers also survive from the Roman Empire, such as those from the Dacian gold mines and the imperial quarries at Mons Claudianus in Egypt.[18]

Slavery then was not incompatible with the hiring of labour in Rome or elsewhere. In fact, although their mobility may have been somewhat constrained by their legal status, slaves themselves were a part of the labour market.[19] They

13 In Greek, μισθωτοί.

14 As agricultural workers: e.g. Varro, *Rust.* 1.17; in a domestic context, see, for example, the hired servant Corax in Petronius' *Satyricon* (see esp. Petr., *Sat.* 117.11; also Dio Chrys., *Or.* 7.114; *Dig.* 48.19.11.1); as a porter: Apul., *Met.* 1.7; as muleteers: Fest. p.258m; in construction, see *Dig.* 45.1.137.3; in a bakery: Plin., *Ep.* 10.74.1; miscellaneous tasks, e.g. guarding a corpse, Apul., *Met.* 2.21–30, discussed further below; throwing dice for a man with gout in his fingers, Hor., *Sat.* 2.7.15–18; see also Plut., *De vitando aere alieno* 6; Epict., *Ench.* 3.26. In general *Dig.* 47.2.90.

15 Explored in this volume by Groen-Vallinga and Tacoma.

16 Not all payment is in the form of daily wages; some payments were made per action or per task (e.g. per animal for the clipping and preparing of hooves, or per man for a barber; per pupil for a teacher; per item for a fuller etc.).

17 The introduction to the edict (pr. 15–17) allows for variations in prices between places.

18 Cuvigny (1996).

19 E.g. Plaut., *Vid.* 25; Col., 1. pr. 12; Sen., *Ben.* 7.5.3; *Dig.* 19.2.42–43; 45.1; 48.1 and 60.7; 32.73.3; 47.5.1.5; *P.Wisc.* 16.5. See also Athens: Davies (2007: 354–355).

could either be hired out by their owners, or hire themselves out, paying a part of their daily earnings to their owners.[20] In this context it is worth noticing Chrysippus of Soli's definition of a slave (cited by Seneca) as a *perpetuus mercennarius*.[21] Slave, free, and freed were all part of the same functioning labour market, and must often have worked alongside each other, although it is difficult to gauge the relative proportion of slave, freed, or free workers in the labour force (and in the population of Rome in general).[22]

Many of the free workers in Rome will have worked independently, be it in retail, manufacturing, or the service industry, but others must have found work on the labour market. The structure and organisation of this market, however, remains unclear, as does the overall proportion of workers in Rome (and in the Roman world more broadly) who were employed by others. This paper marks the beginning of a wider project exploring the labour market of Rome in its entirety, although here the focus is on one particular aspect: the finding of labour. For a labour market to function, employers and workers must have some effective means of finding each other, and this paper considers the dissemination of information about employment opportunities in the city. To a certain extent, the method used must have depended on the type of work concerned. For one-off unskilled roles, for example, ad hoc methods would probably have sufficed, while for short-term but more regular roles, such as in construction, a more reliable and organised system must have been in place; the finding of skilled labour must also have been a more complicated process. The following discussion does not aim to be definitive but reflects some initial thoughts on how labour might be found and engaged. The paper considers four distinct but overlapping methods of finding labour in an urban context: advertising, congregation, networks, and clientelism.

Advertisement

The simplest way to advertise a potential job opportunity would have been orally. A character in Apuleius' *Metamorphoses*, Thelyphron, for example, tells a story which begins with him running out of money in Larissa in Thessaly. He wanders about looking for work and when he comes to the forum he finds an old man standing on a stone, making a public announcement that he is

20 E.g. *Dig.* 19.2.60.7; Col., 1. pr. 12.

21 Sen., *Ben.* 3.22.1.

22 See, for example, Scheidel (2005a: 64–67) for a discussion of the difficulties of estimating the number of slaves in Rome and in Roman Italy. Also Scheidel (2012b: 91–92).

looking for somebody to guard a corpse for an agreed fee.[23] This is fiction and the task itself may appear unusual (although the protection of corpses from witches may have been felt to be particularly necessary in Thessaly), but this part of the story at least appears plausible, if not what happens afterwards.[24] Criers were used in streets and fora as a means of spreading information in urban centres, informing people about lost or stolen property or runaway slaves,[25] and perhaps also about employment opportunities. This would be a quick, cheap, and effective way of finding workers, particularly for occasional and short-term tasks.

Written advertisements for work are another possibility, but are less probable than oral advertisements; the latter give immediate results, while the former would only be useful if workers were required for longer-term projects at some point in the future. Ideally, potential workers would also need to be literate. It is worth noting that although advertisements abound on the walls of Pompeii, offering goods, services, rental units, rewards for the return of stolen items, and electoral recommendations, to the best of my knowledge no work opportunities are offered.[26] Oral advertisements are likely to have been more effective, but while these were perhaps important at an individual level and may have played a significant role in the labour market of smaller communities, particularly for one-off short-term roles, overall, it is difficult to know how significant such means of engagement would have been in a city the size of Rome.

Congregation

A more efficient method would be for workers to congregate in particular areas, enabling employers and potential employees to find each other quickly and effectively. Oral advertisements could then reach their intended audience immediately. This is a practice with a long history, stretching from antiquity up to the present day, where contemporary studies in the United States document

23 Apul., *Met.* 2.21.

24 In Apuleius' novel, the corpse is reanimated and describes how witches put Thelyphron in a deep sleep and cut off his nose and ears, replacing them with wax (Apul., *Met.* 2.21–30). Thessaly was particularly connected with witches in Latin literature: Ogden (2001: 143–147).

25 E.g. Dio Chrys., *Or.* 7.123.

26 For example, rental inscriptions: *CIL* IV 138; 1136; rewards for return of stolen items: *CIL* IV 64; electoral recommendations: see the detailed study of Mouritsen (1988).

workers waiting on street corners of busy intersections, in squares, in parks, and in car parks; most jobs offered to contemporary workers are in construction, gardening, and painting.[27] In the Roman world, the most famous example of this practice must be the parable of the vineyard workers in the Gospel of Matthew, a story based around the idea that potential workers could be found congregating in the agora waiting to be hired.[28] The vineyard owner returns repeatedly throughout the day to hire additional workers, with the message of the parable resting on the workers' belief that they would be paid different rates based on the number of hours worked. Here, in what is presumably a small urban centre, workers are waiting in the agora, and it is probable that in many places the agora or forum acted as a sort of informal labour exchange. In classical Athens, day labourers appear to have waited on the *kolōnos agoraios*, the hill overlooking the agora, a place sometimes just called the *misthōtērion*, or place of the hired labourers / the hiring place. It apparently became so synonymous with hiring that wage workers at Athens could also be referred to as *kolōnetai* rather than *misthōtoi* (the hired) or the *mistharnountes* (workers).[29]

Claudius (as Pontifex Maximus) ordering the withdrawal of slaves and *operarii* from the forum before offering up supplication from the rostra may hint at day labourers waiting there to be hired.[30] In such a large city, however, it is unlikely that one single place sufficed, and the size of ancient Rome probably encouraged specialisation, with the place of congregation depending upon the type of work sought.[31] Wet-nurses, for example, may have been hired from the *columna lactaria* in the *Forum Holitorium*, where Festus says that infants who needed milk were taken, although this is the only mention of this location and it may also have been the place where feeding took place, rather than solely a point of hiring.[32] According to Pliny the Elder, cooks used to wait in

27 For a brief history of this practice, from medieval England to the contemporary United States, see Valenzuela (2003: 312–314). Also see Fevre (1992: 10–13); Granovetter (1995: 121); Rosser (1997: 26) for this practice in medieval Rouen.

28 *Ev. Matt.*, 20.1–16.

29 Pherecr. fr. 142, Harp. p.181.16, *s.v.* kolonetai. See Fuks (1951); Taylor (2011: 120).

30 Suet., *Claud.* 22. This was in response to the sighting of a bird of ill-omen on the Capitol. My thanks to Rens Tacoma for alerting me to this reference.

31 A passing reference in Plautus (*Curc.* 482) to men who sell themselves in the Vicus Tuscus almost certainly refers to male prostitutes rather than labourers.

32 Festus, p. 118 (ed. Müller = p. 105 ed. Lindsay). Palmer (1997: 102) relates this to the Punic cult of milk-offerings, rather than wet nursing, and he also suggests that the monument was destroyed to make way for the Theatre of Marcellus.

the *macellum* in Rome to be hired.[33] He claims that by his own time this practice was confined to the past, as households now included cooks among their slaves, but Pliny is making a moralising point here and in any case, this may not have been true of everybody in Rome. Some households may still have hired cooks for special occasions; congregating in the *macellum* would make sense, as a potential employer could then pick up a cook along with provisions for the meal.

In a similar way, construction workers often congregate in the car parks of DIY stores in contemporary cities in the United States, enabling employers to pick up materials and labour in the same place.[34] In Rome also, those looking for work in the building trade, particularly as unskilled labourers, may have waited in places linked to the importation, manufacture, or storage of building materials. Lumber yards and timber merchants, for example, appear at one time to have been concentrated in an area in the Aventine district. According to Livy, a *porticus* was built in 192 BC outside the Porta Trigemina *inter lignarios* (among the woodworkers or dealers in (fire)wood; Liv. 35.41.10), while a *Vicus Materiarius* (street of the timber merchants) is also attested in this area (*CIL* VI 975).[35] Marble must also have been unloaded in this district, since state *tabularii* were based here, recording imports of imperial marble (*CIL* VI 301; 410).[36]

Somewhat more tentatively, Coarelli has suggested that an open area on the slopes of the Piccolo Aventino depicted on the Severan Marble Plan of Rome was a brick storage area, linked perhaps to *figlinae* and *tegularia* alongside.[37] Many bricks also came down the Tiber from brick yards in the Tiber

---

33 Plin., *HN* 18.108 (xxviii). Plautus, with the action ostensibly set in Athens, describes the hiring of cooks from a *forum coquinum*: Plaut, *Aul.* 406–408; *Merc.* 741–782; *Pseud.* 790–825. The hiring of cooks is a classic comic motif, with cooks commonly portrayed as boastful and untrustworthy.

34 Valenzuela *et al.* (2006); Valenzuela (2003: 319).

35 Meiggs (1997: 186); Rodríguez Almeida (1984: 33); Holleran (2012: 66). See *Dig.* 32.55.pr for a distinction between *lignum* as primarily firewood, and *materia* as timber for building.

36 A dealer in marble (*negotiator marmorarius: CIL* VI 33886) was also based in the *horrea Galbana*, where nineteenth-century excavations revealed a considerable quantity of worked and unworked marble. Lanciani (1897: 533–534); Holleran (2012: 75–76).

37 *FUR* 2a and 2b. A Renaissance drawing of the now lost fragment 2b depicts an open area labelled 'NAVELEMFER'; Coarelli (2000: 376–378) argues that rather than depicting a 'lower *navalia*' (*navale inferius*), *navalia* here is a colloquial expression for brickyard (cf. *CIL* III 11382) and the legend should be read as *Navale M(arci) Fer[ocis]*. For associated *figlinae* and *tegularia*, see *FU* 201. Discussed also in Graham (2005: 109–110).

Valley, and these may have been distributed from further up the river.[38] As Graham suggests, it is probable that particular areas in Rome specialised in the unloading and storage of particular commodities, enabling the collection of taxes and customs duties.[39] Furthermore, heavy building material such as marble and brick may have required particular dock facilities, such as ramps, pulleys, cranes and so on, and therefore came into the city regularly at the same place, enabling potential construction workers to know where to wait.

Those seeking work as porters most probably also waited in such areas, at the docks, or around the gates, where goods came into Rome.[40] The Area Carruces, for example, located just outside the Porta Capena, may have been an area where carts were parked and unloaded before produce was carried into the city, and would have been a logical place for porters to gather.[41] In Milan[42] and in Fossombrone[43] at least, *collegia* of dealers or drivers of mules (*collegium iumentariorum*) were also based at city gates.[44] At Cales, *cisiarii* (carriage drivers) were associated with city gates.[45]

Furthermore, Rome was a large enough city to have specialised quay areas and storage facilities for particular commodities or goods, as well as specialised markets. There was, for example, a *horrea chartaria* (paper warehouse), a *horrea piperataria* (pepper warehouse), a *portus vinarius*, a *portus olearius* (facilities specialising in wine and oil respectively), and numerous commercial fora (e.g. Forum Boarium, Forum Suarium, etc.), as well as some clustering

38 Graham (2005). See also *Ibid.* p. 111 for the 'Tor di Nona', a mole that jutted into the Tiber near the Campus Martius, as a possible specialised dock for bricks.

39 Graham (2005: 110–111). For a discussion of customs duties in Rome, see Holleran (2012: 89–92).

40 See also Broughton (1938: 56–57) for groups of porters based in specific locations in eastern cities, organised in associations, e.g. the porters of the harbour at Cyzicus. At Portus in the fourth century, a corpus of *saccarii* had a monopoly on the movement of goods; if a private citizen was found to have employed his own porters, a fifth of his wares was confiscated, although this probably reflects increased controls in late antiquity rather than earlier practice (*Cod.Theod.* 14.22.1; Sirks (1991: 258–259)).

41 Holleran (2012: 89).

42 CIL V 5872.

43 CIL XI 6136.

44 MacMullen (1974: 70; 175). Further inscriptions from Verona also record *iumentarii Port(ae) Iov(iae)*. My thanks to Scott Perry for this reference and for sharing with me his paper, 'The Go-Between(s): Transportation Workers, Status, and Burial in Roman Italy', delivered at the AAH Annual Meeting, Columbus, May 2013. For the potential role of *collegia* in the allocation of work, see below.

45 CIL X 4660 (here *gisiarii*).

of trades in the city.[46] Potential workers who wished to find work within the movement, manufacture, or sale of particular goods could then have congregated in particular areas.

Contemporary studies, particularly in the United States, indicate that congregating in particular places is a cheap and potentially effective way of employers and employees finding each other, although it remains a relatively marginal practice. Indeed, the vast majority of those who find work in this way are day labourers, and these studies demonstrate the fluidity of the day labourer market and the changing composition of workers. However, within the apparent randomness of the system, there is space for relationships to flourish and trust to develop between workers and employees, with some day labourers being hired repeatedly by the same employer.[47] In Rome also, it is probable that while working relationships between day labourers and employers may have remained casual, being negotiated on a daily or short-term basis, the hiring of workers was not entirely random, but was based on reputation and personal relationships. The building trade in particular was probably organised into small 'firms', which may have then hired day labourers on a casual basis; regular hiring of the same individuals must have allowed relationships to develop.[48] The practice of congregating, however, may have put workers at a disadvantage when it came to negotiating payment since it would be immediately obvious to an employer that other workers were available, although this could of course work both ways.[49]

Networks

The development of such relationships points to the importance of networks in finding employment, a phenomenon that has long been the subject of research in the social sciences. Granovetter, for example, has argued extensively that social ties play a key role in finding employment. In his influential analysis, he distinguished between 'strong ties' between close friends and 'weak ties' between acquaintances, contending that weak ties are more

46 Holleran (2012: 71–72; 78–80; 93–97). On the clustering of trades in general, see Holleran (2012: 51–60).

47 Valenzuela (2003: 319); Valenzuela *et al.* (2006: 9).

48 *Dig.* 45.1.137.3. See DeLaine (1997: 199) for small firms and the hiring of day labourers. Also DeLaine (2000: 132) and Bernard in this volume.

49 See Plaut., *Pseud.* 804–809. Also Cic., *Brut.* 257 discussed above. In comparative terms, see Granovetter (1995: 121).

important in the spread of new information about employment opportunities. Since close friends tend to move in the same circles, they share the same information, while acquaintances move in different circles and have access to different information, thus acting as bridges between groups.[50] Burt reformulated this argument to suggest that ties between groups can be strong or weak, but the important point is that these ties act as a bridge for information, through what he terms 'structural holes' in a network.[51] In both these analyses, individuals with ties to multiple groups are at a particular advantage when it comes to gleaning information about potential employment opportunities. If we apply this analysis to Rome, an inhabitant of the city might be a member of numerous networks, based on factors such as family links, neighbourhoods, religious practices, trade, ethnicity, and (for migrants at least) place of origin, many of which would potentially overlap; comparative evidence would suggest that these networks were all potentially important for the transmission of information about work opportunities.

Studies of contemporary migration, for example, have demonstrated that migrant networks play an important role not only in facilitating migration in the first place, but also in assisting new migrants to find work. The monopolisation of particular trades and the residential clustering in neighbourhoods by certain ethnic or migrant groups can also help new migrants to establish themselves within communities and find work.[52] Yet aside from a Jewish community based in Trastevere, Tacoma has demonstrated that there is no substantial evidence to suggest that other ethnic or migrant communities clustered together in neighbourhoods in Rome.[53] Furthermore, there is no indication of the monopolisation of particular trades and industries by certain groups, although there were provincial commercial representatives based in Rome (as there were in other trading centres of Italy).[54] We might think, for example, of the groups of Tyrians resident in Rome and in Puteoli, or the renting of

50 Granovetter (1973; 1983; 1995; 2005). See also Yakubovich (2005). The advantages gained from social networks are also sometimes referred to as 'social capital'.

51 Burt (1992: 8–49, esp. 25–30).

52 See, for example, Munshi (2003) on the role of networks in finding jobs for Mexican migrants in the USA. Poros (2001) for Asian Indian migrants in London and New York (with useful general discussion and further reading). See also Marett (1989: 80) for Ugandan Asian refugees finding work in Leicester (UK) in the 1970s through relatives and friends rather than formal labour exchanges.

53 Tacoma (2014). See also Lott (2004: 22–23).

54 Although see the *Neapolitani citrarii* in Rome (*CIL* VI 9258).

tabernae near the forum to representatives of certain states.[55] Pliny the Elder talks of *stationes municipiorum* (municipal offices) in the Forum of Caesar,[56] and *stationes* in Rome are attested from the Eastern cities of Anazarbus, Claudiopolis, Ephesus, Heraclea, Mopsuestia, Nysa, Sardis, Tarsus, Tiberias, and Tralles, and from the western province of Noricum.[57] MacMullen suggested that new migrants could receive a welcome from such groups, enabling them to find out important information about their destination, such as where to find suitable housing, work opportunities and so on.[58] It is difficult to know how willing such groups would be to act as unofficial 'welcome committees', particularly to those of a lower social status, although they may have charged for their services.[59] In short, language, ethnicity, or place of origin could be a potential point of entry into certain networks, which would primarily be composed of 'weak ties', but such factors may have been of less importance in Rome than in other historical periods or places.[60]

For many in Rome, including new migrants, neighbourhood networks may have been far more important in the transmission of information about employment opportunities. According to Pliny, there were 265 *vici* in Flavian Rome (*Nat.* 3.66) and although the term *vici* is ambiguous, a *vicus* probably

---

55 For the Tyrian groups, see *IG* XIV 830, lines 1–19 (= *OGIS*, no. 595 = *IGRR* I 421); Lewis and Reinhold (1990: 109–110): the inscription dates to AD 174. For further discussion, see Sosin (1999). See also *CIL* VI 9677 for a *corpus negotiantium Malacitanorum*. For *tabernae* as headquarters at Rome, see Suet., *Ner.* 37.1.

56 Plin., *HN*. 16.236 (lxxxvi).

57 Anazarbus: *IGUR* 78; Ephesus: *IGUR* 26; Heraclea: *IGUR* 88; Mopsuestia: *IGUR* 24; Nysa: *IGUR* 162; Sardis: *IGUR* 85; Tarsus: *IGUR* 79: Tiberias and Claudiopolis: *IGUR* 82–83; Tralles: *IGUR* 84. These Greek inscriptions date primarily to the late second and third century AD, and were found in the area of the Via Sacra. For further details, see especially Moretti (1958); Noy (2000: 160–161); Ricci (2005: 59). See also *CIL* VI 250=30723 for a dedication to the *genius* of Noricum by one L. Julius Bassus, a *stationarius*. For an interesting parallel, see the shippers based in the so-called Piazzale della Corporazioni in Ostia: *CIL* XIV 4.549; Lewis and Reinhold (1990: 110–111); Meiggs (1997: 283–288); Noy (2000: 161–164). On *collegia* of resident aliens, see also Verboven (2011a).

58 MacMullen (1974: 84–85).

59 For charging, see Verboven (2011: 339), although he is referring here primarily to merchants and shippers. Some notion of 'group solidarity' (although not necessarily residential clustering, *contra* Gruen (2002: 263, n. 45)) is perhaps hinted at by Cicero's comment (*Flac.* 17) about Phrygians and Mysians disrupting *contiones*, and Suetonius' claim (*Iul.* 84.5) that after the death of Caesar, groups of foreigners in Rome mourned in their ancestral fashion.

60 See also Tacoma (forthcoming b).

encompassed a street and the dwelling places which adjoined it.[61] If we assume a population of one million, this would give us a figure of around 3,800 inhabitants in each *vicus*. Of course in practice, some *vici* must have been more densely populated than others, and the population was unlikely to be stable, but this figure at least gives us some sense of the potential size of neighbourhoods in Rome. It is doubtful then that everybody in a neighbourhood knew each other personally, but it is probable that many of them would be connected somehow.[62] People must have interacted within neighbourhoods in Rome in different ways, meeting at the water basin, frequenting the same shops and street sellers, and eating and socialising within the same bars. Within apartment blocks also, residents may have formed ties with each other; there were, for example, communal altars set up in at least some *insulae*.[63] This is a community based above all on proximity. Many of these links will have been what Granovetter would class as 'weak ties', and it is precisely these kind of informal networks that can be beneficial in spreading information about potential employment opportunities; even with a transient and changing population, close proximity would enable messages to spread quickly by word of mouth. If we think of workers such as those in construction, who were organised into small work 'gangs', it would only take one member to hear about a project for the possibility of employment for the whole group to arise.[64]

More formal networks in *vici* were based in the Republic around the local cult of the *lares compitales* and the annual festival of the *compitalia* (*ludi compitales*), organised by local magistrates known as *vicomagistri*. The *vici* already appear to have been convenient administrative units, at least informally, but they were also linked with political violence in the late Republic, with Cicero claiming that political agitators were collected *vicatim*, or *vicus* by *vicus*.[65] Augustus then reconfigured and formalised the neighbourhood associations, adding a new focus on the imperial regime and the *lares Augusti*, and

61 Lott (2004: 4; 13–18).

62 Even in the crowded and constantly changing neighbourhoods of nineteenth-century London, there was some sense of community: Winter (1993: 57).

63 In the *insula Bolani*, for example, in the 14th Region, residents set up an image of the Bona Dea for communal acts of ritual (*CIL* VI 67 and 65).

64 See n. 48.

65 According to Livy, oil and corn was distributed to the *vici* on occasion (e.g. in 213 BC (25.2.8) and 202 BC (30.26.5–6)), while Caesar took a census of the population of Rome *vicatim* (Suet. *Iul.* 41.3). See also Plin., *HN* 33.132 (xlvi); Sen., *Dial.* 5.18.1.4 for statues to Marius Gratidianus being voted *vicatim* in the 80s BC, and Front. *Aq.* 97.8 for the upkeep of public fountains organised through the *vici*. For Cicero and political agitators, see *Att.* 4.3.2.9; *Dom.* 129; *Sest.* 34; see also *Dom.* 54.

assigning four *vicomagistri* to each vicus, many of whom appear to have been freedmen.[66] These officials played a role in the organisation of the local cult, but were also concerned with matters of civic administration, such as the local administrative divisions for the census and fire prevention.[67] The *vicomagistri*, who numbered over a thousand in the imperial period, must have formed one of the main lines of communication between the central administration and the people.[68] They were perhaps also able to gather men from neighbourhoods to work on public building projects, or at the very least (given the practice of contracting building out to *redemptores*) to disseminate information about potential employment opportunities on these projects.

Collegia were another potentially important source of information in Rome, particularly for employers.[69] There are overlaps between all of these potential networks, but this is perhaps most marked in the case of *collegia*, associations that might be based around a neighbourhood, a shared cult, or a shared profession, and sometimes all three.[70] Shared cult practices might also reflect a shared ethnicity, as with the group of Phrygians in Rome who worshipped Cybele, while Patterson has suggested that membership of a *collegium* would help integrate new migrants into civic life.[71] All *collegia*, regardless of their basis, must have helped transmit information between members, but it is *collegia* based around shared professions that are particularly relevant for the

66 Suet., *Aug.* 30.1; 40.2. For more on the *vici* and the *vicomagistri*, see Robinson (1992: 11–12). For the religious aspect, see Beard, North, and Price (1998: 184–187). In general, see Lott's detailed 2004 study of the neighbourhoods of Augustan Rome. See also Wallace-Hadrill (2008: 264–290).

67 Census: Suet., *Aug.* 40.2 (cf. *Iul.* 41.3); Fire: Dio Cass., 55.8.6–7; see Lott (2004: 100; 230 n. 124). Games and shows were also sometimes put on *vicatim*: Suet., *Iul.* 39.1; *Aug.* 43.1; Tac., *Hist.* 2.95; see also Tert., *Apol.* 35.2 for feasting. Augustus also dedicated statues of the gods *vicatim*: Suet., *Aug.* 57.1. For the increasing formality of the *vici* from the late Republic onwards and their role in civic administration, see Lo Cascio (2008: 69–76); Tarpin (2008: 52–58).

68 Four *vicomagistri* in each of the 265 *vici* of Flavian Rome (Plin., *HN.* 3.66 (v)) would give a total of 1,060 local officials.

69 For a discussion of the potential role of the *collegium* of the *fabri tignarii* in organising the workforce for major imperial building projects, see DeLaine (2000: 132). For members as 'employers' rather than 'employees', see Patterson (2006: 255); also discussion in Liu (2009: 162–163), with references. See also Liu (2009: 161–212) for the mixed social and economic status of *collegia centonariorum*.

70 Patterson (2006: 252).

71 Patterson (2006: 261–262). He draws a comparison with migration to towns in eighteenth-century England. See also Rosser (1997: 9–10) for a medieval comparison. See *IGRR* I 458 for a body of Phrygians devoted to Cybele; Harland (2013: 27).

present study. There is debate about the extent to which such *collegia* should be viewed as economic rather than social institutions, but they almost certainly had some economic benefits for their members.[72] One of the potential benefits of occupational *collegia* was access to important professional information, with members able to share knowledge about techniques, markets, the supply of raw materials, and perhaps also about potential workers.[73] As Hawkins has argued, the demand for goods in Rome fluctuated, as, consequently, did the demand for labour, both skilled and unskilled; short-term workers may then have been required to enable the completion of a particular order or to meet a period of high demand.[74] Finding good skilled workers was a more complicated and potentially more expensive process than finding unskilled labourers, particularly in a large urban centre such as Rome, where workers were less likely to be known to each other.[75] The information networks of a *collegium* may have gone some way towards simplifying the process, enabling an employer to find reputable workers quickly and efficiently, and lowering the transaction costs associated with recruiting good skilled labour for short-term roles.

Clientelism

Although the households of the elite in Rome were large, with high numbers of slaves, they were not entirely closed entities, and some of the better-connected inhabitants of Rome will have had links with these households. When Tacitus describes the reaction to Nero's death in Rome, for example, he says that the respectable part of the common people, that is, those attached to the great houses, the clients and freedmen of those who had been condemned and driven into exile, were all roused to hope.[76] Some people in Rome then were part of yet another network, and one which was probably of great

72 For a summary of recent scholarship on the debate about the economic role of *collegia* and their similarity (or otherwise) to medieval / early modern guilds, see Liu (2009: 13–18) and the chapters by Verboven and Liu. Also Patterson (2006: 252–253).

73 For a potential comparison with medieval English towns, see Rosser (1997), especially 19–20 for the role of craft organisations and voluntary clubs in the negotiation of labour contracts, and 31 for such groups providing access to financial credit, primary materials, hired labour, and the market.

74 Hawkins (2006); see also Hawkins in this volume.

75 See Liu (2009: 22–23) for the need to distinguish between larger and smaller urban centres in thinking about *collegia*.

76 Tac., *Hist.* 1.4; in contrast to the *plebs sordida*, who were interested only in the theatre and the circuses.

economic benefit to them. Being within the patronage of an elite household in Rome brought obligations and responsibilities, but it also brought rewards, such as financial donations, gifts, food, and meals.[77] Indeed, acting as a client could in itself be a way of securing an income, or at least supplementing an income, but such links are unlikely to have spread too far down the social scale in Rome;[78] those whom Tacitus describes as attached to the great houses were perhaps synonymous with the *plebs media*, and were by no means the poorest in Rome.[79]

For a select few, however, such links may have provided access to employment opportunities. Certainly Lucian suggests that in order to get a role within one of the great houses as a salaried intellectual, it was necessary to ingratiate yourself with the household as a client until such time as your services might be engaged.[80] It is unclear if other more prosaic jobs—for example, domestic roles such as door keeping, commercial roles in *tabernae*, or labouring work—were also distributed in this way.[81] Yet although clients may have been prepared to present themselves at a daily *salutatio* and act as an escort, as well as offer numerous (unpaid) services, it seems less likely that they would have found themselves performing domestic tasks or labouring work for their patrons in return for direct payment in the form of wages.[82] However, a wealthy patron in Rome may have provided access to useful business networks through

---

77 See, for example, Verboven (2002: 64–65 (on the obligations of *amicitia*); 71–115 (on gifts and presents)).

78 For gifts as a form of income, or at least supplementary income, as well as the argument that clients are primarily made up of the cultural elite and the 'Roman middle classes', see Verboven (2002: 104–113). See also p.11 for those involved in networks of *amicitia* and patronage making up at most 10–15% of the Roman population. Cf. Skydsgaard (1976: 46) who argues that there were both direct links between upper and lower strata in Rome, primarily through *tabernae*, and indirect links through different levels of clients. For the *taberna* and their links with the elite, see also Purcell (1994: 660–668). See also Guilhembet and Royo (2008) for a suggestion that vertical relations existed between the elite and the inhabitants of particular districts, at least in the Republic.

79 For the *plebs media*, see Plin., *HN* 26.3 (iii).

80 Luc., *Merc. Cond.* 10.

81 For employment as doorkeepers, see Plut., *De vitando aere alieno* 6, 830b; Epictetus, *Dial.* 3.26. For *tabernae* and links between upper and lower classes, see n. 78 and 83.

82 Although remuneration may have occurred indirectly, services performed by clients were free; this is the difference between a service performed as a *mandatum* and one performed under a contract of hired labour (*locatio conductio operis/operarum*): *Dig.* 17.1.1.4; 1.36; 19.5.13.pr; 5.22; Verboven (2002: 228; 341). The latter case (*Dig.* 19.5.22) refers to the cleaning and mending of clothes, however, suggesting that some of the services performed could be relatively menial.

recommendations, as well as assisting with access to credit, and perhaps also offering opportunities for the formulation of *societates*, with the client providing the labour and the patron (or another) providing the necessary capital investment.[83] Thus rather than providing jobs *per se*, being linked to one of the great houses in Rome could have provided income assistance in the form of gifts and donations, as well as assisting with the creation or expansion of a client's business interests, whatever they might have been.

Conclusions

Assuming a population of c. 1 million, there must have been hundreds of thousands of free workers in the city of Rome. A significant, albeit unknown, proportion of these people worked for themselves, most commonly in sectors such as retail, manufacturing, and the service industry. However, many (again the numbers are difficult to know) will have been in the employ of others, and sought work through the labour market in the city. This paper has focused on some of the ways in which employers and workers might have found each other, namely through oral advertisement, congregating in suitable areas, by means of a variety of different networks, and finally, through clientelism and links to the great houses in Rome. The first two methods of engagement would be best suited to the finding of workers for short-term unskilled roles, while the latter two would probably be more useful in locating skilled workers for more long-term roles. Given the low regard in which wage labour was held in the Roman world, our written sources display little interest in the engagement of labour. Much of the evidence employed here is, therefore, anecdotal or circumstantial, and relies heavily on comparative material drawn from studies of historical and contemporary labour markets. This makes it difficult to say with any certainty how labour was engaged in Rome. Other methods than those discussed here are likely to have existed, but are even less documented. There may, for example, have been 'agents' in the city, who matched workers

---

83 For recommendations linked to trading interests, see Verboven (2002: 299–300), although these are rare, reflecting the social standing of those involved. For *societates*, see *Dig.* 17.2.5; Verboven (2002: 276; 281). See also Skydsgaard (1976: 46) for the rental of a *taberna* as a *beneficium* and the payment of rent as an *officium*; if this were the case, we would either have to consider *tabernarii* to be part of the top 10–15% of the urban population, or accept that the patronage links with the elite in Rome spread much further down the social scale.

with employers, something Noy suggests for migrant workers.[84] Comparative evidence also points to the possibility of labour contractors; these tend to be linked in particular with short-term seasonal work, gathering groups of workers who are then hired out to different employers.[85] In late republican Italy, contractors do at least appear to have been involved in the movement of labour from one place to another, as indicated by Suetonius' comment that some believed Vespasian's great-grandfather to be a contractor (a *manceps operarum*) for the seasonal labourers who moved annually from Umbria to the Sabine district.[86] It is perhaps best to conclude that there was a functioning labour market in Rome—albeit one that must have been distorted by the presence of slavery and the ability of elite households to extract services from clients through the pressures of social obligation—and that there were methods in place to ensure that employers and employees could find each other. Furthermore, these methods must have been effective, however they worked in practice. It is telling that we do not hear complaints of a labour shortage in Rome, even when significant manpower was required for large public building projects; indeed, Vespasian's famous refusal to adopt a labour-saving device in building as it would deprive the plebs (*plebicula*) of food rather suggests the opposite.[87]

84 Noy (2000: 151).
85 Granovetter (1995: 122).
86 Suet., *Vesp.* 1.4.
87 Suet., *Vesp.* 18.

CHAPTER 6

The Value of Labour: Diocletian's Prices Edict

Miriam J. Groen-Vallinga and Laurens E. Tacoma

Introduction

The single most promising document on prices and wages to survive from Late Antiquity is Diocletian's 'Prices Edict' of AD 301.[1] In response to current high prices and no doubt to protect his recent currency reform against the ongoing inflation, the emperor(s) imposed maximum prices for each type of good. According to its preamble, the ambitious Edict was provided 'not for single communities and peoples and provinces, but for the whole world': it was price regulation of an unprecedented scope.[2] Over 1,000 prices are listed, regularly even distinguishing between several grades of quality. The enumeration goes into such detail that it includes goods that are hardly known from other sources. It comes as no surprise that the Edict has been used extensively. The text holds a central place in discussions of the Roman economy and has an importance that transcends Late Antiquity by far.[3]

Next to prices, the Edict also lists wages. In fact, the Edict contains more data on wages than can be found in all the Roman literary sources together and is therefore highly instructive for Roman labour.[4] But it is noticeable that this aspect of the text has received less attention than it deserves. Of course wages are cited and analysed in the scholarly literature (and some of the figures are indeed used in the other chapters in this volume). However, the

1 For an excellent introduction see Corcoran (1996: 205–33), see also Giacchero (1987), and Crawford (2002) who includes a useful account of the transmission of the text. A new text-edition of the *Prices Edict* and the earlier *Currency Edict* is currently being drawn up: Cooley, Mitchell, and Salway (2007: 178) and Roueché (2004); for a revised text of the slave chapter, see Salway (2010). In the meantime, we base ourselves on the edition of Giacchero (1974); references in brackets are to chapter and line.

2 *Non civitatibus singulis ac populis atque provinciis sed universo orbi*, preamble ll. 148–9; Noethlichs (2007).

3 Particular names of goods, price levels in respect to rampant inflation, the relation of the Edict to Diocletian's monetary and tax reforms, and the question of its effectiveness have all been debated at length: e.g. Ruschenbusch (1977), Corbier (1985), Wassink (1991), Böhnke (1994).

4 Frézouls (1977: 253).

 | DOI 10.1163/9789004331686_007

broader question how labour is conceptualized in the Edict has not been fully addressed. That is the aim of this paper.

Anyone who wants to use the Edict for historical analysis is confronted by the question of the purpose of the Edict, its method of compilation and how it relates to the outside world.[5] The preamble of the Edict describes the Roman economy in moralizing rather than strictly economic terms: high prices were blamed on greed rather than market forces.[6] It is obvious that the Edict was prescriptive rather than descriptive: by setting maximum prices it tried to impose a ceiling. It is also quite clear that the attempt was a failure and that it had to be abandoned soon afterwards.[7] These facts raise in an acute form the question of how real the world was that is described in the Edict.

The question has no easy answer. Some scholars are more sceptical than others towards the use of the price data from the Edict. Although studies are certainly not lacking suggesting that specific elements in the Edict are realistic,[8] relating the prices of the Edict to prices in the outside world remains problematic.[9] Therefore, we believe that the best approach is to take the document as a whole and discuss on the basis of an internal analysis how labour is conceptualized.[10] We operate from the expectation that at least the range of wages and remuneration found in the Edict was internally more or less consistent. We also assume that the figures of the Edict are indirectly related to the outside world: if in the Edict a figure painter (*pictor imaginarius*; 7.9) earns a

5 E.g. Frézouls (1977: 255–256); Scheidel (1996).

6 E.g. preamble, ll. 64–71: 'For who is so insensitive and so devoid of human feeling that he cannot know, or rather, has not perceived, that in the commerce carried on in the markets or involved in the daily life of cities, immoderate prices are so widespread that the uncurbed passion for gain is lessened neither by abundant supplies nor by fruitful years…' (transl. Graser (1940)). The preamble is interspersed with words like *iniquitas* (excessiveness, l. 74), *laceratrices centensimas* (ruinous percentages, l. 84), and *avaritia* (greed, l. 89). On the rhetoric of the preamble see Corcoran (1996: 207–213).

7 Lact., *Mort. Pers.* 7.6–7; Duncan-Jones (1982: 367), 'Prices were moving so fast by this date that the Edict's stipulations soon became quite irrelevant: for example, a papyrus of AD 335 gives a wheat price sixty-three times higher than the wheat price of the Edict (*P. Lond.* VI 1914)'; cf Böhnke (1994) for a more positive view on Diocletian's monetary reforms.

8 E.g. Scheidel (1996) on slave prices; Scheidel (2013) on maritime freight charges; Bernard, this volume, on builders.

9 Rathbone (2009: 317–21). In addition, there is very little evidence in terms of a demonstrable and direct impact of the prescriptions in the Edict. One such reflection of the *Edict* might be visible in *MAMA* XI 254 (Thonemann (2012)), though the link remains conjectural and, in our opinion, cannot be sustained. We thank the editor, Peter Thonemann, for his helpful comments on this document.

10 So too Frézouls (1977: 255–256).

maximum wage that is six times as high as a water-carrier's (*aquarius*; 7.31), we expect that this difference roughly corresponds to reality. In short, then, we aim to steer a middle course between taking the text at face value and radically rejecting the data as mere numerical fantasies.

Moreover, rather than approaching the Edict as a sign of a troubled Late Antique economy, we tend to see the underlying structure as a reflection of the Roman labour market in general. We argue that the labour relations of the Edict are reconcilable with what we know about its functioning in the earlier Empire. Imposing maximum prices was in itself a drastic measure in a time of great crisis, but the Edict etched in stone structural properties of the labour market that are otherwise difficult to observe in a coherent fashion.

Section one of our paper deals with the question of what is in the Edict, and what is not. The simple fact that labour is included in the Prices Edict at all is remarkable and suggests that labour was only to a limited extent regarded as a separate analytical category. In the text over sixty different occupations are attested.[11] This is an impressive number that in itself surely justifies the present analysis. Nevertheless, despite its pretention to cover the whole economy the Edict lists only a select, and in some cases rather atypical, subset of all known occupations. The obvious focus in the Edict is on labour that could be priced. We argue that the Edict shows the continued importance of hired labour, and thereby points to the openness of the labour market.

In section two we discuss segmentation in the labour market. There is a remarkable absence of strongly demarcated labour boundaries in the Edict. Though some rural work occurs, there is no strong separation between rural and urban labour. Both skilled and unskilled professions are mentioned. Only twice a specifically female job title is mentioned, but otherwise gender differentiation is absent. Slaves are listed as goods that could be bought, but when it comes to the occupations there are no separate categories for slave or free work. Different occupations are valued differently, but the labour market seems not to have consisted of clearly demarcated segments.

In section three we discuss forms of remuneration for labour. With respect to its pricing, it is striking that there are many forms of payment in the Edict: daily wages, payment per action, payment per product, payment per pupil per month, payment by quantity of raw material worked. The assignment of particular types of remuneration to particular occupations seems to be based primarily on practical considerations. What all the methods share is the fluidity of arrangements: all were based on short-term transactions. No work no pay.

---

11 See appendix. Polichetti's 'more than 70' appears to be based on counting the number of lines of the chapter on wages, not the job titles: Polichetti (2002: 220).

One of the other noteworthy elements is the fact that the daily wages included *pastus*, food. Not only does its inclusion remind us of the fact that payment could also be made in kind, it also points to a setting in which labourers may have worked outside their own homes.

In the last section of our paper we analyse wage differentiation. The salaries of day labourers cover a relatively wide range. No doubt the explanation for the marked differences should be sought partly in terms of skills, and partly in terms of status. It has been argued that at the lower end of the range day labourers hardly earned a living that could sustain a family. We argue that this points not necessarily to poverty, but rather to a situation in which many members of a family were forced to contribute their labour, including children and women. The best interpretative tool to understand such a situation is the model of the adaptive family economy, advocated by Wall for preindustrial Europe.[12] In addition we explore the consequences of the high degree of wage differentials on purchasing power. They are indicative of a rather strong internal hierarchy among the working classes of the Roman world.

Paradoxically, in its attempt to fixate the labour market the Edict actually documented its complexity, fluidity, and openness. The Edict shows the importance of hired labour and short-term arrangements, the absence of strong barriers between slave and free labour, the flexibility in methods of remuneration, and it points to strong economic differentiation within the labour force.

The Occupations in the Edict

The fact that occupations were included in the Edict at all is noteworthy. The commodification of labour has become so self-evident to modern scholars that we fail to notice its importance. It is therefore significant that wages are included in the Edict. Clearly, labour was not viewed as a category that was analytically distinct from prices: labour prices too were considered in the enumeration of costs.

Most job titles from the Edict are listed in chapter seven: *de mercedibus operariorum*. The selection included is interesting. The rural worker (*operarius rusticus*; 7.1a) heads the list, which may be significant of their overall presence in the Empire. What goes against this is that it is difficult to pinpoint any such guiding principle in the remainder of the list. Animal-keepers are also listed and may be thought to stem from a rural context: so, there occur a mule-driver (*mulio*; 7.19), hinny-driver, ass-driver, and camel-driver (*burdonarius, asinarius,*

12 Wall (1986); Groen-Vallinga (2013).

cameliarius; all three 7.17), and shepherd (*pastor*; 7.18). Other than that, very few of those we would call rural workers appear to be present. There is a number of construction workers, such as a stone mason (*lapidarius structor*; 7.2) and a bricklayer (*plinthobolos*; 7.15–16), and some decorating artists like a wall-painter (*pictor parietarius*; 7.8), figure-painter (*pictor imaginarius*; 7.9), and a carpenter (*faber intestinarius*; 7.3). Some white-collar officials are named: scribes (*scriptor*; 7.39–40), notaries (*tabellio*; 7.41) and lawyers (*advocatus*; 7.72–3). There is a striking number of teachers, varying from a trainer of architects to teachers in rhetoric and arithmetic (7.64–71, 74). In the service sector, the clothes-guardian (*capsarius*; 7.75) mentioned is specifically a guardian for the clothes of people attending public baths, as he is paid 'per bather'; apart from him, the bath-keeper (*balneator privatarius*; 7.76), and a barber (*tonsor*; 7.22), other service jobs are notably absent from the list.

Other jobs are listed together with the goods that were produced.[13] They include day-labourers as well as piecework. Occupations occur in the separate chapters that the Edict devotes to embroidery and silk (20), wool-work (21), fullery (22), and in a two-line chapter on silk specifically which includes a wage for 'workers for loosening the silk' (*sericum solventibus*) (23). The presence of these chapters explains the predominance of textile workers in the Edict. A substantial chapter is devoted to gold (28), from where comes the distinct presence of goldsmiths, silver(!)smiths, gold embroiderers and the like.

Thus, apart from the fact that jobs are clustered together either with related jobs or with related goods, there is no obvious other organising principle to be found in the way that the jobs are listed. It is therefore not surprising that the Edict shows no concept that even remotely came near the modern distinction of a primary, secondary or tertiary sector of the economy. It also implies that the price of labour was understood to be integral to the cost of the total production process.[14]

Despite its impressive size, the Edict fails to succeed in its attempt to cover the whole economy. This applies as much to occupations as it applies to goods. Over two hundred job titles are known from the Roman world.[15] The Edict contains a mere sixty. These sixty are not confined to the major occupations and, in fact, the Edict appears to be the only attestation for many of them, like

---

13 Conversely, in the chapter on wages (see below) some individual items are included, for instance, a horse blanket (7.53).

14 Furthermore, it may be a reflection of a practice in which workers were hired in locations where products were sold. See Holleran, this volume.

15 See Treggiari (1980: 61–64); von Petrikovits (1981); Joshel (1992: 176–182); and for Greek Drexhage (2004) and Ruffing (2008), specifically vol. 2.

a gymnastics instructor (*ceromatita*; 7.64), or a gold cutter (*auricaesor*; 28.4).[16] In addition, some distinctions are made that border on the pedantic: that a hinny driver (*burdonarius*; 7.17) receives the same wage as a mule driver (*mulio*; 7.19) is entirely understandable, but why they are listed separately at all is less easy to explain.

There is thus a discrepancy between the occupational structure of the Roman world outside of the text, and the occupational structure of the Edict. It is noticeable that omissions of the Edict concern not only marginal occupations that may tacitly have been subsumed under more generic job descriptions, but also important ones. There is a baker, but no butcher; there is a veterinarian, but no doctor. There are no hairdressers—*ornatrices*, which is the job most commonly attested epigraphically for women[17]—but there is a barber. In the absence of another obvious explanation, the omissions probably should be blamed on administrative sloppiness, or at least on the (unknown) methods used in compiling the text. This created a certain amount of arbitrariness in what was listed and what was not, in the same way as happened with respect to goods. The implication is that the list gives a large, more or less random sample of the labour force.

At the same time the aim of the Edict to set maximum prices obviously meant that only those forms of labour were included that lent themselves to some form of pricing. This often concerned a form of hired labour. Why else list a baker with a daily wage? It would make little sense to settle a maximum wage for an independent owner of a workshop, since recording the price of his wares would do. It also would make little sense to list a wage for a slave who was employed by his owner for a particular job in the owner's household: in such cases listing the price of the slaves themselves sufficed. Only when labour was employed by external parties a price needed to be known.

Given that in Roman times a plethora of different forms of labour could be found whose relative importance remains subject to debate,[18] it is certainly noteworthy that in the Edict hired labour played such a prominent role.

16 It appears to be the only attestation for the occupations of hinny driver (*burdonarius*; 7.17); model maker (*plastae imaginarius*; 7.29); sewer cleaner (*cloacarius*; 7.32); polisher (*samiator*; 7.33–39); parchment maker (*membranarius*; 7.38); teacher of palaeography (*antiquarius*; 7.69); teacher of public speaking (*sofista*; 7.71); workers loosening the silk (*sericum solventibus* 23.2 and 24.13); and gold embosser (*auriductor*; 28.5); see appendix.

17 Groen-Vallinga (2013) on the labour participation of women.

18 See in this volume in particular the introduction by Verboven and Laes, and the chapter by Zuiderhoek.

However, the exact role of hired labour cannot be determined on the basis of the Edict. In fact, other forms of labour are implicitly acknowledged in the Edict—an independent owner of a *taberna* would find his income regulated because the prices of his wares were fixed. We therefore should be cautious in inferring too much from it, but the emphasis on hired labour is still of real importance.

Thus, labour hardly served as a category that was analytically distinct from other prices. That the list is not complete seems due to administrative oversight. In listing jobs, pricing was what mattered, and this meant that jobs would primarily be listed in a way that allowed them to be employed by others. What the Edict shows is the continued importance of forms of hired labour, and this may suggest indirectly also the relative openness of the labour market.

Segmentation

A labour market may show distinctions between urban and rural labour, between male and female workers, there may occur differentiation with respect to age, skill, and the legal status of the labourers. Such distinctions may be more or less marked. To what extent does the Edict testify to strong segmentation?

The Edict imposed price ceilings for particular jobs. Actual remuneration of individuals could therefore be lower as long as it did not transgress the threshold values. In listing prices of goods, the composers have chosen to specify differences in quality of the work or material.[19] In the case of occupations no such distinction is made. Nevertheless, it may be assumed that significant variation lurked beneath the surface. The labour force consisted not only of freeborn healthy adult male workers, and individuals will have had a considerably different daily output. As a consequence of variations in actual output, but also because of market forces and cultural convention, women may have earned less than men, children less than adults, and slaves might be paid less than freeborn workers.[20] Moreover, rural workers are often thought to have

19 For example, a scribe (*scriptor*) was allowed to ask 55 denarii for 100 lines of his best writing (7.39), and 50 denarii for 100 lines of secondary writing (7.40); and a tailor (*bracarius*) could earn 60 denarii for a hooded cloak of the finest quality (7.42), but no more than 40 denarii for a second-rate cloak (7.43).

20 There is little evidence for women's wages other than that of the *gerdia* and *aurinetrix* in the *Edict* (see below). Only from contracts for wet-nurses in Egypt do we have significant documentation, and they are highly specific to time and place, see e.g. Drexhage (1991:

earned less than urban inhabitants.[21] Some of this variation is in fact visible in the section on the prices of slaves (discussed below), which are differentiated according to gender and age. What is at issue, however, is the extent to which labour was segmented into separate domains for particular groups. Some such demarcation is visible in the Edict, but it has not left many traces.

At first sight, most of the jobs that are listed seem to be urban ones. Rural labour comes to the fore mainly in the presence of a rural worker (*operarius rusticus*; 7.1a). In the remainder of the list, no jobs occur that are explicitly stated to belong to the countryside, though the animal-keepers that are listed may have been more at home in a rural rather than an urban context. It is also noteworthy that the remuneration in these jobs can be placed exclusively at the lower end of the spectrum.[22] It may be that the rather generic term *operarius rusticus* was used to cover quite a range of agricultural tasks. Part of the explanation of the lack of differentiation in rural tasks may then be sought in the urban perspective of the compilers: they simply did not care for precision in what was marginal to them.

Moreover, occupational differentiation and urbanization are intimately connected: those able to pursue a job outside of agriculture tend to cluster where the potential clientele is largest: in the city. It is self-evident that it is here that further division of labour took place in response to market demand.[23]

At the same time, the jobs that we tend to consider urban certainly did not exclusively belong to the world of the cities. A blacksmith could reside in either town or country and could provide for both, and the same applies to many of the jobs that are listed. In that sense the distinction between urban and rural work was not as clear-cut as it is today, and town and country flowed naturally into one another.[24] It is easy to see how the urban/rural distinction did not solicit explicit mention.

Slaves executed a significant part of the available labour in the Roman Empire. Slavery features prominently in our sources about the Empire, but not

411–412, 437–439). The papyri collected by Drexhage (1991) indicate that the payment for παῖδες, that is children or slaves, was significantly lower than that for adult men.

21 Rathbone (2009: 314).

22 Though note that if the conjecture of Salway (2010) on the first line in the slave chapter is right—he proposes to read *mancipium rus*]*ticum* [*sive urbanum*—the implication is that on the one hand a distinction would be made between urban and rural slaves, but on the other hand both were priced the same.

23 Jongman (1988: 49), and Scheidel (2010a: 597). This has been well demonstrated in the case of Roman Egypt, see e.g. Alston and Alston (1997).

24 E.g. Wallace-Hadrill (1991).

in the Edict—except as a commodity. Maximum prices for slaves of both sexes and of different age groups are mentioned in a separate section.[25]

TABLE 6.1 *Maximum prices for slaves (in denarii, Prices Edict chapter 29.1–7)*

Age	Male	Female
0–8	15,000	10,000
8–16	20,000	20,000
16–40	30,000	25,000
40–60	25,000	20,000
60+	15,000	10,000

A young adult male slave age 16–40 was most expensive, which presumably has to do with the expectation that he would be most productive.[26] It also indicates a thorough understanding of the fact that it mattered who did the job: in fact, it forms one of the best indications from the whole of antiquity that labour was valued differently according to gender and age.

No distinction in remuneration was made according to legal status, however. The Edict simply states that a tailor earns a maximum of 4 denarii for folding and sewing a fine garment (7.28), without entering into the question whether the tailor was free, slave or freed. It is now commonly assumed that (barring some exceptions) slave, freed and free could be employed in the same jobs. In economic terms they functioned as substitutes.[27] This seems to be reflected in the Edict's lack of distinction between them. And indeed, many of the jobs that are listed are known or plausibly expected to have been performed

25 For the text of the slave chapter, see now Salway (2010). Scheidel (1996: 67) similarly presents this material in a table. Scheidel rightly points out some peculiarities in the price differential, i.e. that teenage boys and girls age 8–16 were valued equally (boys for physical strength, girls for their reproductive capacity), and that older slaves seem to be overvalued considering contemporary life expectancy. All in all, however, he concludes on p. 77 that 'the edict on maximum prices of AD 301 seems to give a not altogether misleading impression of the relative differentiation of actual slave prices'.

26 Giacchero (1987: 127); Scheidel (1996); Harper (2010: 234): 'The very fact that male slaves were more expensive than female slaves in the Roman slave system is evidence that slave prices reflected the value of labour and not just honour premiums'.

27 Tacoma (forthcoming a: section 3); Hawkins (2013).

by slaves, freedmen and freeborn persons alike. So, tailors of all legal status groups are attested epigraphically.[28] In addition, the sewer cleaner for example receives a daily wage in the Edict, though this is a type of job one would associate with servile work.[29] The Edict may still have tacitly included slaves: slaves would be rented out, or rent themselves out for the recorded daily wage.[30] It is of course still possible that a slave tailor got paid less than a freeborn tailor, but the fact that the compilers saw no reason to differentiate between the two is of some significance.

A similar observation can be made with regard to gender distinctions. Only two female jobs occur in the lists: a gold spinner (*aurinetrix*; 28.6) and a woman weaver (*gerdia*; 20.12–13). Both seem to be special cases. The *gerdia* earns the lowest of all wages attested in the Edict, and in her case it is tempting to explain her extremely low wage of 12–16 denarii by her gender. But this cannot apply to the *aurinetrix*, who could earn the stunning sum of 2,000 denarii or more per pound of gold spun (a price no doubt including the raw materials).[31] All other occupational titles are listed in their male form. Yet we know in many cases that women could also perform the same work: in such cases they are epigraphically recorded with the female forms of the nouns. Conversely, men in the 'weaving trade' (*gerdiakē technē*) are also known.[32] To the compilers of the Edict the two jobs of *gerdia* and *aurinetrix* seemed to belong specifically to the female domain. In all other instances, it seems likely that a masculine noun like *sarcinator* (a mender of clothes) could apply to both male and female indiscriminately. It is possible that female labourers received less pay than male colleagues, but in the occupations themselves gender divisions hardly play a role in the Edict.

The only element that seems to have made a real difference in the Edict, is skill. This is apparent from the remuneration for different jobs. Skilled work typically brought in about twice as much as unskilled work.[33] The composers

---

28 *Sarcinatores: Prices Edict* 7.48–53; CIL VI 6348 (Attalus, slave?); 3051 (M. Vipsanius Maior, freedman)—this inscription may be a forgery, however; CIL V 7568 (C. Farronius C.f. Optatus). See appendix for attestations and legal status for other occupations.

29 Thüry (2001: 8) for brief discussion of the organization of the workforces cleaning the sewers; Jansen (2011: 161–162) for the dangers.

30 They probably had to pay a remittance or the full sum to their owner. On slaves hiring themselves out: Hawkins (2006: 204); *Dig.* 32.73.3; 33.7.19.1; 36.1.80.12.

31 Chapter 28.6: 2,000 or more because the Greek text has 2,500 denarii.

32 See appendix for examples. The only *aurinetrix* we know of epigraphically, however, is a girl who died at age 9: CIL VI 9213 (Rome).

33 Rathbone (2009: 314), 'The perhaps surprising twofold differential of Diocletian's Edict is supported by the two stray figures we have for late Republican Italy... and the Egyptian

of the Edict seem to have worked with a standard of 50 denarii a day for skilled work, and 25 denarii a day for unskilled work (both with *pastus*). This distinction is reflected in the chapter on slave prices: a skilled slave could be sold for up to two times the maximum price for an unskilled slave of the same age and gender.[34]

A number of jobs was headed under either category, that is 50 or 25 denarii a day. Subsequent adaptations were made for specific jobs: thus, a shepherd (*pastor*; 7.18) earns a little less with 20 denarii a day, whereas the specialist artists, a maker of models (*plastae imaginarius*; 7.29; 75 denarii a day) and a figure painter (*pictor imaginarius*; 7.9; 150 denarii a day) were exceptionally well rewarded for their art. The extra skills needed, plus maybe some recognition of risk, explain why a shipwright working on a seagoing vessel earns 10 denarii per day more than a shipwright working on a river boat (7.13–14).[35]

It is quite natural that the skilled types of labour receive a high amount of attention in the Edict. If indeed rural labour served as an umbrella term for many unskilled activities (see above), job differentiation and specialization is more likely to occur in skilled work. Because it entailed a greater variety of job specifications, then, skilled labour naturally becomes more prominent in any list of job titles.

Although caution is needed because some of the underlying structure may be hidden beneath the price ceilings of the Edict, the Edict itself does not point to significant segmentation in the labour market. No strict boundaries between agricultural and urban work are visible. No formal separation existed between labour for slaves and labour for free persons. Only two out of more than sixty jobs are the particular domain of women. The one element that was clearly and unequivocally recognised as a distinguishing property was skill.

---

data ... which point to two to threefold differentials'. See also the papers of Hawkins and Bernard in this volume.

34 29.8: *Pro mancipio arte instructo pro genere et aetate et qualitate artium inter emptorem vel venditorem de praetio placere conveniet ita ut duplum praetium statutum in mancipium minime excedere.*

35 Although we might expect that a *naupegos* is active in the shipyard only, the Greek text is ambiguous. Higher wages for a shipwright working on a seagoing vessel lead us to believe that it may also be a compensation for the risk involved if he actually sailed the sea to perform emergency maintenance.

Remuneration for Labour

The fact that labour was considered as an integral part of the costs of the total production process helps to understand the various forms of remuneration that occur in the Edict. The text mentions daily wages (for example, the shepherd; 7.18), payment per action, payment per product, payment per customer served (for example, barbers per caput; 7.22; teachers per pupil; 7.64–71), payment by quantity of raw material worked (for example, tailor per specified piece of clothing; 7. 42–53, embroiderers per ounce of cloth; 20.2–5).[36]

This variety in remuneration is also attested elsewhere. *Locatio-conductio* arrangements show a similar variety of possibilities: labourers could be paid per period worked, per quantity of goods delivered, per task performed. On the larger estates of Roman Egypt, long-term salaried workers and day-labourers worked alongside each other.[37]

In the Edict specific jobs have specific types of remuneration. In reality specific jobs are known to have been remunerated in various forms.[38] Drexhage's collection of Roman-Egyptian data demonstrates that a wide range of forms was available for hiring labour.[39] In the Edict a shepherd is paid a daily wage of 20 denarii. The papyri show that paying a shepherd by the day was definitely an option. It was not the only option, however, as a shepherd could also be contracted on a monthly basis.[40] Monthly contracts are in fact fairly common in the papyri, whereas monthly payments do not appear in the Edict.[41] Another example is that of the baker, who according to the Edict would earn a daily wage. His services could apparently be hired by the day. At the same time we know that it was much more common to buy a single bread at the local bakery, or that it was even possible merely to rent space in the oven to bake off your own, home-made bread. The bakers' guild (*corpus pistorum*) at Rome and Ostia may have been hired by the state for the free distribution of grain or bread.[42] That production could take place on a large scale is amply demonstrated by the monument of M. Vergilius Eurysaces, who was surely more than merely a

---

36 Cf. Frézouls (1977: 257–9).

37 See, for instance, Kehoe (2012: 121).

38 Corbier (1980) analyses the evidence for the various sectors of the economy.

39 Drexhage (1991: chapter 8).

40 Per day: *P. Lond.* I 131 (= *SB* VIII 9699). Per month: *P. Lond.* III 1171 col. 2; *P. Princ.* III 152.

41 See Drexhage (1991: 425–429); annual wages are enumerated on p. 430.

42 Sirks (1999); cf. the fresco from Pompeii that shows a baker selling his wares. It is now in the *Museo Nazionale*, Naples.

hired hand.[43] The fact that, for example, three slave bakers are also known to have been employed by the imperial household of Livia Augusta completes the spectrum of possibilities.[44]

The mention of a daily wage occurs in no less than thirty-one instances, that is for about half the labourers mentioned in the Edict. Daily wages occur for both skilled and unskilled labour (for example, the stonemason; 7.2). The predominance of wages paid by the day is not entirely surprising as, according to Duncan-Jones, 'that is the way in which [wages] were commonly expressed (and paid) in antiquity'.[45] In this way, Duncan-Jones continues, the employer could work with the most flexible workforce to minimise risk. Perhaps the absence of monthly (and annual) wages in the Edict is only to be expected in a volatile market: it allows small businessmen a more flexible investment in labour. If necessary, a maximum price for a contract deal could still be calculated from the maximum daily wages provided. The Edict, then, appears to be concerned with short-term pacts that could easily be entered into, but that could just as easily be broken off.

In the case of the jobs with daily wages, the Edict consistently adds a food allowance (*pastus*). The pattern seems to be that daily wages included *pastus*, and that none (or almost none)[46] of the other payments did. What the *pastus* comprised was left unspecified and thus was left to be settled by social con-

43 *CIL* VI 1958a.

44 *CIL* VI 4010; 4011; 4012, all found in the *columbarium* of Livia Augusta. The inscriptions are fragmentary, but these *pistores* appear to be slaves. The household of the Statilii also included four *pistores*, see Hasegawa (2005: 45).

45 Duncan-Jones (1978: 160).

46 At first sight, the text seems to suggest that others were eligible for *pastus*, too. In 7.15–16 the bricklayer is paid for every four bricks of 2 feet (or every 8 bricks) plus preparation of the clay, but in addition the text calls this a *diurnam mercedem*, daily wage, *pasto*: with *pastus*. In the Greek version of the text, it says τρεφ(ομένῳ) ἡμερ(ήσια)—'daily wage with food allowance'. If this were correct, the daily wage would be implausibly low, at 2 denarii. Most likely, the text interpolated that it was a daily wage because it was seen that the bricklayer received *pastus*—a case of hypercorrection perhaps. Another such instance concerns the sheep shearer of 7.23 who was paid per sheep. In Latin, he too is paid *with pastus*. There is no mention of it in the Greek, and we may presume that *pasto* is a mistaken interpolation. In fact, the only pieceworkers who are ascribed a food allowance in both the Latin and the Greek version(s) of the Edict are a wool weaver (*lanarius*; 21.1a) who is otherwise paid 40 den. per pound of wool, and a silk worker who is paid an uncertain amount per ounce (23.2). Because of all that has been said before we might surmise that this is a scribal error. It also presses the need for a new edition of the text and commentary, for which see n.1.

vention. The fact that the compilers saw no need for further regulation might be explained by the fact that their aim was first and foremost to protect the currency by fixating prices. Stipulating the contents of *pastus* would not have been relevant for them.

It is good to realise that however monetised the Roman economy was, a significant amount of all transactions was still made in kind. Moreover, '[a] cash wage plus a food allowance has been a common payment scheme in many poor countries'.[47] It was also fairly common in the Roman Empire,[48] notwithstanding the fact that the question whether we are dealing with a 'poor country' here is still open for debate. Incidentally, the standard inclusion of *pastus* in the daily wages in the Edict also points to a setting in which hired labourers may have worked outside their homes: on the land, in small-scale workshops, in a factory-like setting.[49] The food allowance, however, is part of the maximum payment set by the Edict and, as a result, need not always have applied.

The many instances of piecework that are listed display an awareness of practical considerations in specifying the type of remuneration. It makes economic sense that, for example, a tailor was hired only to provide or to mend a specific piece of clothing: such costs would not be part of the daily expenditure of most Romans. Fullers, too, were unlikely to be hired by a private person on a daily basis, as fullers would need a fullery to work. That makes it highly likely that the work would come to them, instead of the other way around. A coppersmith, for example, is paid 6 denarii per pound of copper 'for small vessels of various kinds' (7.26). In all likelihood many of such manufacturers will have worked on a bespoke basis.[50]

Thus, the Edict shows a labour market in which remuneration occurred in more forms than wages alone, and is very much in line with what we know otherwise about hired labour arrangements. However, in tying particular jobs to particular forms of remuneration the Edict was unduly restrictive. The particular choices are understandable: practical considerations were taken into account. In reality particular jobs could be remunerated in more than one form.

47 Allen (2009: 330).

48 Mrozek (1975: 80–82).

49 Flohr (2007: 143–144) suggesting that workers from the larger workshops of Ostia had separate work- and living spaces.

50 Hawkins (2006; 2013).

Economic Differentiation

The Edict is the only substantial source for wages from the Roman period, outside of Roman Egypt.[51] It is no wonder that scholars have often taken recourse to the Edict for investigations of real wage or purchasing power, prosperity, and even gross domestic product for the Roman Empire.

The gist of this line of scholarship can be briefly summarized as follows: the majority of the Romans were not very well off. In the calculations of Duncan-Jones, the purchasing power in the Roman Empire (that is, in the Edict) had dropped four or fivefold compared to fourth-century BC Greece.[52] Allen likewise concludes that the real wages of the Edict were historically low.[53] His comparison with later periods is expressed in terms of welfare ratios: the proportion of a 'consumption basket' a labourer could buy for himself and for his family.[54] According to Allen, an unskilled daily labourer could buy a mere 56 per cent of the 'respectability basket', but 110 per cent of a much less nourishing 'bare bones basket'. Scheidel has argued that the low living standard of an unskilled Roman worker was comparable to that of unskilled workers in various other societies in the period from 1800 BC–AD 1300.[55]

Along similar lines West and, more recently, Polichetti have argued that the wages did not pay for the goods enumerated in the Edict. West points out that the best-paid labourer of the Edict, the figure-painter who was hired at max 150 denarii a day, 'would have to work twenty-two days to purchase the

51 Szilágyi (1963); Mrozek (1975); and see Szaivert and Wolters (2005) for the literary wage data. Roman Egypt: Johnson (1936), Drexhage (1991).

52 Duncan-Jones (1978: 161 table 1); his fourth century BC reference is Eleusis, his calculations are made in wheat equivalent. Cf. however Crawford (2010), who compares price relativities in the Prices Edict with the prices in a series of Attic stelai that record the prices at the auction of confiscated property after the mutilation of the Herms in 415 BC. He argues that the relative price structure remained essentially unchanged between the two. His arguments concern price relations between goods, not between goods and wages, but slaves are included, and their price will have affected wages.

53 Allen (2009) with fig. 16.1 'silver wages'; fig. 16.2 'welfare ratios with European respectability basket'; fig. 16.3 'welfare ratios with bare bones baskets'.

54 Allen (2009: 329), 'the items—and the quantities—they would have consumed in a year.'

55 Scheidel (2010b: 433), who works with prices from Roman Egypt, instead of the *Edict*. His work indicates that an unskilled rural labourer could buy only 25–50 % of the respectability basket or 70–90 % of the bare bones basket. That is slightly less than the rates calculated from the *Prices Edict*. See also Drexhage (1991: chapter 9) on the low living standards in Roman Egypt. But cf. Rathbone (2009: 320) who suggests that the low maximum for wages in the Edict was 'presumably a deliberate attempt to make labour cheaper'.

average piece of wearing apparel listed'.[56] Polichetti adds that an unskilled day-labourer (25 denarii a day) had to work twenty-two days to buy the cheapest tunic—which equals eight days of work for a figure-painter.[57] However, the assumption that 'the list of articles mentioned in the tables was not one intended for the mass of the population' is perhaps a bit too strong.[58] Although it is certainly correct to point out a preoccupation with luxury goods in the text, twenty-two days of labour for a tunic appears to be fairly normal.[59]

In addition, rather than pointing directly to poverty, the low wages of the Edict may imply that much labour was family-oriented. One possibility is that the unskilled jobs functioned as a supplementary source of income, for example for rural families in which the elder sons moved temporarily to the city to earn some additional money.[60] Those people who earned their money predominantly through unskilled labour, however, were probably unable to sustain a family by their own labour alone. If cutting expenditure is no longer an option, the only way to increase income is to increase time worked, either by oneself or with the labour of others.[61] Necessity makes it highly likely that women and children contributed to the family income in some measure.[62] At the same time, more mouths had to be fed. In consequence, the 'respectability basket' would never have been easily attained by an unskilled worker even if his family made a significant contribution.[63] What Richard Wall termed the 'adaptive family economy', the idea that the family would work together to maximise their economic well-being, may very well have operated here too—though perhaps the family aspirations should be adjusted in this context not to maximise well-being, but primarily to ensure survival.[64] It also explains why for many families it must have been very hard to make the transition from

56 West (1939: 241), who then goes on to say that '[i]t is impossible, apparently, to compare the prices of foodstuffs as given in the *Edict* with wages'.

57 Polichetti (2002: 225).

58 West (1939: 241); Polichetti (2002: 225, 228).

59 Drexhage (1991: 449) shows that this is a regular working-day equivalent for buying a simple chiton in second century AD Roman Egypt.

60 Erdkamp (2008); Kehoe (2012: 123, 127).

61 Allen (2009: 339), 'One strategy was to increase time worked. Men could work more days and longer hours. No allowance has been made thus far for the earnings of women and children ... Cutting expenditure was another strategy'.

62 Frézouls (1977: 265); Drexhage (1991: 445); Allen (2009: 339).

63 Scheidel (2010b: 433–435, 454), 'Since wages for adult male workers were often so modest, labour force participation by both adult women and minors must have been high in order to fend off starvation'.

64 Wall (1986: esp. 265).

unskilled to skilled labour: even if the apprenticeship system offered a relatively accessible way of vocational training, parents could not miss the labour of their children.[65]

What has received less attention, is that the Edict not only points to low wages, but also to significant income variation. The wages of the Edict take up a wide range, from the figure-painter earning 150 denarii to the *gerdia* (female weaver) who, at 12 denarii a day, earned 12.5 times less; in terms of annual income the *gerdia* might expect a mere 3,000 denarii, the figure-painter 37,500 denarii.[66] Even if we eliminate these two extreme cases as outliers, we still see a significant amount of wage variation (see below). Similar divergences can also be observed in the jobs which pay per item (for example the fullers earn from 60 to 600 denarii per item), or per pupil per month (various categories of teachers earn from 50 denarii to 250 denarii per pupil per month). Many jobs provide at least twice the income of the unskilled labourer whose wage of 25 denarii formed the basis for the calculations of Allen.[67]

In fact, many of the jobs listed could generate an income well above threshold levels. At a maximum wage of 50 denarii, a carpenter (*faber tignuarius*) would have been able to buy 112 per cent of Allen's respectability basket (or 220(!) per cent of the bare bones basket).[68] People in such occupations had the possibility of adding items to their respectability basket.[69] Our *faber tignuarius* earning 50 denarii a day could buy the items listed by Allen, and would still have enough money left to supplement his family's diet every month with, for example, a pair of chickens (60 denarii; 4,23), ten dormice (40 denarii; 4.38), a first quality river fish (12 denarii; 5.3), five artichokes (10 denarii; 6,1), four small melons (4 denarii; 6.31) and eight eggs (2x4 denarii; 6.43). If he chose to save up the extra money, he could buy himself, his wife and their son a (third-quality) shirt of course linen ('for the use of common people or slaves') once a year (3 × 500 denarii; 26,31a–33); or, if he felt particularly innovative perhaps trying to set up an extra business, he might even invest in a horse mill with

65 Hawkins, this volume.

66 At 250 working days per year, which is the number Allen (2009: 337) works with.

67 Allen (2009: 330). Because wages for unskilled workers are far more standardized, Allen, but also Duncan-Jones (1978) and Scheidel (2010b) calculated real wages for unskilled labourers.

68 2 × 56 %, see above.

69 In our calculations we included Allen's addition for the food allowance of 11.1 den./day (Allen 2009: 330) to calculate an annual wage of 61.1 × 250 working days = 15,275 den./year, which as we saw buys 112 % of the respectability basket. This leaves the worker ca 1637 den./year to spend on utensils and/or luxury goods. For ease of calculation we refrained from his use of silver equivalent in computation of wages.

stones (1500 denarii; 15.56a) and almost have enough left to buy an embroidered first-quality horse blanket for 250 denarii the same year (7.53).

Playing around with such somewhat frivolous scenarios in which the Edict easily becomes a mere shopping list, points to the more serious fact that even within the labour force very substantial differences in well-being and lifestyle could arise. It also points to the fact that in such cases more mouths could be fed from a single income. In terms of Wall's family economy, it suggests that at the higher end of the spectrum much less additional labour would be needed by family members: instead, wives could remain at home, children could be educated for longer periods of time, a teacher could be employed, children might be apprenticed out. In fact, it also shows why it would be feasible to employ external labour by hiring others or buying slaves. The Roman city dotted with small workshops where free artisans worked side by side with one or two slaves or freedmen can readily be reconciled with the data from the Edict.[70]

At the same time we should not be too optimistic about standards of living of the labour force in general. If we categorise those occupations of the Edict that receive a daily wage into pay scales, the distribution of income should be pictured as a pyramid with a very small top layer and then widening to a broader base (table 6.2, in which the lowest level incomes below 20 denarii are clearly exceptional). The difference in income has already been explained above as resulting mainly from an individual's skills.[71]

TABLE 6.2 *Wage range for daily wages in the Prices Edict*

Wage range in denarii	Occupations (examples)	Attestations (%) N = 31
≥ 76	*Pictor imaginarius*	1 (3.2%)
51–75	*Pictor parietarius, marmorarius*	6 (19.4 %)
26–50	*Pistor, faber ferrarius*	11 (35.5 %)
20–25	*Aquarius, cloacarius, mulio*	11 (35.5 %)
≤ 19	*Gerdia*	2 (6.4 %)

70 For which see Hawkins, this volume. The wage differentials in the *Edict* pertain of course primarily to hired labourers, but it does not seem wildly speculative to assume that they also reflect income differentiation of independent artisans.

71 It may be that this double ratio also points to the relative scarcity of skilled labour (as Hawkins argues in this volume), but if so, the data presented by Bernard in this volume suggest that such scarcity would be a structural feature in many societies.

It is important to emphasise that these levels refer to different numbers of jobs attested in the Edict, not to percentages of the population working in such jobs. In order to get a sense of scale, we may take recourse to the model devised by Scheidel and Friesen of overall income stratification in the Roman Empire.[72] Leaving elite income outside our scope for now, Scheidel and Friesen place at least 55 per cent of the population around subsistence level, at most 19 per cent only just above it and 10–22 per cent below subsistence level. The richer 'middling sector' includes only around 5–10 per cent.[73] If their income stratification is even roughly correct, the great majority of the labour force was holding jobs of 25 denarii or less. Put differently: the Edict overrepresents the higher end of the labour market by a wide margin. This fits in well with what was said above about the probable bias towards the inclusion of skilled, urban occupations in the Edict.

The wages in the Edict, in sum, seem to reflect relatively low earnings and relatively low living standards for the larger part of the population, and particularly for unskilled labourers. At the same time, the Edict also points to the fact that some workers could have a lifestyle that was well above subsistence levels. Skill paid off.

Conclusion

Diocletian's Prices Edict unintentionally provides an interesting insight into the Roman labour market. In its listing of predominantly daily wages, the text shows a preoccupation with hired labour, and therefore with short-term labour arrangements that reflect a fluctuating market. The piecework that recurs may also reflect a bespoke economy. The composers seem to have given some thought to the practicalities of the production process in their choice of payment for any efforts. However, in reality arrangements for remuneration could vary more widely and were more flexible.

There is no strong segmentation of the labour force in the text: all occupations are attested under a single header with one standard wage, with no regard for age, gender or legal status. The absence of such segmentation may suggest that the labour market was relatively open and may thus imply significant labour mobility. Only in the slave chapter does it show that the Romans did value such characteristics differently in a worker.

72 Scheidel and Friesen (2009). Note that their model pertains to the late second century AD.

73 Excluding soldiers, who probably belong to the middling part. Scheidel and Friesen (2009: 84–85, with tables 8 and 9).

The Edict also attests to a relatively wide differentiation of income. Many of the jobs included in the Edict would allow a family to support itself, even if for many families the labour input of women and children was a necessity. It is likely, however, that the Edict overrepresents the middle and top layers of the labour market. The majority of the people will have lived at or under subsistence levels: the Edict has given us an insight into what such income variations could imply.

Obviously, the aim of the Edict was not to write down a structural overview of the Roman labour market in AD 301: it had quite a different purpose as the emperor Diocletian attempted to fixate the price of labour in a time of rampant inflation. More in general the Edict is to be placed in a context in which social and geographical mobility was discouraged. It is no wonder that the list of occupations drawn from the Edict is far from complete, and that it displays a certain arbitrariness and a bias towards the urban outlook of the composers: unskilled labour and rural labour—as often as not the two can be equated—are less well represented than the more differentiated and specialized workers of the urban labour market.

That the Edict was such a spectacular failure is blamed in modern scholarship on market forces: these were too strong to allow regulation. Prices simply could not be controlled in the fashion Diocletian had in mind. If our arguments are correct, the fluidity of the labour market also formed an obstacle. It makes clear why market forces were so strong: market integration may have been incomplete, but it still resulted in a relatively open market where price formation could and did take place. That is, until Diocletian tried to curb it.

Appendix 1: Catalogue of Job Titles in the Edict, Set Off against Their Attestations in Epigraphy

Prices Edict					Selection of other attestations
	Latin	*Greek*[a]	*Translation*[b]	*Wage (in denarii)*	
7.1a	*operarius rusticus*	*vacat*	Farm labourer	25/day	Cato *Agr.* 4
7.2	*lapidarius structor*	λιθουργός τεχνείτης	Stone mason	50/day	*Lapidarius*: CIL XI 6838 (M freeborn) *Structor*: CIL VI 6353; 8795 (M imperial slave)
7.3a	*faber tignuarius*	λεπτουργός τεχνείτης	Carpenter	50/day	CIL VI 9411 (M freedmen, brothers) CIL XIV 299 (M freedman)
7.3	*faber intestinarius*	τέκτων	Cabinet maker, carver/inlayer (fine woodwork)	50/day	CIL VI 9401 (M Slave) CIL X 1922 (M freeborn)
7.4a	*calcis coctor*	χαλικοκαύστης	Marble burner	50/day	*Hi qui calcem cocunt:* *Dig.* 50.6.7
7.5	*marmorarius*	μαρμαράριος	Marble mason	60/day	CIL VI 6318 (M slave?) CIL VI 9551 (M free[c])
7.6	*musaearius*	μουσιάριος	Mosaicist	60/day	CIL VI 9647 = AE 1997, 160 (M imperial slave)
7.7	*tessellarius*	ψηφοθέτης	Worker in tessellated floors	50/day	*artifex artis tessalari(a)e / lusori(a)e*: CIL VI 9927 (M free)

Prices Edict					Selection of other attestations
	Latin	*Greek*[a]	*Translation*[b]	*Wage (in denarii)*	
7.8	*pictor parietarius*	τοιχογράφος	Wall painter	75/day	*Pictores*: *CIL* VI 4008 (imperial freedman) *CIL* VI 9791 (M slave?)
7.9	*pictor imaginarius*	εἰκονογράφος	Figure painter, portrait painter	150/day	See *pictor parietarius*
7.10	*carpentarius*	ἁμαξοπηγός	Wagonwright	50/day	*CIL* V 5922 (M freeborn)
7.11	*faber ferrarius*	σιδήρευς	Blacksmith	50/day	*CIL* VIII 4487 (M unknown) *CIL* XI 4236 (M freeborn)
7.12	*pistor*	ἀρτοκόπος	Baker	50/day	*CIL* VI 1958a (M freedman? (Eurysaces)) *CIL* VI 6687 (2 x M slaves)
7.13–14	*naupegus*	ναυπηγός	Shipwright	50–60/day	*CIL* XI 2135 (M free)
7.15–16	*–description–*	πλινθοβόλος	Bricklayer	piecework	*Caementarius*: *AE* 1997, 1591 (uncertain attestation, M free) *CIL* X 3414 (M free, military) CIL V 8110, 425 (fragmentary)
7.17	*cameliarius*	καμηλάριος	Camel driver	25/day	*Camelariis*: *Dig.* 50.4.18.11

(cont.)

Prices Edict					Selection of other attestations
	Latin	*Greek*[a]	*Translation*[b]	*Wage (in denarii)*	
7.17	*asinarius*	ὀνηλάτης	Ass driver	25/day	CIL X 143 (*collegium mulionum et asinariorum*)
7.17	*burdonarius*	βουρδωνάριος	Hinny driver	25/day	–
7.18	*pastor*	νομεύς	Shepherd	20/day	*Pastor pavonum* Var. RR 3.6.5 *Pastor gallinarum* Col. 8.2.7
7.19	*mulio*	μουλίων	Muleteer	25/day	AE 1945, 112 (M imperial slave) CIL VI 7409 (M slave?)
7.20–21	*mulomedico*	ἱππιατρός	Veterinary	Piecework	CIL VI 9611 (M slave?) CIL VI 9613 (fragmentary)
7.22	*tonsor*	κουρεύς	Barber	Piecework	CIL VI 4359 (M imperial slave) CIL VI 5865 (F freedwoman?)
7.23	*tonsor pecorum*	κουρεύς	Shearer	Piecework	Vulg. Genes. 38.12
7.24a–28	*aerarius*	χαλκουργός	Coppersmith	Piecework	CIL VI 9135 (M freedman) CIL IX 1723 (M freedman)
7.29	*plastae imaginarius*	πλάστη […	Maker of models	75/day	–
7.30	*reliquis plastis gupsarii*	τοῖς λοιποῖς πλάσταις γυψαρίοις	Maker of other plaster casts	55/day	*Gypsarius:* CIL IX 5378 (M freedman) CIL XII 4479 (M freedman)

Prices Edict					Selection of other attestations
	Latin	*Greek*[a]	*Translation*[b]	*Wage (in denarii)*	
7.31	*aquarius*	ὑδραγωγός	Water-carrier	25/day	CIL VI 131 (M freeborn?) CIL VI 551 (M imperial slave)
7.32	*cloacarius*	ὁ ἐργαζομένος ἰς τ[ὰς ὑπορ ρύσεις]	Sewer cleaner	25/day	–
7.33–37	*samiator*	ἀκονητής	Polisher	Piecework	–
7.38	*membranarius*	διφθεράριος	Parchment maker	Piecework	–
7.39–40	*scriptor*	καλλιγράφος	Scribe	Piecework	Only a *scriptor titulorum* is attested epigraphically—and that appears not to be a calligrapher, but an epigrapher. *Librarius:* CIL VI 6314 (M slave?) *Actarius:* CIL VI 6224 (M slave)
7.41	*tabellio*	ἀγοραῖος	Notary, scrivener	Piecework	*Tabularius*: CIL VI 9925 (M slave?) CIL VI 33796 (M freedman)
7.42–47	*bracarius*	βρακάριος	Tailor	Piecework	*Pap. Marini* 88.8 (AD 572) *Pap. Lond. Ined.* 2176 (6th c)

(cont.)

Prices Edict					Selection of other attestations
	Latin	*Greek*[a]	*Translation*[b]	*Wage (in denarii)*	
7.48–53	*sarcinator*	ῥάπτης	Tailor	Piecework	*CIL* VI 9037 (F slave?) *CIL* VI 6348 (M slave?) *CIL* V 7568 (M freeborn)
7.54–63	[*color*]*ator*[d]	κοροράτωρ	Dyer	Piecework	*AE* 2009, 202 (M freedman) *CIL* VI 3953 (M slave of Livia)
7.64	*ceromatita*	κηρωματείτης	Gymnastics instructor?	50/pupil/ month	–
7.65	*paedagogus*	παιδαγωγός	Pedagogue	50/boy/month	*CIL* VI 5563 (M slave of Agrippina) *CIL* VI 6327 (M pedagogue of Messalina Tauri)
7.66	*magister institutori litterarum*	χαμαιδιδάσκαλος	Elementary teacher	50/boy/month	*Magister litterarum*: *InscrAqu* III 293 (M freedman)
7.67	*calculator*	καυκουλάτωρ	Teacher of arithmetic	75/boy/month	*CIL* XIV 472 (M slave, 13 yrs) *Dig*. 38.1.7.5 (freed, minors)
7.68	*notarius*	νοτάριος	Teacher of shorthand-writing	75/boy/month	*notarius* is epigraphically attested but appears to mean something else in inscriptions. σημιογράφος: *P. Oxy* IV 724 (AD 155 M free (apprenticeship contract for a slave boy))

Prices Edict					Selection of other attestations
	Latin	*Greek*[a]	*Translation*[b]	*Wage (in denarii)*	
7.69	*antiquarius*	ἀρχαιολόγος	Teacher of palaeography	55/pupil/ month	–
7.69	*librarius*	λιβράριος	Teacher of manuscript writing	55/pupil/ month	*CIL* VI 7293 (M slave) *CIL* VI 37802 (F freedwoman)
7.70	*grammaticus Graeco sive Latino et geometrae*	γραμματικός	Teacher of Greek, Latin or geometry	200/pupil/ month	*CIL* VI 9454 *Grammaticus Graecus* (M freedman?) *CIL* VI 19071 (M slave?)
7.71	*sofista*	σοφιστής	Teacher of public speaking	250/pupil/ month	–
7.71	*orator*	ῥήτωρ	Teacher of rhetoric	250/pupil/ month	*CIL* II 354 = *AE* 2000 679 (M freeborn) *CIL* VI 1434 (M freeborn (senator))
7.72	*advocatus*	δικολόγος, νομικός	Lawyer	Piecework	*CIL* VIII 2393 (M freeborn (*eques*)) *CIL* III 15158 (M freeborn)
7.74	*architectus magister*	ἀρχιτέκτονι διδάσκαλος	Teacher of architecture	100/boy/ month	*Architectus CIL* V 3464 (M freedman) *CIL* VI 4884 (M slave)
7.75	*capsarius*	καψάριος	Clothes-guard	Piecework	*CIL* V 3158 (M freeborn) *CIL* VI 3952 (F slave)

(cont.)

Prices Edict					Selection of other attestations
	Latin	*Greek*[a]	*Translation*[b]	*Wage (in denarii)*	
7.76	*balneator privatarius*	βαλανεύς πρειουᾶτος	Keeper of a private bath	Piecework	*Balneatrix* AE 2001, 964 (F freedwoman) *Balneator* CIL VI 6243 (M slave)
20.1–4	*plumarius*	πλουμάριος	Embroiderer	Piecework	CIL VI 7411 (M slave?) CIL VI 9813 (M free)
20.5–8	*barbaricarius*	βαρβαρικάριος	Brocade maker, embroiderer	Piecework	CIL VI 33766 (M slave/freedman) CIL V 785 (M free?)
20.9–11	*sericarius*	σειρικάριος	Silk worker	25–40/day	CIL VIII 9891 (F slave?) *Siricarius* (!)CIL XIV 3712 (M free)
20.12–13	*gerdia*	γερδία	Weaver (f)	12–16/day	*P. Mich.* V 346a (AD 13, F slave, apprentice in the γερδιακή τεχνή) *P. Mich.* III 172 (AD 62 M freeborn, apprentice)
21.1–4	*lanarius*	λανάριος	Wool weaver	piecework	CIL VI 33869 (M free) CIL XI 741 (M free)
21.5–6	*linteonus*	λίνυφος	Linen weaver	20–40/day	*Lintearia* CIL II 4318a (F slave) *Lintiarius* CIL VI 7468 (M unknown)
22.1–26	*fullo*	φούλλων	Fuller	Piecework	CIL VI 4445 (M freedman?) CIL VI 6290 (M slave)

Prices Edict					Selection of other attestations
	Latin	*Greek*[a]	*Translation*[b]	*Wage (in denarii)*	
23.2	*sericum solventibus*	τοῖς τὸ σηρικὸν λύουσιν	Those unravelling silk	Piecework	–
24.13	[*sericum solventibus*]	μεταξαβλάττην ἤτοι ἐν χρώμασιν ἀγένητον λύουσιν	Those unravelling silk	Piecework	–
24.14–18	*vacat*	πορφύραν νήθουσιν	Those spinning purple	Piecework	*Purpurarius, -ia:* *CIL* VI 9846 (F, freedwomen) *CIL* VI 37820 (M, F, freedmen)
28.3	*artifex brattias faciens*	τοῖς τεχνείταις τοῖς εἰς τὸ πέταλον ἐργαζομένοις	Gold-leaf beater	Piecework	*Brattiarius, -ia:* *CIL* VI 6939 (M, F, freedmen) *CIL* VI 33836 (M freedman)
28.4	*auricaesor*	αὐρικαισωρ	Gold cutter	Piecework	–
28.5	*auriductor in lamina*	χρυσελάταις εἰς λάμνας	Gold embosser on sheets of gold	Piecework	–
28.6	*aurinectrix*	χρυσονήστρια	Gold spinner	Piecework	*CIL* VI, 9213 (F slave?)

(cont.)

Prices Edict					Selection of other attestations
	Latin	*Greek*[a]	*Translation*[b]	*Wage (in denarii)*	
28.7–8	*aurifex*	χρυσοχόος	Goldsmith	Piecework	CIL VI 3927 (M freedman) CIL VI 3950 (M imperial slave)
28.10–12	*argentarius artifex*	ἀργυροχόος	Silversmith	Piecework	*Argentaria* CIL VI 5184 (F slave?) *Faber argentarius* CIL VI 9390 (M free)

a The Greek cited here follows the text of Giacchero (1974). We suspect that the new text edition (see n.1 above) will solve some of the inherent textual problems.

b Translations Graser (1940), Von Petrikovits (1981), Joshel (1982), *LSJ*, ours.

c 'Free' throughout this appendix means that the *tria nomina* or another indication of free status are present, but that there is no definite mention of filiation or libertination, or any other hint in the text that may ascertain freeborn or freedman status.

d If Giacchero's conjecture is correct. Von Petrikovits (1981) lists *lavator*—washer—instead. The Greek is more legible, but appears to be a *hapax legomenon* and is no help in deciding what job title is meant.

CHAPTER 7

Roman Workers and Their Workplaces: Some Archaeological Thoughts on the Organization of Workshop Labour in Ceramic Production

Elizabeth A. Murphy

The relationship between Roman archaeology and Roman history can be defined in terms of qualitative difference; an archaeology of objects vis-à-vis an history of texts.[1] Yet certain topics lie at the shared border of text and material culture, and in so doing become suitable for an interdisciplinary approach. In the case of Roman work and workers, investigations of labour specialization, workplace structure, and production organization provide an example. Historians and archaeologists now find themselves posing similar questions concerning the nature and organization of labour in the Roman world, both in terms of its economic and social significance. Archaeology in particular has much to contribute, both because production activities are often reflected in an extensive—yet too often underappreciated—material record, and because recent research is drawing attention to the diverse ways that work and labour was organized throughout the Empire at different periods of its history. Crucially, this material evidence very often derives from industries only rarely or obliquely referenced in textual sources, and presents unique means to reconstruct how work was experienced in the Roman world through its spatial organization and temporal contextualization.

Considering this research potential and the context of this volume, this paper highlights current research themes in the archaeology of Roman workshops and proposes a new direction—drawing inspiration from developments in household archaeology—in order to re-evaluate Roman workshops and workers in terms of socialised workgroups. Evidence of Roman ceramic production sites from Gaul and Italy, which are especially well documented, will provide the primary case studies for the application of this approach.

1 Sauer (2004).

 | DOI 10.1163/9789004331686_008

The Archaeology of Roman Workplaces

Archaeological investigations of workshops and workplaces have been motivated by a variety of different research interests.[2] Yet some general trends can be discerned from the range of studies performed, and these trends provide an intellectual context for the argument developed in this chapter.

The identification of workshops as production centres of known types (particularly ceramic types) has been vital in refining typological chronologies, establishing the range of artefact types from the site, and indicating point-sources from which to build distribution maps (such mapping exercises utilise the production site as the central point from which distribution lines radiate).[3] Production sites and their organization have also achieved prominence as, in part, a function of larger debates by archaeologists and historians regarding the nature and scale of the Roman economy. Accordingly, spatial dimensions of workplaces, range of product distribution, and type and scale of technology are argued to have wider relevance when assessing the scale and efficiency of Roman production.[4]

Moving beyond purely economic approaches, workplaces have—more recently—begun to be investigated by archaeologists with more explicitly social questions in mind. Such studies encompass a wider variety of working contexts (including commercial shops, workshops, quarries, and storage depots), and have largely focused on reconstructing work activities in order to better understand the lived experience of labour in antiquity. Broader issues involve: the relationships among workers based on worker specialization and power relations;[5] commercial and productive landscapes;[6] and ideologies and *dignitas* of Roman occupations as expressed in the visual arts.[7]

Growing concern over the social experience of ancient workplace environments mirrors discussions currently taking place in household archaeology which have implications for the study of Roman work. For instance, much in the way that the archaeology of crafts production has employed the 'workshop'

---

2 Clearly, the approaches outlined here do not exhaustively encompass all production studies of the Roman world, and this broad sketch to some extent glosses regional traditions in scholarship.

3 Biegert (2010).

4 Rostovtzeff (1957); Finley (1999); Fülle (2000; 1997); Greene (2007; 2003); Dark (1996); Wilson (2002b); Poblome (2004).

5 Flohr (2009); Robinson (2005).

6 Sekedat (2010); Delaine (2005); Graham (2005).

7 George (2006).

as a primary unit of economic activity, domestic archaeology has used the 'household' as a fundamental unit of social organization, and the ways in which these units are characterized fundamentally colours our modern perception of ancient society and economy. In the case of households, contextual analyses of domestic sites have begun to recognize an unexpectedly wide range of activities (social, ritual, and economic) that might take place at and were structured by the household level, and houses have consequently begun to be seen as more dynamic structures, inhabited by ever-changing collectives of actors. Consequently, these studies call for a more flexible concept of both architectural and social household units.[8] The potential for these studies to similarly illuminate the archaeological investigation of workshops frames the following discussion.

Workgroup Organization and the Workplace

Physical Units v. Social Units

Scholars specializing in the archaeological study of domestic activities have differentiated between houses ('the physical structures of dwellings',[9] i.e. physical units) *versus* households ('an activity group whose members share in production, consumption, transmission, distribution, reproduction, and co-residence',[10] i.e., social units). This distinction is crucial as households (or workgroups for that matter) are not directly observable in the archaeological record, but rather are inferred by associating physical remains with activity patterns.[11] This has implications for our assumptions concerning the organization of work in antiquity, as well as its relationship to built structures and spatial patterning of work activities.

Many archaeological studies have centred on the 'workshop' as the basic analytical unit of production sites. As workshops typically form discrete, architecturally delineable spaces, they present an easily identifiable unit of production organization. By emphasizing the architectural workshop over the labour workgroup, however, some forms of organization have come to be lumped together based on certain expectations. In such cases, the 'workgroup' may directly correspond with the 'workshop'; however, as will be discussed

---

8 Bermejo Tirado (2010); Hales (2003); Allison (2004); Perring (2002); Lavan, Özgenel, and Sarantis (2007); Bon and Jones (1997); Lawrence and Wallace-Hadrill (1997).

9 Allison (1998: 17).

10 Alexander (2006: 81).

11 Allison (1998).

subsequently, this relationship should not necessarily be assumed. Still, this distinction should not be seen to undermine the utility of the workshop as a unit of analysis for understanding spatial organization of economic activities. Rather, its utility is best suited to address specific sets of questions, such as those related to property rights and elite investment, and less for the study of small-scale relationships among workers and their internal organization within the workplace.[12]

Following this approach, the 'workgroup' (rather than the workshop) forms a basic economic and social production unit. From an economic point of view, our interest lies in their size, internal organization, product output, and task responsibilities. From a social point of view, the workgroup forms a collective of individuals whose collaborative work activities require intense daily interpersonal interaction. Yet in the context of the workplace, the social and economic are inextricably entangled. Such interaction can serve either to reinforce or deflate differences between workers based on specializations, skill level, legal responsibilities, ethnicity, and social status. Analyses of stamps on *terra sigillata*, tile, and brick have provided important information on ceramicists and workshop owners; only occasionally, however, is it possible to attribute other work specializations and establish hierarchies of workers at known production settings.[13] Yet this is not to say that understanding the inner mechanics of production organization at a site is beyond the reach of archaeological study. Indeed, in the setting of a workplace, both specialization in work tasks and collective work activities can be inferred from the material record.

One reason that the workgroup is difficult to employ as a primary analytical unit is that its archaeological identification requires a highly detailed level of excavation analysis that reconstructs the production process through its 'chaîne opératoire'[14] (sequence of operations) within the architectural context. In this way, by identifying the distribution of production activities within a workshop, it is possible in some cases to spatially distinguish the production activities of individual workgroups and compare them to the overall workshop plan.[15] Repetitious infrastructure can thereby be identified, highlighting the

12 But see Flohr in this volume.

13 A few examples can be suggested by kiln docets from other sites, such as Arezzo and Pisa. See Camodeca (2006); Johnston (1985).

14 Leroi-Gourhan (1993).

15 The interpretive basis of these reconstructions also is predicated on a large sample of comparable sites with which it is possible to discern meaningful patterns in the archaeological record and appropriate consideration of the formative processes of the archaeological record (Schiffer 1987).

number of individuals performing similar tasks and the relationship between craft specialists within a workgroup. Furthermore, the spatial relationship between individual workstations and their spatial distribution can be used to infer the practicalities of working together and the intensity of day-to-day interaction among workers. Establishing the distinction between the built environment and workgroup organization is especially important in situations where the workgroup does not appear to strictly correspond to architectural confines of the workshop.

These points are best brought out through a quick comparison of two cases in which the workshop perimeters do not exclusively correspond to workgroups. In this case, two production sites of red slipped table ware will be used as examples—La Graufesenque (ancient Condatomagus, southern France) and Scoppieto (western Italy). Both sites were large-scale production centres for red slipped ware, during the first century BC to second century AD, and their wares were widely distributed. Regarding the locations of the sites, La Graufesenque's ceramic workshops were located across the Dourbie River from the centre of a *vicus*. It can effectively be considered a part of the larger community with the town's theatre and several cultic buildings situated in and around the workshops. Scoppieto was situated in the territory of Todi. Its location along the Tiber River connected it to a wider network including Rome and Ostia. Generally, these production centres cannot be easily classified as either urban or rural industries, but nevertheless both should be seen as important components of larger communities.

When we turn to the workshop remains at La Graufesenque, the organization of the production cycle is largely centred on the small-scale production unit. Most workshops here are modestly sized units containing the necessary equipment for processing and preparing clay, as well as for throwing vessels.[16] Small work rooms contain the remains of one, two, or (in relatively uncommon instances) three wheels, as well as a clay processing basin. The size of the clay basins is also relatively modest (c. 1 m by 1 m). Each production unit employed the same clays and shared access to water sources through wells or canals. The excavators distinguished production units around groupings of rooms. Small kilns were often provisioned in the vicinity of the work units.

In addition to the kilns associated with specific work units, other signs of organization could be involved in the firing stage of the production cycle. Indeed, one of the reasons that La Graufesenque is so well known among production sites is largely due to the preservation of kiln docets—vessels with graffiti scratched through the slip prior to firing and then subsequently fired in

---

16 All excavation details from Schaad (2007).

the kiln. The docets in many cases record the numbers of vessels contributed by individual potters to kiln firings operated by a specialised 'maître-fournier'.[17] These are believed to be a sort of accounting practice maintained among the workshops, whereby different potters contribute their wares to a communal firing.[18] This interpretation of the docets has been corroborated by the discovery of several large kilns and, in particular, the 'grand four' (an especially large kiln excavated at the site measuring c. 6 m by 7 m in plan).[19] Whether or not every production unit pooled their vessels according to this kiln organization, the presence of the 'maître-fournier' nonetheless demonstrates a high degree of task-based worker specialization, at least in the final, firing stage of production. This is of particular note as the overall size of the workshop units remained rather modest and seems to have been provisioned with adequate infrastructure to perform all other stages of the production process.

When turning to the production site of Scoppieto, the built environment strongly contrasts that of La Graufesenque. Like La Graufesenque, spaces can be attributed to different stages of the production process, but at Scoppieto, they are distributed in a very different way. There are large clay basins with channels provisioning water, a long gallery of over 20 potters' wheels, and a large kiln.[20] This built environment offers some important points in terms of considering interaction among workers and workgroups. In the case of Scoppieto, the workgroups seem to be organised according to a spatial division of the primary labour tasks (i.e., clay preparation, wheel throwing, and kiln firing). Moreover, the potters were spatially restricted from other work activities. Preparation of the clay and firing was not visible from the workstations of most of the potters, and clay preparation and firing were of scales large enough to provision the suite of potters, collectively. The use of distance and spatial restriction served to reinforce difference among groups, in this case based on work task.

This is most conspicuous at Scoppieto in the case of the potters, who are tightly clustered next to one another.[21] Each was provisioned with a small (c. 1 m by 1.5 m) workstation including a wheel, window, and small hearth. The potters were crowded together and give the appearance of a workgroup (or perhaps a nested workgroup within the larger operation). The independent nature of

17 Marichal (1988).

18 This is a term coined by Marichal (1988).

19 Recent scholarship by Schaad and Vernhet (2007: 203) has reinterpreted this kiln as a tile and brick kiln, yet the traditional interpretation cited above still generally holds traction.

20 Excavation details from Bergamini (2007).

21 *Ibid.*

the potters is further suggested by the presence of decorative stamps made in a foreign clay type. These stamps are believed to have been transported to the site by potters from other production sites.[22] Information retrieved from stamp markings on vessels at Scoppieto provide names of individuals known to have been active at another Italian *terra sigillata* site, Arezzo.[23] The potters at Scoppieto, although part of a larger workgroup of potters at their wheels, appear to have been operating also as artisans moving individually from one production site to another.

In both the above cases, the internal organization of workgroups seems to be reflected in architectural and spatial distribution of activities, yet they do not strictly correspond to the unit of 'workshop'. Repetitious infrastructure highlights the number of individuals performing similar tasks and the intensity of interaction with craft specialists within and between workgroups. The spatial relationship between individual workstations and task-specific activities reflects different levels of face-to-face engagement among specialised workers. Both of these cases have been used as examples of large-scale *sigillata* manufactories, which have been characterised as a sort of common industry with shared features of large-scale production.[24] Yet, although output at each site was undeniably great, the organization of workers producing those goods was quite divergent, as would have been the lived experience of workers at these two sites. At La Graufesenque the workgroup seems to centre on smaller numbers of workers potentially performing a wider range of work tasks, while at Scoppieto, the workgroup seems to be based on a group of individuals performing the same task with less accessibility to other parts of the process.

Dynamic Structures

Households, like workgroups, are not static entities through time. Allison has noted that the life histories of houses can be quite complex and their form can be adapted and redefined according to the needs and decisions accumulated through several generations of inhabitants.[25] As such, they represent palimpsests of domestic decision making, both at the individual level and across generations. Recognition of these complex histories has even prompted some scholars to use the 'household series' (i.e., 'the sequence of households that

22 Bergamini (2007: 64).

23 *Ibid.*

24 Peacock (1982).

25 Allison (1998).

successively inhabit a given structure or house over a span of more than one generation')[26] as a basic unit of analysis.[27]

Turning to the case of workshops, with over century-long occupations documented at some sites, the built environment acquired for manufacturing would in many cases not have been designed by later generations of workers or by artisans at a property. Structural renovations and adaptations to meet the changing needs of different workgroups can thereby be witnessed archaeologically. The ethnographic study by Papadopoulos on pottery workshops on Thasos demonstrates that architectural and infrastructural changes to a workshop can reflect changes in the very personal histories of the people working there (e.g., individual disputes, growth of families).[28] The size and composition of workgroups could be dependent on a variety of other factors as well, such as the lifecycle of workers, the season of the year, and economic investment or downsizing. The dynamic nature of Roman workgroups likewise has been archaeologically observed in the case of La Graufesenque, where stamps have been used to reconstruct relationships between potters working in the same workshop.[29] Those studies have demonstrated the movement of individual craftsmen between workshops and changes in position of individuals within the workgroup.

Occasionally, production sites offer highly detailed chronological evidence for the rates at which productive spaces were changed through time. For instance, at the tile, brick, and amphora production site of Amphoralis (southern France) expansion and contraction of the rural facilities could be tracked through three centuries of activities. During that time, the site experienced a series of structural phases in which major changes were made to the organization of workspaces.[30] Floor surfaces were re-levelled, old kilns were dismantled or left in disrepair and new kilns constructed—sometimes even in the remains of abandoned workshop rooms. In terms of economic growth, these changes have been tracked archaeologically. Kiln volumes were calculated by Laubenheimer and were used as proxies to gauge increased output up until the final phase of production at the site.[31] The phasing of structural alterations shows that expansion of the workshop facilities did not occur steadily over time. Rather, within relatively short periods of time, major modifications were

26 Smith (1992: 30), as cited in Alexander (2006: 81).

27 For an overview of this discussion, see Alexander (2006: 80–81).

28 Papadopoulos (1995).

29 Dannell (2001: 232).

30 All excavation details from Laubenheimer (2001).

31 Laubenheimer (2001: 24).

made to the workshops that seem to have dramatically affected the composition and organization of the workgroups. The excavators note some of these changes as occurring within 10–15 year periods, i.e. within the career of individual workers.[32]

Many of these alterations represent major investments in production infrastructure, such as the construction of an entirely independent workshop area with two large kilns (dated from c. AD 30 to 40, Phase 3A).[33] Over time there seems to be a shift from multiple small-scale workshop units capable of supporting the entire workshop cycle (from c. 10 BC to AD 50/60, Phases 1–3) to a consolidation of the potters within large, gallery-styled throwing rooms (from AD 50/60 to 300, Phases 4–5).[34] These gallery-style throwing rooms are reminiscent of the organization found at Scoppieto for table ware production, in which wheels were lined up along the walls of a long room.[35] These changes do not represent a sort of total replacement of one organizational structure with another, however. In fact, from AD 50/60 to 200 (Phases 4A and 4B) small-scale workshop units operated alongside the newly constructed gallery-styled throwing rooms.

When we compare the detailed phasing at Amphoralis with that of another rural production site at Yvelines (southern France), we see that the built environment of production at Yvelines also expanded from the first to the third centuries AD. Here, relatively small-scale production units increased in number over time in a concentrated area.[36] Newly built workshops were associated with new domestic structures nearby. In contrast to the barrack-style housing at Amphoralis, the households (like the workshops) at Yvelines were independent structures. The small Yvelines workshops were never integrated into larger facilities. Instead, the work organization appears to have been based on parallel, independent workgroups that was echoed in its organization of domestic spaces.

The historical development of these two production sites took very different trajectories, about which a few points should be raised. First, dramatic changes in the organization of work could occur relatively quickly (even within the lived experience of a single potter). Second, different types of worker organization could be in operation contemporaneously at the same production site.

32 *Ibid.*

33 *Ibid.*

34 Phasing designations and dates are from Laubenheimer (2001).

35 For Scoppieto reference, see Bergamini (2007). Schaad and Vernhet (2007: 154) also reference a similar throwing gallery at the sigillata production site at Rozier (Lozère).

36 Excavation details from Dufaÿ, Barat, and Raux (1997).

Third, expansion of industry at a site can be expressed in different ways. At Amphoralis, expansion gradually resulted in the integration of workers into larger, gallery-style work spaces, while at Yvelines expansion was expressed entirely through the construction of small, parallel production units. Perhaps just as importantly, some of these changes correspond to the internal arrangement and distribution of households at the two sites suggesting that work and domestic life in these rural communities reflected broader patterns in socio-economic organization.

The above comparison is based on changes at chronological resolutions that could be experienced by individual labourers, but other changes would also probably have been experienced within shorter periods of time. In a work environment, such as a pottery workshop, different temporal rhythms co-occur. On the one hand, time can be inferred from the cyclical nature of the production process. That cyclical nature is punctuated at certain points. For instance, ethnographic studies suggest that during the ceramic production process, kiln firing represents the most precarious point in the entire production cycle.[37] It is typically the most expensive stage, and it is a point of no return—from then on the clay can no longer be recovered from the vessel. On the other hand, ethnographic studies have also demonstrated that issues of seasonality have practical concerns related to meteorological change that adversely impact working conditions (e.g., the difficulties of extracting clay from a frozen ground, the time necessary to dry vessels in wet months, the amount of fuel consumed by winter kiln firings).[38] Seasonality is also critical to the agricultural cycle, which might likewise dictate a schedule to ceramic production.[39]

Evidence for such co-occurring temporal rhythms can be found in the archaeological record, as well. Marichal, in his study of the kiln docets from La Graufesenque, has noted that any given 'maître-fournier' would only perform 10 to 11 firings per year, and that there was a strong seasonality to the firings—occurring between the months of March and October.[40] Thus, he calculates that firings would have occurred approximately once every three weeks. This type of organization probably set a very specific 'clock' for the La Graufesenque production process, against which that potters would have had to work. When turning to the issue of workgroups, as the ties holding the labourers together (i.e. ceramic production) influenced by seasonal patterns, this suggests that

37 Sheppard (1956: 74–75).

38 Arnold (1985: 61–98).

39 *Ibid.* (99–108).

40 Marichal (1988: 98).

ceramic workgroups may have been seasonally influenced as well, with workgroup size fluctuating with periods of high and low activity.

This concern over seasonality and rhythms of productive time certainly held even greater relevance to other ceramic industries, such as amphora production. As containers of perishable goods, it was imperative that the production cycle of such ceramics was 'one step ahead' of the agricultural harvest. This is echoed in one of the few lease contracts of a pottery extant from the Roman period preserved on a papyrus from Oxyrhynchus, Egypt, and dated to the second century AD.[41] Its stipulations between the owner of the property and the potter are interesting for a number of reasons, but the point to emphasise here is the explicit timeline placed on production activity. This was to be performed in the offseason (in this case, winter) in order to be pitched and ready for filling by the wine harvest. Vessel counts were also specified in this contract thereby establishing not only a productive 'clock' but also a productive output. This evidence for production cycles and social and economic perceptions of time at La Graufesenque and Oxyrhynchus demonstrate that different workshops functioned under differing and yet co-occurring rhythms of production. Such rhythms set timelines of work intensity and also might impact different compositions of workers at different points in the production cycle.

Wider Communities and Flexible Spaces

As the household has come to be viewed within larger, contemporary social conglomerations, the experience of living is seen not to stop at the threshold of the house, but to extend to larger social groups, most notably to the neighbourhood, town, village, or city. Moreover, activity patterns within household spaces fail to fall neatly into predefined categories of behaviour (i.e. social, economic, or ritual). Houses are consequently viewed, not simply as isolated settings of dwelling, but also as venues for social, economic, and ritual activities.[42] Just as the household was part of larger social spheres, workshops were also part of larger communities that reinforced the nature of relations among workers. Furthermore, as evidenced archaeologically, workshops could be venues, not only of work tasks, but also ritual activity.

These considerations are of merit as we know that many of these potters, particularly in rural settings, were not only co-workers, but they were also neighbours. Again, at Amphoralis and Yvelines, small housing units were situated adjacent to the workshops.[43] Excavations of these structures at Amphoralis

41 *P. Oxy.* L 3595–3597, in Cockle (1981) and Bowman (1983: 234–244).

42 Bermejo Tirado (2010); Allison (1998); Gasparini. (2010); Es-Sadra (2010).

43 For Amphoralis, see Laubenheimer 2001. For Yvelines, see Dufaÿ, Barat, and Raux (1997).

suggest that workers lived with their families on-site in a sort of barrack-style arrangement. Thus, the workshops were not only workplaces; they were the foci of communities. This tie can be further witnessed in the burial of fourteen infants (less than 6 months of age) inhumed within the walls and under the floors of active workshops. The use of work spaces for the interment of children even continued after their disuse.[44] This association is echoed at La Graufesenque where a burial containing several infants was found under the front doorstep of what is believed to be a workshop,[45] and at Lezoux stillborns were interred in buildings near the kilns.[46] Laubenheimer has even posited a connection between the burial of infants in workshops with those often found associated with houses.[47] Although the meaning of these interments is still not clear, such practices undeniably demonstrate a close tie between these workplaces and the social history of the local community.

Other forms of ritual activity are also evident at some of these production sites. At La Graufesenque, ritual activities were situated in close proximity to the workshops in the 'aire cultuelle central', whereby cult buildings were constructed immediately adjacent to the industrial areas.[48] In addition to these well-known cultic structures,[49] a small votive deposit was also found in one of the workshop units.[50] These ritual activities demonstrate that the workshops were not only integrated into communal cultic areas, but that ritual activities were brought into the workshops. Such evidence for domestic structures and ritual activities demonstrates how intimately work activities could be tied to social practices and community topographies.

Broader Implications: Economic Strategy and the Production Unit

Thus far, social aspects of workshops have been emphasised in this chapter. However, the distinction between production workgroups and workshops also holds relevance for broader discussions of economic organization and

44 Coulon (1994: 141–142, 160–162).

45 The burial was located in 'Piece 2' as referenced in Schaad and Vernhet (2007: 155).

46 Coulon (1994: 162).

47 Laubenheimer (1988).

48 Schaad and Vernhet (2007: 92–133).

49 Significant attention has been paid to the two 'Gallo-Roman *fana*' (dated to late second / mid first centuries BC and the first century AD); a small 'Greco-Roman temple' (dated to the second century AD); and a 'sanctuary' (dated to the first and second centuries AD). See Schaad and Vernhet (2007: 165–171).

50 Designated 'Pièce 9' in Schaad and Vernhet (2007: 158–159).

investment strategies during the Roman period. In fact, several scholars have come to see the small-scale work unit as the basic organizational unit of production activities in the Roman period, with industry expansion typically occurring laterally through the establishment of parallel, small-scale workshops.[51] As Robinson argues, elite investment strategies in urban workshops at Pompeii tended to favour small-scale workshops.[52] He interprets these patterns as reflecting elite strategies that maintained a diversified and divisible body of investments. Such property investments could thereby be more easily distributed for inheritance purposes. McCormick also notes the trend as being prevalent in economic systems of Late Antiquity, which he sees as being unable to maintain the large-scale units of earlier Roman periods.[53] He argues that competition among small-scale establishments encouraged greater production and kept rents high for landlords. Additionally, in a contract based system, potters may not have had the capital to rent large-scale facilities, and landlords may have preferred to keep the production units small in order to protect their interests from highly successful (and thereby potentially competitive) renters.[54] In these discussions, the small-scale production unit is seen to represent property investment strategies.

Certainly elite investment, particularly in urban or estate properties, played an important role in the scale of production facilities. However, as this paper argues, workgroup decision making concerning to the practicalities of work experience in some cases also seems to have been taken into consideration. From the examples cited in this paper, even when certain parts of the production process were integrated into bigger organizations, such as with the large-scale kiln firings at La Graufesenque, it does not necessarily imply that every other part of the production process was likewise integrated into larger production units; nor were small and large workgroups mutually exclusive. As the case of Amphoralis shows, production units following different organizational structures could operate alongside one another at the same site. Finally, the scale of production units, when centred on temporal rhythms of production and the workgroup, could fluctuate—not only within the time span of a single potter's career, but also within short-term production work cycles and seasons. These observations suggest that the analytical distinction between workshop

51 Dannell (2002: 214–215); McCormick (2001: 58–59).

52 Robinson (2005).

53 McCormick (2001: 58–59). It is important to note that McCormick also identifies these trends in the mining industry, the organization of which was based on workgroup and mine-shafts units, rather than a more property-based workshop structure.

54 *Ibid.*

and workgroup are therefore not only germane to deconstructing the social experience of work, but also its implications on economic organization.

Conclusion

This paper has attempted to demonstrate some of the potential that the archaeological investigation of production sites offers in developing our understanding of workers and their organization in the Roman world. Drawing upon recent trends in household archaeology, the study of workgroups as a unit of analysis offers a means to reconstruct workshops as places of both economic and social activity. As has been demonstrated in just the few cases presented here from Gaul and Italy, workers and their activities could be organised in numerous ways, and across various configurations of workgroup. Such workgroups were dynamic bodies themselves, employing different sets of agents at different points in the production cycle and at different times of the year. These organizational patterns were contingent on the historical development of each site, which experienced unique series of transformations that could even contemporaneously bring together different types of organization. Moreover, as few textual references to workers in industries, such as ceramic industries, are extant from the period. Such investigation of production sites offers an area where archaeology uniquely has much to contribute to questions of ancient work and its organization.

CHAPTER 8

Constructing Occupational Identities in the Roman World

Miko Flohr

Perhaps the most complex issue in the history of work and labour in the Roman world is to understand how the everyday working lives of craftsmen impacted upon the way in which these people came to shape their occupational identities. While, in recent years, there has been a decent amount of literature on the way in which occupational identities played a role in (semi-)official public discourse in urban communities, particularly through professional associations, and while some have explored the way in which work and legal status interacted in shaping personal identities that were commemorated on funerary plaques and monuments, there can be no doubt that the most significant context in which occupational identities were negotiated actually was the shop floor and its direct urban environment.[1] This is an environment that has been very hard to grasp for modern scholars: it is almost completely invisible in our textual sources, and any argument has to be constructed on the basis of generally badly preserved and often badly published remains of workshops identifiable in the archaeological record. In the large majority of cases, these material remains only reveal partial and indirect information about what was going on in workshops on an everyday basis, and the number of archaeological sites that has returned high-quality evidence for urban manufacturing and retail is exceptionally limited: outside the Vesuvian region and the metropolitan area of Rome and its port cities, only a limited number of production processes has been reliably identified, and the evidence is, besides a few exceptions, of much lower quality than the well-preserved workshops of Pompeii, Herculaneum, Ostia and Rome.

Yet this should not deter us: the spatial context within which people spend their working days conditions the impact, and thus, the meaning of formal labour relations, and plays a key role in the construction of social lives. Indeed, scholars discussing modern factories have emphasized how their spatial layout

1 On professional associations see e.g. van Nijf (1997) and the chapters by Verboven and Liu. On epigraphic commemoration of craftsmen see esp. Treggiari (1975b; 1976; 1980); Joshel (1992).

 | DOI 10.1163/9789004331686_009

could contribute to processes of social control.[2] The spatial disposition of the work environment shapes the communicative landscape during working hours and has a decisive impact on the social effects of task allocation: where you work determines how and with whom you can most easily communicate.[3] Spatial factors also determine the degree to which workers could publicly negotiate occupational identities with outsiders: it matters whether you are mending clothes in a small shop on a busy street, or in a large hall in a factory on an enclosed property, even if all other aspects of your working life—such as task, employment and civic status—are roughly equal.[4] Indeed, one could question what, really, can be said of the everyday world of a worker on the basis of epigraphic information about occupation and legal status, or on the basis of brief references in literary texts written by authors who themselves were mostly proud not to know this world from inside.[5] Tellingly, one of the most detailed descriptions of a workshop focuses not on the people, but rather on the sad life of the donkeys who were operating the flour mills.[6] Without any detailed and reliable information about the place where somebody worked, it is very hard to grasp the socioeconomic meaning of the craft performed: its precise impact was to a considerable extent negotiated on and around the shop floor.

The aim of this chapter is therefore to discuss how the spatial organization and contextualization of shops and workshops in the Roman world conditioned the working lives of the people who spent their days on the shop floor, and how this relates to our view on the history of labour in the Roman world. A little bit of work has been done on this topic in recent years; the present author has discussed, to some length, the way in which the everyday working lives of *fullones* were conditioned by the spatial layout of fulling workshops in Ostia and Pompeii; Lauren Hackworth-Petersen and Sandra Joshel have to some extent further developed this approach in discussing how the material conditions of work places had an impact on the working lives of Roman slaves.[7] The aim here is to discuss a more general model for the spatial

2 Newbery (2013: 19–20). Cf. Rofel (1992); Stein (1995: esp. 289–291). See also Mellor (2005).

3 Cf. Newbery (2013: 24–26).

4 Cf. Mellor (2005: 51–55) on the spatial hierarchy in modern factories, where those doing the actual work were also the furthest removed from the entrance ('backstage'), while business was done much closer to public space ('front stage').

5 The proverbial reference is, of course, Cic., *Off.* 1.150. On this reference see esp. Finley (1999: 41–42). Cf. Treggiari (1975a); Morel (1989: 235); Flohr and Wilson (2016: 1–3).

6 Apul., *Met.* 9.11–14.

7 Flohr (2009; 2013); Joshel and Hackworth-Petersen (2014: esp. 118–161). See also Beavis (2015).

infrastructure of occupational identity and apply it to a broader selection of evidence for manufacturing from Roman Italy. Particular focus will be on the material remains of shops and workshops. The study this evidence has flourished over the last two decades, and both the amount and the accessibility of the evidence has increased dramatically.[8] More than in the past, archaeologists in the field include the visually less impressive remains of everyday life into their investigation, or even specifically focus on datasets related to economic activities.[9] This has to some extent begun to change the scholarly field, though the amount of analytical models available for the material remains of shops and workshops is still much smaller than for example is the case with houses and public monuments.[10] Indeed, most scholars studying the material remains of shops and workshops have focused on identifying production processes and, beyond that, on issues of output level and production technology.[11]

The increased attention for shops and workshops has however made quite clear that there was some variation in the scale and context of investment in retail and manufacturing in the Roman world. For the cities of Roman Italy, it seems sensible to distinguish three key models of investment:

1. The *taberna*: these small-scale, shop-like structures consist of a main room with a wide opening from the street and, sometimes a couple of back rooms or a small upper floor for living space.[12] Typically, *tabernae* were part of a larger whole—a house, or a public building—and rented out or filled by the owner of the complex.
2. The medium-sized domestic workshop: in this model, a workshop was attached to or incorporated in a house, with both the workshop and the house taking up a significant proportion of the property. Domestic workshops tend to take up more space than a *taberna* provided, and included more equipment.[13]
3. The large-scale production hall: this concerns large-scale investment in manufacturing in large, purpose-built structures which did not also have

8 Cf. Flohr and Wilson (2016).

9 See, for example, the 'Artifex' programme of the Centre Jean Bérard. Cf. Brun (2016); Borgard *et al.* (2003).

10 For houses see e.g. Wallace-Hadrill (1994); Hales (2003).

11 E.g. Wilson (2002b); Poblome (2004); Monteix (2011). See for a parallel in the study of modern industry Mellor (2005: 49). See also Murphy in this volume.

12 Pirson (1999); Laurence (2007).

13 Flohr (2007: 136–141).

significant space for domestic purposes attached to them, and were completely tailored to their productive needs.[14]

These models can be found throughout the Italian peninsula and beyond, but not in an equal manner. Small-scale units like *tabernae* arguably represent the norm: they are commonly found throughout the Roman world, and are the standard architectural form for retail and manufacturing in Roman Italy.[15] The two other models were considerably less common. Domestic workshops have been found in a variety of places, most prominently Pompeii, but also in, for example, Volubilis and Saepinum, though they appear less frequently in smaller urban centres.[16] Production halls have, in an urban context, mostly been identified in the metropolitan area of Rome, and seem to have been highly exceptional elsewhere.[17]

These three investment models will be the basis for the following discussion of the way in which everyday life on the shop floor had an impact on the social lives and occupational identities of workers. It is convenient to think of the shop floor in terms of an 'infrastructure of identity': the physical work environment created a platform on which the actual processes of identity negotiation could take place. Obviously, other factors, such as status, background and personal histories, also played a role in this respect: a similar work environment could lead to different outcomes for each individual. However, this does not mean that the spatial configuration of the workshop did not make certain outcomes more (un)likely than others; the issue at stake in this chapter is how this process worked.

To understand this, it is essential to discuss the professional network in which people spent the working day. In the model proposed here, this professional network of craftsmen is envisaged as consisting of four key social layers, which, in decreasing order of direct impact, are:

1. The work group: these are the people with whom workers were most frequently in touch during the working day because they were working in the same establishment. It is of course essential to discuss how work groups may or may not have functioned.

---

14 Bakker (1999); Pietrogrande (1976); De Ruyt (2001). On the terminology see now, correctly, Joshel and Hackworth-Petersen (2014: 151).

15 See e.g. Adam (1994: 320–322).

16 Volubilis: Riße (2001: 75). Saepinum: De Caro (1991).

17 See also Wilson (2008: 406–409). His only urban example outside Rome is the third century AD Chemtou marble workshop, which probably was imperially owned.

2. Clients and customers: the degree to and the way in which workers were able to interact with people consuming their products defines their everyday social experience and the relation they could develop with the product they made or sold.
3. Social superiors: proprietors may have an impact on the functioning of the workshop even if they were not (or not always) present: how independent were work groups, actually, and what does this (in)dependence mean in practical terms?
4. The outside urban community: the possibilities provided by the spatial embedding of a workshop to negotiate occupational identities with other inhabitants of the city are fundamental to the social status and occupational identity of workers.

In what follows, the impact of each of these four social layers will be explored.

The Work Group

To understand the role of the first social layer—that of the work group—in identity construction, four factors are crucial. First, the possibilities for communication on the shop floor; second, the social background of the staff network; third, the composition of the work force, and last but not least, the division of labour.

Communication on the Shop Floor

For the communicative landscape of the workshop, it is both the physical layout of the workshop that matters, and the size of the work group.[18] Small work groups working in one small room function differently from larger work groups or from work groups divided over a larger number of rooms.[19] The lower the amount of people, and the smaller the space, the closer the communicative ties during the working day. Conversely, in larger work groups, the communicative atmosphere would normally be more fragmented: individual workers would be able to communicate directly with a much lower proportion of their colleagues, and the amount of conversations developing simultaneously was, potentially, much higher. *Tabernae*, generally consisting of one or two rooms, and manned by a staff of only a few people, must be thought to have

18 For a case study of the communicative landscape of the *fullonicae* of Roman Italy see Flohr (2009; 2013a: 247–265).

19 See also the comments by Stein (1995: 289–291).

FIGURE 8.1 *Rome, Tomb of Eurysaces: detail of frieze depicting kneading, bread-shaping and baking.*

had a closely integrated communicative atmosphere. The opposite tends to be true in the case of the large-scale production halls, and the layout of the shop floor tended to reinforce this. For instance, the largest bakeries, like the one depicted on the monument of Eurysaces, had multiple bread-shaping tables, which impeded interaction between workers as you could only communicate with the people on your own table (fig. 8.1). Similarly, the linear arrangement of work installations in the largest fulleries in Rome and Ostia limited the communicative possibilities of workers.[20]

The domestic workshops take up an in-between position in this respect, though generally, their communicative landscapes seem closer to those of *tabernae* than to those of production halls. Often, they had more than one work room, but the size of their work rooms, and the number of workers, was limited, and the atmosphere within these rooms must have been rather intimate. Moreover, work rooms were often (though not always) clustered together in one part of the house.[21] For example, the workers in what probably

20 Flohr (2013a: 258–264); Joshel and Hackworth-Petersen (2014: 152–155).

21 Exceptions are cases where the workshop was situated in the back of the house while there also was a shop in front of the house, as is the case in *fullonicae* I 6, 7 and VI 14, 21–22 at Pompeii. On these specific cases, cf. Flohr (2013a: 162–163).

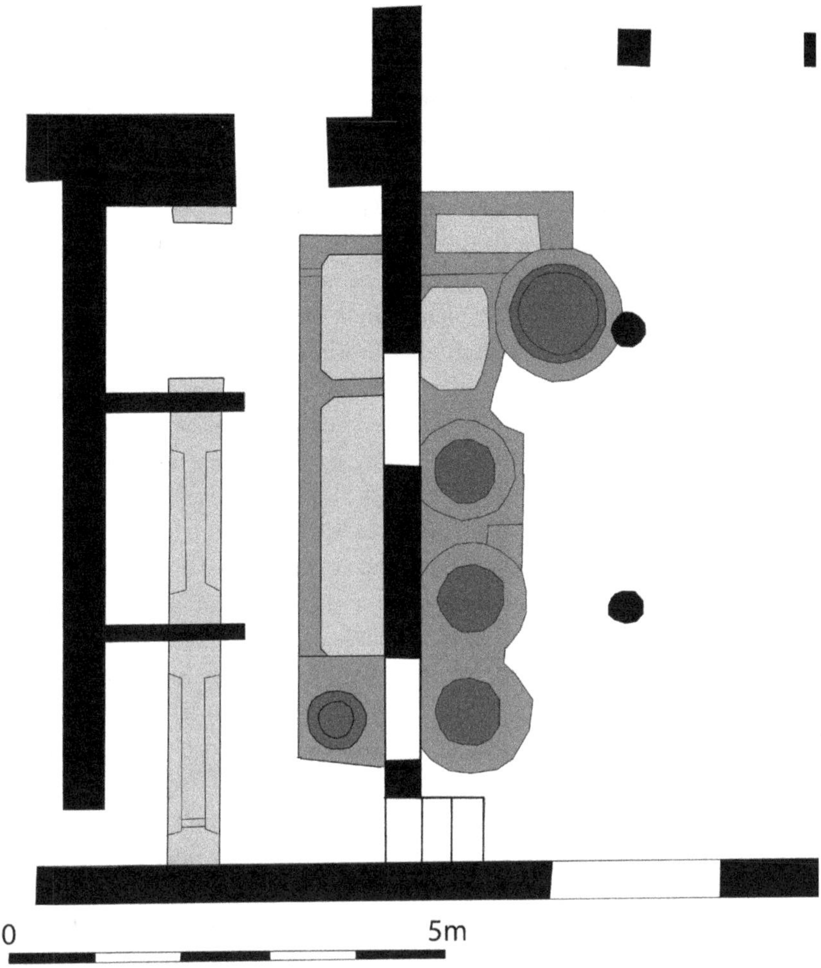

FIGURE 8.2 *Pompeii, workshop I 8, 19. Plan.*

was a felt-making workshop in the basement of house I 8, 1 at Pompeii could easily communicate with each other, and while communication with the dyeing workshop in an adjacent second work room was impeded by the wall separating the two, all workers in the basement were still within hearing distance of each other (fig. 8.2).[22]

22 On the interpretation of the felt-making workshop see Dickmann (2013); Flohr (2013b, 64–66). For a different view see Monteix (2013: 84–86). The exact interpretation of the

The Social Basis of Staff Networks

Besides the role played by the communicative landscape on the shop floor, the social ties between workers were also strongly influenced by the social basis of the staff network. Key question in this respect is whether or not workers also lived together and formed a household: belonging to the same household, and sharing private life beyond working hours, is likely to have made the social ties within the work group significantly stronger.[23] For *tabernae*, there seems to be a tendency towards the integration of working and living, but this is not always true: a substantial number of *tabernae* was not inhabitable, so that it remains unclear whether or not their workers shared more with each other than their working lives. Arguably, however, the limited number of people involved makes this less relevant: the intimate atmosphere on the shop floor made sure that social ties were close anyhow. This was different when workshops were larger. In the case of domestic workshops, evidence of kitchens and decorated rooms tends to suggest that the core of the staff network was made up by a household. In most cases, the social basis of this household is likely to have been a family, perhaps extended with some servants. At Pompeii, artefacts recovered from some houses with a workshop strongly suggest the presence of women.[24] In other cases, there is iconographic evidence suggesting the house was inhabited by a family. This may have been the case with the famous picture of the baker and his wife from bakery VII 2, 3.6 in Pompeii, and with the paintings from *fullonica* VI 8, 20–21.2, which show men, women and children involved in the work in the fullery (fig. 8.3).[25] While it cannot be excluded that the labour force in these workshops was occasionally supplemented by hired labourers, the staff network as a whole is likely to have been dominated by people actually living on the spot. A strong indication of this is that work areas are often situated closely to kitchen and other domestic service facilities (see e.g. below, fig. 8.6).

The large production halls that have been found in Rome and Ostia have no living accommodation attached to them: inhabitable upper floors are absent, unconnected or antedate the workshop. This strongly suggests that, when these establishments were first built, the housing of future workers was no issue, and consequently, that the people managing these workshops recruited their staff from a variety of sources. Given the generally abundant availability

---

function of the workshop in this case does not matter for the interpretation of its communicative landscape.

23 This elaborates upon Flohr (2013a: 265–273).

24 Flohr (2013a: 268–270).

25 On these paintings see Clarke (2003: 112–117); Flohr (2013a: 269).

FIGURE 8.3 *Paintings from fullonica VI 8, 20–21.2 at Pompeii showing fullers at work.*

of unskilled labour in the metropolitan area, this might also have been the most logical option.[26] The people working in these workshops thus generally did not belong to the same household and did not usually share all of their lives beyond working hours. It is important to emphasize that this adds to the already difficult communicative situation: for newcomers in these large work groups, it would take more time to get to know their colleagues on the shop floor than it would take in the smaller domestic workshops and *tabernae*, as they only saw their colleagues during working hours, and it was harder to talk to each and every one of them.

Composition of the Work Force

The social background of the staff network of a workshop had more consequences than just the intensity of ties between workers: it also had implications for the homogeneity of the work group. Obviously, family-based households tend to exist of more than one generation, including parents, children and perhaps the odd grandparent, and they include both sexes. Thus, households represent a naturally varied environment in which people could adopt to a more-or-less clearly defined social role depending on gender and age. The evidence at Pompeii also suggests that in many cases, households were relatively small, so that members of the family are likely to have participated actively in the everyday work.

An example is bakery VI 14, 33–34 in Pompeii (fig. 8.4), which had a small domestic zone around the *atrium* and an attached bakery that took up at least as much space. There is no reliable artefact record to prove this, but the house does not seem to provide enough space to envisage a scenario in which the main occupants spent their days with activities unrelated to the bakery.[27] It is true that there are examples of large elite households where one could imagine that the workshop was completely run by slaves—an obvious example is the bakery in the House of the Labyrinth in Pompeii—but such cases

26 Cf. Hawkins (2013: 347) for Rome. Joshel and Hackworth-Petersen (2014: 160–161) appear to assume, without further argument, that the workers in these establishments were slaves. See, however, Flohr (2013a: 270–272).

27 Many domestic artifacts were discovered on 14 september 1877 in room c, and reported by Fiorelli (1877: 221–222), but this may have been an arranged show excavation in honour of the French ambassador who visited the excavations on that day, so the reliability of the record is questionable.

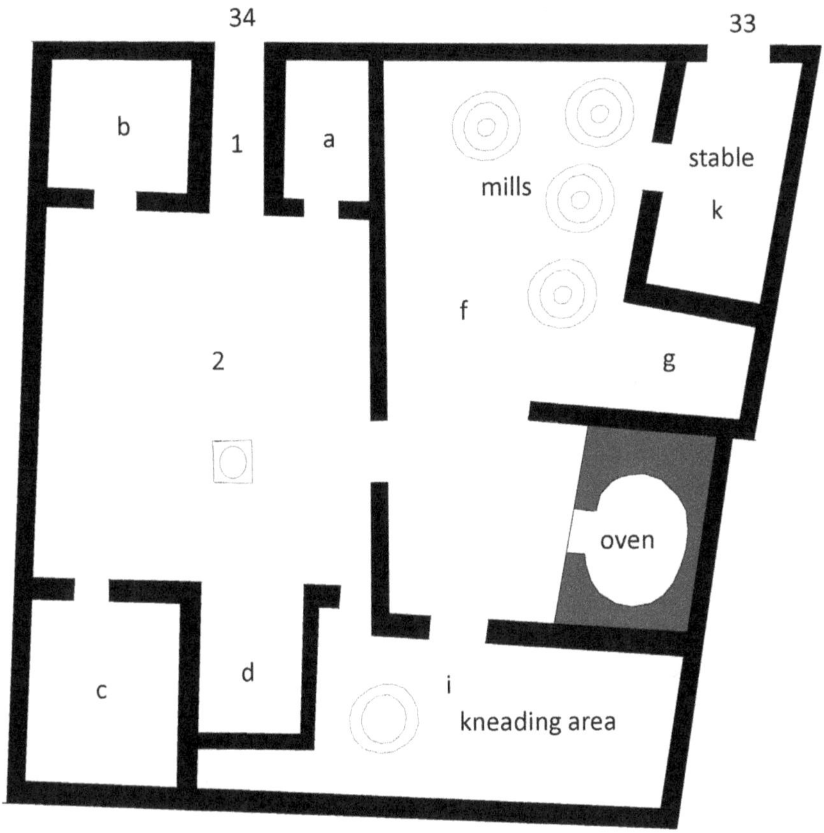

FIGURE 8.4 *Pompeii, house VII 14, 33–34. Plan.*

seem exceptions rather than the rule: most houses with workshops are of relatively moderate size.[28]

Staff networks were much less varied when they were based on hired or bought labour, as probably was the case in the large production halls. Here, workers were selected purely on the basis of their suitability for the job: while pre-existing social ties may occasionally play a role in this process, it is likely to result in much more homogeneous work groups, and in most manufacturing contexts this probably meant: more adult men. This also shows, rather clearly, on the reliefs on the tomb of Eurysaces, which depict 39 people involved in

28 On the House of the Labyrinth (VI 11, 8–9) see Strocka (1992). On the dimensions of houses with workshops in Pompeii see Flohr (2007).

the bakery, who are all male (fig. 8.1).[29] There may be differences in age and seniority within these work groups, obviously, but the social landscape is likely to have been much less articulated, and social roles were much less precisely defined. The contrast between the scenes on the tomb of Eurysaces (fig. 8.1) and the paintings from *fullonica* VI 8, 20–21.2 at Pompeii (fig. 8.3) is telling in this respect.

Division of Labour

As far as the division of labour is concerned, it is especially relevant to zoom in on the degree to which individual workers were able to master all aspects of the craft they performed. The standard cultural image in manufacturing seems to have been that of the skilled craftsman, who mastered the entire craft in all of its aspects.[30] Commemorative reliefs tend to depict craftsmen as working alone, implying that they were personally involved in the entire production process, and no doubt it was true that many small-scale workshops in *tabernae* were organized around the skills of one master craftsman—who then may have been assisted by a couple of servants or apprentices. Yet, this is not the whole story.

Already in the domestic workshops at Pompeii, there is evidence, especially in bakeries and fulleries, for a basic division of labour, with workers predominantly focusing on one specific phase of the process.[31] The size of these workshops, and the composition of the work force, implies that they must have had a basic system structuring task allocation limiting the range of activities for which each staff member was used. Yet it is also likely that there was some room for variation—work groups were still relatively small, so that task allocation was easily manageable. In the large production halls, logistics required a rigid division of labour, which for workers is likely to have resulted in a much narrower action radius. For example, in the large metropolitan bakeries of Rome and Ostia, it is likely that many people spent most of their days kneading or shaping bread, whereas in the large fulleries, most workers never did anything else than trampling textiles. Something similar may be happening in the large production centres of pottery, such as la Graufesenque, where the shaping of vessels is disconnected from their firing, and where the increased use of stamps and moulds reduced the production process to a repetition of

29 Cf. Zimmer (1982: 107–108).

30 See the papers in Monteix and Tran (2011).

31 For fulleries see Flohr (2013a: 281–285). For the bakeries see Monteix (2016).

rather simple tasks.[32] Such rigid divisions of labour meant that people specialized in a small part of the production process, which inevitably led to deskilling. This, in turn, put restrictions on the degree to which workers could develop an occupational identity: if you only knead the loaves or mill the grain, you probably are less inclined to call yourself a baker; if you spend your day trampling clothes, you may not identify a fuller, but rather as a labourer.

Customers

The relation of a worker with the final product and its consumer is one of the most defining aspects of his professional identity. This relation, of course, is partially defined by the nature of the product: the relation between a baker and a passer-by buying bread is fundamentally different from that of a goldsmith working on a commissioned piece of jewellery with its future owner, and so, probably, is the occupational pride attached to it (see Tran in this volume). Generally, one could expect that intensity of the relation between producer and consumer was positively related to the exclusivity of the craft performed: if a product was more expensive, or had to be tailor-made, interaction and trust between producer and consumer was more urgently needed. Arguably, the nature of interactions between producer and consumer also played a key role in the construction of professional identities: dealing with customers involved a semi-public evaluation of one's professional capacities. To some extent, this also shows in the (commemorative) epigraphic record, which clearly privileges craftsmen catering for more exclusive markets.[33] However, the location and spatial organization of the workshop itself also played a role in this respect: to which extent was the production process, actually, visible to customers, and to which extent could workers visibly identify with the final product that was sold? The crucial parameter, in this respect, is of course the presence of a space that can be identified as a shop—that is, a space with a wide opening onto the street and, ideally, a threshold equipped with the characteristic groove that held the wooden shutters.[34]

32 On mass production in the pottery industry see Peacock (1982: 114–128); Greene (1986: 159–161).

33 Cf. Flohr (2013a: 330–331, esp. Table 6).

34 Adam (1994: 320–321).

Working with a Shop

In the case of *tabernae*, the workshop itself often functioned as a shop. Workshops situated in *tabernae* generally seem to have interacted directly with customers, and the small size of the work group, as well as the modest dimensions of the place ensured that most workers got their fair share of the interaction with customers that took place. As individual workers, due to the small size of the work group, are likely to have been involved in a variety of phases of the production process, they also could identify rather strongly with the final result. Conversely, customers saw how the product that they were interested in was produced, and could assess the quality of the product on the basis of what they saw on the shop floor.

In other contexts, the situation was more complicated. While the large production halls of Rome and Ostia generally did not have shops, about half of the domestic workshops at Pompeii and Herculaneum did.[35] However, in these establishments, the proportion of the workers that stood in direct contact with customers was much lower: often, the main working area was in another part of the house, and not directly connected with the shop. For example, in two of the larger *fullonicae* of Pompeii, and in several bakeries, the workshop was in the back of the house, and direct communication with the shop was impossible.[36] This meant that workers did not see customers, and that customers could not see the production process, or only part of it. Nevertheless, if necessary, there was the possibility for customers to interact directly with those responsible for the work.

Manufacturing without a Shop

When there was no shop related to a workshop, there were two possibilities: either, products were sold elsewhere in the city by people involved in the workshop, or they were sold on and reached the consumer through trade and retail. Both scenarios are, of course, impossible to identify in the archaeological record on the level of individual workshops. The first scenario is, however, attested on the funerary altar of Lucius Cornelius Atimetus, which seems to come from Rome.[37] The altar shows two scenes from the work of a craftsman involved in metalworking. On one side, we see the craftsman at work in his workshop, hammering on a piece of metal held by a co-worker. On the other

35 In Pompeii, 42% (11 out of 26) of the workshops situated in atrium houses had a shop. Cf. Flohr (2007: 148).

36 *Fullonicae* I 6, 7 and VI 14, 21–22. Cf. bakeries VI 14, 28–32 and VII 1, 37.

37 *CIL* VI 16166 (p. 3519, 3913); Zimmer (1982: 180–182). See also the contribution by Hawkins in this volume.

FIGURE 8.5 *Altar of Atimetus and Epaphra. 18th century drawing showing the two scenes from Atimetus' professional life depicted on the sides of the altar. Left: retail scene with market stall. Right: manufacturing scene in the workshop. Drawing ascribed to Vicenzo Dolcibene. British Museum (AN1047418001).*

side, we see the same two people—or so it seems—standing in front of a cupboard full of knives and sickles (fig. 8.5). While the precise context is unclear, the environment seems to be that of a market rather than a workshop: the two people wear everyday clothes rather than a working outfit, and there are no visual references to the production process. Other, indirect, evidence for this scenario comes from Pompeii where several of the largest bakeries also did not have a shop, while the very nature of their business implies that their products were consumed locally and distributed on the same day.[38] It is likely that the people operating these shops sold (or distributed) at least some of their bread elsewhere in the city, e.g. around the forum. In such cases, the link between consumer and producer was more indirect, but still, ties were relatively close. This was different in the second scenario. This is most obvious in the case of the large production centres of pottery, of which the products have been found in significant quantities in regions far away. Yet it is also true for some of the

38 Flohr (2007: 134).

large fulleries of the metropolitan region around Rome, and for the tanneries that have been identified at Pompeii and Rome.[39] The lack of direct interaction with customers in such establishments meant that workers may have had only a very vague idea of who used their products, and they probably had no idea of how their work was appreciated, and by whom. Combined with the limited degree to which individual workers were responsible for the final result in these workshops, this is likely to have had a strongly negative impact on the development of their professional identity. It is important to point out that the increasing proportion of goods that were traded over longer distances in the Roman world meant that this second scenario became quite a bit more common—the proportion of craftsmen whose products were sold on markets that they did not personally know is likely to have increased considerably. This is not only true for potters at La Graufesenque or Arezzo, but also for weavers in the Po area whose products were exported to Rome, or for the bronze-workers in Campania whose products were found as far away as Denmark.[40] To a certain, unquantifiable, extent, thus, there was a change in the relation between producer and consumer in the Roman world, and one that had consequences for the social capital of some of the people involved in manufacturing.

Social Superiors

The third group of people that plays a role in constructing the social identity of workers and work groups consists of their social superiors. There has been a tendency among scholars to emphasize the large proportion of economic agents of servile or freed status, though it is often acknowledged that freeborn craftsmen and traders existed, and there are few hard indications allowing us to establish the relative proportion of freeborn, freed, or servile labour.[41] Nevertheless, the idea that shops and workshops must—as a rule—be seen as dependent pervades scholarship on crafts and trade in the Roman world. Yet without contesting the existence of dependence in itself, it is essential to assess its practical impact in everyday life—rather than an absolute, unchangeable fact, dependence was negotiated territory, and complete dependence was as

39 Flohr (2013a: 84–87). On the two tanneries of Pompeii see Borgard *et al.* (2003); Devore and Ellis (2008: 9–10). A tannery that was recently excavated in Trastevere in Rome remains unpublished. Marzia di Mento, pers. comm. 2015.

40 For weaving in the Po area cf. Strabo, 5.1.7. For the bronze workers of Campania see Kunow (1985), cf. Wallace-Hadrill (2008: 406).

41 On the role of freedmen in the economy see esp. Mouritsen (2001b; 2011: 205–247).

rare as complete autonomy. Legal status is just one factor that played a role in this, and probably one that has been quite a bit overrated: there are other, less 'official' aspects to dependence that may play a much more defining role on an everyday level than whether one was slave, freed, or freeborn.

A crucial, but underrated, factor in negotiating social (in)dependence is the spatial relation between workers and their social superiors: if social superiors were spending their day in the direct environment of workshops, they could have a direct impact on everyday processes on the shop floor; if the dependence of a shop or workshop was visibly expressed through architecture, this also made the relation explicit to the outside public. Conversely, if social superiors were further away, and if ties were not physically visible for the outside public, the impact of social dependence was less direct, and work groups were—their internal hierarchy apart—more autonomous. These issues are likely to have had a deep impact on the ways in which they could shape their professional identities. Practically, in the archaeological record, they tend to depend on the architectural context in which commercial spaces were constructed. Key distinction is that between dependent facilities, mostly *tabernae*, and independent buildings.

Dependent Facilities

Almost without exception, *tabernae* were part of a larger whole. Yet there are differences in the contexts in which *tabernae* were constructed, and these had consequences for the nature of the ties between the shop holder, who indeed often may have been dependent in some way or another to the owner of the complex, and the proprietor.[42] A brief case study of the Pompeian evidence is instructive.

At Pompeii, most *tabernae* were related to medium-sized *atrium* houses with a limited number of shops—the canonical number is two.[43] When such *tabernae* functioned independently from the main house, it is likely that connections were very close: there was an obvious visual association between the *tabernae* and the main entrance, and the house owners were often near to keep a close eye on what was happening. They also had a clear interest in doing so, as the state of the shops around their main entrance had an impact on their personal standing and prestige. The same is true for larger domestic complexes with a larger number of shops, which dominate part of Pompeii's city centre. Yet, in complexes such as the 'Casa del Torello di Bronzo' (8 *tabernae*), the 'Casa

42 Cf. Mouritsen (2001b).

43 This is true for 607 of Pompeii's 892 *tabernae* (73%); the average number of *tabernae* per house is 2.2 (i.e. 279 houses).

dei Postumii' (10 *tabernae*), and the 'Casa di Arianna' (11 *tabernae*) the amount of subordinate units is so large that it becomes very hard for the proprietors to completely control what is going on on the shop floor.[44] It also becomes less urgent: not all *tabernae* of these complexes could be visually associated with the main entrance of the house—as some were around the corner, and if one *taberna* happened to be performing a bit less well, it could easily be compensated for by the others. Hence, those in charge of *tabernae* in large complexes perhaps in practice had a bit more autonomy than those working in *tabernae* belonging to medium-sized houses.

Crucially, however, not all *tabernae* were related to houses. Of the about 892 excavated *tabernae* at Pompeii, 88 were related to public buildings, and another 115 were part of independent *tabernae* complexes that were unrelated to an *atrium* house.[45] In these cases, it is not only much more likely that the property was simply rented out on the commercial property market, but it is also obvious that there was no proprietor around to check how *tabernae* were doing. Also, there was considerably less personal interest at stake for the proprietor: any malfunctioning did not necessarily directly, and visually, affect his personal standing, even though local people may have known who owned a complex. Thus, in Pompeii, the landscape of dependence was rather varied, and many shop holders are likely to have enjoyed considerable autonomy on the shop floor—even if they were not completely independent.

Here, it is important to briefly reflect on the specific position of Pompeii within the Roman world. It may be argued that large *atrium* houses with more than five or six *tabernae* were a phenomenon that was not commonly found in every Roman city. Indeed, in small urban sites such as Saepinum, even *atrium* houses with two *tabernae* were exceptional.[46] At Paestum the largest urban villas have only two or three shops.[47] The amount of *tabernae* attached to public buildings also seems to have been relatively large at Pompeii, which thus seems to have been relatively densely commercialized. This can be understood

44 The Casa del Torello di Bronzo (V 1, 3.7) occupied most of the south half of *insula* V 1 at Pompeii, including *tabernae* V 1, 1–2, 4–6 and 8 along the south side of the *insula*, as well as *tabernae* V 1, 29–31 along the west side of the *insula*. On the House of the Postumii see Dickmann and Pirson (2001).

45 On *tabernae publicae* see Tran (2011b), Monteix (2013), Flohr (2016).

46 For an overview of the excavations at Saepinum see De Benedittis, Gaggiotti, and Matteini Chiari (1993).

47 Exemplary for the situation at Paestum is the large domestic complex immediately south of the main platea in the third block from the forum: like the house of the Faun at Pompeii, it has two *atria*, but, despite the central location in the city centre, it has a partially closed façade (pers. observ. 2011).

from its size, and its central position in the wealthy southern bay of Naples zone.[48] For people hiring *tabernae*, this commercialization thus seems to have brought a bit of independence. Yet at Rome and Ostia, and perhaps at Pozzuoli and Naples as well, the scale of urbanism was of course much larger still. These cities, in the imperial period, lacked the *atrium* houses that characterized the landscape of Pompeii, and had a commercial landscape was dominated by *insulae*, of which the owner generally was *not* living inside the building.[49] Thus, throughout these cities, *tabernae* were functioning more or less independently from any social superiors. As far as *tabernae* are concerned, there thus seems to be a relation between the scale of urbanism and the relative independence of work groups operating in *tabernae*.

Independent Buildings

Independently constructed buildings—houses with a workshop, or purpose-built production halls, of course were not necessarily used by a socially independent work group. In the case of domestic workshops, it is however generally obvious that the complex to which the workshop belonged functioned as a fully independent unit: houses did not lose their domestic function once a workshop was inserted, and, at Pompeii, there often is a place identifiable as a kitchen (fig. 8.6; room n). Moreover, such houses also were visibly independent—unlike *tabernae*, houses rarely looked like they were a subordinate part of another building. Indeed, many houses had their own *tabernae* associated with them. Still, of course, the complex may fall under the legal ownership of members of the elite, who may have had a say in its destination and may have played a role in the composition of the household. Yet, in many cases, houses with workshops tended to have their own specific historical development and seem to have been tailored to their user's specific needs and wishes. Many Pompeian houses with a workshop also had rooms that were (re)decorated after the construction of the workshop.[50] Looking at the archaeology of these houses, it therefore generally seems as if the households inhabiting them not only were independent on an everyday level, but also had considerable autonomy when it came to decisions about the layout of their domestic environment. At Pompeii, it is also much less clear than was assumed by Mouritsen some time ago that houses with workshops were generally inhabited by freedmen: it is very hard to derive the legal status of actual occupants

48 On the Bay of Naples see D'Arms (1970).

49 On the *insulae* in Rome and Ostia see e.g. Meiggs (1997: 235–262); Packer (1971); Ellis (2000).

50 See esp. Flohr (2007: 136–141; 2011a).

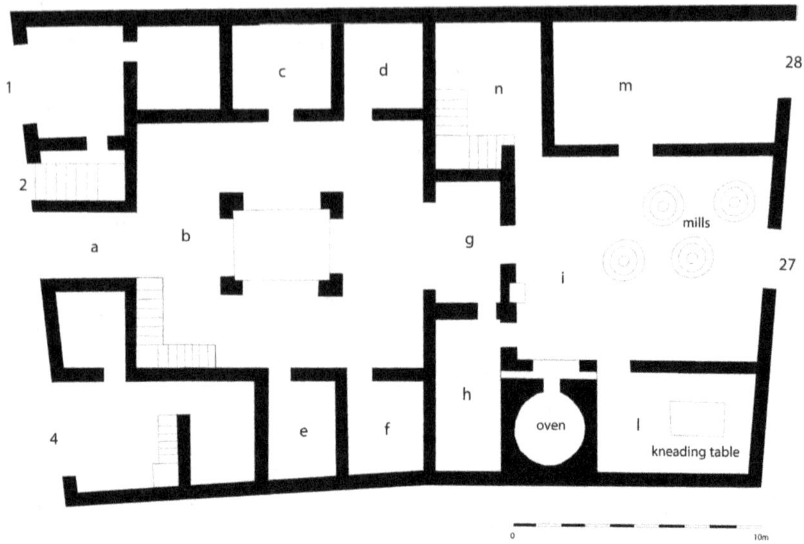

FIGURE 8.6 *Pompeii, house VI 3, 3.27–28 with a bakery in the back yard. The kitchen is in room n.*

from often decontextualized epigraphic evidence painted on the facade.[51] Still, however, it is likely that the main occupants of these houses were involved in bonds of patronage that enabled them to secure loans or concessions from the elite and the government.

As far as the production halls are concerned, it is obvious that they were owned by people living elsewhere. Moreover, in those cases that we know best—the bakeries and fulleries of Ostia and Rome—there was, in the workshop, little or no space reserved for administrative purposes.[52] Thus, while the workshops themselves operated independently during the working day, the important decisions about their management were probably taken elsewhere and by people who were not part of the core work group spending the day on the shop floor. For the workers, this situation brought both liberties and constraints. It brought liberties in the sense that most practical decisions could be taken within the work group itself—the owner of the complex is unlikely to have been around continuously. It brought constraints in that the absence of the owner meant that strategic information about the workshop may have been known to those working on the shop floor only to a limited extent, and the possibilities for workers contributing to strategic decision

51 *Contra* Mouritsen (2001b).

52 Flohr (2013a: 306–307).

making were much more limited. This, of course, had also to do with the size of the labour force.

All in all, while work groups operating shops and workshops were generally not completely independent and often had to deal with some kind of social superiors, they enjoyed considerable autonomy on a practical level. It should be stressed in this respect that expertise and craftsmanship could further enhance this: the know-how that was necessary to turn the business into a success was often firmly concentrated in the work group. While social superiors may have had the legal possibilities to intervene, it was often not in their interest to do so. Only when important decisions had to be taken, or when things started to go wrong, it made sense for them to intervene. The best way to describe this situation is to think of it as a 'bounded autonomy': work groups operated autonomously on the everyday level, but they were not completely independent: there were possibilities for outsiders to intervene when necessary.[53]

The Wider Urban Community

The wider urban community was the fourth and final social layer that played a role in the negotiation of occupational identities by workers. This opens up the issue of the relation between the work environment and public space. Of course, the shop floor was not the only place where people could be associated with their work. There is evidence that some professional associations of craftsmen had their own *schola*, and people who could be visually associated with a certain *schola* could also be associated with a certain craft.[54] Moreover, there were certain annual occasions in which professional associations or groups of craftsmen held processions through the city. However, not all workers involved in a certain craft may have had free access to the building of their professional organization—if there was one—and processions and festivals were no daily occasions. Moreover, outside their workshop, people could not be seen while they were performing their craft. Thus, the way in which the place of work itself was interconnected with the public realm was of crucial importance for the occupational identity of workers.

53 Cf. Flohr (2013a: 307–309).

54 On *scholae* see esp. Bollmann (1998); on *scholae* in the urban landscape at Ostia see Stöger (2011). See also Verboven in this volume.

FIGURE 8.7 *Pompeii, street view from taberna* VI 3, 19–20.

Visible Labour

With their wide openings, *tabernae* of course were very much integrated into the surrounding public realm. Working in a *taberna* meant that you were generally able to take note of what was happening on the street, and that you could be seen whilst at work (fig. 8.7). Moreover, as *tabernae* were generally close to other *tabernae*, there were close natural ties with other workers—especially with those on the opposite side of the road. At Pompeii, many *tabernae* also did not have their own internal water source, which meant that people relied on public fountains for their water. This further integrated people into their public environment: public fountains became hotspots of social interaction of people at work, and, by consequence, places where people negotiated not only their personal but also their professional identity.[55] The world of *tabernae* was a world of publicly negotiated professional identities in which workers could easily relate to other people of comparable socioeconomic status.

However, the role of urbanism and urban geography in these processes should not be underestimated: in streets with fewer shops, interaction was less intense, and integration with the urban community was more limited. For example, in Pompeii, it mattered whether you were working in one of the many shops along the Via Consolare near the forum, or whether you worked

55 On public fountains see Laurence (2007: 38–39).

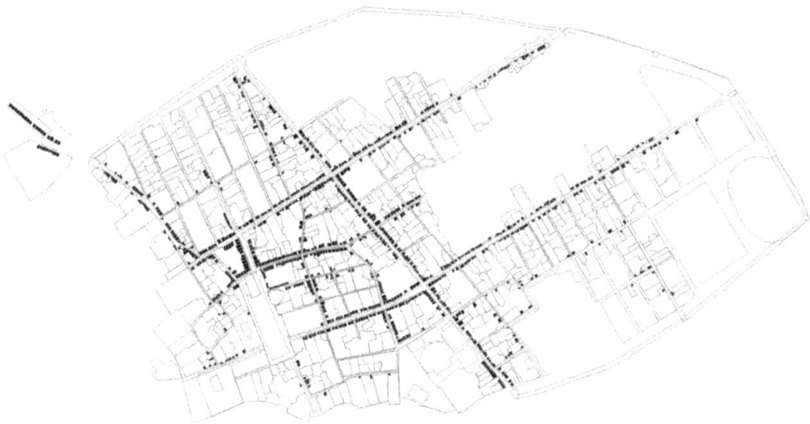

FIGURE 8.8 *Pompeii, map showing the distribution of* tabernae *over the city.*

in one of the few shops in the south-eastern half of the city (fig. 8.8). If a road was very wide, as was the case with the Decumanus at Ostia, or if there were porticoes in front of the shops, as was common in Rome as well as in Ostia, interaction with the opposite side of the street was much more restricted. Nevertheless, overall, workers in a *taberna* were well-off in terms of negotiating a public occupational identity.

Invisible Labour

Domestic workshops and production halls often had work areas that were partially or completely invisible from the street. This, of course, complicated the possibilities for workers to interact with the outside public. Domestic workshops sometimes were directly accessible through a back door, but in many cases these opened off back streets where traffic was limited. This is especially obvious in the region just east of the forum in Pompeii where many domestic workshops have openings on the quiet streets in the central part of the area, whereas the houses to which they belonged had their main entrance along the much busier roads (fig. 8.9). This is not necessarily a matter of consciously 'hiding away'—reasons seem to have been practical rather than ideological—but in terms of interaction with outsiders, the effect was significant.[56] The only exception in this respect is made up by those workshops that had a shop. Here, the production process itself may have been invisible, but the neighbourhood

56 On the handling of potentially inconvenient elements related to the workshop see Flohr (2012).

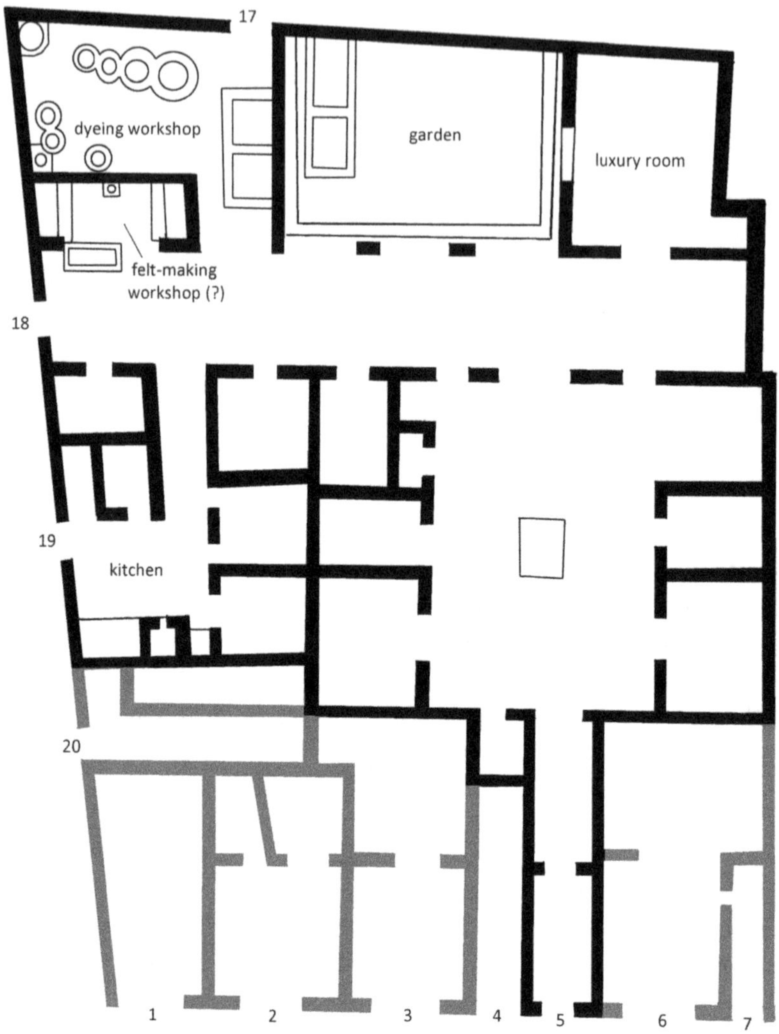

FIGURE 8.9 *Pompeii, house VII 14, 5.17–19. Plan.*

penetrated the workshop indirectly: information is likely to have circulated in the workshop, and some workers may have spent part of their time in the shop, which meant that they could be publicly associated with their work—though the practical aspects of their craft were invisible. The large production halls at Ostia and Rome were almost completely invisible to the outside public. For instance, the Severan-period bakery in the 'Caseggiato del Molino' in Ostia was

FIGURE 8.10 *Ostia, bakery* I III 1. *View from the street towards milling room.*

situated behind a row of shops, and only one of the mills was easily visible from the nearby street (fig. 8.10): passers-by can hardly have guessed the scale of the workshop inside.[57] Sometimes, they could only be accessed from an inner courtyard, as was the case with the large *fullonica* of the Via della Fullonica.[58] As these large workshops were barely visible, chances are high that their existence was known only to a limited number of people.

One should not underestimate the social consequences of invisibility for workers. Especially in the large production halls, but to a lesser extent also in the 'invisible' domestic workshops at Pompeii, the invisibility of work meant that workers lacked a platform on which a public occupational identity could be negotiated: nobody saw them while they were doing their work, and as soon as they left the workshop, they were not recognizable as being involved in any specific craft. In other words, any occupational image that these people may have developed on the shop floor lacked a public audience.

57 On this complex see also Meijlink (1999).

58 *Fullonica* II 2, 2; Cf. Pietrogrande (1976: 15–17, 27–42).

Discussion

From this overview it is clear that the spatial circumstances of labour could differ radically, and that these differences could have profound consequences for the lives and identities of those doing the work. Overlooking the evidence, it is attractive to see the *tabernae* and the production halls as two opposite poles: with the open nature of their workshop, and their frequent interaction with customers, people working in *tabernae* were well-integrated into the urban economy. The intimate communicative landscape and the close personal ties between workers enhanced identity formation, as did the craft-based division of labour, which made sure that workers got experience in many aspects of the production process. Conversely, workers in the production halls of Rome and Ostia could not interact with outsiders, and spent their days in an anonymous environment doing simple, repetitive tasks. In these workshops, the circumstances on the shop floor did not provide a very powerful infrastructure of identity. The domestic workshops stood, on average, somewhere in the middle, though they generally share more characteristics with the *tabernae* than with the production halls.

While *tabernae*-like working environments seem to represent the broad basis that, from early on, was common throughout Roman Italy, the larger-scale environments seem products of specific historical developments that must be seen as a result of the unique economic conditions in a certain number of cities under the Roman Empire. The increased urbanization, and the increased standards of living, enhanced demand and made in certain crafts and industries an increase in scale feasible. This led to the larger workshops, and thus to work environments that hitherto had been rare or even unknown. It can be argued that the emergence of these large-scale working environments in an urban context is one of the more significant developments in the economic history of Roman cities, and the present discussion suggests that the social effects of this development for those involved could be fundamental. Thus, while scholars in the past have often emphasized how economic life in the Roman world was 'embedded' in social and cultural processes, the reverse is, to some extent at least, also true: changing economic circumstances led to patterns of investment that had a deep impact on social life.[59] In terms of the history of labour in the Roman world, it is this change that may be one of the bigger stories.

---

59 On the embeddedness of the Roman economy see Flohr (2013a: 351–353).

CHAPTER 9

Guilds and the Organisation of Urban Populations During the Principate

Koenraad Verboven

Ancient historians have long preferred not to compare Greco-Roman professional associations to the guilds of pre- and early modern Europe. From Waltzing to Finley and after, the orthodox view was that *collegia* were social and religious clubs; important for the emotional well-being of their members, occasionally acting as social support groups, but not protective or regulatory agencies for economic interests.[1] Only recently have scholars begun to question this view. Occupational *collegia* defined themselves through the professional identities of their members. Like all voluntary associations they were multi-dimensional communities that strengthened trust and cooperation by stimulating norms of good behaviour and sanctioning trespassers. They directed collective action and pooled resources. Even if economic interests and motives were not an explicit concern it was inevitable that occupational *collegia* affected and were affected by them. Scholars so far have focused on how *collegia* reduced transaction costs and on how they raised their members' social status.[2] There has been relatively little attention, however, to how occupational *collegia* fit in and changed the institutional framework of Roman cities.[3] Roman *collegia* never enjoyed the formal privileges and powers that some medieval guilds had. They were never formally part of public administration and received no delegated authority from it. I will argue, however, that *collegia*, as collective agents, had a strong potential for effective performative action. Their appeal or resistance to the enforcement

* This paper was extensively reworked and adapted during a research stay at Brasenose and Merton College in Oxford in 2013–2014; I warmly thank Alan Bowman, Ed Bispham, Nicolas Purcell, Jonathan Prag and the fellows of Brasenose and Merton college for their hospitality and stimulating discussions. All remaining errors, of course, are mine alone.

1 Waltzing (1895–1900); Finley (1999: 138); see also Hasebroek (1928: 66).

2 For a short survey see Verboven (2011b). On the multidimensionality linking both economic and social functions see Monson (2006); Pleket (2008); Venticinque (2009; 2010); Arnaoutoglou (2011). For the craftsmen guilds in particular Hawkins (2006), and his paper in this volume. See also the chapter by Liu for a critical assessment.

3 But see van Nijf (1997).

 | DOI 10.1163/9789004331686_010

of public regulations carried weight. So did their praise of public officials who acted magnanimously and scrupulously in the exercise of their duties. Conversely, elites found *collegia* useful to control workers and to mobilise their efforts for public services and duties.

I will begin by analysing how Roman guilds structured citizen populations. Starting from the mythical stories about the origins of the professional associations in early Rome, I will proceed to analyse how the ideals contained in these stories related (or not) to social reality in the early Empire. The second part studies how professional associations in the late first and second century AD acquired a public persona justified by the services they provided to the state and local communities. I will argue that Roman cities from the early second century onwards relied on professional guilds to function. The last section studies how guilds empowered their members and most of all their own officers. Thus, while officers of important guilds were never formally a part of administration they nevertheless wielded considerable influence.

Structuring Urban Populations

According to Plutarch Rome's second king, Numa Pompilius, distributed the people in private associations based on economic occupation:

> He distributed them by arts and trades, into musicians, goldsmiths, carpenters, dyers, leather-workers, curriers, braziers, and clay workers. The remaining trades he grouped together, and made one body out of all who belonged to them.[4]

Each received their own 'communities' (*koinōnias*), assemblies (*sunodous*) and rites of worship (*theōn timas*). Thus, Numa forged Latins and Sabines into a single (citizen) body.

The details of this story, the king's motives and their supposed rationality are influenced by Greek philosophy,[5] but Pliny the Elder confirms the Roman

4 Plut., *Num.* 17: ἦν δὲ ἡ διανομὴ κατὰ τὰς τέχνας, αὐλητῶν, χρυσοχόων, τεκτόνων, βαφέων, σκυτοτόμων, σκυτοδεψῶν, χαλκέων, κεραμέων. τὰς δὲ λοιπὰς τέχνας εἰς ταὐτὸ συναγαγὼν ἓν αὐτῶν ἐκ πασῶν ἀπέδειξε σύστημα. Κεραμέων here does not refer only to simple 'potters' but rather to tile and brick makers, makers of *dolia*, tubes etc., cf. Plin., *HN*. 35.159 and below on the public utility of clay workers.

5 Gabba (1984).

core of the story.[6] In an alternative version, told by the second century historian Florus, king Servius Tullius registered the people on census-rolls, arranged them in property classes and distributed them according to their 'crafts and offices' (*artium officiorumque*) in *decuriae et collegia* to facilitate public administration.[7]

Both stories are legends, of course, but they show how Greco-Roman intellectuals c. AD 100 saw *collegia* not primarily as disruptive and potentially violent militias (as they had been in late republican Rome), but ideally as peaceful groups, sanctioned by *mos maiorum*, that integrated urban workers in the citizen body. The stories probably became part of the canonical narrative of early Roman history only in the Augustan period, but the antiquity—and therefore the legitimacy and respectability—of *collegia* had been acknowledged much earlier. Cicero described them as rooted in ancestral custom (*mos maiorum*).[8] Caesar's and Augustus's ban on *collegia* excepted those that were 'established in ancient times'.[9]

How real was the distribution of urban populations in occupational guilds in historical times? Private associations had thrived in classical Athens, in the Hellenistic world, and in the Roman Republic. Most, however, had defined themselves as cult associations.[10] There is often no reason to suppose that members shared the same profession. Most of the well documented associations in late republican Campania, for instance, were based on neighbourhood relations.[11] This picture may be somewhat misleading because religious labels sometimes (but not always!) covered up occupational identities. Thus, the officers of the guild of merchants (*conlegium mercatorum*) mentioned in an inscription from Capua from 112/111 BC are called the 'Masters of Mercury' in

6 Plin., *HN* 34.1 (i); 35.159 (lx), for the bronze workers (*fabri aerarii*) and clay moulders (*figuli*).

7 Flor., *Epit.* 1.6; *decuriae* were organisations of public servants (*apparitores*), cf. Purcell (1983).

8 Cicero, *Dom.* 74. On the role of *collegia* in structuring the electorate at Rome in Cicero's time see also Q. Cicero, *Comment. pet.* 30. For a discussion see Mouritsen (2001a: 83–84, 141–143); Yakobson (1999: 23–24, 86–87).

9 Suet., *Iul.* 42.3: *Cuncta collegia praeter antiquitus constituta distraxit; Aug.* 32.1 *collegia praeter antiqua et legitima dissolvit.*

10 Leiwo (1997); Jones (1999); Gabrielsen (2001); Monson (2005; 2006); Baslez (2006); Ismard (2010). For older surveys see Poland (1909); Ziebarth (1896). See also Gaius' commentary on the XII Tables cited in *Dig.* 47.22.4 where a law of Solon is cited as the inspiration for a clause allowing freedom to form private associations.

11 Frederiksen (1959: 83–94); Flambard (1983).

an slightly later inscription (105 BC).[12] Merchants and foreign residents who shared commercial interests, may have felt little need to include these in the name of their associations.[13] Whether a *collegium* presented itself as an occupational or as a cult association could also depend on context and intentions. The *collegia* of cattle merchants, fullers, butchers, and other professionals who set up dedications in the republican temple at Praeneste, for instance, may have preferred to use their professional identity to avoid reference to another deity in Fortuna Primigenia's most important sanctuary.[14]

Nevertheless, from the Principate onwards the number of *collegia* openly defining themselves through occupational titles rose dramatically. By the early third century the jurist Callistratus distinguished occupational *collegia* as a separate category of 'associations or corporations to which a person is admitted on the grounds of his trade, as is the case for a corporation of craftsmen'.[15] The diversity among occupational titles of *collegia* is huge, but the spread is highly uneven. Roughly a quarter of all Latin inscriptions mentioning professional associations refer to one or more of the so-called 'Three Foremost Associations' (*Tria Collegia Principalia*): those of the 'tree-carriers' (*dendrophori*), clothmen (*centonarii*) and craftsmen (*fabri*).[16] Callistratus, cited above,

---

12 CIL I 2947 (p 930); 672 (p 930, 931). See also CIL IX 23 (*Mercuriales* from Rudia); CIL VI 10234 (p 3502, 3908) (early second century AD, doctors forming an association for Aesculapius and Hygia in Rome).

13 But see the merchant guilds on Delos; ID 1520: 'The Delian Community of Worshippers of Poseidon from Beirut, Merchants, Shipmasters and Residents' (τὸ ἐν Δήλῳι κοινὸν Βηρυτίων Ποσειδωνιαστῶν ἐμπόρων καὶ ναυκλήρων καὶ ἐγδοχέων); ID 1519: 'The Community of Worshippers of Herakles from Tyre, Merchants and Shippers' (τῶι κοινῶι τῶν Τυρίων Ἡρακλειστῶν ἐμπόρων καὶ ναυκλήρων. On the Delian guilds see Flambard (1982); Hasenohr (2002; 2007); on similar groups in the western Mediterranean Verboven (2012a: 23–24); Díaz Ariño (2004).

14 CIL XIV 2878 (cattle merchants); CIL I 1455 (p 991, 993) and 1456 (p 993) (fullers); ILLRP 105b (butchers); CIL I 3066 (litter bearers); ILLRP 106b (p 319) (pork dealers); CIL I 3068 = ILLRP 106c (scrap dealers and blacksmiths); ILLRP 106d (p 319) (vine planters); CIL I 3071 (basket makers)... cf. also CIL I^2 364 (a *gonlegium* (sic) of cooks (*ququei*), second century BC, the oldest Latin inscription mentioning a *collegium*, cf. Tran (2006: 1–2); Peruzzi (1966); Bakkum (2008: no. 217–218).

15 *Dig.* 50.6.6.12–13 (Callistratus): *in quibus artificii sui causa unusquisque adsumitur, ut fabrorum corpus est*; the same applied to the associations of clothmen (*centonarii*), cf. AE 1920, 69; for a discussion and further literature see Liu (2009: 57–60).

16 The term *Tria Collegia Principalia* occurs only CIL XI 5749; but the concept of these three together forming prime prestigious local *collegia* was widespread, see Waltzing (1895–1900 I: 129–130; II: 193–208).

and an inscription from Solva[17] confirm the occupational basis for membership of the associations of *fabri* and *centonarii*. Nevertheless, the professional nature of these three highly prestigious guilds has been much disputed. Some have argued that they merely served as semi-public fire-brigades or fulfilled other public services.[18] Sirks sees them as organisations created by the state for 'the fulfilment of communally determined duties or obligations'.[19] Van Nijf compares them to the Civic Guards of 17th century Holland, whose prime purpose was to confer status upon successful craftsmen and tradesmen *from various occupational backgrounds*.[20] There is no doubt that the associations of *fabri* and *centonarii* (as well as others) provided important public services and received public recognition for that reason (see below). However, this is no contradiction to their being established on the basis of common occupations, nor does it imply that they did not defend shared professional interests. Van Nijf's point, however, is relevant: was membership restricted to persons in the same or functionally related profession? How strong was the professional identity of the *Tria Collegia Principalia?*

It was certainly weak in the case of the *collegia* of *dendrophori* ('tree-carriers'), whose religious identity was much more pronounced than that of other professional associations. They were created when Claudius reformed the cult of *Magna Mater* (Cybele). Their Greek name refers to the carriers of the sacred pine tree in the yearly procession for the goddess.[21] In addition to Cybele, the *dendrophori* venerated Silvanus, god of the woods, who was honoured with the epithet *Dendrophorus*.[22] They remained under supervision of the state priestly college of *Quindemcemviri Sacris Faciundis* at Rome. Contrary to the *fabri* and *centonarii*, the *dendrophori* were banned as pagan cult associations by Theodosius II.[23] We find no recognisable indication of professional activities or status for the *dendrophori*, apart from their connection to the guilds of craftsmen and clothmen. Scholars usually identify them as loggers and suppliers of wood for construction and/or firing. Symmachus tells us that in the fourth century AD privileged *collegia* guaranteed the supply of wood for

17 *AE* 1920, 69; cf. Liu (2009: 57–59) for a discussion.

18 Hirschfeld (1884); Kneissl (1994); Lafer (2001) (see there for the historiography). For a critical discussion Liu (2009: 125–160).

19 Sirks (1991: 93–94).

20 van Nijf (2002).

21 Lydus, *Mens.* 4.59; *CIL* X 3699; as depicted in a relief now in the Musée d'Aquitaine at Bordeaux (Inv. 602107); Van Haeperen (2010; 2012).

22 Cf. Dorcey (1992: 31).

23 Salamito (1990); for the view that they were only a religious brotherhood see Van Haeperen (2012); van Nijf (2002: 312).

the baths. But he doesn't mention the *dendrophori*.[24] While there was clearly a link with forests, nothing positively links the *dendrophori* to the provision of timber or fire-wood. Wilson recently argued that the geographic distribution of *dendrophori*-inscriptions indicates a link with woodland areas providing timber for construction.[25] The link, however, is not very strong. Wilson himself notes the absence of *dendrophori* in Spain and western Gaul, where we would expect them. The concentration of *dendrophori* in northern Africa, moreover, is suspicious for a professional guild, since African inscriptions rarely mention professional titles or occupational *collegia* (even those of the *fabri* and *centonarii*).[26]

We are on more secure ground for the associations of *centonarii* and *fabri*. There have been doubts about the occupational identity of the clothmen (*centonarii*), because their name is nowhere positively attested to denote a profession. This induced Kneissl to argue that the title was merely honorific.[27] Since Liu's masterful book on the *centonarii*, however, their identification as 'tradesmen and/or manufacturers engaged in the production and distribution of low- or medium-quality woollen textiles and clothing' seems secure.[28]

The identity of the *collegia fabrum* (craftsmen guilds) was openly occupational, but eminently vague. The lack of specificity (which craftsmen?) has been used to argue that occupational interests were irrelevant and that their function was merely to organize the urban plebs more conveniently in order to make it easier to assign public duties and to confer distinction upon successful middling class businessmen.[29] Against this view, it may be argued that the *fabri* were synonymous with the *fabri tignuarii* (builders/carpenters) and grouped various craftsmen attached to the building industry.[30] In 7 BC the

24 Symm., *Relat.* 14.3 *pars urenda lavacris ligna comportat* (cf. Hirschfeld (1884: 249)); Waltzing (1895–1900 I: 240–253); Salamito (1987); Rubio Rivera (1993).

25 Wilson (2012: 139–140).

26 [*cent*]*onari*(*i*) *et subaedian*(*i*) are mentioned in Uthina together with *universae curiae* (*CIL* VIII 10523); a military *collegium fabrum* is documented in Lambaesis (*CIL* VIII 2690; 3545; cf. Sander 1962: 147 and compare *RIB* I 156). These are the only examples documented in northern Africa. See also Verboven (2007a) on the absence of *negotiatores* in African inscriptions.

27 Kneissl (1994).

28 Liu (2009: 69).

29 Sirks (1991: 93); van Nijf (2002); the concept of a guild uniting different trades is familiar to Plutarch (*Numa* 17, see above).

30 111 cities had a *collegium fabrum*, 32 had a *collegium fabrum tignuariorum*, 8 may have had both but dating problems make it difficult to decide whether this was simultaneously. For

ancient guild of the *fabri* at Rome, for instance, changed its name (and organization) into that of *fabri tignuarii*.[31]

The size of some *collegia fabrum* seems to indicate a diverse membership.[32] The joint guild of craftsmen and clothmen in Milan in the second century AD, for instance, was subdivided into at least 12 *centuriae* of each at least 5 *decuriae* for an urban population of 20,000–25,000 people.[33] In Ravenna (much smaller than Milan but catering to about 5,000 marines) the guild of *fabri* was divided into at least 28 *decuriae*.[34] In Ulpia Sarmizegetusa, the capital of Dacia, the guild comprised at least 15 *decuriae* for maybe 5,000–6,000 inhabitants.[35] These are impressive figures, considering that a *decuria* usually comprised about 20 members.[36] They are also, however, misleading because the divide between urban centres and hinterland was not strict. The number of city-residents is less relevant than the number of local *cives*, many of whom lived in rural centres. Construction teams relied on labour supplied by the countryside. Many different skills, moreover, were needed in the building trade. In late medieval Florence the builders' guild of the 'Maestri di Pietra e di Legname' united stonecutters, carpenters and wallers with quarriers, kiln operators, roofers, stucco-workers, house painters, vendors of sand, gravel and wood, founders, cesspool diggers and even carters of stone and dirt. Many of these lived and worked outside the city proper.[37] The Roman builder/carpenter guilds (*collegia fabrum tignuariorum*) may, similarly, have included painters, windowpane-makers, plumbers, smiths, etc., besides

---

the list see Liu (2009: 384–390); cf. the enumeration in Symm., *Relat.* 14.3; see Bernard in this volume for the building trade.

31 Pearse (1974); DeLaine (2003); Waltzing (1895–1900 II: 117–118, 193–194).

32 van Nijf (2002: 313–314).

33 Liu (2009: 141–148). For the estimate of the town population cf. de Ligt (2008); based on 120–150 inhabitants per ha and the late third century wall encircling 133 ha, encompassing the suburbs outside the Augustan wall of 80 ha. But the city may have been larger before in the second century. The *fabri tignuarii* at Rome were organized into 60 *decuriae* of c. 22 members each (*CIL* VI 9405), for a population of c. 1 million inhabitants (Pearse (1976); Patterson (1992)). The *fabri tignuarii* of Ostia in the late second century AD had about 350 members (DeLaine (2003)).

34 *CIL* XI 126.

35 Ardevan (1978); population estimate based on de Ligt's parameters (above) for an inhabited area of c. 32.4 ha *intra muros*, 42.5 *extra muros*; cf. Alicu and Paki (1995: 8–9).

36 For the usual size of a *decuria* see Liu (2009: 131); but cf. *CIL* XIII 11313 for *decuriae* of 50 members (Demougin (2012: 159–164)). Cf. also Plin., *Ep.* 10.33, which seems to suggest that *collegia fabrum* were often larger than 150 members. The 'Indoor Craftsmen' (*fabri subaediani*) at Narbo in 149 may have numbered 480 members (*CIL* XII 4393 (p 846)).

37 Goldthwaite (1980: 250–254); peripherals crafts, such as blacksmiths and lock makers, continued to have their own organisations.

craftsmen whose core-business was building (carpenters, masons, plasterers, ...). This would explain why many cities had a guild of craftsmen involved in building, rather than a guild of builders/carpenters.

With the possible exception, therefore, of the *dendrophori*, there is no doubt that occupation was the main criterion for membership of occupational *collegia*, including privileged ones like the clothmen (*centonarii*), the builders/carpenter (*fabri tignuarii*), or the shipwrights (*fabri navales*). The byelaws of a guild of the ivory and citrus wood dealers at Rome (drawn up during the reign of Hadrian) explicitly stipulate that only *negotiatores eborarii aut citrarii* could be accepted as members.[38] That doesn't mean, however, that guild members were all practising artisans. Some inscriptions distinguish practicing members from non-practitioners. A member from the guild of goldsmiths at Mutina donated a burial ground to the goldsmiths, their wives and 'those who are among us'.[39] Pliny's assurance to Trajan that he would make sure that only true craftsmen would join the guild he wanted to establish in Nicomedia, confirms both the principle that membership was granted on the basis of a person's profession, and the exceptions.[40] Membership could, for instance, be given as a mark of honour,[41] as in the case of Cn. Sentius Felix, president of the *curatores navium marinarum*, council member and *duumvir* of Ostia c. AD 100, patron of 15 *collegia*, who was co-opted as a member free of charge by the guild of Adriatic sea merchants (*corpus naviculariorum maris Hadriatici*).[42] The Solva inscription specifies that privileges were granted only to those who practised the trade and were of modest financial means.[43] Callistratus confirms that the immunity granted to members of authorized guilds was not valid for those who were too young or too old to practice the trade, or for those who

38 *CIL* VI 33885 (p. 3896).

39 *AE* 1981, 387. The benefactor was also *decurio* of Mutina. Compare also the burial ground of 'Asian stage workers' at Vienne: *Scaenici Asiaticiani et qui in eodem corpore sunt* (*CIL* XII 1929) and *CIL* VII 11 (= *RIB* I 91, Chichester, reign of Claudius): [*colle*]*gium fabror*(*um*) *et qui in eo* / [*sun*]*t*.

40 Plin., *Ep.* 10.33: *ne quis nisi faber recipiatur.*

41 Verboven (2007b: 883–884); Liu (2009: 203–208).

42 *CIL* XIV 409 (= *AE* 1999, 407); Tran (2006: 68–70, 80–81); Rohde (2012: 147–148); cf. perhaps *CIL* XIV 5154 (a goldsmith in the builders' guild at Amsoldingen); *CIL* XIII, 1978 (Lyon, late second–early third century, a potter/clay-worker in the craftsmen guild). But note that both may have been involved in building projects, resp. as gilder for ornaments and producer of ceramic parts. For other examples, see Waltzing (1895–1900 I: 342–346).

43 *AE* 1920, 69: *ii quos dicis divitis suis sine onere* / [*uti publica subire m*]*unera compellantur neque enim collegiorum privilegium pro*/[*sit aut iis qui artem non*] *exercent aut iis qui maiores facultates praefi*(*ni*)*to modo possident.*

had become too wealthy.[44] Apparently, therefore, some guilds included also children (some no doubt apprentices[45]) and older craftsmen who had stopped practising, as well as wealthy entrepreneurs whose involvement was limited to owning production facilities and slaves. However, both Callistratus and the Solva inscription also suggest that some merely sought to benefit from guild-privileges without practising the trade.

Through the *collegia*, professional activities and identities provided a suitable criterion for organising non-elite populations. But how comprehensive was this? What proportion of urban populations was attached to an occupational guild? The foundation myths present an ideal city in which all working people were tied to a guild. This was certainly not the case when Plutarch and Florus wrote their stories (nor probably ever before). Fikhman estimated the number of craftsmen who were member of a guild in fourth century Oxyrhynchus (when guild membership had become practically obligatory) at c. 640–900, c. 15–25% of the adult male population. Van Minnen thinks this is (much) too low an estimate. He argues that on average 30–50% or urban populations in Egypt were engaged in crafts.[46] Unfortunately we cannot project back these figures to the second century AD or generalise them for other provinces. MacMullen speculated that in the Italian cities of the second century AD one in three free adult males were member of a *collegium*.[47] There is no way of verifying the accuracy of this estimate, but the data we have suggest that the order of magnitude may well be correct. We have already seen how *collegia fabrum* could have hundreds of members. The clothmen guilds (*centonarii*) as well boasted significant numbers. In Ravenna in the second half of the second century AD, it comprised 17 *decuriae*.[48] In the small town of Solva in Noricum in AD 204 they had 93 members.[49] Membership numbers of other guilds as well could be high. The shipwrights (*fabri navales*) of Portus had 353 members around AD 200.[50] The *lenuncularii tabularii auxiliarii* (shippers with small boats in service of the port authorities) had 125 common members in AD 152 and 258 in AD 192.[51] Besides these large privileged guilds numerous

44 *Dig*. 50.6.6.12–13.

45 On apprenticeships see the chapter by Liu.

46 Fikhman (1971: 118–119); Van Minnen (1987: 37).

47 MacMullen (1966: 174).

48 *CIL* XI 125; On the size of the *centonarii* guilds see Liu (2009: 170).

49 *ILLPRON* 1450–1458; for an extensive bibliography see Liu (2009: 340); following de Ligt's criteria the town of c. 39 ha could have accommodated c. 4,500–6,000 inhabitants.

50 *CIL* XIV 256.

51 *CIL* XIV 250; 251.

smaller guilds are on record. Few had more than a few dozen members.[52] The stage workers (*scaenici*) at Bovillae had 60 members in AD 167.[53] Roughly the same number can be assumed for a fullers guild at Ostia in AD 232.[54] Taken together smaller guilds may have matched the larger ones in membership numbers. Guilds of craftsmen/builders (*fabri* (*tignuarii*)) or clothmen (*centonarii*) are attested in 107 Italian towns, roughly a quarter of the total number of towns in Italy.[55] Considering the incompleteness of the epigraphic record, this suggests that by the second century AD it was standard for an Italian town or city to have at least one *Collegium Principale*.[56] There can be little doubt, therefore, that by the second century AD all Italian-type towns and cities had important occupational *collegia* and a sizeable portion (1/3?) of the urban population was member of one.

How voluntary was guild membership for a practising craftsman? Guild membership was not a legal requirement to practice a trade. Roman law generally upheld the principle that free persons could exercise any profession they wished.[57] Guilds could make it hard on outsiders. The ferrymen of Smyrna in the first or second century AD, had fixed a high price for ferry-services and illegally prevented outsiders from offering the same service.[58] In AD 309, a donkey owner in Oxyrhynchus complained that he had been harassed by the guild of donkey sellers (*onomangōnes*), who claimed he was a donkey seller

52 Cf. Zimmermann (2002: 76–77). See also Liu's chapter.

53 *CIL* XIV 2408. Presumably both performance artists and logistic hands.

54 *CIL* XIV 4573 = *AE* 1909, 215: 37 names are preserved, of which 30 in a first column. There appears little room for more than two columns. Compare the cult association for Jupiter Cernenus in Alburnus Maior (Dacia): originally 54 members, but only 17 remained in AD 167 (*CIL* III p. 924 = *IDR* I 31).

55 If we add the *dendrophori* the number rises to 125; 84 have a major craftsmen guild (*fabri, fabri subaediani, fabri tignuarii, fabri navales*), 65 have *centonarii*, 55 have *dendrophori*; see Waltzing (1895–1900); Mennella and Apicella (2000); Liu (2009: 384–390).

56 Gallia Narbonnensis and the Alpine provinces are comparable. Other provinces show much lower figures. In many cases this can be related to the poorer epigraphic record, but not in epigraphically rich Baetica and Africa Proconsularis. Whether this is due to local differences in epigraphic culture (which caused the *collegia* to remain unrecorded), or to real differences in the institutional set-up of cities in these provinces cannot be made out at this point.

57 Not even a patron could prevent his own freedman to practise the trade learned as slave, cf. *Dig*. 37.14.2; 18; 38.1.4.

58 *ISmyrna* 712. The city council and popular assembly took action against the cartel but the outcome is unknown. See also Liu in this volume on the disruptive influence of occupational *collegia*.

and therefore had to supply the required number of animals that the guild collected for the government.[59] We should beware, however, to overestimate the possibility of guilds to institute *de facto* monopolies. Wealthy aristocrats commonly invested in training slaves to set them up as craftsmen. Manumission served as a prime incentive for such skilled slaves. With a powerful master or patron to back them up they would have been hard to intimidate.[60] There were, however, also positive incentives. The prevalent organization in small workshops, the interdependence of specialized craftsmen and the general condition of insecurity of demand, made membership desirable.[61] Since the second century AD privileges and immunities for craftsmen and traders were distributed through their guilds.[62]

Both pull and push factors, therefore make it likely that the majority of independent professionals preferred to be member of a guild. But, the situation is further complicated because, although Roman law was opposed to monopolies and cartels, the administration did use licenses to supervise and regulate economic activities. For instance, even though Rome gave a much wider scope than the Ptolemies to private enterprise and free trade in Egypt, it continued to regulate economic activities by imposing licenses. Hunting and fishing rights, for instance, as well as the right to gather papyrus had to be purchased.[63] Fish breeding too was subject to license fees.[64] So was the exploitation and trade of salt and sodium carbonate.[65] Even manufacturing trades were (sometimes) regulated through licensing. A papyrus from the Arsinoite nome from AD 172, for instance, contains an application to obtain the (sole?) concession for weaving in a village for one year.[66] As usual, Egypt is the best documented province,[67] but, the organisation in other provinces was probably not so very different. The municipal charter of Urso (in Spain) stipulated that no one had the right to exploit a tile workshop of more than 300 tiles or similar products. All such exploitations

---

59 *P. Oxy.* XLIV 3192 (= duplicate of *P. Oxy.* XLV 4491); Adams (2007: 94); Gibbs (2008: 53–54). See also below Liu on guilds barring outsiders from lucrative contracts.

60 Verboven (2012b: 93–95); Temin (2004).

61 Hawkins (2006); and his contribution in this volume.

62 *Dig.* 50.6.6.12–13.

63 Fishing and hunting: *P. Giss.* 12 (AD 87/8); *P. Tebt.* 359 (AD 126); Papyrus: *P. Giss.* I 12 (AD 87/8).

64 *SB* 13150; Parassoglou (1987) (here for fishing rights more generally).

65 See Gibbs (2011: 297); *P. Abinn.* 9.

66 *P. Ryl.* II 98; Johnson (1936: 386, no. 239).

67 Wallace (1969: 181–190).

(*figlinae*) were public property and were leased to concessionaires.[68] In the mining district of Vipasca shoemakers, barbers, and fullers had to purchase a license, of which only a limited number were available.[69]

Licenses could be bought both by individual practitioners and guilds. How common it was for *collegia* to step in cannot be made out, but since they routinely collected taxes owed by their members, it seems likely they also routinely bought licenses.[70] In AD 47, the guild of salt merchants from Tebtynis bought the sole license to sell salt in the district and thus acquired a local monopoly.[71] Around AD 200, the guild of 'Fishermen and Divers' (*piscatores et urinatores*) at Rome acquired a license to sail the Tiber.[72] Sirks believes the guild was identical with the 'Corporation of Skiff-Men' (*corpus scaphariorum*) and suggests they acquired a monopoly on river transport. Unfortunately, the inscription is inconclusive.[73] True legal monopolies, however, are attested only in Late Antiquity for corporations working for the *annona*. Only members and associates of the porters' guild (*saccarii*) at Rome, for instance, were allowed to load and unload cargo.[74] Whether this was the case already in the second and third century cannot be made out.

Taken together, the potential intimidation of outsiders, the enhanced security through guild solidarity for insiders, the legal privileges, and the joint taxation and licensing system show an institutional setup that made guild membership highly attractive for craftsmen, professional services providers, and local traders.

Government Control and Public Personae of Guilds

It should be noted that privileges, monopolies, licenses and concessions were obtained from imperial or provincial authorities, not local ones. The objective was for the authorities to facilitate taxation and regulation. The initiative, therefore, probably came from public authorities, not from the guilds

68 *Lex Ursonensis* 76; Crawford (1996: 404, 424, no. 25).

69 CIL II 5181 = *IRCPacen* 142.

70 See in this sense Gibbs (2011: 298); cf. Joh. Mal., *Chron.* 10.23 (246) for involvement of guilds in collecting the hearth tax in Antioch under Claudius.

71 *P. Mich.* V 245; Van Minnen (1987: 64); Gibbs (2011: 296–297). But note that salt is an exceptional commodity, cf. Tsigarida (2015).

72 CIL VI 1872 (p. 2879, 3820); see also *IParion* 6 (purchase of fishing rights in the sea of Marmara); cf. Purcell (1995: 146–147); Marzano (2013).

73 Sirks (1991: 269–279).

74 *Cod. Theod.* 14.22.1; Sirks (1991: 258–259).

themselves. This brings us to the second part of our paper. How independent were Roman occupational guilds? What (or who) was behind the surge of occupational *collegia* from c. AD 100 onwards?

The foundation myths ascribe the establishment of the first occupational *collegia* to an initiative of the kings. According to Livy the first *collegium mercatorum* would have been instituted in 495 BC by order of the senate to attend to the new temple of Mercury.[75] The religious guild of the *Capitolini* would have been created by the dictator M. Furius Camillus to organise the *ludi Capitolini*.[76] These are legendary foundations, and the two latter were religious rather than professional associations. But under the Principate, as well, public authorities were sometimes involved in the establishment of a *collegium*.[77] Under Domitian the senate deliberated on the institution of craftsmen guilds (*de instituendo collegio fabrorum*).[78] As governor of Bithynia, Pliny asked imperial permission to set up a craftsmen guild in Nicomedia.[79]

The creation itself of a *collegium*, however, was always a private act. The municipal 'dictator' of Lanuvium, L. Caesennius Rufus, inspired the establishment of a cult association for Diana and Antinous in AD 136, but he did so as a private benefactor (donating 15,000 sesterces), not as a municipal magistrate, and asked the members to draw up a charter 'by themselves' (*legem ab ipsis constitutam*).[80] According to the second century jurist Gaius, the law of the XII Tables had given *collegiati* the power (*potestatem*) to make internally binding agreements, providing they were not in breach with public legislation.[81] Caesar and Augustus curtailed the freedom to create private *collegia*, but the ban was not absolute and did not affect the binding power of collegial statutes

75 Liv., 2.27.5. Livy speaks of a *collegium mercatorum*, but the group in question was no doubt the priestly college of the *Mercuriales*, cf. Combet Farnoux (1981).

76 Liv., 5.50.4: *constitueret ex iis qui in Capitolio atque arce habitarent.*

77 Cf. Waltzing (1895–1900 II: 248–254); Royden (1988: 10–11). Sirks (1991: 81–107) believes the *corpora* working for the *annona* were public bodies, created by the state/emperor, but see against this Lo Cascio (2002); De Salvo (1992: 261–298).

78 Plin., *Pan.* 54.

79 Plin., *Ep.* 10.33; 34; cf. also Aur. Vict., *Caes.* 13.5; Sirks (1991: 313–322): Trajan (re)formed (*reperto firmatoque*) the guild of bakers in Rome to cooperate with the *annona*; against Sirks' view that Trajan also established the *Corpora Naviculariorum* as public bodies to assist the *annona* (1991: 81–107) see now Broekaert (2008); see also SHA, *Alex. Sev.* 33.2 (Alexander Severus establishes (*constituit*) *collegia* for all professions in Rome); SHA *Aurel.*, 47.3 (Aurelianus increased the number of Shippers on the Nile and created a guild of *Navicularii Amnici* on the Tiber); cf. Sirks (1991: 139–140, 288–289).

80 *CIL* XIV 2112; Ausbüttel (1982: 23–29).

81 *Dig.* 47.22.4. (*Gaius libro quarto ad legem duodecim tabularum*).

for legally authorised groups.[82] Doctors, teachers and athletes had a general permission to form private associations since at least the reign of Vespasian.[83] Other groups applied for specific permissions. Thus, the guild of *centonarii* of Hispalis thanked the emperor for allowing it to be formed.[84] A number of guilds affirm that they had been given the right to convene by the Roman senate (*quib(us) ex s(enatus) c(onsulto) / coire licet*).[85]

Florus' version of the foundation story asserts that artisans were assigned to *collegia* by the magistrates responsible for assigning the people in *census* classes. This was certainly not true in the late Republic or early Empire. Pliny assured Trajan that he would see to it that only workmen would join the *collegium fabrum* that he wanted formed in Nicomedia.[86] This implies that supervision was possible, but also that admission was normally left to the guild. The statute of the guild of ivory and citrus wood dealers' at Rome stipulated that admissions were handled by the group's own officers.[87] When, however, in the third century AD guild membership became obligatory for some professions that were necessary to ensure the capital's food supply, the autonomy of these guilds to select their members may have become more limited. Caracalla is the first emperor who is said to have appointed members to the guild of bakers in Rome.[88] Similar appointments are on record for Late Antiquity to guarantee the food supply of Rome and Constantinople.[89] Obligatory and imposed membership, however, was never extended to all occupational *collegia*. Craftsmen and clothmen guilds, as well, faced stronger controls in Late Antiquity. Constantine decreed that the members of the *dendrophori* had to be added to those of the *fabri* and *centonarii*.[90] By AD 369 clothmen (*centonarii*) were no longer free to leave their guild.[91] In the second century AD, these evolutions lay well in

82 Asc., *Corn.* p. 67 (ed. Clark); *Dig.* 47.22.1–3.

83 *FIRA* I: 420–422, no. 73; cf. *Dig.* 27.1.6.8; 50.4.18.30; Sen., *Ben.*, 6.15–17.

84 *CIL* II 1167; *AE* 1987, 496; see also *CIL* III 7060 for Cyzicus during the reign of Hadrian sending a delegation to ask the senate's 'confirmation' (*confirmetur*) of the city's *Corpus Neon*).

85 E.g. *CIL* V 7881; VI 85 (p 3003, 3755); 2193; X 1642; 1643; 1647; for a full list see Liu (2009: 105).

86 Plin., *Ep.* 10.33; 34.

87 *CIL* VI 33885 (p 3896).

88 *Fragmenta Vaticana* 235 (*creatis pistoribus*); cf. Sirks (1991: 322–325).

89 Cf. *Cod. Theod.* 13.5.14pr. (AD 371); cf . Sirks (1991); Broekaert (2009).

90 *Cod. Theod.* 14.8.1 (AD 329): *quoniam haec corpora frequentia hominum multiplicari expediet*; for a discussion see Salamito (1990) and Liu (2009: 282–283), who links the decree with a policy to remedy a shortage of skilled craftsmen, mainly in the building and textile trades.

91 *Cod. Theod.* 14.8.2; they are forbidden to 'withdraw' (*subtrahere*) to the city council, implying that they could not leave their guild; on guilds and their *munera* and privileges in Late

the future, but the seeds were sown as local and imperial authorities came to depend on guilds to ensure the provision of basic necessities and public works.

The attempts by public authorities to regulate the guilds reflect the increased importance of some *collegia* to public life. In the first century AD laws and senatorial decrees had banned all *collegia* except a few that were required for the sake of their public utility, such as those of craftsmen (*fabri*) and clay workers (*fictores*).[92] By the early third century AD associations instituted for the provision of 'necessary work for public utilities' (*ut necessariam operam publicis utilitatibus exhiberent*), such as those of the craftsmen (*fabri*), enjoyed special privileges.[93] The first such immunities were probably given by Trajan to guilds working for the *annona*, Rome's food supply system. Over the course of the second century (possibly under Marcus Aurelius) the main local craftsmen guilds as well received legal immunities.

Pliny's idea to provide Nicomedia with a craftsmen guild to combat fire indicates that fire-fighting could be a public service.[94] But ancient authors had a much broader view on why occupational *collegia* were useful. Pliny the Elder, for instance, writes that king Numa had instituted the guild of clay workers (*collegium figulorum*) because of the manifold blessings provided by earthenware products, such as wine containers, water pipes, conduits, roof tiles, bricks and pottery.[95] The builders/carpenters guild (*fabri tignuarii*) was crucial for construction projects and repairs.[96] Liu argued that the clothmen guilds (*centonarii*) received public recognition because they were important as suppliers of clothes to the army.[97] Much later, in AD 400 Honorius and Arcadius prohibited (craft) guild members to leave their cities., which had lost their former

Antiquity see Carrié (2002); Cracco Ruggini (1971); Sirks (1991) for the guilds working for the *annona*.

92 Asc., *Corn.* p. 67 (ed. Clark).

93 *Dig.* 50.6.6.12–13.

94 Plin., *Ep.* 10.33; 34. Cf. also *Notitia Urbis Constantinopolitanae* 3.21 referring to *Collegiatos viginti quinque, qui e diversis corporibus ordinati incendiorum solent casibus subvenire* (see also above n. 18).

95 Plin., *HN* 35.159 (lx): *propter quae Numa rex septimum collegium instituit.* According to Pliny, the establishment of the guild of bronze workers was inspired by the fact that its price most closely reflected its utility, whence it was also used as money and held in high esteem (*HN* 34.1 (i)).

96 See Bernard in this volume.

97 Liu (2009); Egyptian papyri show that authorities addressed the textile guilds not just to requisition clothes or collect them as taxes, but also to buy them; cf. *P. Oxy.* XII 1414 (AD 271–272); XIX 2230 (AD 119–124); LXIV 4434 (AD 154); *P. Ryl.* II 189 (AD 128). More examples in Sheridan (1998: 137–146).

splendour as the flight of the *collegiati* had deprived them of their supporting work force (*ministeria*).[98]

In the early Severan period, services by guilds working for the *annona* became obligatory *munera*.[99] The *munus naviculariorum* made guilds of shippers responsible for shipping fiscal and imperial grain, olive oil and perhaps wine to Rome. The *munus pistorium* obliged the guild of Bakers in Rome to mill grain and bake bread for the imperial distributions.[100] The guilds were paid for these services but the fee was not subject to market prices.

The recognition that they were necessary for public welfare gave some guilds a public identity, which they prominently advertised through architecture, collective munificence, seating arrangements and social ceremonies. Property owned by *collegia* is attested already c. 100 BC in Italy,[101] but its semi-public character becomes explicit mainly in the second century AD when visually prominent guild temples, club houses and monuments shaped the urban landscape.[102] Important guild complexes were large and lavishly decorated. The temple of the builders/carpenters guild in Ostia (*fabri tignuarii*), dedicated in AD 194, was over 25 meters long and 15–22.5 meters wide.[103] In addition the guild owned a town house, built around AD 120, with a courtyard of 13.5 × 21.5m, a public latrine, shops, dining rooms and various other rooms.[104] The divide between public and private was particularly blurry in the case of religious buildings. In late second or early third century Trier the guild of 'axe-workers' (*fabri dolabrarii*), for instance, built a temple for the Divine Augustan Powers, the God Intarabus and its own *Genius* on public land in a temple precinct.[105] The most spectacular example is the 'Piazzale delle Corporazioni' in

98 *Cod. Theod.* 12.19.1: *Destitutae ministeriis civitates splendorem, quo pridem nituerant, amiserunt: plurimi siquidem collegiati cultum urbium deserentes agrestem vitam secuti in secreta sese et devia contulerunt*; see for instance Lib., *Or.* 1.205–210, 226 for fear that the bakers would abandon the city. See also Symm., *Relat.* 14.3 for the city of Rome.

99 Sirks (1989).

100 Sirks (1991).

101 Cf. CIL I² 687 (c. 100 BC, *Magistri Herculei*).

102 Patterson (1994); Bollmann (1998); Tran (2006: 241–261); Zänker (1994: 273–277); Gros (1997); Slater (2000).

103 Bollmann (1998: 340–345).

104 Bollmann (1998: 284–288); compare also the so-called *basilica* of the Ostian guild of the *lenuncularii*, Bollmann (1998: 275–278). On the Ostian *collegia* buildings see also Zevi (2008).

105 CIL XIII 11313. Cf. CIL VI 40414 (Romae AD 47). They were presumably the local variant of the *fabrii tignuarii*. Cf. CIL V 908 for a *dolabrarius* who was member of the *collegium fabrum* at Aquileia. Cf. also the temple in honour of the Imperial House in Aventicum built

Ostia where 61 guilds of traders, merchants and shippers had meeting rooms (*stationes*) in Severan times.[106] The statement made by these guilds—and condoned by local authorites—is unmistakable: professional *collegia* were as much the pillars of society as political elites claimed to be.[107]

Some *collegia* contributed to public building projects. Part of the cost for renewing the pavement at the Cattle Market (*forum pecuarium*) in Falerio in AD 199, for instance, was paid by the *collegia* whose clubhouses and temples were situated there.[108] Towards the end of the second century the *centonarii* at Lyon repaired 500 seats in the circus.[109] We don't know how common such collective munificence was, but the frame of mind behind it—that *collegia* were stakeholders of their city's public image—was widespread. It went back to at least the late Republic. In Capua c. 100 BC, the council of the Herculanean district (*pagus*) asked the cult association for Jupiter Compagus to rebuild a portico. In return their magistrates were awarded seats of honour in the theatre.[110]

The public role of guilds was celebrated also in immaterial ways. Tanners, goldsmiths, gardeners, grain merchants, as well as neighbourhood clubs and other associations had reserved seats in the theatre of Aphrodisias.[111] In the theatre of Nîmes seats were reserved for the guilds of river shippers of the Ardeche and Ouvèze' (*nautae Atricae et Ovidis*), of the Rhône and the Saône (*nautae Rhodanici et Ararici*) and of the sea-shippers (*navicularii marini*).[112]

---

by the *Nautae Aruranci Aramici* (CIL XIII 5096) and the temple of the Craftsmen guild in Cetium (CIL III 5659).

106 The square dates to the time of Augustus and underwent several changes. At least one guild of rope makers (*stuppatores restiones*) had a *statio* on the site in the first century AD (CIL XIV 4549,58). Meiggs (1997: 283–288); Rohde (2009). For a similar allocation of public space to guilds see, for instance, the central street in Ephesus between the theatre and the stadion (van Nijf (1997: 84–85)).

107 Cf. Symm., *Relat.* 14,3: *noverat horum corporum ministerio tantae urbis onera sustineri.*

108 CIL IX 5438. See also *IANice* 73 for a stairway and portico financed by the *collegia* of the town of Cemenelum.

109 CIL XIII 1805.

110 CIL I^2 682 (the *magistri* in question were all freedmen); cf. also CIL I^2 674; 677; 678; 683. Note how these associations are often recorded also as financing public games; cf. Flambard (1983); Frederiksen (1959: 83–94); cf. also construction of port installations in Carthago Nova, CIL II 3434; cf. Díaz Ariño (2004: 467–468).

111 Roueché (1993: 124–128). See also the four rows reserved for the 'Porters devoted to Asklepios' in the theatre at Smyrna (*ISmyrna* 713 = IGRR IV 1414) and the seats reserved for the goldsmiths at Miletus (*IMilet* 940; cf. Dittmann-Schöne (2001: II.5.4–7)).

112 CIL XII 3316; 3317 (barge skippers); 3318e = EAOR V 45^e (*navicularii*, presumably members of the *Corpus naviculariorum marinorum Arelatensium* (*quinque corporum*), cf. CIL III 14165, 8); cf. Virlouvet (2004); Tran (2011a). See also the reserved seats for the *diffusores*

Seating arrangements in theatres, amphitheatres, stadia and circuses reflected social order. They had been subject to legal regulations since at least the *Lex Roscia theatralis* of 67 BC and Augustus's *Lex Iulia theatralis*. Local regulations added on to these, as just illustrated by the seats of honour given to the magistrates of the guild of Jupiter Compagus.[113] Of course, we cannot infer from these instances that *collegia* had reserved seats everywhere. But they indicate that such arrangements were accepted as a proper acknowledgement of the social role played by the guilds.[114]

Guilds actively participated also in public ceremonies. The guild of 'Divers and Fishermen' at Rome co-organized the yearly 'Fishermen Festival' (*ludi piscatorii*).[115] The Tyrian residents at Puteoli paid for the yearly bull sacrifice at the games and lavishly adorned their *statio* (no doubt also a temple)—the largest and most splendid in the city—at imperial holidays.[116] *Collegia* figured prominently in public processions.[117] Several inscriptions mention flag-carriers.[118] A stele for Jupiter Dolichenus records the solemn procession in Sarmizegetusa of the craftsmen guild (*fabri*) led by a high ranking local aristocrat.[119] Guilds with their *vexilla collegiorum* marched in the triumphal parades of Gallienus and Aurelian.[120] The banners and insignia of the guilds of Autun welcomed Constantine's jubilant entry.[121] The famous fresco from Pompeii showing a procession of carpenters carrying a figure of Daedalus does not explicitly refer to a guild. It does, however, illustrate the role of professional

olearii in the theatre of Arles (*CIL* XII 714,1). In Rome public servants (*apparitores*) had reserved seats (cf. Tac., *Ann.* 16.12.1 for *viatores tribunicii*, but not doubt valid for all *apparitores*). Cf. Purcell (1983) on the *apparitores* as a status group and their organization in *decuriae*.

113 Kolendo (1981); Edmondson (1996); Rawson (1987).

114 van Nijf (1997: 211–240); Verboven (2011a: 345–346).

115 Waltzing (1895–1900: I 237–238).

116 Verboven (2011a: 336). On the Tyrian residents' club see Sosin (1999).

117 Waltzing (1895–1900: I 237–240, 425); van Nijf (1997: 191–206) (see here for more examples); van Nijf (2002: 322–324).

118 *CIL* III 7900; 8837; 8018. See also the banner stand of an association of ξυστοπλτειταί from Smyrna (*IK* XXIV 714; Kubitschek (1934: 44–45) (late second century AD). Note the separate 'band' of *vexillarii* within the guild of *fabri* and *centonarii* of Comum (*CIL* V 5272, c. AD 200). On the *vexillarii* see van Nijf (1997: 200).

119 *CIL* III 3438 (p 1691).

120 SHA, *Gall.* 8.6; *Aurel.* 34.4.

121 *Panegyricus Constantini* 8.

groups in public ceremonies. *Collegia* of *fabri tignuarii* (builders/carpenters) were surely involved in processions as these.[122]

Important *collegia* were prominently present also at the inauguration of temples and other monuments. Sometimes hand-outs of money reflecting social hierarchy accompanied these occasions: *decuriones* received most, the common *plebs* least. Members of important *collegia* received more than the rest of the *plebs*, but always less than the *Augustales* and the *decuriones*.[123] The city patron of Urbino, for instance, at the inauguration of a statue in his honour during the reign of Commodus, gave five *denarii* to council members (*decuriones*), four to members of the *collegia* and three to common citizens.[124] In Misenum a freedman member of the *Augustales*, who was honoured with the *ornamenta decurionalia* (the highest distinction possible for a freedman) distributed twenty *sesterces* to council members, twelve and eight sesterces respectively to the *Augustales*, eight to freeborn members of the *corpora* (i.e. the *collegia*) and four to the citizens of the town.[125]

As a counterpart, guilds joined local institutions in honouring public benefactors and members of the elite. By doing so, they asserted their legitimate capacity to bestow public honours.[126] City councils confirmed this claim by granting a prominent public location for such honorific monuments. In AD 149 for instance the 'indoor craftsmen' (*fabri subaediani*) of Narbo erected a statue in honour of their patron Sex. Fadius Musa—one of the town's most illustrious notables. The local senate agreed to place the statue in front of the new temple of Augustus.[127]

122 Pompeii VI.7.9; cf. Leach (2004: 188, 309, no. 16); Burford (1972: pl. 12).

123 Patterson (1994: 229–232, 234); Verboven (2007b: 882).

124 *CIL* XI 6053. Clearly, only the officially recognized *collegia* received anything, among which at least a 'builders/carpenters' guild (*collegium fabrum tignariorum*, *CIL* XI 6075) and a clothmen guild (*CIL* XI 6070). Compare *CIL* XI 6378 (Pisaurum): 5 *denarii* to the *decuriones*, 2 for the *collegiati* and 1 for 'ordinary' *plebs*; *CIL* V 7920 (Cemenelum): 2 *denarii* for *decuriones, Augustales* and *officiales* and 1 *denarius* to the guilds.

125 *AE* 2000, 344, cf. D'Arms (2000) for a discussion. Cf. also *CIL* IX 23 (Rudia, time of Hadrian).

126 van Nijf (1997: 111–128); Verboven (2007b: 881).

127 *CIL* XII 4393 (p 846); Cels-Saint-Hilaire (1976); Bouet (2001); Verboven (2012a: 28). See also the statues set up for city patrons by guilds of *fabri tignuarii*: *CIL* IX 2213 (Telesia); *AE* 1935 (Minturnae); *CIL* X 5198 (Casinum) or the *Tria Collegia*: *AE* 1965, 194 (Cemenelum). See also *TAM* V 991; van Nijf (1997: 88–89) (the dyers of Thyaitera in Asia honour civic benefactor for constructing aqueduct); *CIL* V 7881 (*Tria Collegia* of Cemenelum honour provincial governor for restoring aqueduct and solving food crisis, cf. Arnaud (2007)). For more examples see van Nijf (1997: 72–128).

Power to the People?

By the second century AD, therefore, occupational guilds had become a part of the institutional framework of Roman cities. But what did this mean for local power relations? Were guilds able to weigh on the political agenda? Could they force governments to take decisions in their favour? *Collegia* were never formally involved in public administration. Executive and judicial powers were in the hands of yearly elected magistrates who had to comply with minimum property qualifications. Voting usually took place in geographically defined units.[128] The highest political institution was usually a local senate (*curia*), hierarchically structured with senior ex-magistrates at the top and co-opted members at the bottom. Guild officers were occasionally co-opted—presumably because of their influence among the plebs—but the office and dignity of guild magistrate did not entitle the holder to a place in the *curia*.

Whatever informal influence or power some (!) of the guilds had derived from their importance to the working of the city and the social capital they commanded. How far could such informal power stretch? How common was it? When did it arise? Electoral posters in Pompeii show a total of 28 professional groups promoting a particular candidate.[129] Scholars long identified these groups as *collegia*, deducing from that that occupational *collegia* were a prominent feature of Pompeian politics.[130] Mouritsen, however, convincingly rejected this interpretation showing that the electoral posters were part of the candidates' campaigning activities.[131] None of the posters mentions guild officers or other associative structures. More than half of the occupational groups mentioned are nowhere else attested as *collegia*. According to Mouritsen, many were simply workshop-teams in the vicinity of where the poster was painted. Those that were *collegia* were clients of the campaigners and were mentioned to enhance the candidate's prestige.[132]

Liu took Mouritsen's argument a step further.[133] She notes that *collegia* are practically absent from the epigraphic record at Pompeii. Even the famous

---

128 On local elections, see Mouritsen (1988); Levick (1965); Gonzales and Crawford (1986).

129 Fullers (*fullones*), bakers (*pistores*), porters (*saccari*), barbers (*tonsores*), ... For a full list see Mouritsen (1988: 175); Mennella and Apicella (2000: 56–58); note CIL IV 7838, connected with a fresco showing fullers at work (Zimmer (1982: 128, no. 42)).

130 Waltzing (1895–1900 I: 169–172, III: 115–118); Schulz-Falkenthal (1972: 114–117); Castrén (1975: 114–117).

131 Mouritsen (1988; 1999).

132 Mouritsen (1988: 66–67); for the view that not all groups are *collegia* see also Franklin (1980: 21–22).

133 Liu (2008a).

honorific inscription on the pedestal of Eumachia's statue, set up by the fullers in the early first century AD, makes no mention of a *collegium* or its magistrates.[134] This absence of *collegia* has nothing to do with the dissolution of illegal *collegia* by the senate after the riot of AD 59, since the inscription in honour of Eumachia, as well as a number of electoral posters, predate the riot.[135] Liu concludes that formal *collegia* as such were (largely) absent from Pompeii and probably elsewhere in Italy until the late first century AD.

Liu's conclusion, I think, is going too far. There is no reason to doubt that the illegal *collegia* banned by the senate in AD 59 were what Tacitus claims they were, viz. *collegia*.[136] An unpublished funeral inscription describes a member from the prominent family of the Alleii as 'well deserving from all *collegia*' (*omnium collegiorum benemeritus*).[137] Nothing indicates that these were public priestly colleges, as Mouritsen and Liu believe.[138] The quality *benemeritus* is a standard description mentioned in the Pompeian electoral *tituli*, but hardly occurs elsewhere in the town.[139] At least one other inscription, in which the servants of the *Augustales*, the percussionists (*scabiliarii*), skippers (*nates*) and *forenses* honour a local aristocrat, suggests that professional *collegia* were active in the town during the reign of Claudius.[140]

The meagre Pompeian evidence for *collegia* is not exceptional. Inscriptions mentioning *collegia* are rare (but not inexistent) in Italy before the late first century AD.[141] They were, nevertheless, familiar to authors of literary texts. Significantly, however, *collegia* in the Julio-Claudian period did not embrace public epigraphic culture as they would later—maybe because they were less affluent and prominent or because they were still looked upon with too much distrust by the elite to be allowed a public *persona*. It seems, therefore, that the prominence of professional *collegia* within the institutional fabric of Roman cities—and hence any informal power they may have had—grew only in the Flavian period and matured in the Antonine period.

Roman authorities were apprehensive about *collegia* as political action groups. In the turmoil of the late Republic, popular politicians had used

134 CIL X 813.

135 on the riots see Moeller 1970. See also Castrén (1975: 112); Mouritsen (1988: 32–36).

136 Obviously, this does not imply that they were the groups who set up the electoral posters.

137 Castrén (1975: 116, 133), from tomb no. W 11e near the Porta di Nocera.

138 Mouritsen (1988: 195, n. 241); Liu (2008a: 57); contra Ausbüttel (1982: 20) (private *collegia*).

139 CIL IV 3367; 7460; 7687; 9248; 9831; 9832; 9906. For variants: CIL IV 706; 768.

140 AE 1994, 398. The *forenses* may be retail traders. Note also the *magister Mercurialis* mentioned in AE 1992, 285 (c. 60–20 BC) of a predominantly (?) religious *collegium*, prefiguring/linked to the *Augustales*, cf. Combet Farnoux (1981); Degrassi (1937).

141 Patterson (1994).

collegia as private militias. This had led to a ban on *collegia* by the senate in 64 BC, which was later confirmed and extended (?) by Caesar and Augustus. The third century jurist Marcianus refers further to unnamed 'imperial mandates' ordering governors to ban *collegia* in their provinces.[142] Trajan refused his permission to establish a guild of craftsmen in Nicomedia because he believed it would inevitably become a political club (*hetaireia*), and these had caused much trouble in the province the previous years.[143]

The ban, however, was not absolute. A senatorial decree, probably from the (mid?) fist century, permitted 'humble folk' (*tenuiores*) to form *collegia* and pool funds for social purposes.[144] In his description of the riots in Pompeii in AD 59 Tacitus relates that the senate disbanded all *collegia* formed *contra leges*, which local authorities apparently had allowed to exist. But the senate's intervention only occurred after serious rioting and even then it was satisfied with merely disbanding the groups without actively punishing members or officers.[145] The Flavian municipal law only prohibited *collegia* formed as political pressure groups.[146]

Were *collegia* really a threat to public order? How common was public action by guilds? MacMullen thought it was self-evident that if labour disputes led to strikes or riots, the guilds would be involved.[147] The apprehension felt by authorities suggests the threat was real. Yet, only a handful of cases are known where guilds seem have put pressure on public authorities. The most famous (but exceptional) case is that of the 'Guild of Marine Shippers from Arles' (*Corpus naviculariorum marinorum Arelatensium*). When they felt slighted by the provincial tax administration, they wrote a letter to the prefect of the *annona* threatening to stop their cooperation. The head of the provincial fiscal administration was quickly ordered to back off.[148] The case is unique, however, and while it is telling about the influence of guilds that were vital for the capital's food supply, it doesn't tell us much about local guilds.

142 See Liu (2005); Arnaoutoglou (2002).

143 Plin., *Ep.* 10.33; 34.

144 CIL XIV 2112. Septimius Severus later confirmed that this general exemption was valid throughout the empire (*Dig.* 47.22.1).

145 Tac., *Ann.* 14.17.

146 *Lex Irnitana* § 74: *ne quis in eo municipio coetum facito neve sodalicium conlegiumve eius rei causa{m} habeto.*

147 MacMullen (1963); cf. also Baldwin (1963).

148 AE 1899, 161; Virlouvet (2004); Tran (2011a: 207–209).

Around AD 200 the governor of Asia intervened to break a strike of the bakers at Ephesus that may have been organized by their local guild.[149] Most other documents attesting labour disputes, however, don't mention guilds being involved. We know the silver-smiths of Ephesus were united in a guild, but it is not mentioned in connection with St. Paul being nearly lynched by these craftsmen. Instead the riot is said to have been stirred by a large scale entrepreneur and quenched by the city magistrates.[150] The alabaster workers from a quarry in second century Egypt organized a sit-down to protest against the employment of new labourers. Scholars often assume that they were organized in a guild, but the papyrus documenting the case is inconclusive.[151]

While it is true that monumental inscriptions rarely document civil conflicts,[152] we would expect to hear more of it if collective public action by guilds was common. Dio Chrysostomus and Libanius consider strikes and riots by craftsmen as a common feature of urban life, but they don't connect this with the guilds.[153] Respectable guilds (especially the important ones) may have preferred to stay aloof from rioting or stand on the side of the municipal councils in trying to prevent or suppress social unrest.[154]

Instead, potential conflicts could be avoided or handled through negotiations between guild officers and their patrons on the one hand, and the authorities on the other. Or by means of orderly trials in which the guilds were represented by their officers or by designated *defensores*. The *Historia Augusta* credits Severus Alexander for 'constituting' all trade and crafts *collegia* in Rome, and ordering them to appoint *defensores* to represent their interest in court.[155] This is not a reliable source, but the organisation whereby guilds as *universitates* were represented in court by *actores* or *syndici* is confirmed by

149 *IEphesos* XII 215 = *SEG* XXVIII 863; Buckler (1923); Zimmermann (2002: 83–85). Compare the conflict between the bakers' guild of Antioch and the governor in AD 382–384, Libanius, *Or.* 1.205–210, 226–230. See also *P. Oxy.* XXII 2339 (middle first century AD), documenting criminal procedures against a weaver who incited his fellow workers to revolt. But the case may be related rather to anti-Jewish riots in Alexandria than to a professional dispute; see Harker (2008: 80–81).

150 *Act.* 19; for the guild of silversmiths of Ephesus see *IEphesos* IV 2212; for a discussion see *New Documents Illustrating Early Christianity* IV, no. 1 (p. 7–10), other examples of labour disputes cf. Buckler (1923); *CIL* VIII, 14428 = *ILTun* 1220; *P. Oxy* XIV 1668.

151 *PSI* 822; see Gibbs (2011: 297); for another example (without guilds) see *P. Oxy* XII 1414 in which the *stratēgos* orders the banks to reopen.

152 Buckler (1923); cf. Waltzing (1895–1900 I: 191–192).

153 On Dio see Jones (1978); on Libanius see (Norman 1958).

154 Cf. Ausbüttel (1982: 100); in this sense also Zimmermann (2002: 83–86).

155 SHA, *Alex. Sev.* 33.2.

Gaius for the second century.[156] We find a similar form of legal representation already in the early first century BC.[157]

Guilds were routinely involved in collecting trade taxes and distributing liturgies in Egypt.[158] This simplified administration for the authorities, but also allowed the guilds to defend their members' interests. In the 160's AD, the fullers and dyers of the Arsinoite nome filed a complaint against a tax inspector for overcharging them. The complaint mentions a similar conflict in the past that had been resolved in favour of the guild by the *epistratēgos*—the second highest official in the province—under whose jurisdiction the Arsinoite nome fell.[159] In the early 270's AD the guild of linen weavers of Oxyrhynchus successfully presented a petition to the municipal council asking a higher reimbursement for weaving linen for the temple.[160] The situation outside Egypt was not fundamentally different. In Rome a fullers' guild on the Esquiline had been entrusted with the care of a sacred well. In return they enjoyed tax immunity for using the water for fulling. When in AD 226 a tax collector tried to force them to pay for the water, the guild disputed the claim. The affaire dragged on for 18 years but was finally resolved in favour of the fullers.[161] The guild of 'Divers and Fishermen on the Tiber' honoured a former president and (current) patron because he had succeeded in obtaining sailing rights for the association.[162]

Guilds, therefore, served as intermediate formations between craftsmen and other professionals and local and imperial authorities. But *cui bono*? We already noted that a limited number of prestigious guilds dominate the epigraphic record. They were arguably the only ones that really mattered in the institutional make-up of ancient cities. The thousands of largely invisible small professional associations were too insignificant to have an impact on public life.

156 *Dig.* 3.4.1; cf. Aubert (1999).

157 *CIL* I[2] 687 (a trial over property rights won by the *magistri* of an association dedicated to Hercules).

158 Gibbs (2011); Venticinque (2009: 47–49); *SB* XVI 12695 (Oxyrhynchus 143 AD); *P. Tebt.* II 287 (Tebtynis, AD 161–169). See also Joh. Malal., *Chron.* 10.23 (Antioch during the reign of Claudius).

159 *P. Tebt.* II 287; cf. *P. Phil.* 1 (c. AD 108–130).

160 *P. Oxy.* XII 1414; cf. Van Minnen (1987: 49).

161 *CIL* VI 266; 267: 268; see most recently (Tran 2007) and there for more references (the bibliography on the case is huge).

162 *CIL* VI 1872; Sirks (1991: 269–279) (see above); cf. also the builders' guild at Sardis in the mid-fifth century AD, who appear to have negotiated salaries, *ISardis* VII 1.18; Buckler (1923: 36–45); Garnsey (1998c).

A rigid hierarchy prevailed also inside important guilds—even though they were formally democratic and certainly much opener than civic institutions. Only the wealthiest members could afford to be magistrate of a prestigious *collegium*. Magistrates had to pay honorary fees (*summa honoraria*) and assume part of the group's expenditure. Venticinque showed that guild elites and civic elites in Roman Egypt largely belonged to the same social class in terms of relative wealth and social status.[163] In Gaul, as well, the magistrates of important guilds, such as that of the river shippers on the Saône (*nautae Ararici*) or the wine merchants based in Lyon (*vinarii Lugduni consistentes*), were close to the civic elite. L. Helvius Frugi, for instance, was twice *curator* of the river shippers on the Rhône in the second century. He became *duumvir* of Vienne and patron of the river shippers of the Rhône and of the Saône. His wife, Nameria Titulla, may have been the patroness of Namerius Euprepes, who was *magister* of the guild of *hastiferi* of Vienne. Frugi was related to another *decurio* of Vienne, P. Helvius Masso, who was married to Apronia Sabini f. Casata. She in turn was related to C. Apronius Blandi f. Raptor, a *decurio* of the Treveri living in Lugdunum as a wine merchant (*negotiator vinarius Lugduni consistens*) and river shipper on the Saône (*nauta Araricus*). Raptor was patron of the corporation of the Wine Merchants based in Lyon (*negotiatores vinarii Lugduni consistentes*) and like Helvius Frugi of the corporation of the River Shippers of the Saône (*nautae Ararici*).[164]

The economic wealth of guild elites in Italy matched the lower levels of the civic elites. The property qualification for membership of the *ordo decurionum* (100,000 sesterces) in Italy was relatively low.[165] Yet, some council members hovered only little above it. In the 160's AD, Marcus Aurelius and Lucius Verus relieved *curiales* of slender means (*tenues*) from the obligation to accept local magistracies.[166] Royden argued that c. 20% of all senior guild officers in Italy came to hold some municipal position, while c. 10% pushed through into local

163 Venticinque (2009: 86–129).

164 *CIL* XIII 1918 (Helvius Frugi); XII 2220 (Nameria Titulla); 1814 (Namerius Euprepes); 2243 (Helvius Masso); 2259 (Apronia Casata); *CIL* XIII 1911; *AE* 1904, 176 = *CIL* XIII 11179 (Apronius Raptor). See Verboven (2009: 163–164; 2012a: 29–30); see there also for more examples.

165 On the property qualification of 100,000 sesterces see Patterson (2006: 202); Duncan-Jones (1982: 147, 243). A fortune of 100,000 sesterces invested exclusively in productive wealth (in itself *not* a realistic scenario for an elite household!) would yield c. 5,000 sesterces a year of reliable profit. This is barely enough to maintain elite social standards. Compare for instance the Pompeian 'household list' of *CIL* IV 5380 which suggests a yearly expenditure for three *plebs media* adults of c. 2500 sesterces, 75% of which on food.

166 *Dig.* 50.4.6.

senates. These figures are not statistically reliable, but they show that the chance for guild magistrates of important *collegia* to enter the local city was realistic.[167]

Collegia were socially important not just because they were part of the structure of ancient cities, but because they institutionalized social mobility. They allowed successful businessmen to transform economic capital into social and symbolic capital—influence, honour and prestige.[168] Thus the guilds laid out paths of social mobility that were firmly embedded in the civic community. By the second century AD guild elites were socially close to—but not part of—civic elites. They moved in the same circles and shared overlapping social networks.

This was not just the result, however, of the *collegia* becoming wealthier and more respectable, but also of a reverse trend within civic elites. The public duties (*munera publica*) attached to the dignity (*honor*) of *curialis* became more burdensome in the second century AD. Membership of craftsmen and clothmen guilds became desirable as a way to avoid being charged with the *munera* of council membership. Emperors had to decree that the immunities granted to these guilds did not apply for those who were rich enough to take up the decurionate. Severus did so in a response to the governor of Noricum regarding the clothmen guild at Solva.[169] The problem occurred also elsewhere since Callistratus applied the same rule to all guilds who, like those of the craftsmen, had been instituted to provide 'necessary work for public utilities'. In a similar vein Pertinax confirmed that the immunities enjoyed by members of the shipper guilds (*corpora naviculariorum*), did not apply to the *munera publica* attached to the *honor decurionatus*.[170]

Significantly, the privileges of important municipal guilds were established and upheld by imperial laws. The license required for guilds who aspired to be more than private assistance groups was given by the senate or by the

---

167 Royden (1988: 228–231) (but heavily skewed (91%) towards Rome and Ostia); for a broader discussion see Tran (2006: 211–240). About 26% of Royden's sample were excluded from entering the *ordo decurionum* because they were freedmen (Royden (1988: 233)), but servile descent was no obstacle: c. 21% of the council members in Pompeii descended from freedmen, c. 15% in second century Puteoli and Beneventum, 13% in Ostia; cf. Patterson (2006: 238); López Barja de Quiroga (1995); Lós (1996).

168 Verboven (2007b).

169 *AE* 1920, 69.

170 *Dig.* 50.6.6.13; Sirks (1989). Although Septimius Severus did decree that shippers, contrary to other wealthy persons, could not be forced to become *curiales* against their will (Dig. 50.2.9.1).

emperor.[171] The clothmen of Hispalis honoured the emperor in thanks for the 'indulgence' he showed for allowing their establishment.[172] Eighteen other guilds mention authorisation by the senate.[173] The top local guilds, therefore, had direct symbolic and legal links with provincial and imperial institutions, bypassing the institutions of their home towns. How this affected their local position is unclear, but it must have given their officers leverage towards local authorities.

The top members of guild elites often became *patroni* of their guild, which raised them above its magistrates. Some, like Helvius Frugi, had risen through the ranks of the *collegia*.[174] In other cases a hierarchy is apparent between guilds. The freedman M. Frontonius Euporus, for instance, became *curator* of the marine shippers (*navicularii marini*) at Arles—a powerful guild working for the *annona*. As a freedman he was excluded from the local senate, but he was conferred the alternative dignity of *sevir augustalis* in Aquae Sextiae, and he was elected patron of the river shippers of the Durance and of the *utriclarii* of Ernaginum.[175]

Most patrons of important guilds, however, belonged to the local aristocracy; such as M. Iunius Sabinus, municipal *quattuorvir*, who was patron of the clothmen of Padua,[176] or L. Egnatius Victorinus Sagittius, *quattuorvir iure dicundo* at Carsulae and patron of the town's craftsmen guild.[177] They defended the guilds' interests and were in turn supported by them.

The most important guilds had direct relations with provincial or imperial authorities. This was obviously the case for the guilds working for the imperial *annona*. The guild of marine shippers' at Arles, for instance, co-opted an imperial procurator and high ranking officer in the imperial army as their patron.[178] But it was also the case for supra-local guilds as the 'Most Splendid

---

171 *Dig.* 47.22.3.2.

172 CIL II 1167 (p. 841); AE 1987, 496. Note also Pliny's suggestion to establish a craftsmen guild in Nicomadia (cf. supra).

173 See the list in Liu (2009: 105).

174 Clemente (1972); Liu (2009: 213–245); Verboven (2007b: 885–887); van Nijf (1997: 95–100); Waltzing (1895–1900 I: 425–446).

175 CIL XII 982 (p 820) = AE 1998, 876; Verboven (2007b: 876). The *utriclarii* were (probably) local land transporters.

176 CIL V 2864.

177 CIL XI 4589. Cf. CIL V 5295 (a *sevir augustalis* patron of the *Nautae Comensium*); for many more examples see Clemente (1972); for a discussion *ibid.* 164–167 (Gaul), 186–188 (Italia), 204 (Ostia and Portus).

178 CIL XII 672 (p 817) (Cominius Bonus Agricola Laelius Aper); cf. Alföldy (1986); Demougin and Christol (1984).

Body of Cisalpine and Transalpine Merchants' (*corpus splendidissimum negotiatorum Cisalpinorum et Transalpinorum*), which controlled the land routes over the Alps and had members and agents in important cities both in northern Italy and the Gallic and German provinces. They were under the protection of some of the most influential provincial aristocrats like Otacilius Pollinus from Aventicum, top aristocrat and patron of his home town, *Inquisitor Trium Galliarum* at Lugdunum and personally privileged by the emperor Hadrian. Descendants of some of their presidents even made it into the Roman senate.[179]

Lugdunum was the seat of some other important merchant and shipper guilds that enjoyed protection from provincial nobles. Prime among these were the river shippers of the Saône and of the Rhône (*nautae Ararici et Rhodanici*) and the wine merchants based in Lyon (*vinarii Lugduni consistentes*). We already mentioned how two of their officers, Helvius Frugi and Apronius Raptor, became prominent council members in their home towns. One of the illustrious patrons of the river shippers on the Saône and Rhône was Q. Iulius Severinus, a high ranking aristocrat from the Sequani who like Pollinus for the Helveti represented his people in Lugdunum as *Inquisitor Trium Galliarum*.[180]

High protection paid off. In AD 119 the river shippers of the Rhône' (*nautae Rhodanici*) set up an inscription at the customs' office on the confines of the *civitates* of Valentia and Vienna, honouring the emperor Hadrian for his 'indulgence'.[181] In Spain the 'skiff-men' (*scapharii*) of Hispalis honoured the imperial procurator responsible for the Baetis river (Guadalquivir) for his integrity and exceptional justice (*ob innocentiam iustitiamque singularem*).[182]

Links between municipal guilds and imperial and provincial authorities are less visible, but did exist. The guilds of *fabri* (craftsmen), *centonarii* (clothmen), and *dendrophori* from Cemenelum, for instance, elected the (former) governor of their province, Alpes Maritimae, M. Aurelius Masculus as patron.[183] A former consul and high imperial official accepted patronage over the craftsmen of

179 Walser (1991); Alföldi (1952); Kolb and Ott (1988); Verboven (2007b: 876–877; 2012a: 30–31); Tasser (2005) believes there were several 'Cis- and Transalpine Merchant Guilds'.

180 CIL XIII 1695; Wierschowski (2001: 303, no. 424); cf. also Besius Superior of the Viromandui, an *allector arcae Galliarum* (CIL XIII 1688; Wierschowski (2001: 302–303)).

181 CIL XII 1797; Tran (2011a).

182 CIL II 1180; cf. Remesal Rodríguez (1991); Verboven (2012a: 31) (see here for more examples of the guilds' relation with imperial and provincial authorities).

183 CIL V 7881; see above.

Aquileia early in the second century AD.[184] The builders guild of Praeneste was even given (*datus*) a president for life by the emperor Hadrian.[185]

In other cases we find local guilds co-opting as patrons officers from provincial guilds or from those connected to the *annona*, such as the freedman M. Frontonius Euporus we already encountered, *curator* of the marine shippers (*navicularii marini*) at Arles, patron of the river shippers of the Durance and of the *utriclarii* of Ernaginum.[186] The shippers of Lake Como (*nautae Comensium*) elected a member of the guild of Cisalpine and Transalpine merchants as patron.[187] Another was prefect of the craftsmen at Lyon.[188] Although not on the same level as the imperial or provincial elites, these members and officers of supra-local guilds, and their social networks, clearly surpassed the municipal level on which the local guilds were active.

Conclusion

Voluntary associations had a long history in Mediterranean cultures. In the early first century AD Roman imperial authorities were apprehensive about them as political pressure groups and potential disturbers of the peace. By the end of that century, however, their positive role as constituent parts of urban populations was recognized. Professional associations brought common people together, who thanks to their skills, hard work and co-operation enjoyed a respectable income and in exceptional cases even gathered a small fortune. Local, provincial and imperial authorities had come to recognize that urban culture—the backbone of social and political organisation throughout the empire—was impossible to maintain without help from occupationally organized associations. Occupational guilds were allowed, stimulated and put to work for the public good. Although guilds were never formally part of public administration, leaders of important guilds gained prominence and the divide between guild elites and city council grew thin.

---

184 *CIL* V 865 (T. Caesernius Statius Quinctus Macedo Quinctianus).

185 *CIL* XIV 3003; Tran (2006: 303–304); cf. Waltzing (1895–1900 I: 377–378).

186 *CIL* XII 982 (p 820) = *AE* 1998, 876; Verboven (2007b: 876) (and see here for other examples). Guilds of *utriclarii* are found in 18 locations in Gaul and Dacia. In Cemenelum at some point in the second century they were put on a par with the craftsmen, clothmen and *dendrophori*, thus forming together the *Quattuor Collegia*. Cf. Kneissl (1981); Deman (2002).

187 *CIL* V 5911.

188 *CIL* XIII 2029; Wierschowski (2001: 355, no. 492).

The differences between guilds, however, were huge. A plethora of small guilds provided intermediate structures for allocating corvées and taxes but little more. Besides these, however, prestigious local guilds were honoured and symbolically involved in public life. Guilds of craftsmen (*fabri*), clothmen (*centonarii*), and 'tree-carriers' (*dendrophori*), took pride of place in the Latin provinces. Merchant and shipper guilds, organized on a provincial and inter-provincial level, were directly in contact with provincial and imperial authorities and outstripped the reach of local communities. Leaders of guilds working for the *annona* wielded more influence than many local notables. Significantly, however, important local guilds as well received privileges and immunities that were guaranteed by imperial decrees rather than by local town councils. These imperial and supra-local connections are perhaps the most striking feature of the Roman guild culture. Although guilds structured local communities, their direct links to imperial and provincial authorities gave some of the more important guilds prestige and leverage that did not depend on local administrations.

CHAPTER 10

Group Membership, Trust Networks, and Social Capital: A Critical Analysis

Jinyu Liu

Scholarship over the past twenty years or so has significantly improved our understanding of the positive and active roles voluntary associations (*collegia, koina, sunodoi*, and so on) played for both their members and society at large, especially their importance in creating a space for construction of prestige among the craftsmen and tradesmen, facilitating the lower classes' participation in civic life, socializing upward mobility, facilitating 'Romanization', fragmenting social hierarchy, and facilitating business.[1] There is now a growing tendency among ancient historians to emphasize associations as private-order enforcement mechanisms that institutionalized trust networks and hence had the effect of reducing transaction costs, defined as all the frictions and expenses (search and information costs, bargaining and decision costs, policing and enforcement costs) involved in facilitating an exchange.[2] Informed in particular by social capital theory and the New Institutional Economics, these analyses approach associations as reputation-building, risk-averting, and efficiency-enhancing mechanisms for craftsmen and tradesmen against the ancient markets, which were characterized by uncertainty and unpredictability. This reputation mechanism has been afforded such significance that it was claimed recently that 'manufacturers were able to mitigate high transaction

* I would like to acknowledge my gratitude to Humberto Barreto, Sarah Bond, Wim Broekaert, Danielle Kane, Daniel Hoyer, Philip Katz, Catharina Lis, Hugo Soly, Miriam Groen-Vallinga, Andrew Monson, Michael Peachin, Tara Perkins, Manu Raghav, David Ratzan, Giovanni Ruffini, Koenraad Verboven, Tracy Yun, and Arjan Zuiderhoek for their insightful comments, and Christel Freu for sharing an unpublished paper with me.

1 For instance Kloppenborg and Wilson (1996); van Nijf (1997); Harland (2013); Tran (2006); Patterson (2006); Liu (2008b); Verboven (2007a: 861–893; 2011a; 2012); Perry (2011: 499–515); the dossier by Koenraad Verboven, Matthew Gibbs, Nicolas Tran, Wim Broekaert, and Ilias Arnaoutoglou in *Ancient Society* 41 (2011); Dondin-Payre and Tran (2012); and Fröhlich and Hamon (2013).

2 Monson (2006: 221–238); Hawkins (2006, esp. 78–138; 2012: 175–194); Venticinque (2010; 2013); Bang (2006: 51–88; 2008); Kessler and Temin (2007: 313–332); Broekaert (2011: 221–256; 2012c: 222). Cf. Gabrielsen (2007).

 | DOI 10.1163/9789004331686_011

costs by using voluntary associations—particularly professional *collegia*—as private-order enforcement networks, thereby forestalling the need to create integrated firms'.[3] While these analyses provide important new ways to understand how ancient economic life intertwined with social structures and practice, more data input and micro-level realities need to be incorporated to refine the analyses and take full advantage of theoretical tools.[4] This chapter represents an exercise to complicate the ideal theoretical scenario by bringing into focus some operational and efficiency issues of *collegia*. The goal is not to deny altogether the positive roles of associations or the validity of applying these theories, but to guard against an overly optimistic assessment of the voluntary associations' role in reducing transaction costs and to suggest some ways to initiate a more contextualized and nuanced understanding of the complex relationship between associative life and trust networks in antiquity.

Introducing the Questions

The extensive social capital literature has elaborated on the varied causes and effects of social capital, which can be defined as 'the ability of actors to secure benefits by virtue of membership in social networks or other social structures'.[5] Among social scientists, opinions diverge on the benefits of associative life, with some seeing it as a crucial force for positive social outcomes[6] and others emphasizing its negative social consequences, especially social exclusion and inequality.[7] Harking back to Bourdieu,[8] a number of recent studies have criticized Robert Putnam, the leading advocate of seeing involvement and participation in groups as a source of civility and trust, for not giving sufficient attention to the possibilities that 'social capital can divide as well as unify', and that 'associativeness may contribute to producing, maintaining, or eroding the social capital of a society'.[9] Not only has 'the correlation on the individual level between involvement in voluntary associations and high social trust' been called into question, but finding 'a working distinction between the kind of

3 Hawkins (2012: 197). But see Broekaert (2012a), who argues that vertical integration did happen in a number of economic sectors in the Roman Empire.
4 For preliminary discussions, see Liu (2009: 18–24); Venticinque (2013).
5 Portes (1998: 6). Cf. Easley and Kleinberg (2010); Ferragina (2012).
6 For instance Coleman (1988); Greif (1989); Putnam (1993; 2002); Migheli (2012).
7 For instance Kaufman (2002); Li, Savage, and Pickles (2003; 2005); Daly and Silver (2008).
8 Bourdieu (1980; 1985).
9 Li, Savage, and Pickles (2003: 500); Rothstein (2005: 102).

organizations that produce social trust and those that produce the opposite' has also proven to be difficult.[10]

Even if associations produce trust—an important form of social capital—all trust is not the same. Social capital may produce either positive or negative externalities. In other words, the social capital generated by a particular group may benefit or harm the society at large, depending on whether the radius of trust extends beyond the group itself or the trust resides only within the narrow circle of the group at the expense of the outsiders.[11] In the on-going debate about whether to rehabilitate guilds, Sheilagh Ogilvie urges to distinguish generalized trust and particularized trust, the latter of which, she believes, the guilds tended to generate.[12] Supported by multi-faceted analyses, Ogilvie challenges a wide range of claims, including the notion that guilds offered private-order enforcement mechanisms as an efficient alternative to other mechanisms available,[13] and focuses on demonstrating how institutions like the merchant guilds and craft guilds did not make the economic pie larger or generate positive social capital that benefited the society at large. Questioning the validity of interpreting the pre-modern institutions as a beneficial and efficient solution to one or more obstacles to possible transactions, Ogilvie has proposed other explanations for institutions: 'accidental events and personalities, cultural beliefs and values, and conflicts over the distribution of resources'.[14] Her recent book of the European merchant guilds (1000–1800), for example, argues that the prevalence and long survival of these institutions should be explained by how they served to allocate/distribute a disproportionate share of resources to benefit the guild members and their rulers.[15]

It must be noted that closed networks such as voluntary associations are not the only types of networks or mechanism that may facilitate information flow and trust. Approaching social capital as a tension between closure and brokerage, Ronald Burt emphasizes the importance of bridging across structural holes.[16] For Nan Lin, while closed networks may have a relative advantage in preserving or maintaining resources, accessing and extending bridges in the network may be more useful in searching for and obtaining resources.[17]

---

10 Rothstein (2005: 101).
11 Fukuyama (1995; 2002: 23–37).
12 Ogilvie (2003; 2004; 2005; 2007; and 2011) vs, for instance, Epstein and Prak (2008).
13 For instance Ogilvie (2011: chapters 5 and 6).
14 Ogilvie (2007: 658).
15 Ogilvie (2011).
16 Burt (1992; 2005).
17 Lin (2001: 10).

The issues of how associations interacted with other networks as well as the personages who played the role of either intra-association or inter-networks brokers must, therefore, be given sufficient attention.

In light of the development and complexity of the scholarly views on associations, trust networks, and social capital, the study of Roman associations, especially in terms of their relation to society and economy, would benefit from scrutinizing the following issues more closely: Were the Roman associations actually efficient in the sense that they helped cut transaction costs? For whom might they have been efficient? What type of social capital did they generate? Did associations benefit only specific groups of people or the society at large? It is impossible to answer all these questions in one chapter. In fact, a thorough investigation requires collaborative efforts, especially since the factors that contribute to explaining the development of associations and their institutional diversity range from urbanization, political economy, human capital, and social relations to (deficiency of) public-order institutions.[18] Nor does it need any reminding that the sparse and fragmentary state of our sources for the Roman *collegia* more often than not prevents us from performing analysis at the same level of detail or depth as the historians of the later period. This chapter focuses on 1) the factors that may have affected, impeded, and reduced efficiency of associations to foster trust networks or generate social capital; 2) associations as a possible mechanism of exclusion and separation; and 3) the relation between associations and other types of social networks.

Collegia: Cost Benefit Analysis

A wide range of factors may affect the efficiency of an association to generate social capital. The ability of an association to remain sustainable and durable, in particular, would directly impact its ability to enforce norms, foster and sustain a trust network, and sanction rule breakers. We do know of the existence of numerous associations from the Roman world. But many of them were frozen in time, being recorded in one or two extant inscriptions or papyri. We only know their particular concern, achievement, member base, or status at a specific moment but are in the dark about their lifespan or survival rates. There were certainly *collegia* whose longevity was well-documented, such as the *collegium centonariorum* of Mediolanum, *collegia fabrum tignariorum* (of Rome and Ostia), *collegia fabrum* (especially of Ostia and Mediolanum),

18 For a global approach to the factors that impact the formation of associations, see Lucassen, de Moor, and van Zanden (2008).

collegia naviculariorum, and the associations of the Dionysiac artists and travelling athletes. Some of these *collegia* had their own eras:[19] the *collegium fabrum tignariorum* of Rome, for example, counted at least forty-three *lustra*, each *lustrum* being a five-year cycle.[20] The *collegium aromatariorum* (pharmacists) of Rome lasted for at least twenty-eight *lustra*.[21] The publicity intention is certainly plausible in displaying these dating schemes on inscriptions. There is no need to believe that all these collegial dates accurately reflected the reality. But for some of the *collegia*, where there were a series of inscriptions over an extended period of time, a relatively long lifespan of these *collegia* can safely be assumed.[22] Most of these *collegia* had official backing behind them, with privileges granted from Rome, and/or had wealthy or powerful patrons, which was the case with many *collegia* at Ostia.[23]

It remains to be known whether many of the other *collegia* were ephemeral. Due to the public nature of inscriptions, they were particularly prone to publication bias, which means that they did not tend to record unhappy stories but often exhibited advertising orientation.[24] Furthermore, upon the dissolution of a *collegium* either due to internal problems or external pressure from public authorities, it is unlikely that the members would want to spend money on a stone monument. The rarity of the records of dissolution of an association in the epigraphic sources, therefore, would have been due to the nature of the sources, rather than the rarity of dissolution per se. As for the papyrological evidence, most of the relevant papyri represented the registrations of association bylaws, which were made on a yearly contractual basis, as well as expenditures related to group activities.[25] Hardly any reference to dissolution of an association can be found in the papyrological sources. Conceivably, the dissolution of an association would result in not renewing the contract and

19 Waltzing (1895–1900 IV: 280–285).

20 *CIL* VI 9034 and 9415b; *ILS* 3776 and 7240.

21 *CIL* VI 384.

22 For instance the *collegium fabrum tignuariorum* of Ostia: *lustrum* II, XVII, XXII, XXI, XXVI, XXVIIII, XXXIII, XXXVI (*CIL* XIV 299, 370, 371, 374, 418; *ILS* 1428; *AE* 1988, 204; 1989, 124). For more examples, see Waltzing (1895–1900 IV: 272–274).

23 For instance *CIL* XIV 246; see also Verboven in this volume.

24 Liu (2009: 24–26); Arnaoutoglou (2011: 259).

25 The bylaws of the associations in Roman Egypt and/or their registrations with the local registration offices would commonly mention the president of a given year (see, for instance, *P. Mich.* II 121 Recto, col. IV. vi; II 127, l. 20; V 244). For some of the associations such as that of the salt dealers (*P. Mich.* V 245), the specific arrangements that they wrote into their agreement must have been contingent on the duration of the concession that they had obtained from the state. Cf. Gibbs (2011: 297).

not registering with the *grapheion*, which means there would be no record in the documents.

We are fortunate to have a wax tablet that details the internal problems experienced by a *collegium* and documents what amounted to its dissolution. On 9 February AD 167, the president (*magister*), along with the two treasurers (*quaestores*) of the *collegium* of Jupiter Cernenus at Alburnus Maior—a mining town in Dacia—deposited a notice (*libellus*) concerning the depressed state of the *collegium*.[26] The main problems were as follows: 1) no more than seventeen of the fifty-four members of the *collegium* now remained at Alburnus, and even the co-president had not come to Alburnus or to the *collegium* since the day he took office; 2) there was not enough for burial expenses (*funeraticis*), and the *collegium* was running out of burial slots; and 3) over all this time, no one had been willing to come to meetings on the days prescribed by the bylaws or to contribute burial money or dues (*funeraticia sive munera*). At the end of the notice, the magistrates warned that no one should count on the *collegium* for burial service any longer.

The mining business in Alburnus Maior might have been in a particularly depressed state at that time, and the region might have felt the impact of the Marcomannic War,[27] which might have been the reasons why the *collegium* ran into trouble. This peculiar background, however, does not vitiate the general illustrative value of the document. It is illuminating in several respects, especially at the methodological level.

First, it serves as a warning that we cannot always take the prescriptions in the collegial bylaws as reliable indicators of collegial activities. Many historians have come to acknowledge the normative and idealistic nature of the guild statutes in the medieval and early modern eras.[28] The gulf between what the collegial bylaws had established and what actually happened should also be taken into serious consideration by ancient historians. The collegial rules indeed often had penalty clauses that imposed high fines or other forms of punishment such as expulsion for failure to participate in collective activities or for disruptive behaviours.[29] If strictly enforced, the penalties would have indeed caused damage to the reputation of the rule-breakers and increased

---

26 *ILS* 7215a = *IDR* I 31; *AGRW* no. 69.

27 Hirt (2010: 231).

28 Rosser (1997: 5).

29 *IG* IX/1^2 670 = *AGRW* no. 30 = Kloppenborg and Ascough (2011) no. 61; *IG* II^2 1369 = *AGRW* no. 8; *SIG*^{3} 985 = *AGRW* no. 121; *P. Lond.* VII 2193 = *AGRW* no. 294; *P. Mich.* V 243 = *AGRW* no. 300; *P. Mich.* V 244 = *AGRW* no. 301. Venticinque (2010; 2013); Arnaoutaglou (2002: 43–44).

the potential costs of the violators in their business affairs.[30] The sanctioning mechanisms could be costly to achieve and maintain, however.[31] In the Dacian case, the *collegium* was incapable of penalizing members who were in arrears or failed to come to meetings, as a consequence of which the *collegium* went into bankruptcy in all its senses.

This brings me to my second point, that is, the costs of being a *collegium* member must not be forgotten when we look at the possible benefits of membership. On one hand, upon joining a *collegium*, a member received a package deal, which offered access to banquets, burial, connection with patrons, possible low-interest loans, and aid in times of difficulty or financial crisis, or at least the combination of some of these.[32] On the other hand, scholars have long emphasized that it was not cheap to be a member.[33] We are not informed of the amount of dues for the *collegium* of Jupiter Cernenus in question, but data from other *collegia* suggest a wide range of admission fees. A miner could earn 70 *denarii* in addition to board for about half a year.[34] The entrance fees of 100 *sesterces* to the *collegium* of the *cultores Dianae et Antinoi*, Lanuvium (AD 136) were almost two and a half months' pay for a miner, who would not have necessarily been employed year round.[35] Lower entrance fees have also been attested. The *thiasos* of the worshippers of Dionysos at Physkos in the second century AD seems to have only charged 14 obols, although other contributions were also required.[36] Apart from monetary costs (admission fees, monthly dues, *ad hoc* contributions and subscriptions, and so on),[37] time commitments (to meetings, administrative work, participation in funerals, and so on) and labour for collective activities may also be seen as costs. For an individual member, if these costs exceeded gains, willingness to commit to the *collegium* would decrease, unless he was constrained by other considerations (perhaps family tradition, cultic allegiance,[38] unwillingness to forfeit the entrance fees too soon, and so on). It has been suggested that in order for a network to generate valuable social capital, one of the conditions is 'that member-

30 Hawkins (2006: 121).

31 Hechter (1987: 20).

32 Liu (2008b); Venticinque (2010).

33 Ausbüttel (1982); van Nijf (1997: 31–69); Tran (2006); Patterson (2006: esp. 260–263); Verboven (2007a; 2012: 19–20); Venticinque (2013).

34 *IDR* I 41.

35 *CIL* XIV 2112 = *ILS* 7212. Higher entrance fees: *ILS* 9100; *P.Lond.* 1178; *P. Oxy.* XXVII 2476.

36 *IG* IX/1^2 670 = *AGRW* no. 30.

37 For *ad hoc* contributions, see, for instance, *P. Mich.* V 243 (*BL* IX 160).

38 Religious activity did not always produce social capital, see Putnam (1993: 107; 2000: 65–79); Rothstein (2005: 102).

ship in the network is a privilege and is costly enough that participants remain invested in preserving that membership'.[39] Precisely because membership was costly, however, it not only barred a large number of the lower classes[40] from entry but there was also no guarantee that all of the current members would be capable of maintaining membership. A letter from Karanis dated to AD 184, for example, recorded a member's resignation (*aporrēsis*) from an association (*sunoditai*) due to his impoverishment or feebleness or perhaps both.[41]

My third point thus follows that the ability to remain solvent was crucial to the long-term survival of a *collegium*. The sources of income for a *collegium* could be diverse, including stipulated admission fees and monthly dues, *summa honoraria* (compulsory or voluntary contributions by magistrates) and other *munera*/liturgies, yields from collegial properties (*tabernae, horti*, etc.) and perpetual endowments, donations from patrons and benefactors, fines stipulated for inappropriate behaviour or other violations of the bylaws of the association, and subscriptions (*aere conlato*).[42] It is clear from the epigraphic records of gifts that the larger donations were reserved for the wealthier and more prominent associations. The wealthier the members of a *collegium* were, the easier it was to attract gifts either from them in the form of *summa honoraria* or voluntary donations or from higher ranking benefactors. The poorer *collegia*, on the other hand, would have fewer outside sources of income, which means that they had to depend primarily on membership dues. Because the members of such *collegia* were relatively poor, there was a higher chance for them to default on the dues, making it difficult for the *collegium* to function properly, not to mention participate in civic life. The recurring interactions and exchanges within a *collegium*—the convivial, religious, and funerary activities—can indeed be seen as repeated transactions in multiple spheres which constituted multiple means for the members to get information about, punish deviance in, and urge collective action on one another.

39 Hawkins (2012: 189).

40 Tran (2006: 105–109).

41 *P. Mich.* IX 575: ἀσθενῶς / ἔχων κοὺ δυνάμενος / νέμιν τὴν κοινήν; *AGRW* no. 289. Epiodoros, who addressed the letter to the supervisor and members of the association, was not necessarily the patron of the association, as often assumed. The Greek expression σύνοδον ἔχειν / νέμειν was equivalent to *collegium habere*, which may mean to form an association, to be part of an association, or to have corporate identity, cf. Joseph., *AJ* 14.235; *Gnomon of the idios logos* 108; Liu (2005: 287 note 44). As to the meaning of ἀσθενῶς, it may be related to impoverishment or feebleness. If we take νέμιν τὴν κοινήν as indicating being part of an association rather than physical presence at meetings, ἀσθενῶς most likely meant impoverishment.

42 Liu (2008b: 231–256). Cf. Waltzing (1895–1900 IV: 624–671).

These norm-fostering activities, however, involved investment; the operating expenses could be very high for the following transactions or a combination of some of them: multiple convivial activities throughout the year, sacrifices and other religious ceremonies, purchase of burial slots, burial ceremonies for members, maintenance of a collective graveyard, and bailing out members in trouble.[43] The higher-end activities, which not only communicated but also reinforced the strength of a *collegium*, would involve honorific inscriptions and/or statues for emperors, patron deities, patrons, and benefactors; maintenance and decoration of collegial meeting-places (*scholae*); banners and signets/*tesserae* as symbols of membership; and financial participation in civic events.

Economic downturn, mismanagement of funds, inflation, failure to recruit members, and so on may all have affected the economic viability of a given *collegium*. In AD 174, for example, the Tyrian merchants, who had long been operating at Puteoli but now had fewer members, ran into financial difficulty maintaining their station and had to make a request to Tyre for help, which they may have eventually received after much debate.[44] The *collegia* of small artisans and businessmen would have been even more vulnerable. Even though in many ways *collegia* were resource-pooling institutions, their limited financial ability necessarily circumscribed their ability to aid their members, provide opportunities for collective activities, enforce collegial rules, and maintain stability of the organization. Not only did the higher perils of insolvency make it more difficult for the poorer *collegia* to generate social capital but financial stress could have also weakened those *collegia* and eroded existing social bonds of trust and mutuality.[45] The feedback effect would have been particularly salient and damaging in those weaker *collegia*.

The less vulnerable *collegia* tended to be the wealthy ones and those that had been granted privileges, which not only made it easier for the members to accumulate patrimonies[46] but also helped to ensure durability of the organization. Rules may have been more self-enforcing in these associations because it was undesirable to lose membership. In such cases, the fear of being punished by the association would encourage the members to behave properly: they would, in theory, resist the temptation of opportunistic behaviours or short-term gains from cheating because those actions would have jeopardized the

43 For instance *CIL* XIV 2112 = *ILS* 7212; *P. Mich.* V 243.

44 *CIG* 5853; *AGRW* no. 317; Sosin (1999: 275–285); Verboven (2011a: 335–348, esp. 336); Terpstra (2013: 70–84).

45 Cf. Daly and Silver (2008: 561).

46 Tran (2006: 422–426).

long-term steady benefits of being a part of that group. *Collegia* as institutions would, therefore, have particularly benefitted the better-off among the sub-elite, but not necessarily the poorer members, who were in a vulnerable position regarding their recovery ability after a financial crisis and their access to credit and information.[47]

Collegia: Rivalry, Exclusion, and Separation

If *collegia* produced social capital at all, the state of our evidence does not allow us to investigate in any depth the externalities or the radii of trust produced by such social capital.[48] It may be helpful, however, to look at how *collegia* may create exclusion and separation, which, in contrast to integration, has not been sufficiently explored in current scholarship.

Collegia were competitors for resources including donations and other forms of benefactions.[49] A *collegium* was sometimes designated as the alternative beneficiary of a gift if the original recipient had failed to observe the stipulations. This can be seen as both manifestation of the inter-*collegia* competition and the benefactors' self-interested manipulation of the competition between various potential beneficiaries.[50] In Pisa, M. Naevius Restitutus left a legacy of 4,000 *sesterces* to the association of the ship-builders (*collegium fabrum navalium*), who were expected to feast beside his tomb every year during the *parentalia* and *rosalia*. Should they fail to observe this condition, they would lose the money to the carpenters/builders (*fabri tignarii*) as a punishment (*pro poena*).[51] The *fabri tignarii* were thus assigned the role of monitoring the behaviour of the *collegium* of the ship-builders. It is hard to see how this could be beneficial to inter-*collegia* trust or the trust between craftsmen in related trades. Even sub-divisions within the same *collegium* were used as checks against each other. In Ravenna, for example, a gift of 1,000 *sesterces* originally designated to the seventh division (*decuria*) of the *collegium fabrum* would be taken over by the eighth *decuria* of the same *collegium* if the former neglected the stipulated duties.[52] With twenty-eight *decuriae*, the *collegium*

---

47 See also Verboven above.

48 Cf. Bang (2008: 287).

49 Harland (2003: 53–63).

50 Liu (2008b); Kloppenborg and Ascough (2011: 324–329, no. 69).

51 *CIL* XI 1436 = *ILS* 7258 = *InscrIt* VII 1.19. Other examples: *AE* 1987, 198 and 199 (Ostia, AD 256); Waltzing (1985–1900 III: no. 1600).

52 *CIL* XI 132 = *ILS* 7235.

fabrum at Ravenna was a sizable organization.[53] The donor was perhaps taking advantage of existing intra-*collegia* rivalry or competition to ensure the proper use of the donation.

It has long been recognized that the occupationally based associations in the Roman world did not necessarily include all the practitioners in a given trade.[54] The *sunodos* of the weavers at the village of Kerkesoucha Orous in AD 42, for example, had only five members and one president/secretary [*hēgoumeno*(*s*) *gr*(*ammateus*)]. They were all men between 30 and 40 years old,[55] which points to the selectivity and exclusivity of the organization. The members were most likely the well-established, most active master weavers in the village, excluding the older and younger master weavers and apprentices. Two of the members were sons of a Papontos, and two others were sons of a Herak(l---), and they were most likely two pairs of brothers.[56] The small size of the association made it easy for these weavers to form a tightly-knit group, the cohesion of which was reinforced by drinking activities. In AD 42, they seemed to have budgeted a sizable amount of ninety-two *drachmae* for beer.[57] Presumably, they could all have engaged in exchanging sons or other relatives as apprentices, or even formed marriage alliances. What we would like to know is whether the existence of this association increased the barrier to entry or difficulty in obtaining weaving concessions for the other weavers, including the occasional weavers in the village.[58] Unfortunately, we do not have any evidence to work with nor do we know how a vacant spot in these small associations was filled.

Associations could play complex roles vis-à-vis their own members, nonmembers, the city or village, and the state, as illustrated by the case of the weavers of Philadelphia. In AD 139, twelve weavers were the recipients of a public order, most likely for military clothing, with advance payment. Since four of the twelve had been assigned other duties, the weavers submitted a complaint to the *strategos* and requested that he restore the four weavers and

53 *CIL* XI 126 and 127.

54 Kloppenborg and Ascough (2011: 5); Verboven's chapter in this volume.

55 *P. Mich.* II 121, Recto, col. IV. vi: Petheus (president and secretary), son of Petheus, c. 35 years old; Papontos, son of Herak(l---), c. 36; Harpa (?), son of Papontos, c. 35; Ptollis(?), son of Ptollis, c. 30; Papontos, son of Papontos, c. 30; Ptollis, son of Herak(l---), c. 40.

56 Associations of less than ten members were not rare in Roman Egypt. The well-known *koinon* of the salt dealers at Tebtynis had only five members (*P. Mich.* V 123 and 245) in AD 47. See further, van Minnen (1987: 31–88, esp. 50).

57 For beer drinking among the Egyptian associations, see Gibbs (2011: 301).

58 See *P. Ryl.* II 98 for an application for weaving concession (AD 172). See above Verboven on *de facto* monopolies.

confirm the exemptions from compulsory public services for the weavers.[59] Although the tone of the petition gave the impression that the weavers were hard-pressed due to shortage of hands, the question arises as to why they could not try incorporating other weavers to help fulfill the order. This question is reasonable because the weavers did not cite specific qualifications or expectations of special skills as arguments, which means that they were not irreplaceable, and because the twelve weavers could not have been all the weavers in Philadelphia; two first-century documents listed at least twenty-eight and eighty-eight weavers in Philadelphia respectively.[60] The twelve weavers in question may most likely have belonged to a preexisting association, although the petitioners did not explicitly called themselves an association (*koinon*) in the petition. Dealing with an association of weavers rather than individual weavers was an economical method of communication for the government and was also in line with the common practice regarding public orders. The letter from the Philadelphia weavers indicated that not only were they in anticipation of more orders from the state but they may have had prior experience working with the government. On one hand, the association, whether preexistent or *ad hoc*, provided an organizational structure to secure exemptions and preemptively protect the members from having further liturgies imposed on them.[61] On the other hand, it is very likely that these weavers blocked out the other weavers' access to public orders and reserved the business for themselves with the help of their wives, apprentices, slaves, and other assisting hands. Public orders certainly did not come by on a daily basis. But the Philadelphia case serves as an example of how an occupationally-based association may have used the structure to its own economic advantage, to the exclusion of the other practitioners in the same trade. With a variety of exemptions, it would have been easier for the incorporated weavers to accumulate wealth, leading to their increased ability to control raw materials and labour, and influence resource allocation in general.

Outside of Egypt, we see a greater degree of openness in terms of occupationally-based *collegia* recruiting members. In large port cities or commercial centers, however, another sort of exclusion can sometimes be detected, which

---

59 *P. Phil.* 10 = *AGRW* no. 296.

60 *BGU* VII 1615 (AD 84). Based on the understanding that papyri did not strictly apply duals, I count 'sons' (υἱοί, which appeared twice) as at least two weavers. *P. Corn.* 23 (l. 38): (γίνονται) γέρδ(ιοι) πη. In terms of the population size of Philadelphia, Rathbone (1990: 133) gave 935 as the average of poll-taxpayers in the period AD 32 to 50.

61 For the interactions between weavers and the officials in Roman Egypt, see the collection of references in Sheridan (1998: Appendix 2).

was directed at the resident aliens (*consistentes*), whose presence was conspicuous in these places.[62] We are ill-informed of whether the preexisting, local *collegia* systematically blockaded immigrants or rather provided low-cost ways of integrating them on an *ad hoc* or more systematic basis.[63] Being keen to build up local networks in their host city, the various *collegia* of resident aliens seem to have been happy to enlist locals, the *Augustales* in particular, as members, magistrates, and patrons, who functioned as important conduits to local society and networks.[64] The evidence is far less the other way round. An example of resident aliens being incorporated in local *collegia* was Apriclius Priscianus, a resident alien and potter [*exserc*(*ens*) *art*(*em*) *cret*(*ariam*)] in Lugudunum (*consistens Luguduni*), who paid for his position as *quaestor* [*redempto s*(*ibi?*) *honor*(*e*) *quaestor*(*io*)] in the association of the *fabri* with which he was affiliated [*pertinens ad collegium fabror*(*um*)].[65]

The fact that there were separate organizations of the local craftsmen and the resident aliens in the same trade speaks against smooth local integration of the resident aliens. In Lugudunum, the *fabri tignarii consistentes*, for example, formed their own *collegium*,[66] distinct from the corresponding local *collegium*.[67] Similarly, there were two types of *collegium centonariorum* in Lugdunum.[68] Did the coexistence of these parallel organizations point to the local *collegia*'s propensity to exclude the nonlocal craftsmen and tradesmen? Was the formation of a separate *collegium* of the *centonarii consistentes* or a *collegium* of the *fabri tignarii consistentes* a response to their relationship with the local *collegia* marked by exclusion? If so, to what extent did such exclusion, or possible rivalry, raise the cost of doing business at Lugudunum?

Compared with the locals, the resident aliens were faced with more limitations and particular challenges.[69] Not only did they lack the intricate web of long-established family and personal ties, but it was also difficult for them to join alternative networks. In the host cities where they were marked as

---

62 For the meaning of *consistentes*, see recently Todisco (2007: 1447–1454).

63 For examples of regulated integration of resident aliens in later periods, see Ward (1997: 126): the weavers' company of London admitted between eight and ten aliens in a typical year in the early seventeenth century, allowing four looms to each alien member.

64 *CIL* XIII 1939, 1961, 1966, 1967, 1972, and 2039.

65 *CIL* XIII 1978.

66 *CIL* XIII 1939 and 1967; *CIL* XIII 1966 = *ILS* 7028.

67 *CIL* XIII 2036 = *ILS* 7723; *CIL* XIII 2029 = *ILS* 7279; *CIL* XIII 1734 = *ILS* 7263; possibly *CIL* XIII 1734 = *ILS* 7263.

68 The local *centonarii* (*CIL* XIII 1805); the *centonarii Lug*(*uduni*) *consistentes* (*CIL* XIII 1961; 1972; *AE* 1982, 702). Liu (2009: 132–135, 210).

69 For discussions of these challenges, see Terpstra (2013: passim, esp. 79–84, 223).

outsiders,[70] the resident aliens needed to strike a balance between credibility to the locals and loyalty to their place of origin. For them to effectively function as a trading bridge between their home and their adopted community,[71] they must neither have been too assimilated to alienate the traveling members from their native city nor have distanced themselves from the local customs too much for them to be perceived by the locals as suspicious and untrustworthy. An individual member's lapses or failure could easily hurt the collective reputation of the networks of resident aliens with which he was associated. At the same time, the principle of 'economies of scale in publicity that make reputation-pooling a means of augmenting individual reputations'[72] had particular significance for the resident aliens. It would have been beneficial for the resident aliens to observe the rules and customs of the *collegia* they belonged to. The *collegia* would also have had a strong position vis-à-vis their individual members, which would have facilitated compliance with collegial rules.[73] *Collegia* as reputation-based, private-order enforcement mechanisms may have been best applicable to the organizations of the resident aliens.[74] It is reasonable to think that these *collegia* functioned as support structures for resident aliens, especially the new immigrants and commuters.[75] It is, however, important not to exaggerate the benefits of formal associations of resident aliens. Sociological studies of immigrant communities have warned us of the possible effect of social closure created by bonds to family and community, which may 'create cumulative disadvantages for the most marginalized group members', forming part of a 'downgrading process' instead of producing upward mobility.[76] Indeed, not all resident aliens in the Roman cities necessarily formed or belonged to structured organizations or formal associations.[77] The epigraphic evidence also provides anecdotes of individuals extending their connections into the local society by marriage, among others.[78]

---

70 Todisco (2007: 1452).

71 Verboven (2011a: 338–339).

72 Brennan and Pettit (2004: 196).

73 Cf. Terpstra (2013: 223–224).

74 Verboven (2011a); Broekaert (2011); cf. Terpstra (2013).

75 See also Holleran's chapter in this volume.

76 Daly and Silver (2008: 562); Cranford (2005: 393).

77 Explicit references to collegial affiliations are rare (*IG* XIV 2499; and p. 453) on Wierschowski (2001)'s catalogue documenting the movement of private individuals to, within, and from the Gallic provinces in the first three centuries.

78 Broekaert (2012b: esp. 50–52).

Collegia and Other Networks

Collegia did not exist in isolation but intersected and interacted with other social networks such as family, kinship, and friendship.[79] Historians of the medieval and early modern eras have long highlighted the high endogamy as a strategy to strengthen multiplex ties within guilds.[80] Our data, however, do not allow us to perform the same level of qualitative or quantitative analysis. It is also important to point out a gap in the study of the interactions between *collegia* and other types of networks or institutions; that is, apprenticeship and collegial life have more often than not been discussed separately from each other. While the status attached to skilled labour and to those able to transmit these skills to others has been made abundantly clear,[81] the dynamics between occupational training and the organization and inner working of the occupationally based associations are yet to be sufficiently explored. Since the medieval and early modern guilds took great pains to regulate apprenticeship, investigating into or modelling the connection between apprenticeship and collegial life is also essential for understanding the structural similaries and differences between ancient occupational associations and the guilds of later periods. This section provides an experimental case study of the weavers' networks in first-century Oxyrhynchus—where the prosopographical and biographical data are relatively rich, thanks to the dossiers of the two weaving families of Tryphon and Pausiris[82]—to illustrate how close-knit trust circles connected and sustained by multiplex ties including apprenticeship were formed among craftsmen and how these ties may have impacted the intra-association relationship.

The social ties of the weavers in first-century Oxyrhynchus that we know of are presented visually in Figure 10.1 The data present two sets of connections that are likely to be denser and more interconnected than the average set of connections in the entirety of the weaver population. One centres on Pausiris; the other on Tryphon. Tryphon himself, his grandfather, father, two uncles, his younger brother (Onnophris), and two of his sons (Apion and Thoonis) were all weavers.[83] Onnophris was apprenticed to Abarus in AD 36. Within ten

79 Tran (2006); Venticinque (2010); Broekaert (2012b); cf. Ogilvie (2007: 675).

80 De Roover (1948: 22); Sarnowsky (1999: 223–232, esp. 230–231); Ogilvie (2011: 11).

81 Tran and Monteix (2011); Tran's chapter in this volume.

82 About these two dossiers, see the introduction to *P. Oxy.* II 267; Brewster (1927: 132–164; 1931: 19–45); Biscottini (1966: 60–90; 186–292); Gagos, Koenen, and McNellen (1992: 181–205); Bradley (1991); Rowlandson (1998: 112–118); Piccolo (2003: 197–213); Hawkins (2006: 176–179); Venticinque (2010: 289–291).

83 See Rowlandson (1998: 113) for Tryphon's family tree.

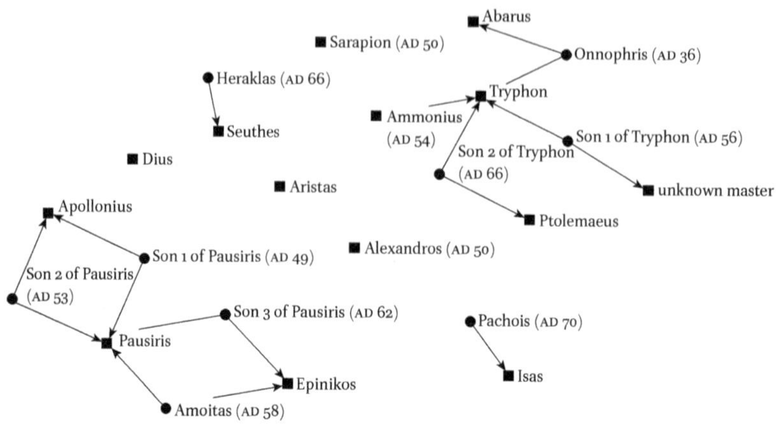

FIGURE 10.1 *Weavers at Oxyrhynchus (AD 36–70); square = master weaver; circle = apprentice.*

years, Tryphon's sons were apprenticed to an unknown master and Ptolemaeus respectively.[84] As far as the papyri can tell us, the networks of Tryphon and Pausiris, insofar as those connected by neighbor relations, business transactions, family, and apprenticeship are concerned, appear to have been distinct and isolated from each other.

Pausiris, Apollonius, and Epinikos were all master weavers of Oxyrhynchus, the connections among whom were characterized, sustained, and strengthened by multistranded ties that were closely intersected and intertwined. Apprenticeship, in particular, played an important role in linking these weavers. The links between them extended beyond the duration of a given apprenticeship term. Pausiris and Apollonius were residents in the same quarter—the Cavalry Camp Quarter—of the city; and Pausiris apprenticed two of his sons, Ammonios and Dioskos, to Apollonius in AD 49 and 53 respectively.[85] In AD 58, Epinikos' wife's nephew, Amoitas, was apprenticed to Pausiris,[86] whose son (also named) Pausiris was apprenticed to Epinikos four years later in AD 62,[87] attesting to the on-going, long-term mutual goodwill and high level of trust between these two families. Apollonius may have been too old or weak

84 In AD 56, Tryphon paid the weaver's tax for Apion, who was specified as an apprentice (*P. Oxy.* II 310). Whether he was the apprentice of Tryphon or another master weaver can be debated. Tryphon's name in the genitive may be a patronymic.

85 *P. Mich.* III 170; *P. Wisc.* I 4.

86 *P. Mich.* III 171.

87 *P. Mich.* III 172.

to take apprentices at that time; or perhaps he had already died. In order to fully understand how apprenticeship could foster and cement trust networks among artisans, it is important to look more closely at apprenticeship as a social institution.

Papyrological, inscriptional, legal, and literary sources indicate that apprenticeship was a widespread and well-established practice in the Roman world. This material has been used to inform discussions of a wide range of subjects including child labour, transmission of professional knowledge, investment in human capital, family as a productive unit, taxation of minors, and social mobility.[88] Scholars of apprenticeship in other cultures and later periods, for which documents are more abundant, have provided insights about how the apprenticeship had implications beyond economic benefits or the issue of appropriate training or transmission of skills. Apprenticeship has been emphasized as a vehicle of socialization, and transmission of the language, codes, value systems, and life styles associated with individual trade.[89] It has also been stressed that an apprenticeship was not merely a contract between economic actors but was an agreement between neighbors, families, fellow professionals and/or fellow association members. Munck, Kaplan, and Soly's observation that '[b]oth parties might have material as well as nonutilitarian concerns. Institutional and socio-cultural contexts were similarly essential factors with respect to the economic added value of the contracts'[90] may also be applicable to the Roman period. The ritualized and symbolic side of apprenticing a son or sons to another artisan, especially to a practitioner in the same trade, must be considered. Both apprenticing one's son to a fellow practitioner, and the acceptance of that child from a fellow practitioner as an apprentice, can be interpreted as tokens of trust, especially since they involved sharing trade secrets as well as information about clients, credit, and supplier networks.[91] Giving one's son to another craftsman as an apprentice amounted to certifying the qualification of the chosen fellow craftsman. Accepting a fellow practitioner's son as apprentice was a gesture of not only reciprocating

88 For discussions on apprenticeship in the Roman period, see the introduction to *P. Oxy.* LXVII 4596; Westermann (1914: 295–315); Zambon (1935: 3–66); Wipszycka (1965: 57–63); Pearl (1985: 255–59); Goody (1989: 233–256); Bradley (1991: 103–124); Bergamasco (1995: 95–167); Dixon (2000: 217–230); Rawson (2003: 192–194); Saller (2007: 109; 2012: 75–77); Venticinque (2010: esp. 288–294); Laes (2011: 191–195); Gibbs (2012: 38–56, esp. 44–45); Freu (2011: 27–40; and 2016: 183–199); Tran (2013: 146–185). Cf. Smits and Stromback (2001). See also the chapters by Hawkins and Tran in this volume.

89 For instance Munck, Kaplan, and Soly (2007). See also Humpheries (2003; 2010).

90 Munck, Kaplan, and Soly (2007: 5).

91 Freu (2016).

the trust but also extending the trust to the next generation, especially since an apprentice could be a potential competitor, whose reputation as a decent, reliable, and dutiful worker the instructor helped build, certify, and circulate.[92]

It was far from uncommon for the master's family and the apprentice's family to share the disciplinary obligations as well as the obligations to 'nourish' the apprentice. Due to the relatively short duration of the term in most cases,[93] as well as the facts that most of them had families nearby[94] and that not all the apprentices boarded with the master,[95] apprenticeship was not as uprooting an experience for most of the apprentices in Roman Egypt, who usually started their term between ages 12 and 14 (*aphēlikes*), as it was for their counterparts, especially those who apprenticed in metropoleis, in late medieval and early modern eras.[96] All the apprenticeship contracts in weaving from first-century Oxyrhynchus were for one or two years in length. In AD 53, Pausiris apprenticed his son Dioskos to Apollonius for the duration of one year. Dioskos was to board with Apollonius; but the two families perhaps did not live far away from each other, especially since they were from the same quarter. Apollonius received a pre-determined amount per month for the boy's food and clothing, respectively.[97] In AD 66, Tryphon apprenticed his son to Ptolemaeus, who was to pay five *drachmae* each month and twelve *drachmae* for clothing at the end of the whole period. Tryphon's son lived and ate at home instead of with Ptolemaeus.[98] In either case, the information flow between the apprentice's family and that of the master's would be constant. In addition, since the expenses in the latter case as well as in a number of others[99] seemed much

92 Wallis (2008: 845); Laes (2011: 192); Tran's chapter in this volume.

93 Various explanations have been proposed to account for the variations of the lengths of the training period: aptitude of an apprentice, the apprentice's previous knowledge/training, the level of specialization, the possibility of an apprentice having more than one master, and especially the starting age of the apprentice and the expertise of the instructor. See, for instance, Wipszycka (1965: 50–63); Bergamasco (1995); Bradley (1991: 111); Freu (2011).

94 Only in one of the apprenticeship contracts do we see a child apprenticed to a master who lived sixteen miles away. Pearl (1985: 255–259); *SB* XVIII 13305 (AD 271).

95 Westermann (1914: 310); for instance *P. Oxy.* II 275 (AD 66); *P. Tebt.* II 385 (AD 117); *P. Oxy.* IV 725 (5 years, free boy); *P. Oxy.* XXXI 2586 (AD 264); Wipszycka (1965: 59).

96 See, for instance, Hanawalt (1993: 131).

97 *P. Wisc.* I 4.

98 *P. Oxy.* II 275.

99 *P. Mich.* II 121 recto II, 8; *P. Oxy.* II 275, XXXVIII 2875 and XLI 2971; *P. Ox. Hels.* 29; *P. Tebt.* 385.

lower than the necessary maintenance costs for teenage boys, Sabine Huebner has reasonably suggested that the master and parents must have split the costs for feeding the child, with 'half the expenditure in cash going into whomever the boy lived with'.[100] Apprenticing the son to another master weaver, therefore, did not necessarily relieve the family of the maintenance costs of the child. Quite often, the family was also responsible for the taxes levied on the apprentice (weaver's tax, poll tax for apprentice above 14 years of age, and so on), and a small registration fee at the notary office.

During the term, what the apprentice's family lost in the short run was the boy's labour; what it would gain in the long run was the boy's increased productivity as well as a formalized relationship with his teacher. There were no immediate monetary gains on the part of the master, because the cash he received from the apprentice's family was to be spent on feeding and clothing the boy. As for the master, what he gained was a helping hand at no monetary cost; the compensation he provided was transferring the knowledge in the weaving trade to the child, and perhaps more importantly, providing a service to the child and the child's family by certifying the child and helping to initiate him into the business.[101]

The network that was linked by apprenticeship was both intragenerational and intergenerational. The intragenerational relationship not only existed between the fellow masters but may have also been fostered between the apprentices and the masters' children, and among the apprentices of the same master. When Amoitas was Pausiris' apprentice in AD 58–59, Pausiris' three sons were perhaps close to 23, 19, and 10 years old, respectively. Amoitas would certainly have had occasions to interact with Pausiris, Jr, if not all three of the brothers. When Pausiris, Jr was Epinikos' apprentice, Amoitas was probably about 18 years old. We do not know whether Amoitas, whose father had died before AD 58, was living with his aunt and her husband Epinikos or was working for Epinikos. In any case, it is quite likely that Pausiris, Jr and Amoitas would have had opportunities to meet at Epinikos' house. Apprenticeship as an institution had an important role to play in shaping the connections among the next generation of craftsmen, the future masters.

How, then, did these networks impact the workings of *collegia*? To address the question, it is necessary to first consider to what extent the associations

---

100 Huebner (2013: 62).

101 Cf. the later parallel, Munck, Kaplan, and Soly (2007: 15). There may be other costs on the part of the masters, including loss caused by damage due to the apprentice's lack of skill or experience.

regulated apprenticeship. Based on a papyrus now known as *P.Carlsberg* 53, which seemed to be a tax-list of fullers and dyers and mentioned a *hegoumenos gerdiōn* of Tebtynis in connection with the *diakrisis mathētōn*, van Minnen suspected that the document suggested that the guild had a say in the screening of apprentices of individual members, and that government officials were involved as well.[102] Reasonable as it is, the suggestion is far from conclusive due to the absence of parallels from the first four centuries and any context of the document. Nor is it clear what the *diakrisis* in question entailed. In general, the associations' interference with or regulation of apprenticeship seemed far from extensive. There did not seem to have been any significant regulation of the length of the term,[103] which was an area of intense control for the guilds of later periods with a general tendency to prolong the apprenticeship duration.[104] In terms of whether apprentices, newly-graduated apprentices, and young masters had access to membership in a *koinon*, there does not seem to have been a consistent or detectable system. There was certainly no established three-stage progression from apprentices to journeymen to masters.

If associations did not have a significant restrictive impact on apprenticeship, we can return to Figure 10.1, which visualizes the better connected weavers, the less connected weavers, and the 'isolates'. I do not claim, however, that Figure 10.1 is an accurate depiction of the ties of all the weavers. Our knowledge of their social networks is necessarily conditioned by the survival of papyri. We lack three types of information: 1) the possible connections of the more

102 Van Minnen (1987: 70); Bülow-Jacobsen (1989: 125–131). The κατὰ τὸν νόμον in the apprenticeship contracts from Karanis in AD 50 (*P. Oslo* III 141) should be understood as 'all over the nome' rather than 'according to the law', whether it was general law or guild law. Cf. *P. Mich.* V 355; van Minnen (1987: 69–70); Wipszycka (1965: 60).

103 We have too few examples to be assertive on whether the term of apprenticeship in Roman Egypt became longer in the later centuries. Short duration is also attested for all the centuries. The few apprenticeship arrangements that lasted for four to five years also came from all centuries. Length of terms also varied within the same trade, there being no clear correlation between the duration of the apprenticeship with trade. Take weaving, for example—the duration ranged from one to two years (five cases), two years (five cases), two and a half years (two cases), three years (two cases), four years (two cases), five years (three cases), to even longer terms.

104 The bibliography is extensive. See, for instance, Quimby (1985: 40); Lane (1996: 16–17); Smits and Stromback (2001); Munck, Kaplan, and Soly (2007); Wallis (2008: 832–861).

'isolated' weavers;[105] 2) the total number of weavers in Oxyrhynchus;[106] and 3) the size of the association of weavers in Oxyrhynchus, if there had indeed been a weavers' association there in the first century.[107] But the presence of clusters would be in line with the findings of social network analysis.[108]

Three different scenarios of the relationship between such clusters and the weavers' association may be postulated. It is possible that one of the clusters significantly overlapped the weavers' association in terms of membership, which in turn functioned as a mechanism of advancing the benefit of one particular group of weavers. Alternatively, there is also the possibility that the association was dominated by the otherwise isolated members. In that case, the association functioned as a mechanism to counter-balance the tightly knit trust networks of some weavers. If hypothetically all of the known weavers belonged to the same association, the following questions arise: How did the presence of clusters within an association influence information flow and knowledge transfer?[109] Which ties took precedence in case of conflict? How did clusters shape the evolution of the association itself? Empirical data for the Roman world are not easy to come by. It is easy to forget that competition and rivalry may have coexisted with coordination and cooperation. Theoretically, these different sub-groups may have been potential competitors not only in business but for status within the association as well. Rising up within the association was no small matter for an artisan, especially since collegial magistracy was

---

105 For some of the weavers, we only have one papyrus for each of them. In AD 48–50, four Oxyrhynchus weavers—Dius, Alexandros, Sarapion, and Aristas—sent petitions to the *strategos* individually to complain about the extortion (διεσείσθην) by former tax collectors (*P. Oxy.* LXXIII 4953; II 284–285 and 393). In AD 54, Ammonius sold a loom to Tryphon (*P. Oxy.* II 264). Isas, who took Pachois as apprentice in AD 70 (*SB* XXIV 16186; the names are transcribed differently in *P. Lond.* inv. 1407), may well have been an apprentice of another master some time ago, whose name was simply not available to us. In AD 66, Seuthes took Heraklas as apprentice (*P. Oxy.* XLI 2971).

106 Van Minnen (1987: 76) once suggested, although not followed by everyone, that 20% of the total population of a town like Oxyrhynchus, which was estimated at 30,000, would have been engaged in the textile trade.

107 For evidence of weaving guilds in Roman Egypt in the first century, see, for instance, *P. Ryl.* II 94 (AD 14–37, Euhemeria), *BGU* VII 1615 (AD 84, Philadelphia); *P. Mich.* II 121 recto IV.vi; 123 recto iii.41 and 124 recto ii.19; *Chrest. Wilck.* 57 (AD 92, Soknopaiou Nesos); Bradley (1991: 107); Arnaoutaglou (2005); Hawkins (2006: 122–130).

108 Brautbar and Kearns (2010). See also Holland and Leinhardt (1971: 107–124); Watts and Strogatz (1998: 441).

109 Helms *et al.* (2010: 62): 'Sub-communities are undesirable in a learning network as it hinders the free flow of knowledge through the network'.

considered as an accepted source of social status and prestige in the society at large.[110] Competition and rivalry could lead to discord, impeding or reducing trust between groups within a given association. We have never been under the illusion that collegial banquets and other social events were simply harmonious occasions for sociability. The ordinances of the associations made it quite clear that they anticipated unruly and disruptive behaviours, including causing disturbances, speaking abusively, and insulting the collegiate magistrates, and as a norm they preemptively set a fine on such behaviours.[111] If these rules were enforced, those who may have suffered most would have been the isolated or the least connected members, that is, those who were either excluded from the clusters or those at the bottom within the guild hierarchy, and these two categories may have overlapped to a great extent.[112]

If this analysis is legitimate, membership may have further enriched those with high social capital but further impoverished those without. For the latter, the social cost of being punished within the association would have been particularly high. Alternative hypothetical scenarios may also be possible, however. The structural holes may create opportunities for brokerage. Benefits may have accrued for members who functioned as bridges between sub-groups.[113] Detecting brokers and bridgers would be a useful exercise in the future study of Roman associations.

Conclusion

Collegia can be broadly described as resource-pooling and reputation-pooling organizations. Their ability to have any impact on their members and the society depended to a great extent on how successful they were in these two areas. A certain number of *collegia* distinguished themselves in terms of wealth, reputation, and durability. The epigraphic evidence clearly suggests that it was a matter of pride to be associated with those *collegia*. Not only did they carry reputations on which the members could ride but they also served as honour-generating bodies, bestowing honour on patrons and benefactors. It is important not to forget that there were certainly more people outside of these *collegia* than those within. While these *collegia* were able to provide significant benefits, including access to public contracts and protection for their

110 MacMullen (1974: 119); Joshel (1992); van Nijf (1997); Verboven (2007b); Perry (2012).

111 For instance *CIL* XIV 2112 = *ILS* 7212; *P. Lond.* 2710.

112 Cf. Burt (2005: 30).

113 Burt (1992; 2005); Easley and Kleinberg (2010: 68–70); Stovel and Shaw (2012: 139–158).

members, they barred a large number of craftsmen and tradesmen from such benefits. *Collegia* as a mechanism of exclusion went hand in hand with their being a mechanism of protection. The local *collegia*'s roles in integrating resident aliens seemed ambiguous at best, and probably even hostile at times.

Not all the *collegia* worked effectively as reputational mechanisms or collective punishment schemes. The ability of many *collegia*, especially the poorer ones, to enforce rules, foster trust networks, generate social capital, take collective action, and hence contribute to reducing transaction costs could be affected, impeded, or circumscribed by a variety of factors. These factors included lack of stability or durability, financial difficulty or high enforcement cost, and internal competition and rivalries between cliques, which were usually tight-knit clusters connected by multiplex relationships (apprenticeship, kinship, neighbor relations, and so on).

Finding trustworthy persons and intermediaries was a constant need for craftsmen and businessmen. It is important to remember that they were not only concerned with issues directly related to business (raw materials, equipment such as looms, suppliers, buyers, prices, and so on) but lending and borrowing money also consumed a sizeable amount of their energy. A large part of the dossiers of Tryphon and Pausiris, in fact, involved loan transactions.[114] When Tryphon failed to get back a loan of 52 *drachmae* he had made to Dioskoros,[115] for example, he asked his 'dear friend' (*philtatōi*) Ammonas to 'worry' (*ochlēson*) Dioskoros and make him pay; and if Dioskoros gave Ammonas the money, the latter was to give it to someone 'reliable' (*asphalēn*) to bring to Tryphon. It is not clear whether Ammonas was a fellow weaver. What is clear is that Tryphon was mobilizing his trust network, and in this process, Dioskoros' credibility or lack thereof was being circulated and scrutinized. There were indeed numerous ways that a craftsman or businessman's credibility, integrity, trustworthiness, and reliability came to be cross-checked and circulated.[116] Through the networks of neighbors, apprentices, parents of the apprentices, relatives, creditors, and friends, a craftsman's reputation—especially in terms of whether he could provide high-quality training to his apprentices, whether he treated them appropriately, and whether he was able to repay loans in a timely manner—was repeatedly monitored and communicated. His reputation in these areas would directly impact his access to credit, labour, and

114 Tryphon as debtor: *P. Oxy.* II 304, 318, and 320; as creditor: *P. Oxy.* II 269 and 319. Loans and repayments made by Pausiris, Jr: *P. Mich. inv.* 84–92 (AD 73–74). Gagos, Koenen, and McNellen (1992).

115 *P. Oxy.* II 269 (AD 57); Brewster (1931: 42–43).

116 *P. Mich.* VIII 485. See also *P. Oslo* II 47.

business opportunities. Social capital literature has emphasized the importance of informal networks.[117] The unstable or weak ties formed through membership in some *collegia* may have served as possible conduits to networks that may not have otherwise overlapped.[118] The reputation mechanism of the ancient *collegia*, however, may not have been any more effective than the less formal networks. Not only did *collegia* by no means replace those networks, especially in smaller cities and villages, but inter-member and member-association relationships were impacted by those networks in complex ways.[119]

This chapter in no way exhausts all the possible scenarios concerning the working of the Roman associations as social networks. I hope, however, that it has sufficiently demonstrated the complexity of the factors that may have impacted the internal workings of the association, intra-association relationships, and the relationships between the association and other networks or institutions, so that we may exercise caution when interpreting the association's efficiency in reducing transaction costs.

---

117 Lin (2005: 101); Li, Pickles, and Savage (2005).

118 For the value of weak ties, see the seminal article by Granovetter (1973: 1360–1380). See recently, Easley and Kleinberg (2010), especially chapter 3. See also Holleran's chapter in this volume.

119 Venticinque (2010: 273–294); Lin (2001: 10–11).

CHAPTER 11

Currency and Control: Mint Workers in the Later Roman Empire

Sarah Bond

Following their meeting at Milan in 313, Constantine remained in control of the Roman Empire in the west, while Licinius oversaw the east.[1] Although they were ostensibly partners, the rivalry between them visibly continued in a number of spheres, including their coinage reforms. In his earlier struggle to be recognized as Augustus in the west, Constantine had advertised his legitimacy by introducing a new gold coin called the solidus. For his part, Licinius had rejected Constantine's solidus and struggled to sustain the minting of the heavier aureus.[2] This 'valorised' solidus would eventually emerge as the standard within the empire; however, it could not be fully implemented in the east until after the defeat of Licinius in 324.[3] It is within the broader context of both emperors' patent attempts to ensure the supply, authority, and legitimacy of their imperial coinage that we must consider legislation that dictated the status of imperial mint workers known as *monetarii*. It was probably Licinius who sent a rescript dated to 21 July 317 to the Bithynians declaring that the *monetarii* were to maintain a lowly status into perpetuity; moreover, he barred them from attaining the dignities of the equestrian order.[4] The

* I would like to thank Richard J.A. Talbert, Michael Peachin, and John Melville-Jones for their helpful remarks in the writing of this chapter. All mistakes are my own.

1 This meeting would result in a new policy of religious toleration labeled the Edict of Milan, as well as the marriage of Constantia, Constantine's half-sister, to Licinius. See Lact. *De mort. pers.* 48; Eus. *Hist. eccl.* 10.5.4.

2 See Abdy (2012: 591–592). It does appear that Licinius went along with reforms to *nummi* around 318.

3 The introduction of the *solidus* began in 309. See Depeyrot (2012: 237–240). Although it was of lesser importance than gold to his monetary program, Constantine also reinvigorated the minting of silver coinage, through the *siliqua* and *miliarensis*, and in addition reformed billon and base metal coinages. See Vagi 1999: 485–486.

4 The rescript was later attributed to Constantine in the *Theodosian Code*, but if the date and place are correct, it is probable that it is Licinius' work. *Cod. Theod.* 10.20.1 (=*Cod. Iust.* 11.8.1): *Imp. Constantinus a. ad Bithynos. monetarios in sua semper durare condicione oportet nec dignitates eis perfectissimatus tribui vel ducenae vel centenae vel egregiatus. dat. xii kal.*

 | DOI 10.1163/9789004331686_012

equestrian grades of *perfectissimatus* and *egregiatus* in particular carried with them special exemptions from *munera*, and could thus be used to escape curial duties—an increasingly pervasive problem in the fourth century.[5] The rescript indicates that minters were already considered as having a degraded status by 317, but that this status was not altogether debilitating or base. Though barred from the equestrian orders, freeborn Bithynian *monetarii* perhaps served as curials, suggesting that mint workers could achieve a degree of wealth and civic prominence.

An ostensible reason for limiting the dignities available to minters was to tie them to their positions in the imperial mint; however, an additional reason for overseeing them carefully became evident only a few years later, when Constantine cited the imperial *monetarii* in his pronouncements on counterfeiting. In 321, the emperor alleged that imperial minters were engaged in clandestine minting of money.[6] He attempted to stop the practice through threats directed at the counterfeiters and by proffering incentives for informers. The measures imply that some minters illegally benefitted from their close proximity to the imperial stores of gold, silver, and bronze, but the law may have additionally served as a public strategy to restore confidence in the quality of the currency and hence boost consumer confidence.[7] Positions in the mint did provide a unique opportunity for theft, coin shaving (wherein an individual debased the coin's value by filing the metal down), and stealing official dies to be used externally, but the move also unambiguously asserted Constantine's control over the coinage. Over the course of the fourth century, regulation of the status, prospects, and even conjugal rights of these imperial minters only intensified; however, little modern work has explored the reasons for the changing status of Roman mint workers. This investigation into the legislation concerning *monetarii* will attempt to show how Roman law was employed to construct imperial legitimacy. It will also posit that the legislation in the fourth

aug. Gallicano et Basso conss. (*317 iul. 21*). The code attributes the rescript to Constantine, though if the date of 317 is correct, it must have been from Licinius in the East, then living in Nicomedia. For Licinius' authoring the rescript, see Potter (2013: 208); Millar (1983: 90–91).

5 Millar (1983: 91), noted that by 317, *perfectissimatus* and *egregiatus* were 'equestrian grades' that exempted holders from their curial duties.

6 *Cod. Theod.* 9.21.2pr. (321). A clarification, which concerned property owners unaware of counterfeiting occurring on their property, was issued in 329 (*Cod. Theod.* 9.21.4).

7 For instance, after issuances of lead and iron during the Social Wars caused fluctuation in coin values, in 86/85 BC, a praetor named Gratidianus instituted an office for verifying money and exchanged the base currency for new denarii. With acclaim and statues, the populace lauded these monetary measures and their confidence in the coinage returned (Cic., *Off.* 3.80). See Kay (2014: 250).

century signals a legal shift in the use of legislation and status to secure labour in state workshops during the later empire. As I will argue, legal manipulation of the status of minters served both to systematize a fixed caste of corporally vulnerable workers to staff imperial mints and, more broadly, to affirm legally the emperor's legitimate right to control coinage. Moreover, I hope to demonstrate that the degraded status that accompanied service in some compulsory trades in the later empire did not necessarily inhibit workers from attaining prestige.

Outline and Scope

Mint workers produced the most visible medium of imperial propaganda circulated within the Roman Empire: coinage. Since the term 'propaganda' is itself a loaded term, this article will use a definition similarly utilized by other classical numismatists in order to evaluate coinage as a tool of propaganda: 'The deliberate attempt to influence public opinion through the transmission of ideas and values for a specific purpose, not through violence or bribery.'[8] As I will assert, mint workers were an integral though often overlooked part of numismatic propaganda. Studies of the art and material culture of antiquity often divorce the artwork from the artisans in analyses of visual propaganda. Consequently, studies of Roman art generally treat the artisans separately. In the same manner that the role of the viewer in imperial communiqué has recently been emphasized, I would like to suggest that we must also reflect on the carefully constructed personas of the state-employed artisans themselves.[9] This article aims to illustrate how the legally controlled status of the artisans who crafted Roman coins served to reinforce the message of legitimacy, stability, and continuity that Roman coinage itself intended to advertise.

A few guidelines in terms of subject, scope, and evidence are necessary before embarking on this overview of Roman imperial minters. First, imperial (that is state-produced) coinage was not the only currency available to Romans in the early empire, but there was expansive circulation of this imperial coinage.[10] In the Republic and early Roman Empire, there was a rather laid-back

8 Cull, Culbert, and Welch (2003: 318). See Manders (2002: 28); Noreña (2011: 17–18).

9 Cf. Elsner (2007).

10 Regarding the widespread monetization in the early empire, see Kessler and Temin (2008: 137–159). Note von Reden's caveat (2010: 90) that widespread monetization does not prove there was market integration.

attitude at Rome towards coinage in the provinces.[11] Provincial mints struck coins for local use, which often circulated alongside other forms of coinage, such as the *spintriae* possibly used as entrance tickets redeemable for services in brothels. In terms of the location of the mint and working conditions within it, the evidence is fragmented and diffuse. Recreations of the working conditions of the *moneta* itself must rely to a large extent on textual sources and depictions on coins. For instance, Statius' reference to the ore thrust in a crackling fire to mint coins and Firmicus Maternus' mention of blazing furnaces employed to melt down metal give us some idea of the atmosphere on the workshop floor.[12] Although decidedly later, the Byzantine writer Nicholas Mesarites remarked upon John Komnenos' failed usurpation in 1201 that the workers in the mint at Constantinople were sweaty, with blackened clothing and feet from labouring night and day to control the gold supply—though this scene may also be a nod to the human greed attached to money.[13] Rather than evaluating the conditions within the mint itself, the primary focus of this chapter will remain on a more textually attested topic: the shifting status, associations, and legal regulation of Roman mint workers from the late Republic to AD 565, and how these shifts reflect the anxieties of an empire.[14]

The act of minting itself advertised the power and legitimacy of an individual, but the deed alone meant little unless the people trusted and circulated these coins. In the same way that Alexander's coins had become the model for consistent metal content in the Hellenistic period, it was important for Roman emperors to evoke and maintain trust in their coinage.[15] Emperors or claimants to imperial power needed to establish and then uphold the reputation of their coin. As I will argue, one way to cultivate this reputation was through publicized control of the status of the mint workers themselves. In the Republic, coinage was centralized in the city of Rome, and the surviving records do not indicate the status of the minters. However, under Julius Caesar, servile minters began to be utilized: men directly tied to the master for whom they minted, and corporally vulnerable to physical abuse or even death as a penalty for fraud or pilfering. The early empire saw the regularized use of a mix of freedmen and servile labour organized into *familiae monetariae* within mint workshops called *officinae*, but, as I will discuss, the status of mint workers

11 Metcalf (2006: 40–41).

12 Stat., *Silv.* 3.3.103–105; Firm. Mat., *Err. prof. rel.* 28.6. Also note Luc., 1.380.

13 Heisenberg (1907: 9; 25–26). Morrisson (2002: 916).

14 Klose (2006) notes the static nature of the process up to the sixteenth century and remarks that ancient coins were typically struck rather than cast.

15 See Le Rider (2007).

in the later empire is often unclear. Beyond their status, the actions of mint workers could also have an impact upon imperial policy; it was an uprising of minters under Aurelian that prompted shifts in monetary policy and closer oversight of the minters. As emperors increasingly hoarded and secured gold and silver to ensure quick accessibility, mobile minting escalated, and new hierarchies among the mints developed. By the early fourth century, imperial minters had become so integral to securing the coinage minted for administrative purposes, to pay soldiers, and to repay debts, that laws were enacted to immobilize these workers both legally and socially. The existence of legal evidence of attempts to prevent the elevation of mint workers tends to refute the lowly stature assigned these workers by modern scholars.[16] While this may seem to be an *argumentum ex silentio*, these laws appear to be reactive to mint workers gaining a degree of social and political prominence. An ignoble status and marriage restrictions were used to define a class of minters who—while technically stigmatized with a demeaned status—would acquire prestige from their proximity to the emperor and the exemptions they received as part of their office.

The Mint from the Republic to the Principate

In the Republic, Rome's mint was located near the temple of Juno Moneta, which stood upon the rocky *arx* of the Capitoline Hill.[17] The temple occupied a potent and symbolic space; it looked out over the Roman Forum, allowing shoppers and merchants to gaze up from the Forum and, with a glance, be reminded of the institutional and divine protection over their coinage.[18] Livy notes the dedication of the temple by Marcus Furius Camillus in 344 BC, and it is possible that the association of the temple of Moneta with the guardianship of standards of measurement extended back to the mid fourth century.[19]

16 See Jones (1970: 83), who notes (without supporting evidence) that 'the *monetarii* had always been imperial slaves.' Jones believed that mint workers and others in compulsory labour trades were 'essentially slaves.'

17 Liv., 6.20.13. Coarelli (1994: 23–65).

18 Littlewood (2006: 58), remarks, 'Moneta's guardianship of Roman coinage was an encouragement for Roman moneyers to use coinage...' See *CIL* VI 362 = *ILS* 3108. For the sources and worship of Juno Moneta in general, see Jean Haudry (2002). The idea of Republican coinage as a monument is suggested by Andrew Meadows and Jonathan Williams (2001: 48).

19 Livy's dating (in 7.28) of 344/3 BC is at odds with Valerius Maximus (1.8.3), who records the dedication as occurring after the seizure of Veii in 396 BC by Marcus Furius Camillus.

Between 320 and 280 BC, Rome began to produce more coinage, with minting becoming further regularized after 225.[20] Overseen by administrators called *triumviri monetales*, mint workers were organized into an *officina* of artisans similar to the Greek *sunergion* or *ergastērion*. Livy's reference to the *officina Monetae* may suggest that this workshop organization was employed from early on, but it could also be an anachronism based on the organization in the late first century BC, when he wrote his history.[21] The use of organizing units called *officinae* ('workshops') would endure into Late Antiquity.

Oversight of a mint was an important duty, a point underscored in Plutarch's remark that Sulla entrusted Lucullus to perform duties of the highest significance, 'for instance, the oversight of the mint.'[22] In the Republic, minor magistrates called *triumviri* (or *tresviri*) *monetales* oversaw the mint and often fulfilled the office as an early part of the *cursus honorum*, but later inscriptions suggest that the workshop floor itself was probably supervised by *officinatores* who monitored the *officinae*.[23] In respect to the number of workshops within the mint, beginning in 130 BC, early control marks start appearing on coins that use Latin letters to indicate various obverse and reverse dies. These designate the ways in which the dies were employed rather than the organization of the Republican mint itself; however, Michael Crawford has demonstrated that when these dies are plotted out, it can be reasonably asserted that at first, just one workshop used multiple anvils to produce coinage, since each die is directly or indirectly linked.[24] Two workshops probably alternated years in the late second century BC, shifting between preparing the issues and actually minting coins, and later, two workshops produced the coinage simultaneously.[25] Because we lack any mint records, we possess very little knowledge about the number of men in each *officina* or the status of the workers within them during the Republic, but it can be assumed from later references that they were not at

---

Meadows and Williams (2001: 30), suggest that the connection between mint and temple perhaps extends back to the mid-fourth century BC, as suggested by Livy.

20 Vagi (1999: 24).

21 Liv., 6.20.13.

22 Plut., *Luc.* 2.1: ὧν ἦν καὶ ἡ περὶ τὸ νόμισμα πραγματεία.

23 The six boards of minor magistrates were known collectively as the *vigintisexviri* by the late Republic. Cic., *Leg.* 3.3.6 notes that holding one of these positions was a precursor to holding the quaestorship, which then ushered a man into a senatorial career. The *officinatores monetae* are cited in a number of later, imperial era inscriptions (*CIL* VI 43; 298; 1145 and 8463), though *officinae* were normally overseen by foremen termed *officinatores*, as was the case in the Roman brick industry.

24 Crawford (1966: 18–19).

25 Crawford (1966: 22–23).

this point *servi*, though their status in the eyes of the senatorial elite does not appear to have been distinguished. Cicero exemplifies this elitist view when he notes the vulgar and illiberal nature of any artisan who worked in an *officina*.[26] However, among the Roman populace not serving as senators or from elite landed families (that is to say, most people within the city), they were probably regarded as perfectly respectable men chosen from among the artisan class engaged in a service that benefitted the *res publica*.

It would appear that just as Caesar's wife had to be above reproach, so too did his coinage.[27] With the ascension of Caesar to a position of power, the status of the workers within the Roman mint shifted. In the wake of the honours bestowed on him after his victory at Munda in early 45 BC, Julius Caesar installed his own slaves as supervisors of the imperial mint, probably in order to provide him with more direct control over the coinage.[28] He was certainly not the first to perceive the value of having servile staffers operating the state mint. In classical Athens, public slaves called *dēmosioi* performed many duties for the public, including the minting of coins.[29] An advantage of using slaves rather than citizens in the Roman mint was their high degree of corporal vulnerability; they could more easily be beaten for stealing or debasing coins. This vulnerability of slaves is illustrated by the legislation regarding counterfeit coinage. Promulgated around 81 BC, Sulla's *lex Cornelia de falsis* had supplied a legal basis for future anti-counterfeit legislation, stipulating banishment for free men caught making silver coinage, but death for slaves.[30] It should be kept in mind that while servile mint workers could more easily be beaten for criminal offenses, this does not mean that they were financially incapacitated. Even servile officials could acquire wealth. The imperial cash tellers, called *dispensatores*, provide a notable example; while usually servile in status, they could, and did, accrue vast wealth.[31] The position of *dispensator* was in such

26 Cic., *De Off.* 1.150: *Opificesque omnes in sordida arte versantur; nec enim quicquam ingenuum habere potest officina.*

27 The modern proverb stems from a quotation in Plut., *Caes.* 10.9. Also note Dio Cass., 37.45; Suet., *Iul.* 6.2.

28 Suet., *Iul.* 76.3.

29 An Athenian decree (*SEG* XXVI 72) of 375/4 BC indicates that testers who checked for counterfeit coinage were to be paid from the same moneys set aside to pay the state mint workers. See Stroud (1974: 157–188).

30 *Dig.* 48.10.8. Grierson (1956: 242). Later, this would be modified to impose exile on *honestiores*, and either sentencing to the mines or crucifixion for *humiliores*. The penalty for gold counterfeits was even harsher: see Grierson (1956: 244).

31 *Dispensatores* could themselves own slaves. See *CIL* VI 5197 = *ILS* 1514. Plin., *HN* 33.145 (liii), notes that a *dispensator* of Hispania Citerior owned the largest known silver plate.

high demand that one slave in the early empire is said to have paid a million sesterces for the privilege.[32] Proximity to money and to the imperial house was apparently worth the price.

In the early empire, Rome's mint continued to be the main producer of imperial coinage. Between AD 70 and the early second century, the mint was relocated near the Flavian Amphitheatre, on the Caelian hill.[33] Inscriptions dating to AD 115 found near San Clemente suggest a range of mint positions predominantly filled by freedmen and slaves.[34] Although the mint as a whole was overseen by an equestrian *procurator monetae* under the supervision of the emperor's *a rationibus* at the time, the highest official listed on these dedicatory inscriptions is a freedman *optio et exactor auri argenti et aeris* named Felix, who was assisted by another freedman *optio* named Albanus, along with 9 other servile assistants.[35] Below the *optio* in the Trajanic inscriptions were 16 freedmen *officinatores* who served as overseers of the *officinae*, 17 freedmen *signatores*, 11 freedmen and slaves who functioned as *suppostores* that probably placed the flans on the anvils so that they could be struck, and 38 intermixed slaves and freedmen *malliatores* who hammered the coins.[36] Other persons variously employed by mints were *nummularii*, who served as moneychangers, but in this context probably checked and bagged coins—men who were probably close in status to the *officinatores*—and the *conductores flaturae*.[37] In addition to a recognizable hierarchy, the inscriptions also illustrate ties to

32 Suet., *Otho* 5.2.

33 Vagi (1999: 133), proposes that this may have occurred early on in Domitian's reign, since a large series of *dupondi* and *asses* with the Moneta Augusti on them were issued from AD 84 until his death in September of AD 96. Howgego (1995: 27) suggests that it was moved after the fire of AD 80.

34 *CIL* VI 42–44. For the *familia monetalis*, see also *CIL* VI 239. See Mommsen (1887: 36–39); LaFaurie (1972: 267–271). *CIL* VI 298 = *ILS* 1636 (Rome) refers to the association of the mint workers as the *familia monetaria*.

35 Cf. *CIL* VIII 9990 = *ILS* 1352. See Peachin (1986: 94–106).

36 For the role of the *signatores* and a fuller explanation of the jobs of each worker listed in the inscription, see Woytek (2013). These freedman would seem to refute Jones' (1966: 164–1655) assertion that *monetarii* during the Principate and thereafter were all 'public slaves'.

37 *CIL* VI 8463 (Rome) commemorates a *nummularius officinator monetae*. Also note *CIL* VI 8461 and 8463 (Rome). For other imperial freedmen who acted as *nummularii*, see *CIL* III 7903 (Sarmizegetusa). *CIL* VI 8455, from 115 AD, notes the *manceps* that oversaw the *officinae* in charge of the *flaturae argentariae*, while *CIL* VI 791 mentions the *conductores flaturae argentariae monetae Caesaris*.

certain deities, as did most voluntary associations.[38] Dedications address Apollo, Fortuna Augusta, Hercules, Victoria, and the *genius familiae monetalis*. Finally, the use of the word '*familia*' for the voluntary association of the minters mirrors the terminology employed to encompass many state enterprises; there were the *familia aquarum*, *familia publicanorum*, and *familia vectigalis*. Although it cannot be deduced from the use of the organizing term *familia* alone, Caesar's shift to employing slaves within the mint appears to have persisted to some degree in the early empire; an inscription from Lugdunum commemorates an *aequator monetae* named Nobilis, who was a slave of the emperor Tiberius.[39] Collectively, the epigraphic evidence demonstrates a great degree of specialization, a recognizable hierarchy, and a strong associative element at work among the mint workers.

Many ambiguities remain in regard to the mint staff, including the estimated number of workers in each *officina*. Due to the difficulty in quantifying the amount of coins circulating at any one time, attempts to calculate the mint staff based upon die issues are similarly hindered by large error margins during the various phases of minting.[40] Likewise, the number of mint workers per *officina* and the aggregate number per mint cannot be deduced from the number of dies in use. Therefore, estimates must rely on the inscriptions of the mint workers. It appears that close to 100 people worked in the Trajanic mint in the administrative and minting areas alone, but, as Philip Grierson and Melinda Mays point out, there must have been almost as many staff additionally involved in melting, refining, and then preparing the blanks.[41] This leads us to estimate around 200 mint workers employed at each of the mints at Rome, Constantinople, Alexandria, and Antioch during the Later Empire.[42] However, an elite group of minters began to form at this time, shadowing the movements of the emperor as he travelled throughout the Mediterranean.

38 For the religious nature of most voluntary associations, often in conjunction with funereal and convivial activities, see Liu (2009: 247–278).

39 *CIL* XIII 1820 = *ILS* 1639. The *aequator monetae* probably tested the accuracy of the weight of the blanks. See Weaver (1972: 116–117). For a list of other administrative and industrial departments filled by imperial freedmen, see Weaver (1972: 7).

40 Buttrey (1993: 338–345), (1999: 342–352); Howgego (1992: 2–3).

41 Grierson and Mays (1992: 51).

42 Grierson and Mays (1992: 51).

Minters in the Later Empire

In his commentary *On the Agrarian Law*, Cicero noted that during the Republic, Romans had originally established colonies as 'bulwarks of empire'; however, the later empire utilized new bulwarks: armies and imperial mints.[43] Whereas minting in the early Roman Empire had been more centralized and focused on the city of Rome, the mid-third century gave rise to an increased diffusion of mints, due particularly to the increasing realization that *monetae* needed to be close at hand in order to pay the soldiers so pivotal to maintaining imperial support during the third century.[44] After all, Septimius Severus' last words had been, 'Be harmonious, pay the soldiers, and scorn all other men.'[45] Moreover, loyalty was a necessary element that came at a premium at this time. As I will now discuss, mint workers were central to the functioning of the state. Consequently, they had to be given both carrot and stick: rewards for staying loyal, combined with a robust threat for deviating from it. Rebellious associations of minters that did reject the emperor or who supported a usurper could pay a heavy price, but could also serve as catalysts for reforms to the minting system. Ultimately, attempts to ensure and to advertise the stability of the coinage culminated in the use of legal statutes and an ignoble status—also attached to other artisans such as weavers, purple dye workers, and muleteers—in order to prescribe and preserve classes of imperial minters confined to their trade and tied almost permanently in service to the emperor.

The mid-third century crisis had an impact on every sector of society, political, social, and economic.[46] Debased coinage was a significant problem that the emperor Aurelian attempted to address, and meeting with resistance, it seems. As had been the case in the Republic and the early Principate, emperors still heavily depended upon the mint at Rome for coinage during this period of flux.[47] This reliance on the Rome mint empowered those who worked within the city's *moneta*, and perhaps provides a partial explanation for the actions of the emboldened mint workers who revolted during the reign of Aurelian in

43 Cic., *Leg. agr.* 2.73: *propugnacula imperi.*

44 Corbier (2005: 348). De Blois (1976: 93–95) argues that destabilization of the coinage stemmed from the profusion of mints outside Rome.

45 Dio Cass., 77.15.2: ὁμονοεῖτε, τοὺς στρατιώτας πλουτίζετε, τῶν ἄλλων πάντων καταφρονεῖτε.

46 Not all scholars agree that the collective events of the third century should be termed a crisis. See Witschel (1999), and Liebeschuetz (2007).

47 Malalas 12.30, who was himself an Antiochene, situated the revolt in Antioch rather than in Rome. See Peachin (1983).

271.[48] It seems that the mint workers in Rome had greatly debased the coinage for their own profit under the aegis of the mint's *rationalis*, Felicissimus. Following Aurelian's challenge to the mint's overseer, the *rationalis* incited the mint workers to rebel. One can only hypothesize that these mint workers might have become accustomed to the illicit perks that Felicissimus had allowed. When these came under threat, he invoked the evidently strong patronage bonds between himself and the mint workers to full effect. Felicissimus died early on in the melee, but the mint workers gained support from disaffected followers in the form of senators and others who perhaps had not supported Aurelian's accession in AD 270.[49] The *Historia Augusta* reported 7,000 dead as a result of the insurrection (a large and suspect number of fatalities), but the impact went well beyond the human toll and might have served as a caveat for future emperors.

The so-called *bellum monetariorum* ('war of the minters') appears to have been a worrisome civil outburst, one that forced Aurelian to take action. Clearly, imperial control over mints and associations of mint workers needed to be tightened. Immediate precautions came in the form of a mass execution of many involved in the uprising, including senators, and the closing of the Roman mint. Aurelian disbanded the twelve *officinae* of the mint, but in fact took some pardoned minters on campaign with him in the Balkans. The immediate fire had perhaps been stamped out, but the long-term smouldering still had to be addressed. The mint at Rome was reopened in 273 and, along with Milan's, began to produce a reformed *antoninianus* called the *aurelialianus* by modern scholars, a radiate silvered coin.[50] Following his movement of the boundary of Dacia to the southern banks of the Danube, Aurelian put a mint at the new capital, Serdica, and after his reconquest of the Gallic Empire in 274, he closed the mints at Trier and Cologne. Although Aurelian died before all of his reforms were in place, the mint workers' rebellion perhaps served as a pivotal example to him and, consequently, to later emperors, that these workers had to be carefully overseen if emperors were to be successful in galvanizing their own power and publicizing a secure coinage.

In many ways, Aurelian emerges as a model for Diocletian, who also undertook coinage reforms. Around 294, Diocletian imposed a new organization

48 The author of the *Historia Augusta* gives a thorough yet (as is the case with the HA generally) altogether specious account of the revolt via a letter from Aurelian to his adopted father (*Aurel.* 38.2–4). Other accounts: Aur. Vict., 35.6; Eutr., 9.14.1; Ps. Aur. Vict., *Epit.* 35.4. Also note Polemius Silvius 1.48. See Conway (2006); Watson (1999: 50–53).

49 Zos., 1.49.2. See Cubelli (2002: 47–50).

50 Zos., 1.61.3: ἀργύριον νέον. Caracalla had originally introduced the so-called *antoninianus*.

of local minting.[51] Whereas local mints had always quite regularly produced coinage for the city or province, the debasement of the coinage was such that the tetrarch felt he needed to close all the local mints and replace them with fourteen imperial mints that would supply standardized coins to the empire as needed. Mints were separated into static *monetae publicae* that continued to be run by an equestrian *procurator monetae* with various *praepositi* who assisted him and the mobile *moneta comitatensis* that shadowed the emperor's movements.[52] These reforms embodied the ideals of organization, control, and cohesion that were the foundation of the tetrarchic system. Following Diocletian, probably in the early fourth century, the *comes sacrarum largitionum* was additionally established to oversee mints and mines.[53] Like many imperial workers, the *monetarii* became increasingly regulated players within the confines of the Dominate.

At many junctures in Late Antiquity, usurpers and conquerors set up mints that required *monetarii*. The act of founding a mint asserted the legitimacy of an imperial claimant, but was a functional move as well, creating coinage to pay the troops in particular.[54] The usurper Carausius is a telling example. In 286, he established five mints, using London as the flagship. In regard to the staff, P.J. Casey has posited that minters may have travelled from mint to mint, and argues that the coinage was so angularly cut and poorly minted that Carausius probably had to hire local sealstone cutters and intaglio artisans to produce the dies.[55] If no previous mint existed and they were not already employing their own traveling *officina* of minters, it is probably that imperial usurpers in particular often had to court local jewellery makers and metallurgists. Since many mints lay dormant for periods of time (with the exception of the especially integral ones, such as Rome's), it is probable that minters frequently worked sporadically. Following the closing of the London mint in 324, for instance, the British minters probably returned to their livelihoods making and selling jewellery or other metal products; the London mint would only be briefly reopened again in the fourth century, under Magnus Maximus, from

51 Grierson and Mays (1992: 48).

52 *CIL* VI 1641 and 1145. Carson (1956: 232–233).

53 Jones (1964: 427–428).

54 Whether true or not, the Historia Augusta's *Vita Triginta Tyrannorum* cites the founding of a mint as a preliminary action taken by many mid-third century imperial claimants, including the Isaurian 'archpirate' Trebellianus (26) and the Gallic Victoria (31). See Ando (2000: 215–228), who notes that, 'The beliefs that legitimate emperors ought to oversee the mints and that their faces ought to appear on their coins reinforced each other through long association' (221).

55 Casey (1994: 61).

383–388. Artisan metallurgists and jewellery makers easily transitioned to being minters, thus providing a valuable skill to potential usurpers.

Disbanding a mint altogether was perhaps one way to control minters, but another method was simply to revoke the elite privilege to mint precious metals. As was glimpsed in the revolt under Aurelian, rebellious minters could sever the indispensable bond between emperor and mint. The fourth-century minters in the city of Cyzicus again demonstrate this fact. In the fourth century, this city was the capital within the diocese of Asia and home to an imperial mint.[56] This is supported by a description from the reign of Julian in the early fifth-century by the ecclesiastical historian Sozomen, who remarked that Christian imperial textile workers and coin minters constituted a sizeable portion of the population there.[57] The historian further noted that these two groups were given special dispensation by the emperor to live with their wives and families in Cyzicus—in other words, to work on a cottage system of production—provided that they gave clothing to the soldiers and coinage to the fiscus. This allowance is important to keep in mind in regard to what happened in 365, when Procopius (later cast by Ammianus and others as a pretender to the throne) seized the city. Procopius acquired the imperial mint in the city and ultimately minted coins in Constantinople, Heraclea, and Nicomedia as well. Although Valens put down the revolt in 366, the Cyzicus mint would be chastised, relegated to producing base metal coinage by the sweeping monetary reforms that Valens was to undertake.

As the fourth century progressed, control over minters appears to have reflected less apprehension over whether they would revolt and greater concern with coin tampering. As the permanent mints in cities like Cyzicus were consigned to producing non-precious coinage under Valentinian I and Valens in 368, the comitatensian mint increasingly minted the precious metals silver and gold. This mint was organized into 10 departments denoted by the Greek numerals A to I.[58] The *Theodosian Code* preserves the reasoning behind the monetary reforms, particularly noting that they were meant to stop the fraud committed by members of the *largitiones*, *prosecutores* (escorts), and *allectores* (tax collectors).[59] Whether real or imagined, coin tampering was a concern in

56 Around AD 297, Diocletian had begun to reorganize the province of Asia, with the city of Cyzicus becoming the capital of the Hellespontus province. Although the city was probably displeased at Constantine's later choice of Byzantium as his *nova Roma*, it remained integral to the late empire.

57 Sozom., *Hist. eccl.* 5.15.

58 Kent (1994: 23–25).

59 *Cod. Theod.* 12.6.12 (366). See Lib. *Or.* 18.138.

the public psyche as well. Written in the 360s, the anonymous treatise *De rebus bellicis* had in fact suggested a number of countermeasures to check some of the state's rampant civil, military, and fiscal problems—for instance, advising that *opifices monetae* ('workers of the mint') should perhaps be placed on their own island in order to preserve, in part, the *integritas* of the service.[60] As Noel Lenski has noted, Valens' reforms did indeed isolate moneyers in gold and silver to a traveling island—one guarded by the emperor himself.[61] Moreover, coinage studies reveal that, with a certain Midas touch, wherever the emperor was, there tended to be an increase in the precious coinage.[62] These comitatensian minters appear to have been more highly regarded than the local *monetarii* in urban mints. A law of 384 outlines the comitatensian departments concerned with coinage; two dealt with gold: the *scrinium aureae massae*, overseen by a *primicerius* and *secundarius* with two *ducenarii*, four *centenarii*, and four messengers, and the *scrinium auri ad responsum*. The first oversaw the bullion and the second the coins and gold exchanged through the mints in each diocese.[63] They employed a staff of *aurifices specierum* (goldsmiths), *aurifices solidorum* (minters of gold coins), and *sculptores et ceteri artifices* (engravers and other craftsmen). The attention to bureaucratic minutiae here is noteworthy, and it has been pointed out that there seems to have been no room for mobility except in cases of seniority or death.[64] Members of the comitatensian mint in particular were meant to be viewed by all as fixed, permanent, and secure entities—much like the coinage itself.

In one of his many expressive metaphors, Augustine of Hippo remarked that while the *moneta* of Christ was man, the Roman emperor had to rely heavily on his minters:

> Caesar, my brothers, did not make the coinage; the *monetarii* make it ... it is commanded to the artisans, [Caesar] issues his commands to his servants. His image was stamped on the coinage; on the coinage is the image of Caesar. And nevertheless he asks what others have minted; that man puts it in his treasury; that man will not have it refused to him.[65]

---

60 Anon., *De reb. bell.* 3.1–3. Lenski (2002: 299–300). For the date, see Cameron (1979: 1–10).

61 Lenski (2002: 301).

62 Hendy (1985: 386–398).

63 *Cod. Iust.* 12.23.7.7.

64 Kelly (2004: 42).

65 August., *Serm.* 90.10: *Caesar, fratres mei, non fecit nummum: monetarii faciunt; artificibus iubetur, suis ministris imperauit. Imago exprimebatur in nummo: in nummo est imago Caesaris. Et tamen quod alii impresserunt quaeritur: ille thesaurizat, ille non uult sibi negari.*

Control radiated from the emperor himself, but depended upon trustworthy workers in the mint as guarantors of his power. As such, these minters received tax exemptions for their service to the emperor, but, by the early fourth century, they also accepted a nominal stigma of disrepute. The purpose and the effects of this ignoble status on Roman minters tell us a great deal about disrepute in the later empire and its uses in defining and restraining workers that were viewed as essential to the economic stability of an increasingly unstable Roman state.

Ignobility and Control in the Fourth Century

The security of gold and silver was of the utmost importance in the later empire, which was the principal reason for the increasing micromanagement of these metals. Legislative control extended even to the details of transporting the coinage on the *cursus publicus*; statutes declared that each wagon was to have two palatine officials and three slaves guarding it.[66] Control also tightened within the mint. From the third century onwards, mint marks indicate the escalating effort to denote not only the place, but also the specific workshop, from whence each coin came.[67] As suggested earlier, the laws concerning coinage could function to advertise legitimacy. Likewise, the degraded status of mint workers served to bond pivotal artisans to imperial service. The use of degraded status to lock in essential workers was part of broader commercial trends in Late Antiquity aimed at securing the state workforce; similarly, purple fish dye workers were prevented from achieving high status and their own status became hereditary.[68] Whereas legal stigmas of disrepute and the deprivation of honour had previously been used in the Republic and early Roman Empire to marginalize moral threats to the socio-political order and to condemn criminals, in Late Antiquity, imperial lawmakers increasingly withheld civic honours and assigned a degraded status in order to secure vital workers in state *corpora*. Thus, being an imperial *monetarius* in the later empire could be a double-edged sword: job security, tax exemptions, and status from imperial service on the one hand, but legal disrepute and social restrictions on the other.

66 *Cod. Theod.* 8.5.48. See van Heesch (2006: 54).

67 Carson (1956: 236) dates the more developed system of *officina* marking that occurred in the later empire to no earlier than the reign of Philip (244–249).

68 These workers were called *murileguli*. See *Cod. Theod.* 9.45.3; 10.20.5 and *Idem* 12, 15–17.

The deprivation of civic offices was a common tool of control employed in the Republic to marginalize persons viewed as threats to the integrity of Roman civic life. The *Tabula Heracleensis*, which probably transmits the *lex Iulia municipalis* of 45 BC, had banned a number of persons deemed disreputable from attaining civic office: funeral workers, criers, gladiators, pimps, and prostitutes, to name a few.[69] However, from the fourth century on, legal disrepute increasingly established social ceilings, delineated hierarchy, and maintained the state's ability to inflict corporal punishment on certain workers. The aforementioned decree of Licinius from AD 317, which noted rather ambiguously that *monetarii* were to remain in their current lowly status and that certain titles could not be extended to them, is just one example of this trend. The law, which effectively created a class of minters with corporal vulnerability, was the precursor to more intense efforts to stop counterfeit coinage. The emperor particularly targeted counterfeits minted by imperial *monetarii* by promulgating new laws stipulating that imperial minters producing *adulterina moneta* (adulterated money) be handed over to authorities and tortured into giving up their co-conspirators, while estate owners and other household members could also be found guilty of abetting counterfeiting more generally.[70] As with other occupations, the minters were part of Constantine's litigious, extensive, and invasive articulation of the socio-legal order.[71]

Oversight of minters extended into their personal life in the late fourth century. In 380, marriage restrictions were placed on *monetarii*; they could wed women of only a particular status group, whereas women of higher status who chose to marry them lost their position.[72] Moreover, the daughters of *monetarii* could only marry men within the trade. The minters became part of the larger movement towards compulsory trades, a movement that included weavers and purple dye makers, to name a few.[73] We should perhaps not overly lament the hard lives of these workers in service to the state. In 440, all *corporati* were in fact exempted from military service.[74] The employment was steady, and by

69 *CIL* I^2 593 = *ILS* 6085 = *FIRA* I^2 no. 13; Crawford (1996: 335–91, no. 24).

70 *Cod. Theod.* 9.21.2 and 9.21.4.

71 *Cod. Theod.* 14.3.1 (319). Later marriage restrictions on *pistores* by Constantius: *Cod. Theod.* 14.3.2 (355). See Humfress (2012: 208–210).

72 *Cod. Theod.* 10.20.10 = *Cod. Iust.* 11.8.7.

73 Free-born women who married weavers became bound to the lowly condition of their husbands in *Cod. Theod.* 10.20.3= *Cod. Iust.* 11.8.3 (365). Purple dye makers were denied civic honours and confined to lowly status in *Cod. Theod.* 10.20.14 = *Cod. Iust.* 11.8.11 (424); *Cod. Theod.* 10.20.17= *Cod. Iust.* 11.8.15 (427).

74 In *Nov. Val.* 5, Valentinian III decreed that they would only be responsible for urban guard duty at walls and gates.

the early fifth century, a loophole existed for *corporati* within the *Comitatenses largitionum*, workers who already derived status from a close proximity to the emperor. These workers could leave the service if they found suitable replacements and received the emperor's consent, although their property and family would remain tied to the state.[75] A hierarchy indeed persisted among minters, with elevated prestige attached to those who served the comitatensian mint within the *Comitatus*, but the benefits of attaining a mint position hint that they were not as socially degraded as the law codes might lead us to believe.

There is strong evidence that the mint and, by extension, the mint masters continued to play a local role. The head of the mint remained a recognizable (if sometimes notorious) figure in the civic life of late antique cities such as Alexandria. This can be gleaned from an episode of 361 recounted by Ammianus Marcellinus, wherein Dracontius, a notably Christian *praepositus monetae* of Alexandria, was killed by a pagan mob and dragged through the streets.[76] Two other officials died at the hands of the mob, but Dracontius stood accused for his removal of an altar from the mint.[77] It is possible that minters still sacrificed to Juno Moneta and pledged to mint coins in loyalty to both the goddess and the emperor, just as the Senate vowed service to the emperor at the Altar of Victory.[78] Like Victory, Juno Moneta symbolized the stability and prosperity of the empire, but *monetae* themselves could also bring prestige to a community. Consequently, local mint masters like Dracontius could become visible imperial figures within the cities that minted coin in the late empire.

---

75 *Cod. Theod.* 10.20.16 = *Cod. Iust.* 11.8.13 (426).

76 Amm. Marc., 22.11.9. See *PLRE* I, 271 D. (1). Peachin (1987: 248–249) has convincingly argued that here Ammianus errs, in all likelihood, in respect to nomenclature by calling Dracontius a *praepositus* rather than a *procurator monetae*. He further notes that Ammianus (14.9.7) similarly errs in calling the head of the Tyrian purple dyeworks a *praepositus Tyrii textrini* rather than the correct term, *procurator*.

77 This controversy closely resembles the conflict over the removal of the Altar of Victory from the *Curia Iulia* in 357 by Constantius II—a political and social debacle that would erupt again just a few years later, thanks in large part to the persistence of the bishop Ambrose. It has been proposed that the altar in Alexandria was dedicated to Juno Moneta; just as the Altar of Victory was tied to the emperor, an altar of Juno Moneta was also closely linked to loyalty to the emperor. See Haas (1997: 288).

78 The Statue of Victory was placed in the newly completed *Curia Iulia* by Octavian in 29 BC. See Dio 51.22.2.

Minters in the Middle Ages

Despite the accompanying limits on occupational and conjugal liberties, mint positions appear to have gained prestige and become increasingly attractive in the later eastern empire, due not only to the office's exemption from military service and compensation, but perhaps also to its proximity to the emperor and the opportunity to pocket some of the precious metals that minters frequently handled.[79] Yet, as in the empire itself, the fractures between east and west were becoming increasingly apparent within the imperial mint organization.[80] In a pivotal article on coinage in the Latin west in the early medieval period, Michael Hendy indicated the significant shift from federal to private spheres that occurred between the state weighting of coin in the Roman Empire and the private weighting of coin in the early Middle Ages.[81] Whereas in the east, a great amount of central control was still exerted over the status and organization of minters (though the number of palatine mints was itself decreasing), in many of the smaller kingdoms in the west, the central secular power did not maintain a monopoly on producing coinage.[82] The Ostrogothic and then Lombard conquests of Italy had greatly disrupted minting, and increasingly, Gothic, Vandal, and Frankish coinages also came into circulation—often attempting to use the iconography of Roman coinage to give them prestige.[83] Amid these lapses in oversight came the resurrection of the private moneyer within these new 'barbarian' kingdoms. When Theodoric acquired power over Spain, Cassiodorus lamented about the moneyers who had abandoned state duties to go out and strike coins for private individuals.[84] Now private artisans

---

79 *Cod. Iust.* 11.8.16 = *Bas.* 54.16.16 notes that no one could be enrolled in a state association without going through the proper procedure for acceptance. Illegal workers were denied the salary, whipped, and exiled from the province. This salary was probably given to all state corporations. The date of the rescript is unknown, but it is also included in the Byzantine *Basilica* from the ninth century. See Heimbach (1850: 140). See Sabatino Lopez (1949: 89–90); Papagianni (2002: 1084).

80 At some point, the minting of gold was transferred from Rome, where the Ostrogoths had minted, to the northern Italian city of Ravenna. From here, we have a document from 572 mentioning a *monitarius auri*. Marini, *P. Dip.* 120 = *P. Ital.* 30. *PLRE*, s.v. Ioannes 76. See Hendy (1985: 400).

81 Hendy (1988: 31–32).

82 Grierson and Blackburn (1986: 98).

83 Harl (1996: 190–191). In the later sixth century, the *solidus* was minted at the palatine mints of Constantinople and Thessalonica.

84 Cass., *Var.* 5.39.8: *Monetarios autem, quos specialiter in usum publicum constat inventos, in privatorum didicimus transisse compendium. qua praesumptione sublata pro virium qualitate functionibus publicis applicentur.*

with highly marketable skills, they began to gain prestige, particularly in the early Frankish kingdom under Merovingian rule.[85] The elevated social stature of the private medieval minter would endure in Western Europe well into the Middle Ages, while in the Byzantine Empire, state minters tied to their *corpora* continued to strike coins in service of the emperor.

Conclusion

In his sixth century *Christian Topography*, Cosmas Indicopleustes argued for the unending, transcending power of the Roman Empire. To Cosmas, the ubiquity of, uniformity of, and trust in Roman coinage were a visible sign that God favoured the Romans: 'I refer to the fact that it is with their coinage all the nations carry on trade from one extremity of the earth to the other.'[86] Six centuries earlier, Julius Caesar had understood that the imperial *moneta* was indeed a barometer for the health and *existimatio* of an administration when he placed his own slaves in the Roman mint. However, this *existimatio* diminished with the growth of mints on the frontiers, which were established to respond to the demand for readily available coinage to pay the troops, an ability that helped to secure an imperial claimant's success. This diffusion of mints during the third-century crisis weakened the government's centralized control over minting and in part enabled events such as the minters' rebellion under Aurelian. In an attempt to reassert authority, limit counterfeiting, and stabilize the coinage, the status of mint workers became more tightly controlled in the fourth century. This was a move commensurate with the anxieties of the emperor over both the reliability of the coinage and his own reputation. Nevertheless, despite escalating checks on their status, marriage opportunities, and outlets for honour, imperial minters still acquired a certain level of prestige. This came in part from their close proximity to the emperor—particularly in the case of the comitatensian minters in the later fourth century—but perhaps also from the opportunity to pilfer or debase coins. As part of the state *corporati* system of the later empire, minters reflect the changing ideas about commerce and labour in the later empire, but also demonstrate that an ignoble status did not always marginalize professionals.

85 See Lopez (1953: 1–43). For example, Gregory of Tours, *Glor. conf.* 105 notes a *monetarius urbis* who had a chapel constructed for S. Crescentia.

86 Cos. Indic., *Top. Chr.* 2.77: λέγω δὴ ὅτι ἐν τῷ νομίσματι αὐτῶν ἐμπορεύονται πάντα τὰ ἔθνη καὶ ἐν παντὶ τόπῳ ἀπ' ἄκρου γῆς ἕως ἄκρου γῆς δεκτόν ἐστι (trans. McCrindle).

CHAPTER 12

Ars and *Doctrina*: The Socioeconomic Identity of Roman Skilled Workers (First Century BC–Third Century AD)

Nicolas Tran

One of the leitmotivs in the historiography of Greek and Roman economy consists of emphasizing the fact that ancient thinkers failed to unify the multiple elements that to modern eyes appear to be work-related. There are no Greek or Latin words that express the entire expanse of the modern concept of work. This view was further elaborated by J.-P. Vernant and his school of historical anthropology,[1] which established a link between the absence of the modern concept of work in Greek thought and the negative perception of crafts and urban occupations that prevailed in ancient Rome—the pursuit of which was considered equivalent to being in a relationship of dependence upon another person.

It is undeniable that no ancient category wholly encompassed the notion of work in its broadest sense. However, this observation invites us to examine how the ancient Romans defined work-related economic activities, and to try to determine whether the names they used to refer to those activities reveal a negative vision of the people who were engaged in them. This is the object of my paper, which will focus on skilled urban workers in the Western Roman Empire between the first century BC and the third century AD.

Producers of goods and food, shopkeepers and traveling merchants, small-scale bankers and barbers, to name only a few examples, were all considered as practicing an *ars*, or *technē* for Greeks. Both words in themselves neither refer to 'work' or even 'occupation', and can often be found in very different contexts.[2] *Artes liberales*, for example, pertained to the realm of culture, as we define it today. Respectable citizens who took part in them were not considered to be working, nor were they expected to derive a living from them.[3]

---

* This text synthesizes a number of theses previously developed in Tran (2013: 147–252). It was translated from the French by Maxime Shelledy.

1 Vernant (1971: 12–18 and 35–43).

2 *TLL* II, 657–673; Gavoille (2003).

3 Thomas (2004: 203).

 | DOI 10.1163/9789004331686_013

However, the fact that real professionals could be called *artifices*, i.e. practitioners of an *ars* mastered after fulfilling an apprenticeship, is indicative of a particular and often positive perception of their work. The status of *artifex* was central to their social identity.

Modern historians have insisted on the contempt that ancient societies would have had for work, particularly for manual and commercial occupations in the widest sense. True, Roman writers have expressed scorn for crafts and trades. Nevertheless, the ancient literary discourses on which these modern historians have based their view, express primarily the viewpoints of specific social categories.

The literary *topos* of the indignity of work emanated from the elite. Its members were brought into disrepute if they did not steer clear of financial, commercial, and manufacturing activities, from which they were allowed to draw indirect profits but not practice personally. Whoever wished to rise to the highest strata of society had to conform to this norm. Its transgression was considered shocking and gave rise to strong disapproval. Furthermore, the rejection of work is even more categorical in ancient philosophical texts, in which the negative portrait of the worker serves to magnify the diametrically opposed figure of the thinker. For the same reasons, Seneca emphasized the vanity of the office of prefect of the *annona* (*praefectus annonae*), who supervised Rome's food supply, even though it was normally reserved for the highest dignitaries of equestrian rank.[4] On the whole, the literary and aristocratic opinions on work (in the modern sense of the term) hardly appear as ends in themselves, or judgments in absolute terms. They say more about aristocrats' reprobation of behaviour that was considered unworthy of their rank or about their hatred for parvenus, than about the general perception of ordinary craftsmen.

Whether contemptuous or not, perceptions of work were above all subjective and plural. In 1963, Fr. M. De Robertis opposed two visions of work revealed by the various epigraphical, papyrological and iconographical sources.[5] In his view, aristocratic psychology disparaged the work that plebeians had to perform to make a living. On the other hand, popular thought valued work and considered it an object of pride. More recent studies also highlight the wide gap that existed between aristocratic and plebeian mentalities. S.R. Joshel has shown that the stereotypes conveyed by a literature produced by and for the elite were opposed to the professional prestige granted to well-to-do freedmen.[6] P. Veyne drew on the *Disticha Catonis* to understand

4 Sen., *Dial.* 10.19.

5 De Robertis (1963: 21–97).

6 Joshel (1992: 4–7 and 79–85).

the 'sapiential moral' ('morale sapientiale') of 'the middle-*plebs*' (*plebs media*) of which skilled workers were emblematic figures. This moral pertained to a popular culture that was in many distinct from elite culture.[7]

The analyses of De Robertis have marked significant scholarly progress. They allow us to go beyond the hackneyed theory of the general contempt felt for work and workers in ancient Rome. However, these analyses must now be taken further to avoid falling into other forms of oversimplification. Although they may be clearly individualized, both value systems should not be considered as hermetically sealed, but rather as being in constant interaction with each other. Most importantly, they must be addressed carefully in order to avoid turning their opposition into a new kind of orthodoxy.[8] Furthermore, if professional pride was intense and widespread among Roman craftsmen and merchants, we need to identify which elements and aspects of their work gave rise to such a sentiment.

Artifices: A Professional Status Recognized by All

In the cities of the Roman world, skilled workers belonged to a larger category: that of *artifices*—practitioners of an *ars*, a special knowledge that they had acquired through apprenticeship and were capable of passing on. Roman skilled workers were especially proud of being *artifices* and of being recognized as such. The concept was characteristic not only of the way these workers considered themselves, as can be seen in epigraphical monuments, but also of how they were considered by Roman society as a whole, elite included. As one of an abundant series of similar inscriptions, a funerary altar in Cordoba commemmorates the marble cutter Valerius Fortunatus by referring to him both as a good man and an *artifex marmorarius*, who died at the age of 98 years.[9] Similarly, in Lyon, the *artifices tectores*, who worked as stuccoers, shared a collective burial place with the local *corpus fabrum tignuariorum*, or professional association of carpenters.[10] In Rome, a Christian sculptor is referred to in his epitaph as an *artifex signuarius*, or statue maker.[11]

Other inscriptions mention particular *artes* to specify occupations not only of craftsmen, but also of persons whose professional activities do not

7 Veyne (2000: 1192–1194).

8 Van den Hoven (1996: 5).

9 *CIL* II^2 7, 348.

10 *CIL* XIII 1734. See Laubry (2012: 117–119).

11 *CIL* VI 9896.

correspond to modern definitions of arts and crafts. Thus, a certain Praecilius from Cirta in Numidia described his banking business in his funeral poem as *argentariam exibui artem*.[12] Elsewhere in the empire, similar mentions of *artes* are abundant in Lyon and North-Eastern Gaul. They were used to designate either certain manual occupations or the products sold by *negotiatores*. One epitaph, for instance, celebrates the everlasting memory of an African from Carthage who settled in Lyon and worked there as an *opifex artis vitrariae*, or glassmaker, before he died in the early third century.[13] In Metz, Caratullius from the *Mediomatrici* was presented as a *negotiator artis clostrariae*. He was a locksmith, who chose to have himself described as a *negotiator*, not in the sense of a merchant, but to indicate that he had his own business, or *negotiatio*.[14]

Many other epigraphical examples could be listed here, but it is more useful to emphasize the fact that manuscript texts reveal a similar perception of urban occupations. Leaving aside their value judgments regarding work, so-called literary authors and Roman jurists placed craftsmen and merchants in the heterogeneous category of *artifices*, along with rhetoricians, poets and doctors. For instance, both Pliny the Elder and Vitruvius use *ars sutoria* and *ars fullonia* to designate shoemaking and fulling.[15] The architect Vitruvius relates these *artes* to his discipline to assert that an *ars vera* could only be practiced by professionals. Likewise, an episode in the life of Elagabalus in the *Historia Augusta* mentions an *artifex claustrarius*.[16] Furthermore, in a narrative referring to ancient Samos, Apuleius mentions *artifices* carving gemstones.[17]

Of course, by opposing *artes sordidae*, *vulgares* or *viles* to the *artes liberales* practiced by worthy and respectable citizens, Roman authors expressed an idea firmly set in the minds of aristocrats and notables. Consequently, historians have tended to focus their attention on the ancient notion of hierarchy and separation between the various *artes*.[18] By doing so, they have repeated the analysis of the same literary evidence an incalculable number of times: a short fraction of Cicero's treaty on duties (*De Officiis*), for instance,[19] and the no less famous quotation by Seneca: *hae viles ex professo artes quae manu*

12 *CIL* VIII 7156.

13 *CIL* XIII 2000.

14 *AE* 1976, 484. The deceased was represented with his tool in his hand.

15 Plin., *HN* 7.196 (lvi); Vitr., *De arch.* 7. pr. 7. See von Petrikovits (1981: 86).

16 SHA, *Heliogab.* 12.2.

17 Apul., *Flor.* 15.13.

18 De Robertis (1963: 51); Treggiari (1980: 48) for instance.

19 Cic., *Off.* 1.150. See Finley (1999), for instance, where this text is of crucial importance.

constant (...) *ad uirtutem non pertinent*.[20] It is of course wholly legitimate to examine the value judgments expressed by adjectives. Nevertheless, urban crafts and trades, although sordid and vile, were included by aristocratic writers and the whole of Roman society alike in a larger category, which grouped all forms of *artes*, however different they may have been. It is quite significant that a single noun was used to refer to those *artes*, as they all shared many common features.

An *ars* was above all a kind of knowledge acquired through apprenticeship, the mastery of which varied from one individual to the next. In the immense majority of cases, inscriptions mentioning Roman skilled workers do not explain the notions they refer to. Most of them were much too brief to do so and, besides, had no such intention. On the other hand, texts do include some general definitions of the notion of *ars*, regardless of various specialisms. Thus, literary authors often associate the notions *ars* and *scientia* (in the sense of 'knowledge'),[21] as the following statement by Cicero explains: *ars enim earum rerum est quae sciuntur*.[22] Furthermore, *ars* was sometimes affiliated with *doctrina*, the type of education a *doctus* had received.[23] The *artifex* could be *magister* (master)[24] of his *ars*, as he was also *peritus* (taught through practice).[25] Thus, he was naturally considered a specialist, which explains why he could also be *idoneus* and fulfil the specific tasks he was assigned.[26] The work of an unskilled worker, on the contrary, could never be compared to that of an *artifex*. This explains the opinions on *mercennarii* held by Cicero, who considered that it was from their *operae*, and not their *artes*, that such wage-earners made a living. Through a somewhat excessive generalization, the latter were thus implicitly associated to unskilled workers.[27] Such conceptions were steeped in the aristocratic awareness of the hierarchical organization that prevailed in the working world among the urban *plebs*.

---

20 Sen., *Ep.* 88.20; see also the next paragraph(21).

21 Liv., 37.30.2 (*arte gubernatorum et scientia remigum*); Tac., *Dial.* 30.4 (*ingenuae artis scientia*); Paul. Fest. 21 (*artifices quod scientiam suam per artus exercent sive quod apte opera inter se artent*); Caes., *BCiv.* 1.58.2: *scientia artificis*.

22 Cic., *De or.* 2.30.

23 Cic., *Cael.* 54 (*artibus atque doctrina*).

24 Cic., *De or.* 1.111 (*magister atque artifex*); Plin., *HN* 26.12 (vii) (*magister in ea arte*).

25 Curt., 4.13.4 (*peritissimus... artium belli*); Petr., *Sat.* 109.7 (*artifex peritus*); Amm. Marc. 28.2.2 (*artifex periti aquariae rei*); Plin., *Ep.* 3.6.3 (*artifices* were opposed to *imperiti*, and knowing them fully required a *tirunculum*); Stat., *Silv.* 4.6.44–45 (*experientia docti artificis*).

26 Cels., *Med.* 3.4.9 (*artifex idoneus*).

27 Cic., *Off.* 1.150: *Illiberales autem et sordidi quaestus mercennariorum omnium, quorum operae, non quorum artes emuntur.*

Moreover, because an *ars* was based upon the mastery and application of a specific kind of knowledge, it represented a ground where the *artifex* could display his skill and ingenuity. Concepts as *sollertia, calliditas, subtilitas* and *ingenium*, among others, designated such qualities,[28] the indispensability of which explains why an *artificium* could sometimes be so difficult to master.[29] The notion of *ars* was so closely linked to those of dexterity and knowledge, that the word *artifex* itself was sometimes used as an adjective synonymous to *sollers* and *peritus*.[30] Most importantly, because an *ars* could be unequally mastered by various individuals, an *artifex* could distinguish himself among his fellow-workers. An *artificium* was seen as a proper ground for emulation, and the best *artifices* were sources of admiration.[31] An *artifex* could be considered as *mirus* (wonderful),[32] *magnus* (great),[33] or *summus* (the greatest).[34] He could be renowned and even aspire to some form of glory.[35]

In their writings on talented slaves and the *operae* of emancipated slaves, Roman jurists did not contradict the assertions made by literary authors. They saw the servile *artifex* as a specialized worker, unlike the *servus mediastinus*, or unskilled slave.[36] However, a *servus artifex* could be more or less educated: hence, according to the edict of the *aediles curules*, a buyer could not consider himself swindled if his newly acquired slave revealed himself a precise worker rather than an *artifex perfectus*.[37] The edict thus confirms the existence of levels in the mastery of an *ars*.

---

28 Man., 1.73 (*doctas sollertia fecerat artes*); Caes., *B. Alex.* 16.5 (*sollertia atque ars*); Paul., Fest. 293 (*sollers*); Apul., *Apol.* 4.8 (*sollertissimum artificium*); Apul., *Mun.* 31.359 (*artificum sollertia*); Cic., *Tusc.* 1.47 (*callidissimum artificium*); *Rhet. Her.* 3.3 (*callidus*); *Rosc. Am.* 49 (*callidus*); *Fin.* 2.116 (*artifex callidus*); Vitr., *De arch.* 4.1.10 (*elegentia et subtilitas artis marmoreae*); 7.5.7 (*subtilitas artificis*); Gell., *NA* 3.1.6 (*subtilis*); Liv., 31.26.11 (*ingenia artificum*); Hyg., *Poet. astr.* 2.7.3 (*ad musicam artem ingeniosissimus*).

29 Petr., *Sat.* 56.1–3.

30 Cic., *Brut.* 96; Ov., *Am.* 3.2.52 and *Tr.* 2.1.522 (*manus artifices*); Cic., *De or.*, 161 (*indoctus* is opposed to *artifex*).

31 Cic., *De or.* 1.130 (*in quo quisque artificio excelleret*); 2 *Verr.* 1.64 (*mirum artificium*); 2.87 (concerning a poet); 4.4; 4.38 (*summum artificium*).

32 Quint., *Inst.* 12.10.6.

33 Sen., *Ep.* 53.11 and 123.7; Juv., 11.102.

34 Fronto, *Arion* 1; Val. Max., 8.11 ext. 5.

35 Cic., 2 *Verr.* 4.12 (*praeclara nomina artificum*); *Fam.* 1.7.7 (*egregius artifex praeclaris operibus*); Plin., *HN* 33.154 (lv).

36 *Dig.* 7.7.6 pr.; *Dig.* 32.65.1 opposes the servant's *officium* to the skilled worker's *artificium*.

37 *Dig.* 21.1.19.4. Interestingly enough, the fragment also displays an assimilation of the *artifex*'s skills to a *scientia*. The notion of difference between the various *artifices* also appears in *Dig.* 46.3.31.

Roman workers, some of whom defined themselves as *artifices*, may have been regarded, and have regarded themselves, along similar lines, since the definitions of *ars, artificium* and *artifex* presented by Roman literature and jurisprudence no doubt applied to their work. At this stage of our demonstration, however, this can only be accepted as a possibility, as most definitions that we have examined so far do not specifically apply to craftsmen and merchants. The hypothesis, nevertheless, merits further consideration.

Ars, doctrina and the Pride of Roman Skilled Workers

Romans defined *artes* and *artifices* in a similar way, whether speaking in general, or referring to liberal arts, or arts and crafts or other urban occupations. In all cases, the *ars* enabled the *artifex* to show his dexterity, ingenuity, and, more generally, to demonstrate his skills. For craftsmen, their *ars* constituted a proper ground for displaying expertise (*peritia*) and excellence. Skilled workers were unanimously considered as men of knowledge, which was for them a source of pride. In literary and legal texts, the excellence of certain craftsmen is indeed based on their knowledge and skill. A good professional worker was called *doctus* or *peritus*. 'He who wins the favour of Pallas becomes a *doctus*', asserted Ovid in his description of the *Quinquatria*, the annual feast of craftsmen celebrated from March 19 through March 23.[38] By means of mythological references, Ovid alludes to spinners (*lanificae*), weavers (*textrices*), fullers (*fullones*), dyers (*infectores*), shoemakers (*sutores*), carpenters (*fabri tignuarii*), chiselers (*caelatores*), painters (*picturam inurentes*) and sculptors (*scalptores*). The goddess rewarded them, or punished their impiety, through the qualities that most characterized how they related to their work, viz. their know-how,[39] their ability to acquire skills through apprenticeships,[40] their well-executed technical manipulations,[41] and their manual dexterity.[42] Statius, in turn, contemplating a statue, sang praises of the *experientia docti artificis*.[43] The jurist Paul describes a slave who earned a yearly income thanks to his work as *arte*

38 Ov., *Fast.* 3.816–818.

39 Ov., *Fast.* 3.816. Likewise, in his *Metamorphoses* (6.23–24), the poet describes Arachne as *docta a Pallade*, the goddess being her *magistra*, whatever Arachne may say.

40 Ov., *Fast.* 3.817–818.

41 Ov., *Fast.* 3.823–824.

42 Ov., *Fast.* 3.825–826.

43 Stat., *Silv.* 4.6.44–45.

fabrica peritus.[44] The skilled worker had to distinguish himself by his *peritia*. Conversely, incompetence was considered a lack of training and knowledge. In a letter to his brother Quintus, Cicero criticizes the poor achievements of a certain Diphilus, who showed himself incapable of lining up the columns of a bath house, and expresses the hope that one day, this person should learn to use a set square and a plumb line.[45] According to Plutarch, the use of such instruments and of numbers revealed the intellectual dimension of the *technai*, and their status of emanations of intelligence (*sophronēsis*).[46] Ulpian attributed the defective work of a jeweller to *imperitia*, a lack of know-how.[47]

Manual workers could be recognized as men of talent. Whatever may have been written about the rejection of work in Roman literature in general, certain writers did consider the technical dexterity that manual work required. Horace makes a pun on the name of the jurist Alfenus Varus, referring to him as Alfenus *vafer* (skilful Alfenus), to allude to his supposed past when Alfenus would have owned a shoemaker's shop equipped with the *instrumentum* of his *ars*.[48] Moreover, the moral condemnation of manual work uttered by Seneca, to which historians continually refer, did not prevent the philosopher from acknowledging, almost admiringly, the *artifex*'s skilful poise that reflected his second nature, his *ars*.[49] According to Seneca, an *artifex* wielded his tools with ease, and the professional worker who showed himself capable of propping up a cracked wall in a building on the verge of collapse deserved to be praised for his *ars incredibilis*.[50] Various activities were based on gestures of which the technical mastery was often recognized. Martial argued that a good barber's hand, expertly wielding a razor-blade, was lighter than the earth in which his remains had been precociously buried.[51] But it is above all the dexterity of painters that gained the praise of Roman writers. Using his eye and his hand, the *pictor* could grasp an image of reality both instantaneously (*celerrime*) and without the slightest apparent difficulty (*facile*). When looking for a professional capable of adorning a library with portraits of writers, Pliny the Younger asked a friend to find him a *pictor diligentissimus*.[52] Furthermore,

44 *Dig.* 33.7.19.1.

45 Cic., *Q. fr.* 3.1.2.

46 Plut., *De fort. Rom.* 4, 99c.

47 *Dig.* 19.2.13. 5.

48 Hor., *Sat.* 1.3.130–131.

49 Sen., *Ep.* 121.5.

50 Sen., *Ben.* 6.15.7.

51 Mart., *Ep.* 6.52.5–6.

52 Plin., *Ep.* 4.28.2–3.

in his ninth Satire, Juvenal mentions two slaves used respectively by their master as vase carver and painter. About the second slave, the poet declares: 'swiftly does he paint many shapes' (*multas facies pingit cito*).[53] In fact, the adverb *cito* conveys an idea of poise and speed enabled only by technical mastery. The theme of skill-related excellence also appears in considerations regarding architecture and construction. According to Vitruvius, whose treaty mentions the notion of *sollertia* on several occasions,[54] one of the three qualitative criteria that were used to evaluate an architectural work was *subtilitas fabrilis*, the fineness of execution resulting from the rigor and precision of the *officinator* (the contractor) at work on the construction site.[55] In another passage, Vitruvius attributes the architect's excellence, that of the *perfectus architectus*, to the combination of two qualities: the intrinsic talent of the *ingeniosus* and the capacity to learn from the *docilis ad disciplinam*.[56] It is thus logical that the protagonists of Cicero's *Brutus* consider that a *faber tignuarius* may be called *optimus*.[57]

Only technical ease could enable the worker to attain satisfying and praiseworthy results, which is why one of the guests in the *Cena Trimalchionis* praises the remarkable (*optime*) quality of the funeral monuments built by the *lapidarius* Habinnas.[58] Similarly, in his *Apologia*, Apuleius laid much emphasis on the talents of Cornelius Saturninus, a sculptor from whom he had ordered a statuette of Mercury.[59] Accused of practicing witchcraft, Apuleius had to convince his judges that he had chosen this craftsman for his skills (*invitatus eius artificio*), and not to acquire an object charged with some evil power. Cornelius Saturninus was thus praised for his art (*arte laudatus*) because he crafted pieces with fineness and dexterity (*subtiliter et affabre*). Similar dispositions of mind also appear in imperial Greek literature. Lucian of Samosata's uncle, for instance, was called an excellent sculptor (*aristos hermogluphos*).[60] The apprenticeship he provided was expected to make a good stonemason, fitter and sculptor.[61] Writers conveyed similar social representations, even though their evocations were not centred on craftsmen of flesh and bones, but on

53 Juv., 9.145–146.

54 In the first paragraph, for instance (Vitr., *De arch.* 1.1).

55 Vitr., *De arch.* 6.8.9.

56 Vitr., *De arch.* 1.3.

57 Cic., *Brut.* 257.

58 Petr., *Sat.* 65.5–6.

59 Apul., *Apol.* 61.5–8.

60 Luc., *Somn.* 2.

61 Luc., *Somn.* 2: … καὶ δίδασκε παραλαβὼν λίθων ἐργάτην ἀγαθὸν εἶναι καὶ συναρμοστὴν καὶ ἑρμογλυφέα.

mythical characters, or historical figures from a very distant past. Consequently, workers were presented in a favourable light, and described in a way that only few Romans would have rejected. According to Ovid, Daedalus was famous for his *ingenium* in *ars fabra*.[62] Likewise, Diodorus Siculus saw Daedalus as the archetype of the talented craftsman.[63] The Athenian hero was an object of admiration: *kata tēn philotechnian thaumazomenos*.

Some texts issued by Roman authorities were based on a similar conception of work. In a letter answering his proconsul in Bithynia, Trajan insisted on the high level of training and genuine talent of provincial architects.[64] Pliny the Younger had informed him that a building site for public baths in Claudiopolis had gotten off to a bad start, and asked him to send an architect capable of evaluating the situation and finding a solution, but Trajan refused, arguing that every province of the empire had its share of architects who were *periti* and *ingeniosi*. Furthermore, the notion of *subtilitas* appeared in the *Edict on Maximum Prices* issued by Diocletian, in regard to the prices assigned to products of goldsmiths depending on their quality, whether they were considered as *opus subtile* or *opus simplex*.[65] As well-informed connoisseurs, aristocrats and notables had an acute perception of the quality of many artefacts. Martial presents a rich and stingy connoisseur when he describes Marmurra's stroll among the abundant and diverse luxury items of the *Saepta*.[66] Thus, persons of high social status could admire the work of craftsmen. To reconcile this idea with the notion of aristocratic contempt for work, can we surmise *artes* to be a source of admiration, and *artifices* an object of disdain?[67] The texts we analysed above prevent us from generalizing such a discrepancy between the acknowledged fineness of an object and the vision of the craftsman.

Roman skilled workers were the first to view their *ars* as a basis for excellence, by means of which they could gain superiority over their fellow-workers. Hence, certain inscriptions engraved at the request of skilled workers echo the literary extracts quoted above. In a funerary poem, the professional excellence (*ars summa*) of the Arlesian carpenter Q. Candidius Benignus is defined by his knowledge (*doctrina*). His superiority was first expressed by his wife and daughter, who declared: 'Nobody was ever more learned than him' (*doctior hoc*

62 Ov., *Met.* 8.159. A redundant expression, as *faber* is here employed as an adjective meaning 'artfully', 'with a sense of technique'. See *TLL*, VI/1, col. 7.

63 Diod. Sic., 4.76.4.

64 Plin., *Ep.* 10.40.3.

65 *Edictum de Pretiis* 28.7–8; see Groen-Vallinga and Tacoma in this volume.

66 Mart., *Ep.* 9.59.

67 Van den Hoven (1996: 68).

nemo fuit). The *ars* of Q. Candidius Benignus could be called *summa*. Similarly, in Konana, Pisidia, a blacksmith's son stated that a *technē megalē* was passed down to him by his father.[68] In Rome, M. Canuleius Zosimus 'excelled in carving Clodian ware'.[69] He was an expert in the fabrication of a certain type of silver vase mentioned by Pliny the Elder.[70]

The same kind of excellence is celebrated when professional workers are simply described as *optimi*. In Alba Fucens, a man named Halicius consecrated the funeral altar of Marcius Faustus by having the civic status of the deceased inscribed on its front face, and by honouring 'the best of cooks', in large capital letters, on both sides of the monument.[71] The excellence of this emancipated slave reminds one of the *cocus optimus, optimus in eo artificio* whom Gaius chose as an example in his comment on the edict of the *aediles curules*.[72] In a similar fashion, M. Ulpius Hera and Valeria Saturnina paid a last tribute to their son, C. Pomponius Heracon, who died at the early age of 25, by honouring him as a *faber navalis optumus*: the best of shipbuilders.[73] To better express their son's professional identity, they had the image of a ship engraved on the lower section of his stele. Such occurrences of self-celebration also appear in Greek epigraphy.[74] Maximus the carpenter lived in Rome until his death at the age of 26, but he was born in Bithynia. Hence he had a poem in Greek composed in memory of himself and had it engraved on a little marble stele, discovered in the vicinity of the *Porta Maggiore*.[75] The poem presents him as a *oikodomos xuloergon* (the equivalent of a *faber tignuarius*), 'irreproachable in the practice of his art' (*amōmētos kata technēn*). In the second century, the sculptor Zenon of Aphrodisias also moved to Rome, after having visited many cities on account of his work. He sculpted his son's gravestone with the utmost care, and the result was a self-proclaimed 'technically remarkable piece of work' (*technassamenos kluton ergon*).[76] The mastery in which *artifices* in urban economies took such pride resulted from the apprenticeship they had received and were capable of offering in their turn. Such vocation, therefore, was central to their professional identity.

---

68 *SEG* XXXI 1284.

69 *CIL* VI 9222.

70 Plin., *HN* 33.139 (xlix).

71 *CIL* IX 3938.

72 *Dig.* 21.1.18.1.

73 *CIL* VI 33833.

74 Burford (1972: 180–183 and 208–209).

75 *IGUR* III 1263 (*SEG* IV 105).

76 *IGUR* III 1222.

The Status of Magister

The mastery of a specific *ars* and the vocation of teaching it to others were closely linked to the hierarchies which structured the working world and, on a microeconomic scale, the businesses of craftsmen and merchants. Indeed, apprentices and former apprentices provided a significant part of the workforce employed by small-scale Roman entrepreneurs. The goldsmith Secundinius Felicissimus had a poem composed in memory of his former *magister*, Iulius Statutus, in which he presents himself as the first of Statutus' *discipuli*, and specifies that the workshop had comprised three *ministri* of the same age.[77] The *minister* assures that the trainees of Statutus continued the latter's work as *suboles* (offspring, literally) of his *statio* (his workshop) and measured up to their *magister*'s *artificium summum*. The vocation to pass on a specific know-how, associated with running a business, outlined a professional status. The apprenticeship system turned an occupation into an educational benefit. The training of apprentices was thus an essential part of the work and status of the master craftsman. (see also the chapter by Liu)

The available documentation presents the image of workshops alive with *discipuli* and *discentes*, apprentices. A dozen fragments from the Digest provide information on apprentices, in texts concerning such questions as *revendicatio*, usufruct, mandate, *locatio* and the master-slave relationship. Regarding the latter, for instance, Ulpian distinguished *operarii* and *discipuli*, among a fuller's employees.[78] The craftsman's know-how was passed down to children and adolescents of diverse legal and familial statuses. In most cases, the apprentice was probably one of the master craftsman's sons, although the available sources fail to prove it, for quite obvious reasons; the hereditary transmission of the craft from father to son was not based on any contract which, in case of litigation, was to be examined by jurists. On steles and gravestones, those who had been taught their craft by their own fathers had no specific reason to define themselves as apprentices or former apprentices. An exception is provided by a lengthy and detailed epitaph found in Lyon:[79] it appears on a third century altar dedicated to Valeria Leucadia and Vireius Vitalis, who died at the respective ages of 6 and 19 at a thirty-day interval. The young man is described as a specialist of *ars fabricae ferrariae*, or ironwork. He owed the mastery of his art to Valerius Maximus, his stepfather and probably the second husband of his mother Iulia Secundina, 'who had adopted him and taught him his art'

77 *RIT* 447.

78 *Dig.* 14.3.5.10.

79 *CIL* XIII 2036.

(*qui eu[m] sibi filium adoptaverat et art[e] educaverat*). The expression 'in whom he had placed the hopes of his old age' (*in quo spem aetatis suae conlocaverat*) suggests that Vitalis was to succeed Maximus as head of the family business. Elsewhere, the brief allusion to the sons of a banker (*nummularius*) in a fragment of Scaevola implies that the man in question had taught his craft to his sons.[80] Whereas any unfinished banking operation was usually cancelled by closing the account, this rule did not apply to outside orders. The jurist thus specified that the execution of a mandate continued to impose itself on the banker and his sons. We can thus infer that the latter worked with their father and had probably also been taught by him.

Slave owners, furthermore, were very concerned about the education of their dependents.[81] J.-Chr. Dumont even goes to the extent of considering 'slavery as the normal form of apprenticeship', especially insofar as arts, crafts and commerce were concerned.[82] According to the expression used by jurists, slave owners 'made' skilled workers, *artifices*.[83] The education a slave received was seen as an investment that increased his value. According to Gaius, if a slave was the object of a claim and his value had to be estimated by a judge, his qualifications acquired through apprenticeship, for instance as a painter, should not benefit the plaintiff, when the adverse party, sued *de rei vindicatione*, had taken the slave's training upon himself.[84] The profitability of a servile workforce thus resulted first from the natural reproduction of the slaves and subsequently from their education and training, the costs of which were justified by the prospect of a more lucrative future exploitation of these new skilled workers.

A third possibility consisted of placing children as apprentices with master craftsmen. Their legal situation was usually based on a contract of hire (*locatio conductio*).[85] Ulpian considers the possibility for the father or guardian of a *discens* to sue a shoemaker (*sutor*) for breach of contract (*ex locato*) who had grievously injured his apprentice. This composite and therefore complex fragment shows that such apprentices could be slaves as well as *ingenui* from respectable

---

80 *Dig.* 2.14.47.1. See Andreau (1987: 560).

81 Morabito (1981: 85–86); Dumont (1987: 744–746) about the general principles claimed by Cic., *Rep.* 5.4–5; Dumont (1987: 519), about actors and Cic., *Com.* 27–28; Hermann-Otto (1994: 335); Rawson (2003: 187–191); Laes (2008).

82 Dumont (1987: 65).

83 See *Dig.* 6.1.32, for instance.

84 *Dig.* 6.1.28. Paul (*Dig.* 6.1.27.5) also mentions a slave's education in a case of *vindicatio* (*sed si puerum meum, cum possideres, erudisses* …).

85 De Robertis (1946: 197–200).

families.[86] The jurist first considers the case of a master who injured a slave *in disciplina*, in the context of his apprenticeship. The second part of Ulpian's text deals with the actual work relationship between a shoemaker and his apprentice who lost an eye through his master's violent treatment. In this particular case, the unhappy *discens* was a *filiusfamilias*. In another text, Ulpian considers the case of a slave apprentice.[87]

Workshop and shop owners liked to define themselves as *magistri*, since the status of *magister* allowed both a position of authority over a group of workers and the transmission of a specialized know-how to one or several apprentices (*discipuli*). Once again literary and legal texts reveal that everyone in the Roman world was aware of this particular aspect of the work and identity of skilled workers. In the *Sententiae Pauli, magistri tabernae* are said to be responsible for the work of their *discipuli*.[88]

The *Edict on Maximum Prices* limited spending to one-hundred *denarii* per *puer* per month for architects working as *magistri*.[89] In Roman mythology, Minerva was the *magistra* of all arts and all craftsmen.[90] Technical excellence was seen as the result of a perfectly assimilated apprenticeship, to such an extent that some writers mention the commonplace figure of the disciple surpassing his master. Pliny the Elder, for instance, described the competition held between two potters from Erythrae, a master and his disciple, as both endeavoured to fashion the thinnest possible amphora.[91] Lucian attributed the brutality of his uncle, a sculptor, to his fear that someday he would be surpassed in his art.[92] Diodorus Siculus explained Daedalus's murder of his nephew, Talos, by the master carpenter's jealousy of his apprentice's creativity.[93]

In epigraphical sources, the word *magister* tends to appear as a prestigious title, sometimes referring to apprenticeship in a more or less explicit way. In Arles, the professional reputation of Q. Candidius Benignus is described by the words: 'whom great artisans always called Master' (*quem magni artifices semper dixsere magistrum*). Similarly, it is as a *discipulus* that Secundinius Felicissimus, from Tarragona, addresses his deceased *magister* Iulius Statutus.[94]

86 *Dig.* 9.2.5.3.

87 *Dig.* 19.2.13.3.

88 Paul., *Sent.* 2.8.3; see Aubert (1994: 88).

89 *Edictum de Pretiis* 7.74. Tac., *Ann.* 15.42.1 also designates as *magistri* both architects whom Nero chose to build the *Domus Aurea*.

90 Front., Str. 3.8.

91 Plin., *HN* 35.161 (xlvi).

92 Luc., *Somn.* 4.

93 Diod. Sic., 4.76.4.

94 *RIT* 447.

Significantly, an inhabitant of Puteoli, M. Perpernius Zmaragdus, uses a possessive adjective when writing a last goodbye to his well-deserving master, thereby stressing his relationship with the artisan whose apprentice he had been.[95] On the other hand, several craftsmen are referred to as *magistri* in inscriptions from the Western Roman Empire, without any mention of apprenticeship whatsoever. In the mid-fourth century, another mason (*structor*), *magister* Generosus, was painted among his workers and next to the commissioner on the tomb that Trebius Iustus ordered to be decorated on the *via Latina*.[96] In late antique Byzacium, in Henchir El-Errich, Bictorianus and Victorinus presented themselves as *magistri* at the head of an *officina* of mosaicists.[97] It was thanks to the mastery of their *artes* that such skilled workers could become *magistri*. Solinus the grammarian describes Daedalus as *fabricae artis magister*.[98] In Cologne, Iulius Verinus worked as a *magister artis fulloniae*, or master fuller.[99] The superiority expressed in his epitaph thus affirms his technical expertise, rather than a position of authority exerted in the workplace.

We may infer from the above observations that the recognition of skilled workers as *artifices* legitimized a discourse of self-celebration and pride, the commonplace notions of which were unanimously acknowledged. Thus, historians have been partly mistaken in opposing a popular and laudatory conception of arts and trades to the contempt that Roman elites supposedly felt for such work. Although firmly rooted within the higher strata of Roman society, writers and jurists echoed some positive representations that were widely shared by the whole of Roman society, when recognizing the master craftsmen's know-how, technical dexterity, and even talent. Such a perception did not abolish or even reduce the gap that separated the elites from plebeian circles. On the contrary, it revealed an acute awareness of social hierarchies. The high aristocracy itself, along with notables of lesser rank, had an acute perception of what, among plebeians, distinguished an *artifex* from an unskilled worker, and an entrepreneur from his workforce. The acknowledgement of this gap in no way altered the feeling of social dominance that characterized the members of the elite. Conscious of their unquestionable superiority, they did not for all that consider the plebs as an indistinct mass but were capable of making contradictory comments on the intermediary social categories. Paradoxically, contempt and praise were not incompatible. Cicero,

95 *CIL* X 1959.

96 Bisconti (2004: 142–144, fig. 79 and 111).

97 *AE* 2001, 2074.

98 Solin., 5.8.

99 *CIL* XIII 8345 (*RSK* 319).

for instance, could in the space of one year declare that no man of high birth could be seen in a workshop,[100] and go into rapture over the manual dexterity required by the *artes*, not only of painters, sculptors, musicians and peasants, but also iron and bronze workers and builders.[101]

---

100 Cic., *Off.* 1.150: *Opificesque omnes in sordida arte versantur; nec enim quicquam ingenuum habere potest officina.*

101 Cic., *Nat. D.* 2.150: *Quam vero aptas quamque multarum artium ministras manus natura homini dedit. Digitorum enim contractio facilis facilisque porrectio propter molles commissuras et artus nullo in motu laborat. Itaque ad pingendum fingendum, ad scalpendum, ad nervorum eliciendos sonos ad tibiarum apta manus est admotione digitorum. Atque haec oblectationis, illa necessitatis, cultus dico agrorum extructionesque tectorum, tegumenta corporum vel texta vel suta omnemque fabricam aeris et ferri; ex quo intellegitur ad inventa animo percepta sensibus adhibitis opificum manibus omnia nos consecutos, ut tecti ut vestiti ut salvi esse possemus, urbes muros domicilia delubra haberemus.*

CHAPTER 13

Work, Identity and Self-Representation in the Roman Empire and the West-European Middle Ages: Different Interplays between the Social and the Cultural

Catharina Lis and Hugo Soly

Social historians specializing in medieval and early modern Europe are fascinated by the funerary monuments and epitaphs constructed to commemorate the dead in public places both in ancient Rome and in many provinces of the Roman Empire.[1] They are intrigued less by the intrinsic artistic qualities than by the texts and especially the visual images, which often refer explicitly to the professional activity of the deceased. Some tombstones list only an occupation, while others also depict tools of the trade or even show the specific actions for which these instruments were used. During the Western Middle Ages before the fifteenth century, on the other hand, nobody set up texts or images in places accessible to the public that contained any reference to the occupation practised by an individual. Professional activities were no longer considered defining elements to be remembered by future generations. At first sight this seems remarkable since according to the standard historical accounts, in Classical Antiquity disdain for work and workers was deeply rooted among the elite, while it was the representatives of Christianity who stressed the value of work. How can the two elements of this grand narrative be reconciled with the changes in funerary representation? In this essay we shall argue that the answer lies in different interplays of the social and the cultural. Anybody in the Roman Empire who took pride in his professional achievements could include this in cultural expressions without encountering any serious objection, while in the Western Middle Ages public manifestations of occupational honour were rigidly bounded by ideological constraints.

1 See on this topic also the chapter by Tran in this volume.

 | DOI 10.1163/9789004331686_014

The Roman Empire: Social Change and Building Occupational Identity

Although we are now well into the twenty-first century, historians stressing negative perceptions of work in Classical Antiquity still invoke the authority of Moses Finley: commercial and industrial activities were of only marginal significance, which meant that aristocratic standards and values remained dominant and therefore excluded appreciation of non-agrarian work. In the past twenty years the Finleyan model has undergone many adjustments, but the discussion has by no means subsided.[2] Some authors continue to assert that the ancient economy was bounded by overriding social constraints.[3] Other authors readily compare the economy of the Roman Empire in the period 100 BC–AD 200 to that of Western Europe between 1400 and 1700, focusing mainly on the similarities.[4] Archaeological excavations reveal high levels of specialization and concurrent high levels of production and trade in the late Republic and the early Principate. Society was very dynamic. Members of the established elite increasingly seized the opportunities for profit that commercial expansion effectively provided for marketing the produce of their estates and—directly or indirectly—for participating in international trade. Still more importantly: epigraphic sources indicate the rise of economically active and successful middle groups, many of whom were organized in occupational associations. Irrespective of whether the concept of 'middle class',[5] is applicable to the merchants, financiers, and master artisans who were economically successful,[6] it is undeniable that the intermediary layers between the elite and popular masses expanded considerably. The social advancement of entrepreneurial freedmen is especially striking.[7]

Put briefly, reasonable grounds are available for questioning whether non-agrarian work was indeed universally disdained in the late Republic and the early Empire. It would nonetheless be incorrect to assume that the foundations

2 For recent critical assessments, see Andreau (2010); Scheidel (2012a); Verboven (2012c); and several contributions to this volume.

3 See, for example, Bang (2008).

4 See esp. Pleket (1990); Grantham (1999); Greene (2000); Temin (2006); Kessler and Temin (2007); Lo Cascio and Malanima (2009).

5 Veyne (2000).

6 Mayer (2012) argues that the commercialization of the Roman Empire led to the rise of a 'middle class' characterized by distinct patterns of economic behaviour and specific cultural values that set it apart from the established elite.

7 See esp. Scheidel (2006); Tran (2006); Verboven (2007b); Scheidel and Friesen (2009); Mouritsen (2011); Mayer (2012).

for revaluing all kinds of human activity were laid in this period. For centuries a strong work ethic had permeated Greco-Roman society. The social changes between 100 BC and AD 200 merely reinforced the demand that everybody should make worthy efforts, as had also been the case in Athens in the fifth and fourth centuries BC.[8] The dominant myths, epic, lyric, tragedy, philosophy, and the acts of heroes and other role models indicate that making worthy efforts was regarded as a duty and a necessity throughout Classical Antiquity, not only because the Gods demanded efforts from everybody, but also and especially because the social value of such efforts was generally recognized. Idleness was harshly condemned in Homeric poetry.[9] In his *Works and Days* Hesiod stated pithily: 'Work is no disgrace: it is idleness which is a disgrace.'[10] His words were repeated centuries later as an adage or slogan, both by Pericles and by Socrates, by Demosthenes and by his adversary Demades.[11] To quote Xenophon: 'The best men and dearest to the Gods are those who do their work well … He who does nothing well is neither useful in any way nor dear to the Gods.'[12]

The positive connotations of the concept *ponos* reveal that efforts, suffering, and pain were associated with virtue and honour. This resounds in the popular myth of Hercules at the Crossroads, insisting that a good, virtuous, honourable, and happy life required continuous efforts: only by so doing can one be self-sufficient, serve society, and observe the will of the Gods.[13] In numerous texts it was emphasized that those at the top of the polis needed to be 'labour loving,' i.e. willing to make serious efforts. Members of the elite were constantly reminded that they were expected to submit to this imperative. Pericles made clear through legislation that the rich also must avoid idleness. The Cynics even argued that poverty, defined as the absence of wealth,[14] merited appreciation, precisely because it implied the inherent need to work. The labour of the poor was associated not only with virtues such as honesty, moderation, and justice but also with inner freedom and self-fulfilment.

8 See Lis and Soly (2012: 13–53).

9 Hom., *Od.* 9.105–9 and 17.225–228. See the pertinent remarks of Meier (2003: 30–31) and Ndoye (2010: 32–33, 135–136).

10 Hes., *Op.* 2.311.

11 See the references in Desmond (2006: 183, n. 17).

12 Xen., *Mem.* 3.9.15. See Marchant, Todd and Henderson (2013: 245).

13 Balme (1984: 151–152); Desmond (2006: 84–87, 97); Csapo (2005: 15). See also Harbach (2010: 91–134).

14 Poverty was thus not equated with destitution, as the latter state was attributed to idleness. Hesiod referred to 'hungry idlers' and 'begging idlers,' while Aesop contrasted the cricket with the ant: own fault, tough luck.

The Stoic philosophers, who deeply influenced the Roman intelligentsia, similarly advocated a life of simplicity and virtue, in keeping with nature, which entailed appreciation for work. They qualified all people as reasonable beings who were alike by nature and should treat each other as brothers. Everybody, regardless of his place in the cosmic order, had therefore to perform specific duties, especially marriage, starting a family, and work. Hercules was a hero who enabled people with very different social positions to interpret the concept of 'effort' in their own way, i.e. in keeping with their specific position. In all cases, however, work was a social and a moral obligation, because its performance served others while achieving personal integrity and self-sufficiency at the same time. A life of service, meaning a life consisting of worthy efforts, was the antipode of laziness, opulence, hedonism, and parasitism.[15]

This meant not only that working to provide for one's own subsistence was a virtuous activity, but also that a life of pure contemplation was tantamount to forsaking one's social and moral obligations. This applied to philosophers as well as peasants. Gaius Musonius Rufus, a great teacher who lived in the first century AD, asserted: 'Pupils would seem to me rather benefited [...] by seeing him [the philosopher] at work in the fields, demonstrating by his own labour the lessons which philosophy indicates—that one should endure hardships, and suffer the pains of labour with his own body, rather than depend upon another for sustenance.'[16] Another Roman Stoic, Maximus of Tyre, argued in the late second century AD that *all* occupations were honourable, including trade in luxury commodities or forms of entertainment. He compared society with the human body, in which all parts were indispensable and equal.[17] Which activity or what work was performed did not really matter: anyone could lead a life of virtue, as long as moral codes were observed. This also held true for all those doing paid work: the wage earners.[18] The question was whether certain occupations led people to stray from the path of virtue too easily. Several Stoics advised avoiding professional activities associated with excessive opulence, but they valued forms of wage labour that had nothing to do with this.[19]

---

15 See esp. Van den Hoven (1996: 21–37).

16 Muson., *Diss.* 11.26–31 translated by Lutz (1947: 83).

17 Max. Tyr., *Or.* 15.2–4; Trapp (1997: 135–137).

18 Indications are available that wage labour was widespread and was still gaining ground in late Antiquity: Temin (2004); Van Heesch (2007); Banaji (2011: 117–30); Flohr (2011b: 92–93); Kehoe (2012). See also Bernard and Holleran in this volume.

19 Van den Hoven (1996: 41, 49–50).

The ideal of the virtuous, hardworking citizen was not new,[20] but during the late Republic and the early Principate, praising hard work and depicting 'poverty' as a positive state countering corruptive wealth was considered more necessary than ever. Seneca the Elder ('the Rhetorician') valued the argument that poverty was desirable, because citizens who had to work were then best protected from all possible forms of corruption.[21] A great many texts glorified honest hard work enabling those engaging in it to provide for their own subsistence. Simple farm life became a rhetorical argument, a recurring *topos* to remedy the purported ailments of the time. Virgil, Horace, Livy, Pliny the Elder, Columella, and many others depicted the life of the small but autonomous and self-sufficient farmer as the epitome of virtue. Figures from the past (in some cases the very distant past), such as Cincinnatus and Cato the Elder ('the Censor'), were presented as exemplary, because they—as legend had it—had never hesitated to dirty their hands. The notions *industria* and *inertia* were defined as antipodes; rest was acceptable only following hard work. The view of the Cynics that poverty, work, and virtue all coincided was widely supported, as is clear from the success of an orator such as Dio Cocceianus or Dio Chrysostom, who told his audiences in the second half of the first century AD that poor farmers who worked the land daily were truly virtuous and therefore merited great appreciation and even admiration.[22] Understandably, prominent Romans tried to demonstrate to everyone that the work ethic was firmly embedded within them. Cicero not only *was* a workaholic: he presented himself as such as well. In 45 BC, after Caesar was assassinated, when Sallust withdrew from public life and took to historiography, he worried that a life without universally visible efforts would compromise his reputation, and he felt the need to account for this change.[23]

This was the background to the explicit references to *productive* work in epigraphic and iconographic sources. Wealthy Roman entrepreneurs readily visualized their economic pursuits. Aulus Umbricius Scaurus from Pompeii, who amassed a fortune by manufacturing and selling a special fish sauce (*garum*), had a mosaic floor built in one of the two atriums of his impressive *domus*. This floor featured large amphorae inscribed with the words *garum* and *Umbricius Scaurus*. His attitude did not discourage public tributes. Around AD 50 Scaurus was honoured as a *duovir* with a publicly sponsored funeral and an equestrian

20 See Osborne (2006: 13).

21 Sen., *Controv.* 2.1.

22 Brunt (1973: 11–13); Van den Hoven (1996: 46–48); Osborne (2006: 13); Woolf (2006: 93–94).

23 André (1966: 122–124); Balsdon (1969: 138–140); Toner (1995: 25–28).

statue in the Forum.[24] Likewise, in the same city, Marcus Vecilius Verecundus and his wife, affluent textile manufacturers and traders, had frescoes with scenes of the production process portraying both the workers and themselves placed on either side of the entrance to their large workshop.[25] The numerous large and small tombstones depicting economic pursuits reveal unambiguously how closely work, virtue, and honour were intertwined.[26] They were to be found throughout the empire, and they were used by people active in very different occupations to demonstrate what they considered worthy of commemoration. Freedmen's reliefs, in particular, evolved from family group portraits listing occupations in the first century BC to elaborate, detailed depictions of professional activities in the first century AD. Some of these new funerary monuments were placed at highly visible sites, primarily along access roads to the cities, and they continued to multiply in the second and third centuries.[27] Freedmen appear to have preferred tombstones with scenes of occupational activities more than freeborn (*ingenui*), but the latter also had such monuments erected. In addition to the visual images, most were inscribed with information on family ties, the course of the deceased's career, public tributes, and other elements of value to the deceased. Combining images with words made it possible to exhibit very specific qualities and accomplishments: talent in practising an occupation, running a business, owning slaves, amassing wealth, starting a thriving family, membership of honourable associations, and the like. The most elaborate monuments told a story, a type of curriculum vitae, and expressed a self-representation intended to demonstrate worldly status.

One most enlightening tombstone is that of the Roman baker and bread contractor Marcus Vergilius Eurysaces, who was probably a freedman. His tomb, dated ca. 50–20 BC, is remarkable not only because of its location—at the convergence of two roads just outside of Rome—and its vast size and the construction materials, but also and mainly for the friezes depicting all stages in the production process, from grinding wheat to baking bread, and the integration of kneading machines in the construction. The visual strategies of Eurysaces' tomb were not fundamentally different from the ones used by prominent Roman citizens at the time. The 'victory' frieze on the grave monument of C. Cartilius Poplica in nearby Ostia, for example, depicted his military

24 Curtis (1984); Campbell (2010).

25 Clarke (2003: 105–12); Holleran (2012: 122–123).

26 On the importance of preserving the memory of the dead in ancient Rome, see Carroll (2006), who concentrates on inscriptions.

27 George (2006).

victories, while sixteen gigantic fasces in relief illustrated his career as a high-ranking official. Eurysaces presented his economic activities as *equivalent* to the efforts by public figures: he, too, had served the common good, as visualized by a scene of a public official inspecting the bread's weight and clarified by an inscription. Lauren Petersen has rightly noted that this was not a specific type of 'freedman art' characterized by exuberant, gaudy self-representation. Eurysaces was not a frustrated freedman, and his tomb was not a manifestation of counterculture, i.e. an attempt to take issue with aristocratic values, especially the presumed disdain of the elite for work and workers. The messages conveyed by his monument may be interpreted in various ways, but there is little doubt that this baker aimed to express values shared among broad social groups.[28]

In many cases, grave monuments of entrepreneurs convey, implicitly or explicitly, in images or words, the message that the deceased had served the common good, which suggested moral integrity. The wealthy merchant Lucius Nerusius Mithres from Magliano in Tuscany, for example, noted in his epitaph that he had started his career selling goatskins, and that he had done this to satisfy the needs of many citizens. He described his merchant occupation as *semper honorificus* and stated that 'as far as was possible,' he had always performed his commercial transactions honestly, had always paid his taxes, and had supported the needy.[29] Such moral virtues were also strongly emphasized on the tombstones of economically active individuals outside Italy. The impressive grave monuments established by affluent local families in the Trier area between the start of the second century and the first quarter of the third century depicted the transport of wine and oil and trade in textile products, often including monetary transactions.[30] The most spectacular example is the 23 metres high 'Igel Column', which was erected by the cloth merchant family of the Secundinii. The richly decorated column portrays several stages in trading textile goods, with special consideration for quality control, because the family hoped to emphasize that they had earned their wealth legitimately, i.e. by working hard, and by braving dangers, as expressed in various scenes. In fact, land ownership is presented as only an incidental element. Hardworking, reliable merchants are the central theme. Several visual images moreover suggest that the family's commercial pursuits had served the common good. Honest work, wealth, public interest, and honourable commemoration were inextricably linked: that was the message of the Secundinii. Their depiction of

28 Petersen (2006: 84–120). See also Mouritsen (2005).

29 *CIL* IX 4796 (p 686) = *CLE* 437; cf. Knapp (2011: 9).

30 Many examples are displayed at the Rheinisches Landesmuseum at Trier.

the apotheosis of Hercules is not purely coincidental: like this divine hero, they had made huge efforts and overcome many obstacles. We agree with Jérôme France's conclusion that the grave monuments of the Secundinii and other Trier merchants should be interpreted as odes to work. The author rightly recalls the view of Rostovtzeff, who argued nearly a century ago that their graves do not suggest a 'parvenu' mentality but reflect the pride of a new local elite aiming to demonstrate that strict fulfilment of obligations in an exemplary life would justify an apotheosis.[31]

What wealthy merchants wished to commemorate was valued in equal measure by craftsmen, as the abundant mentions of skilled labour on tombstones indicate. They also sought to recall to public memory that they had done their duty, i.e. had worked hard. But they often added something, namely that they had always excelled in their occupational ingenuity, meaning they had served the common good by guaranteeing reliable products of quality. The visual images on their tombstones served to disclose great skill and, if possible, technical knowledge. Many artisans insisted that their professional skills had brought them the utmost satisfaction in life. This occupational pride gave rise to statements along the lines of 'nobody better than,' 'the best in,' 'unsurpassed by anyone.' One inscription read: 'What he has ill done in workmanship, who can do better? What he has well done, no one can equal.'[32] Those who commissioned the sarcophagus of Q. Candidius Benignus, a *corporatus* of the guild of carpenters/builders (*fabri tignuarii*) from Arles c. AD 150–250, had the inscription portray him as a man who knew everything about engineering: nobody was more learned (*doctior*) than he; his knowledge was so vast that all eminent specialists (*artifices*) had recognized him as their master (*magister*) in the trade.[33] Conceivably, such an inscription was intended to commemorate the possession and application of 'true' knowledge, i.e. knowledge extending beyond practical skills, as those who could fathom nature, who mastered general principles, and who produced knowledge merited special appreciation.[34] Inscriptions in which skilled craftsmen presented themselves as outstanding tradesmen and as experts moreover corresponded with the views of most Romans on quite a few specialized urban occupations, as Nicolas Tran has

31 *CIL* XIII 4206; Espérandieu 6, 5268; cf. France (2004), endorsing the comment of Rostovtzeff (1957: 611–612 n. 27). See also Schwinden (1989); Young (1999); Liu (2009: 90–91).

32 *CIL* V 5930; quoted in Geoghegan (1945: 52–53).

33 *CIL* XII 722 = *CLE* 483; Cuomo (2007: 85). See also the chapter by Tran in this volume.

34 In this connection, see the comments of Van den Hoven (1996: 81–94) and Cuomo (2007: 98–102).

observed. Several writers assimilated such occupations to *artes* and qualified the individuals who practised them as *artifex doctus* or *artifex doctissimus*.[35]

Skilled manual artisans were also likely to mention their great *physical* exertions over the course of their occupational lives. One case in point concerns the altar that the cutler Lucius Cornelius Atimetus dedicated around the middle of the first century AD to himself, to his most deserving freedman, and to his other freedmen and freedwomen: one of the two reliefs depicts a smith's workshop, where two men toil at activities requiring great physical strength and causing heavy perspiration.[36] The tombstone of the butcher Tiberius Julius Vitalis is equally remarkable: next to his bust is another depiction of him carving open a pig's head with a cleaver.[37] Such scenes were not exceptional. The reliefs on several tombstones of manual artisans, *ingenui* and freedmen alike, depict figures unmistakably toiling away,[38] while the inscriptions often explicitly mention a life of hard work, involving blood, sweat, and tears. Those who had performed manual labour for extended periods and had advanced in social status clearly took pride in their efforts. The altar of a landowner from Dalmatia who long worked as a shoemaker depicts him twice: on one side of the altar he has a bushel of corn ears in his hand, while on the other side he is holding a shoe, with the instruments from his previous occupation beside him.[39] Craftsmen who ultimately achieved social prestige did not repudiate their origins. These and other examples show that craftsmen took pride in their professional achievements and especially in their ingenuity.[40] Their epitaphs reflected variations on the theme: 'We have each made *worthy* efforts in our own way.' This was similarly emphasized by wealthy merchants, bankers, and ship owners: they tried to visualize the merits of *negotium* in some way, associating the grandeur of their *labor improbus* with the works of Hercules.[41]

Even the epitaphs on the tombstones of businessmen and craftsmen who had held public office in their community and had acquired prestige thanks to the associated 'honours' announce that they attributed their social advancement to their hard work. The miller and *augustalis* Publius Nonius Zethus

---

35 Tran (2011b); and his chapter in this volume.

36 *CIL* VI 16166 (p 3519, 3913); Gummerus (1913: 78–79); Clarke (2003: 121–123); George (2006: 26). See also the chapters by Hawkins and Flohr (with drawing).

37 *CIL* VI 9501; Geoghegan (1945: 52, and Plate III).

38 See Turcan (1999: figs. 82–83, 86–87, 89).

39 *ILJug* 1550 = *AHB* p. 213; cf. Patsch (1909: 154–156, no. 21) (with drawing); Rostovtzeff (1957: 224, and Plate XXXIII.4).

40 For other examples, see Zimmer (1982) and (1985).

41 Turcan (1999: 88).

commemorated himself both for his office and for his craft; the depictions on the urn holder included a donkey grinding wheat.[42] A man from Madaurus, a Roman colony in Numidia, who had advanced to equestrian rank, had the following text inscribed on his grave: 'Here lies Lucius Aelius Timminus / hardened by work, moderate, attentive, frugal, / and who elevated a modest family to knighthood.'[43] Equally telling is the tomb of the 'Harvester of Mactar' from late third-century Tunisia. After a life of hard agrarian work, he managed to purchase an estate and was elected to the local office of *censor*, thus becoming a highly respected individual in his town. Still, he had explicitly mentioned in the extended inscription on his funerary stele that he had toiled as a wage worker for many years, and that he had 'reaped the fruit of honours' for his life of work.[44] In short, solid grounds exist for rejecting views holding that the Roman world was imbued with disdain for work and workers.

The West-European Middle Ages: Social Change and Ideological Constraints

Since economic and social developments in the late Republic and the early Principate resembled those in the central Middle Ages, we might expect individual and collective representations of professional activity and occupational identity to have been highly explicit in both periods. The changes occurring in Western Europe from the eleventh century onward in technology, agrarian and industrial production, interregional trade, urbanization, and social relations after all left merchants and craftsmen with comparable opportunities to develop positive self-images to those available to their predecessors in the period 100 BC–AD 200. Nonetheless, few public manifestations of occupational awareness are discernible until around 1400. Even ego-documents intended for family members, close friends, and descendants contain few references to professional activities. The explanation in our view lies in the markedly different ideological context. From the early Middle Ages until the rise of Protestantism in the sixteenth century, the Church of Rome was the primary source of ideological positions in Western Christianity. No single religion or school of philosophy had ever been so predominant in Classical Antiquity. This meant that economically active lay people in the Middle Ages needed to relate their self-definitions and profiles first of all to religious discourses. They might seek

42 *CIL* XIV 393; Mayer (2012: 113–114).

43 *ILAlg* 2195 = *CLE* 1868; Geoghegan (1945: 53, n. 140 (translation), and Plate IV).

44 CIL VIII 11824 (p 2372); Lasserre and Griffe (1996).

support in the fundamentally positive view of the clergy toward work, but the principle that all work should ultimately serve a spiritual purpose was hardly conducive to public manifestations of occupational pride. How the views of Church Fathers, founders of monastic orders, theologians, and bishops influenced representations and self-representations of dynamic occupational groups over the centuries therefore needs to be examined.

The first centuries of Christianity were rife with controversies about how to live the perfect life according to Christ's example, and, more specifically, about whether *all* His followers were required to perform manual labour. In addition to those who focused on the message from the apostle Paul that everybody had the duty to work to provide for their own subsistence,[45] there were 'dissidents' who interpreted his words to mean that whoever proclaimed the Gospel worked and was therefore entitled to rely on alms. The latter referred to passages from the gospels of Luke and Matthew, who in their view legitimized the refusal by members of the clergy to perform manual labour.[46] The 'democratization' of religious experiences, as Peter Brown has characterized the changes in Christian communities in Late Antiquity, gave rise to groups who regarded spiritual work as the ideal way to follow Christ.[47] Still, the dominant view in the fourth and fifth centuries was that members of the clergy needed to buckle down to work as well. Whoever did not and expected that God would care for him anyway was a sinner, argued Augustine of Hippo around 400 in his treatise 'On the Work of Monks', in which he explained in detail that there was no contradiction at all between praying and working; he noted, however, that the two obligations were complementary and not identical.[48] It was essential for lay people that prominent Church Fathers interpreted the story of Genesis as God appearing as the first craftsman-creator, and moreover that they should emphasize that Adam and Eve had worked in Paradise. Such interpretations implied, after all, that after the Fall, mankind had to carry on working on God's creation and had to bring about a 'second nature' in cooperation with nature. This was nothing new, as Stoics such as Panaetius of Rhodes in the second century BC and Posidonius of Apamea (in Syria) in the first century BC had already set against the nature as delivered by Divine Providence a 'second nature,' made by mankind. In his *De Natura Deorum*, Cicero presented a eulogy of human hands, which by transforming raw material made possible

45 Saint Paul: 'If anyone will not work, then let him not eat', 2 *Ep. Thess.* 3.10.

46 *Ev. Matt.*, 6.25–26 and 28; *Ev. Luc.* 12.22, 24 and 27.

47 Brown (1992: 89–103).

48 *De Opere Monachorum*, original Latin text and translation on various websites. See the comment of Lawless (1987).

huge accomplishments. Basil of Caesarea, Gregory of Nyssa, and Augustine praised hands as well and marvelled at the impressive results of human work. The legacy of Classical Antiquity thus came to be linked with the Christian view of the joyful elaboration of Creation.[49]

Influenced by hermitism and early coenobitic monasticism, other—spiritual—highlights gradually came to the fore. Although the desert fathers in the fourth century subscribed to the Pauline imperative that he who does not work shall not eat, their physical exertions were essentially intended to chastise their bodies, with a view toward achieving a higher spirituality; this objective did require work, but only as a form of carnal discipline. The monastic project was based on organized collective manual labour, but asceticism and the spiritual dimension of work were the main focus from the outset. Work, asserted Basil of Caesarea, served to avoid idleness and the related ailments, to cultivate patience and detachment, and to progress along the path toward spiritual perfection. In other words: submission through work and spiritual salvation were related. To ensure material survival, a rational, collective structure was introduced that accommodated manual labour, but in which the exertions essentially derived their significance from each monk's individual pursuit of God. Since this quest was the ultimate objective, activities other than manual labour were very likely to be deemed more appropriate for the purpose, and that is precisely what happened in the sixth century: the *Regula magistri* stipulated that hard physical labour might be entrusted to *conversi* or lay brethren. While according to the famous Rule of Saint Benedict, work was a form of prayer, by 817 most monks were relieved of the obligation to work in the fields; they were henceforth entitled to devote every day to the *opus Dei*, i.e. to spend their days in prayer. Over the centuries that followed, monastic orders operating as large landowners systematically had agrarian activities performed by those who were not monks—from the tenth century in increasing measure by legally unfree farmers. Within monasteries, the work was distributed in a manner that made the monks deemed to be less spiritual perform greater efforts, which in practice meant that duties were passed on to those lower down in the social hierarchy. Subsequent reforms highlighted the need for all monks to perform manual labour, but, time and again, this ambition was abandoned to pursue what were regarded as superior activities, namely *opus Dei*. This coincided with redefining what monks saw as work: intellectual and religious efforts, such as reading the sacred scripture, learning Latin, copying and/or illuminating manuscripts, and, last but not least, praying. Writing was indeed

49 See esp. Spanneut (1957); Ovitt Jr. (1987: 57–68); Bultot (1990); Salamito (1996); MacCormack (2001).

hard work, as some monks took care to mention in manuscripts, but reading was represented as similarly onerous, while preaching happens to have been likened to ploughing or threshing. Understandably, therefore, manual labour was increasingly proclaimed as not being particularly conducive to achieving spiritual objectives. Physical exertion was to be regarded as a cure for *acedia*, for listlessness, boredom, and melancholy.[50]

The twelfth century was a turning point, in that reformed or new orders quickly and explicitly abandoned the old monastic rules that had basically associated the everyday life of the ideal monk with manual labour. While the Cistercian Bernard of Clairvaux initially maintained the duty to work, apologists or chroniclers of new religious orders raised arguments for waiving it in the same period. The perfect monk, they advised, need not bother with things related to the world of the laity. In the *Libellus de diversis ordinibus*, presumably written between 1121 and 1161, the crucial passage from Paul's Second Epistle to the Thessalonians was reinterpreted as follows: 'This was said not only of manual labour but of *all* work suitable for men of the church, that he who does nothing shall not eat.'[51] In other words: manual labour was not suitable for members of the clergy, and the tasks they took upon themselves should qualify as forms of work, as they would then in effect be fulfilling their divinely ordained duty. The Carthusians and the Premonstratensians or Norbertines (canons regular), who attracted an ever greater following, soon became known for their life of ascetic solitude, devoted mainly to contemplation. While their daily schedules accommodated manual labour, it served as an ascetic exercise; lay people were considered far better able to perform manual labour and to care for the physical surroundings in which the spiritual pursuits of the clergy were pivotal.[52]

In his *Summa Theologiae* (1265), Thomas Aquinas explained that not everybody interested in salvation needed to perform manual labour, and that what scholars and teachers did for the sake of knowledge was superior to what was done for the sake of utility. In a Christian society many types of labour were obviously needed, but they were of course highly unequal. Because of their spiritual functions, *oratores* were ranked at the top of the hierarchy, followed by the *bellatores* (the warriors), whose duty was to protect, and at the bottom were all others (the *laboratores*).[53] The fact that this tripartite model,

50 Delaruelle (1948); Ovitt Jr. (1986: 495–497); Sullivan (1989); Milis (1992: 26–27, 94–95); Berman (2000).

51 Translated and quoted by Constable and Smith (1972: 95–97).

52 Chenu (1968: ch. 6); Ovitt Jr. (1987: 143–150); Lawrence (2001: 156–160, 166–171).

53 Ovitt Jr. (1987: 158, 162–163, and 235, with references to the sources).

conceived far earlier, became dominant in the twelfth century,[54] meant that the clergy positioned itself at the top of the social pyramid and made clear that it merited this status, as the only group performing spiritual work. Assigning manual labour solely to the *laboratores* and representing it as their fundamental distinguishing trait, i.e. associating it with those at the bottom of the hierarchy, opened the door for deprecating statements about those performing these 'inferior' duties. While the discourses based on the principle of the tripartite system obviously came about in a clerical context, they nonetheless deeply influenced not only the attitudes of the secular elites toward other lay people but also the ability of the target groups to devise self-images and self-representations that deviated in some measure from the categories and hierarchies prescribed by the Church.

In the twelfth and thirteenth centuries the clergy continued to perceive lay society in religious terms, reflecting an 'ideological blockage,' as Guy Allard has noted.[55] This period was marked by sweeping socio-economic changes, offering both merchants and those practising the *artes mechanicae* opportunities for social advancement, but the clergy viewed the changes primarily as threats to the spiritual wellbeing of the laity. Especially the urban *laboratores* were considered to be at risk of moral degradation and needed to be withheld from engaging in the many sinful activities associated with the cities. The Church was interested mainly in the spirituality of the believer, who would be exposed to the danger of sin when performing work. His identity was defined not by what he did as a worker, but by the extent of his sins. The Church tried to grasp the changing and increasingly complex world of (primarily urban) labour by approaching and evaluating it in familiar categories. Neither the *sermones ad status* nor the treatises of the theologians contained classifications denoting professional groups—the degree of sinfulness was the sole criterion. This led some authors to base their classification on the places that gave the greatest or the least cause for sinful conduct. In cities and especially at markets, the devil constantly lurked, incarnated in fraud, usury, drink, and prostitution. In confession books and *artes praedicandi* (manuals for preachers), parish priests were instructed to impress the concept of sin on urban society and confront each individual believer with the question of whether his daily professional activity guaranteed spiritual salvation.[56]

54 The classic study is Duby (1978). For discussions and critiques, see *inter alia* (Brown 1986) and Constable (1995: part III).

55 Allard (1982: 15).

56 Baldwin (1970: 53–58); Corti (1983: 159–162); Schmidt (1993: 309–310); Van den Hoven (1996: 201–208, 224–227).

The Church thus failed to develop a positive theology of work that might have lifted the sinful connotations from all kinds of professional activities. *Laboratores* were told that the material results of their efforts were by definition subordinate to the path that they had to travel towards Christian self-improvement. As Bernard of Clairvaux submitted in his *De Diligendo Deo* (1126) and other treatises: lay people must never forget that they should not perform work for their own benefit or in pursuit of worldly objectives; if they truly wished to serve God through their work, they needed to manifest a 'cult of work devoid of any self-interest.'[57] Laypersons were encouraged to regard manual labour as an exercise in humility and submission. Nobody incarnated this ideal better than farmers, according to the Church. The objective, however, was not to glorify the self-sufficient *autourgos*, the citizen-farmer from ancient Greece, but the peasant who bowed to the land, not merely as a sign of humility toward God but also as a sign of submission to his lord. After all, the Church was not merely and exclusively the centre of ideological power; it operated as a large landowner and worldly potentate as well. This was expressed in countless public places by the image of the peasant obediently performing his divine and social duty to work.[58]

The ecclesiastical authorities did not hesitate to devise a very aggressive rhetoric about the *laboratores* having a duty to work, consistently emphasizing that they had to be submissive. The concept of *acedia*, which in monastic circles denoted melancholia and lack of religious fervour, was interpreted for laypersons as neglecting both their divine and their social labour duties. Whoever failed to perform these duties was compromising the order consecrated by God and was therefore subject to denunciation by the Church. After the Black Death of 1348–1349 and during the years that followed, when the rural population west of the Elbe River began to extricate itself from its feudal ties through migration, revolt and other forms of resistance, the ecclesiastical authorities supported in word and deed the repressive labour laws proclaimed in various countries. The Benedictine monk and bishop of Rochester Thomas Brinton, who served on a commission responsible for interrogating participants in the English Peasants' Revolt of 1381 stated unambiguously that 'those miserable idle ones who are not occupied [...] and who are not bearing any fruit consequently also deprive themselves through divine justice of the

57 Bernard of Clairvaux, *De Diligendo Deo*, Latin text and English translation online: http://www.pathsoflove.com/bernard/on-loving-god_la.html (accessed 11 May 2016). See the comment of Vignes (1928).

58 See esp. Freedman (1999). Also Lis and Soly (2012: ch. 4).

kingdom of God.'[59] In this context, the figures surfaced of the sturdy beggar and the dangerous vagrant, who from the fifteenth century onward were depicted as unsightly beings, as their bodies were to be regarded as reflections of despicable souls, as carnal embodiments of sins.[60] The Church hallowed only work performed within an intransigent social order, in which each individual continued to occupy the place assigned to him or her by God. Such was the message conveyed by the thirteenth-century stained glass windows in the Cathedral of Chartres: each of the three orders was assigned a separate, distinct place, and the *laboratores* were portrayed as small figures hunched over to perform their work beneath greatly enlarged depictions of saints, whose lives were the main focus.[61] In the central Middle Ages images in sacred places were not intended to call attention to work as such or to tools, practices, or physical efforts. As long as Church buildings were the privileged areas for a large public, the message was consistent that worldly activities needed to be performed by the right persons in the right places at the right times in the appropriate relational context. The objective was to present models, both positive and negative, and to make moral and didactic statements by presenting images of 'good' and 'bad' work/workers.[62] The (rare) twelfth and thirteenth-century tombstones of architect-designers of abbeys and cathedrals figure within this context: their names were recalled on the instruction of ecclesiastical authorities, and they were depicted holding their professional instruments, because their activities had served a religious purpose.[63] This was the reason for the introduction of what was known as the Sunday Christ in the second half of the fourteenth century: a gigantic figure painted on the walls of churches in England and Wales and in Alpine regions and surrounded by all kinds of tools used to wound Him: the new suffering of the Lord was invoked to remind economically active believers to rest on the Sabbath.[64]

The teachings of the medieval Church were questioned repeatedly, but in each instance by religious groups seeking spiritual purity rather than offering an alternative vision of work.[65] Economically active lay people were thus confronted with discourses and images that conveyed a very straightforward and

59 Devlin (1954: sermon 20: 1.83).

60 Vandenbroeck (1987: 117–131).

61 Williams (1993: 141–145).

62 Jaritz (2009).

63 Harvey (1972); Coppola (1998: 49–55); Wu (2000); Binding (2004: 69–71, 83–85, 102–103).

64 Reiss (2000).

65 This also held true for the Cathars and the Humiliati: Paolini (1991); Hamilton (1999: 5–23); Miller and Taylor-Mitchell (2010: 135–137).

virtually undisputed message. Its significance is impossible to overemphasize, as the Church of Rome figured as the gatekeeper of heaven, protector of spiritual salvation, the exclusive servant of the indispensable sacraments, the sole mediator between God and the Saints on the one hand and the pious on the other hand. Could merchants and craftsmen, in a society where they were told continuously by the dominant ideological institution that the earthly and the material was radically subordinate to the heavenly and the spiritual, construct self-images and self-representations that depicted their professional activities from a favourable perspective? Let us consider first the merchants beyond the scope of the tripartite system and not easily captured either within the powerful-versus-powerless or rich-versus-poor contrasts favoured by the clergy.

Some authors in Classical Antiquity and early Christianity condemned commercial endeavours unconditionally, but they were exceptional. Most commentators stressed that trade benefited general wellbeing. The Stoics even believed that Providence had created trade to bring countries and peoples in touch with each other and to transport goods from places with surpluses to places where shortages prevailed,[66] and several early Christian thinkers embraced this argument. The Church Fathers, however, were interested mainly in whether a merchant could trade honestly, and, if so, whether he had performed all his Christian duties in the process. In his response, Augustine argued that virtue and sin were not unique to a specific occupation but depended on the morality of the person in question. He added, moreover, that since mercantile activity was a type of work, *boni negotiatores* were just as entitled to profit as were farmers or craftsmen. He concluded by reviewing the finality of the effort: the primacy of individual responsibility and freedom meant that enrichment should never be an objective in its own right; some of the profit should be donated to charity.[67] His view became the foundation for elaborating principles and practices in the West.[68]

Until the eleventh century, professional merchants attracted little notice. This changed with the marked expansion of interregional trade. The number of merchants rose substantially, and in many places they formed guilds to obtain privileges from the local authorities. Political constellations changed as well. Inhabitants of several towns in Lombardy, Northern France, the Rhineland, and Flanders formed leagues to ensure mutual protection and solidarity. Both the religious and the secular elites tended to label such associations as

66 De Salvo (1987).

67 August., *En. Ps.* 70, *Serm.* 1.17. See esp. Salamito (1996: 47–52); Arbesmann (1973: 252–253); MacCormack (2001: 225).

68 On attitudes toward money and wealth in the late Roman world, see Brown (2012).

conspiracies and directed their venom at merchants, who were often driving forces behind movements of citizens aiming to increase their autonomy.[69] From the late eleventh century onwards, clerics wrote about professional merchants in increasingly negative terms, and during the twelfth century their attitudes toward this occupational group grew still more rigid. Ecclesiastical authorities understood that the positions of power acquired by urban communities in various regions could no longer be reversed, however, and they adjusted their discourse, albeit without taking into account the ambitions of the new emerging groups. The ideal type they constructed was aimed at impressing upon merchants that they were constantly on the verge of damnation, and that going to hell was a very real prospect, unless they behaved like saints. In 1199 Omobono Tucenghi, a merchant-draper from Cremona, who had died two years previously, was beatified by Pope Innocent III—the first non-aristocratic saint in the Western Middle Ages. Why? Because he had never cheated anybody, had always given to charity, had attended mass twice daily, had run a campaign against heretics, and, above all: because after abandoning a successful career in commerce, he had sold his worldly possessions, donated the proceeds to the poor, and spent his remaining days in asceticism and prayer. This pious merchant, as the *vitae* later drafted of him read, was a reflection of Christ; many miracles were therefore attributed to Saint Homobonus.[70] Merchants were expected to derive their identities from values important to and controlled by the Church. They should be workers dedicated to serving God, which entailed faith, humility, and submission, as those relying solely on their own work were challenging Divine Providence. Ultimately, God alone would decide whether their efforts would be successful. The basic message was: thou shalt not sin! The obligation to work should certainly be met, but as it would in the ideal monastery: as a form of penitence. It was not the actual effort that mattered but the course taken to achieve it, the road travelled. It was not the earthly but the spiritual that was rewarded. Amassing wealth should therefore never be an objective in its own right. What mattered was earning admission to heaven. Merchants therefore needed to show generosity in both religious and charitable endeavours: a wealthy man was the manager of material goods that God entrusted to him temporarily.[71] As businessmen became increasingly prominent in economic and social life, the code became ever more elaborate, and scholastics specified which conditions needed to be

69 Schulz (1992); Oexle (1994: 56–57).

70 Webb (1987); Morandi (2010).

71 These principles were proclaimed by the Roman Catholic clergy until well into the eighteenth century. See Groethuysen (1927).

met to profit from trade without sinning. The arguments that came to constitute the canon in the course of the thirteenth century (work, the merchant's intention, transport fees, risks taken, social benefit) were not new but were categorized at this point. In his *Summa*, Thomas Aquinas emphasized above all that profits must always be moderate and should preferably be used to support one's own family, help the poor, and/or serve the common good. They should never be an objective in their own right.[72]

Although theologians argued that religious-moral principles and economic practices were compatible under certain conditions, and the Franciscans even proclaimed that 'good' businessmen were indispensable in a Christian society,[73] the Church took care not to channel favourable messages via the figure of the merchant. The clergy was aware that many businessmen paid little heed to the religious-moral dictates in their daily practice. They readily reaped usurious profits, deceived their suppliers and customers, traded with 'non-believers,' and even cheated their own family members. The few figures depicting merchants in late-medieval murals of churches or in manuscripts therefore always carried attributes that could be interpreted in various ways: scales, a measuring jug, and/or a money pouch. In what was known as a chess book from 1479, the elegant attire and especially the well-filled purse together with a pair of scales showed that this merchant clearly disregarded moral and social codes.[74]

Late-medieval businessmen were nonetheless deeply concerned with their spiritual salvation. Their cultural-ideological dilemma was 'how to achieve spiritual validation while remaining an active member of mercantile society,' as Kathleen Ashley has noted.[75] Even though their daily practices were often hardly compatible with Christian teachings, they were inclined to focus on religious aspects toward the end of their lives. The so-called *ricordi* and *libri di famiglia* of Florentine merchants and bankers indicate that they were not at all ashamed to express their pursuit of profit and display the qualities they deemed necessary to achieve economic success: in addition to being diligent, thrifty, moderate, and prudent, they engaged continuously in reasoning, performing calculations, and organizing, so operating in a rational, calculating, and pragmatic manner with a view toward maximizing their earnings.[76] They took no interest in what theologians had written about foreign exchange

72 Thomas Aquinas, *Summa theologiae*, 2a2ae.77.4.

73 In this connection, see the interesting (but contested) views of Todeschini (2004) and (2008: 20–22).

74 Husa (1967: figs. 110–112); Jaritz (2009: 143–144).

75 Ashley (1998: 374).

76 Bec (1967) and Branca (1986).

operations and showed little concern for the restrictions placed by the Church on usury.[77] On the other hand, their autobiographical writings reveal that when they felt their end was approaching, they embarked on soul-searching missions, and the religious dimension of their life then became decisive.[78] The correspondence of Francesco di Marco Datini, the famous merchant from Prato, reveals that he was a merciless businessman, driven purely by pursuit of profit. Nevertheless, in his ledgers the top of each page reads 'In the name of God and profit.' This rang less hollow when, in 1410, he left almost his entire fortune to the poor in the city of his birth.[79]

In the late Middle Ages, the Church of Rome was increasingly imbued with the calculating rationality of businessmen, with a commercial logic. This emerges not only from the economic activities of the Church, but also from theological treatises and sermons. Members of the clergy were by then willing to praise mercantile values. They emphasized, however, that merchants and financiers should always act with moderation, observe the Christian commandments, and be ethically responsible.[80] In 1425 the Franciscan preacher Bernardino of Siena publicly proclaimed the importance and the utility of trade, and he explained that becoming a merchant required a combination of rare qualities, in particular diligence, efficiency, and responsibility. A few years later the Dominican friar Antoninus (who later became the archbishop of Florence) expressed a similar view.[81] Such eulogies, however, always included the message that money needed to be earned through lawful acts, and that affluent Christians had a special duty to express their religious piety through acts of private charity. The humanists of the 'Trecento' and the 'Quattrocento' advanced a different formulation but similarly emphasized that the pursuit of personal wealth should serve a higher purpose: the *res publica*, which meant that businessmen had to practice virtues of *liberalitas* and *magnanimitas*—virtues greatly valued by the traditional elite as well.[82] By relating enrichment to charity and generosity, members of the clergy and humanists succeeded in justifying wealth and pursuit of profit, but they did so without 'introducing any new cultural values that informed and reshaped economic behaviour.'[83]

---

77 See, for example, Marco and Noumen (2008). Also Jouanique (1996).

78 See the important remarks of Tenenti (1968) and La Roncière (1992).

79 Origo (1992).

80 Hamm (2011: 301–334).

81 De Roover (1967). Note that eulogies always concerned substantial merchants and financiers, never shopkeepers.

82 Lis and Soly (2012: 256–258).

83 Goldthwaite (2009: 592).

The immense popularity of devotional texts in the vernacular in the second half of the fourteenth and especially in the fifteenth century reflected the existential problems facing economically active groups in the cities. The new spiritual manuals blurred traditional boundaries between active and contemplative lives and, more importantly, individualized piety; they encouraged lay people to 'view themselves' and to reflect on what they saw.[84] The available ego—documents show that merchants and financiers hoped to be remembered as extremely hard workers, who had always operated under intense pressure and had taken carefully calculated risks—precisely the elements deemed important by the clergy. The individual in question also stressed that he had 'made' it on his own: he had started with nothing and owed his material success exclusively to his own efforts—references to Divine Providence were rare in this context.[85] Concern with spiritual salvation was apparent from masses intended to commemorate the deceased, from alms for the poor, and from bequests to religious and charitable institutions. Individual businessmen and merchant guilds moreover highlighted their generosity through donations. They had chapels or even churches built or embellished at their own expense or financed the construction of 'maisons-dieu', orphanages, and hospitals.[86] Through these actions they attempted to reconcile mercantile logic with a prayer to God to bless business enterprises and their concern for spiritual salvation and social recognition.

'Interior concerns of spiritual well-being' may be assumed to have initially provided businessmen 'with a socially acceptable opportunity to gain access to portraiture.'[87] The famous portrait that Jan Van Eyck painted in 1434 of the Italian merchant and financier Giovanni Arnolfini and his wife, both residents of Bruges, lends itself to several interpretations. The work was, however, undoubtedly intended as a 'mirror' of an ideal merchant couple, linking the sacred to the profane: the gaze of both characters suggests introspection, and that they participated in meditative practices in the spirit of the *Devotia Moderna*, the new religious movement that was so popular in this region.[88] Portraits of businessmen remained rare and were all situated in a religious context until the end of the fifteenth century. Only in the 1520s and 1530s did

84 See the fine book by Bryan (2008). Also Corbellini (2013).

85 Maschke (1964); Bec (1967); Irsigler (1985). See also Schmitt (2009).

86 For Germany: Maschke (1964). For England: Kermode (1999: 178–179) and Davis (2012: 377–380). For Italy, see *inter alia*: Becker (1974); Cohn Jr. (1994: 57–60, 90–100, 133–158); Nelson and Zeckhauser (2008).

87 Cooper (2012: 5), endorsing the view of Martin (2004).

88 Heck (2009). See also Carroll (1993).

large numbers of wealthy merchants from Germany and the Low Countries commission portraits of themselves from prominent artists, such as Albrecht Dürer, Hans Holbein the Younger, Jan Gossaert, Joos Van Cleve, and Maarten Van Heemskerck. Many had themselves depicted at a desk covered with letters, ledgers, coins, and other objects referring to their professional activities, which was presumably an indication of professional pride. Still, the religious-ethical dimension of doing business was not overlooked: the frequent presence of scales reflected the need to strike a balance between monetary earnings and Christian ethics, while on other canvases *memento mori* devices or more subtle references to the passing of time were visible. The portrait of the Hanseatic merchant Georg Gisze, painted by Holbein in London in 1532, depicts the ideal that the international merchant wished to convey of himself: not only a successful businessman who took pride in being so but also a learned man, a humanist, and a true Christian, who embraced the adage 'No joy without sorrow,' which in this context presumably meant 'No joy without exertion.'[89] Unlike the funerary monuments of Roman Trier, which featured coins as symbols of abundance, artists in the first half of the sixteenth century depicted financial wealth as a manifestation of greed. The well-known scenes of moneychangers and moneylenders painted by Quentin Metsys and Marinus van Reymerswaele were moralizing allegories that made clear that pursuit of wealth and opulence obscured higher spiritual values.[90]

The available evidence suggests that funerary inscriptions were almost exclusively devoted to noblemen and members of the regular clergy until the fifteenth century.[91] After that point, wealthy laypersons appear to have asserted themselves increasingly as well, especially in important commercial centres. In sixteenth-century Antwerp many great merchants stipulated in their wills that they were to be buried in the Cathedral, and that their epitaph should read: *coopman* (merchant), *negociator*, or *mercator*, preceded by epithets such as 'the honourable,' 'the renowned,' or 'the excellent' in Dutch or Latin. But they omitted depictions of objects associated with money or—in more neutral terms—trade.[92] In the light of the hereafter, a reference to worldly affairs was considered to be inappropriate. This also held true around 1520 for Europe's richest merchant-banker and mining entrepreneur: Jacob Fugger. He

89 De Vries (2004: 134–138); Haag *et al.* (2011); Cooper (2012: 81, 83, 86–88).

90 See, for example, Quentin Metsys, *The Moneylender and His Wife* (1514), Louvre Museum, Paris, and the online comment of Guillaume Kazerouni: http://www.louvre.fr/en/oeuvre-notices/moneylender-and-his-wife (accesses 11 May 2016).

91 See, for example, Grillon (2011).

92 Soly (1976: 33–34).

commissioned several portraits of himself: together with his wife on their wedding day in 1498 (painting), in 1518 (medallion), ca. 1511 (woodcarving), and ca. 1520 (painted by Dürer).[93] He and his two brothers founded a burial chapel in the Carmelite Church of St. Anna in Augsburg, with the intention that this should become the final resting place of the three founders and their male descendants. The elaborate architecture and the opulent decorations, to which Dürer contributed, made this large and very costly chapel the most original monument of the early German Renaissance. No single decorative element, nor any single epitaph, however, could be associated with the economic activities of the Fugger; the objective was clearly the 'visualization of a concept of individual salvation.' One telling detail: the wooden bust of Jacob Fugger in the choir stalls depicted the merchant-banker as a general from the Old Testament.[94]

While *nouveaux riches* might try to convince the public through texts, visual images, gifts, and donations as to how their profitable activities were to be seen, individual craftsmen had far greater difficulty demonstrating religious devotion and valorising their work at the same time. Unless they met basic needs or served ritual purposes, products of manual labour were regarded with suspicion by the Church in the central Middle Ages. Theologians believed that the *artes mechanicae* did not contribute to knowledge of God and labelled many manifestations of craftsmanship as superfluous luxury. Members of the clergy who took an interest in artisanal production consistently emphasized that beautiful objects should serve to honour God and inspire religious devotion. Around 1140 Suger, the Abbot of Saint-Denis, had the gilded doors of 'his' church inscribed to advise onlookers: 'Marvel not at the gold and at the expense, but at the craftsmanship of the work.' Craftsmanship, however, had no intrinsic merit: 'Bright is the noble work; but being nobly bright, the work / should brighten the minds, so that they may travel, through the true lights / to the True Light where Christ is the true door.'[95] The Benedictine monk known to us only by his pseudonym Theophilus similarly argued that knowledge of the *artes mechanicae* should serve a higher, spiritual purpose. In *De diversis artibus*, written between 1100 and 1120, Theophilus described in great detail technologies and recipes for painting and drawing, producing stained glass and glass paintings, and metal casting. He proposed that human skill in the arts was a gift from God, and that people had a duty to develop and apply this gift. With respect to the practitioners of such arts, he emphasized that in

---

93 Haag *et al.* (eds. 2011: 76–77, 103–104, 220–221, 230).

94 Bushart (1994) and Scheller (2004: 15, 70, 77, 82–89).

95 Translated and quoted by Frisch (1987: 7).

addition to being an antidote to idleness, manual labour was a means toward achieving personal spiritual perfection.[96] The thirteenth-century *Sermones ad Status* did address the ethics of craftsmen, but the attitude of the clergy toward the profane realities of artisanal work did not change.[97]

If artisans wanted to upgrade the status of their craftsmanship, the overwhelming majority could do so only via collective practices and rituals. From the central Middle Ages onward, demonstrating religious devotion and implementing it in practice was the designated way for associations of craftsmen to attribute a socio-economic meaning to their professional activities. Many urban craftsmen organizing themselves did so initially as confraternities engaging in devotional and charitable activities, and those forming groups based on occupation alone—craft guilds—all honoured a patron saint, who was in some way associated with the occupation concerned. From the fourteenth century onward, many occupational associations founded an altar or chapel in a parish or conventual church. In addition, they participated collectively in religious rituals, processions, and pilgrimages to demonstrate that their secular activities were to be regarded as *opus Dei* as well.[98] This was of the utmost importance for corporative organizations, because religious and moral imperatives with connotations such as honour, trust, and honesty had economic and social consequences as well. Investing in religious life was equivalent to consolidating and making a quality guarantee publicly visible. Professional honour and respectability became inextricably intertwined with piety. Those gathering round this banner were not only pious but also belonged to a collective that guaranteed knowledge, talent, and quality. In corporative petitions, master artisans consistently argued that they could ensure both professional and moral qualities. Connecting economics and religion in this way distinguished craft guilds from nearly all other institutions in medieval Europe.

Individual demonstrations of professional pride remained exceptional and in nearly all cases concerned artists, who invariably expressed their professional awareness within a religious context. Until the thirteenth century, very few medieval works of art are known that bear a name and a date, nor is the role of the individual named always clear. It has been argued that the inscription *Gislebertus hoc fecit* on the western tympanum of the Cathedral of Autun—dated around 1120–1135—refers not to the sculptor but to the principal

96 Dodwell (1961) and Hawthorne and Smith (1963). See also the comments of Ovitt Jr. (1987: 168–173) and Schulz (2010: 107–109, 113–114).

97 Vauchez (1987: 141).

98 See *inter alia* Thijs (2006) and Kluge (2007: 312–321).

or patron,[99] and the most famous twelfth-century portrait of an artist at work, Eadwine, remains an enigma.[100] Only in the fifteenth century did individual craftsmen begin to manifest themselves publicly. Pamela Smith has noted the expressions of self-awareness as revealed in the portraits and self-portraits affixed in places easily visible to the public.[101] Examples include works by the architect Peter Parler in 1378/9 in Prague, the painters Cola Petruccioli c. 1400 in Perugia and Rogier van der Weyden in 1438 in Brussels, the sculptor Lorenzo Ghiberti around the same time in Florence, and his colleagues Adam Kraft in 1485 in Nuremberg and Anton Pilgram in 1514–15 in Vienna. Especially the self-portrait by Kraft reveals how far medieval craftsmen had come. His depiction of himself and his two journeymen was almost life-size; they were clad in their work attire and holding their tools. They were positioned, however, beneath a Sacrament house, and all three were kneeling—supporting the towering structure on their shoulders. In other words: the pride of the craftsman-artist linked to true Christian humility.[102] Other artists displayed the same combination of humility and pride by appropriating specific saints: painters such as Rogier van der Weyden, Dirk Bouts, and Jan Gossaert identified with Saint Luke, who drew or painted the Madonna,[103] while sculptors such as Tilman Riemenschneider depicted himself as Saint Nicodemus. They portrayed themselves as mediators, as pious dispatchers of the sacred message.[104]

In ever increasing numbers, visual artists in Northern Italy, the Low countries, and Southern Germany drew, painted, and/or etched self-portraits, initially inserted into religious scenes, but increasingly as independent presentations. Some images contained no reference at all to spirituality or devotion, but these were exceptional, as most were clearly related to a discourse of piety. Great artists such as Dürer, Leonardo da Vinci, or Michelangelo painted themselves as Christ/God, fashioning an image that was both self-portrait and *vera icon*.[105] The first great monuments since Classical Antiquity that Renaissance sculptors designed to commemorate themselves were pious works as well. They all had a common theme: the sacrifice of Christ. Linking God and the artist was nothing new, but the medieval metaphor now acquired a different meaning: 'Whereas before the artist was used to illustrate God's creativity,

99 Seidel (1999).

100 Heslop (1992).

101 Smith (2010: 28–29).

102 Klamt (1999).

103 Filedt Kok (2006) provides an extensive bibliography.

104 Schmidt (2008: 53–54, 57, 64).

105 Koerner (1993: 131–138).

now [...] the artist's creativity was likened unto God's,'[106] thereby opening up new perspectives.

The growing need of territorial rulers for representations of power, especially propaganda media, and the rising demand from clerical and secular elites for luxury commodities similarly enabled skilled artisans manufacturing valuable objects to acquire prestige. Goldsmiths were highly respected—at princely courts and among the aristocracy, if they were known internationally, or otherwise at least among local secular and clerical elites—because they handled precious metals with virtuosity. That they manifested their social standing both collectively and individually very early on is not purely coincidental. In 1449 the Bruges guild members commissioned a painting from Petrus Christus depicting Saint Eloy, their patron saint, as a goldsmith busy in his workshop. They highlighted their identity not only as a group. In 1436 the Bruges goldsmith Jan de Leeuw, age 35, had himself immortalized by none other than Jan Van Eyck, and half a century later Gerard David painted the portrait of another Bruges goldsmith, presumably his father-in-law Jacop Cnoop the Younger.[107] Still, such expressions of individual occupational pride remained highly exceptional among artisans.

Most late medieval craftsmen continued to present themselves as members of a collective. Nonetheless, subtle trends toward individual self-assertion started to become manifest. Some artisans presented their professional activity not only as a specific skill, but also as the result of particular kinds of knowledge, as is clear from the technical treatises in the vernacular, which were printed from the 1460s and covered a vast diversity of subjects from the late fifteenth century. That the authors (as perceived by the elite and the intelligentsia) practised the *artes mechanicae* suggests a process of emancipation. To quote Pamela Smith: 'These individuals began to take the measure of themselves and sought to make their practical knowledge known, respectable, or in other words, recognizable as 'knowledge' within their culture.'[108] The fact that from the early sixteenth century onward wealthy master artisans not perceived by their contemporaries as artists—according to whatever definition—had tombstones built in the Cathedral of Antwerp featuring inscriptions of their occupation in the vernacular: pastry baker, plumber, tinsmith, soap boiler, and the like, is equally indicative of this process.[109] Not until the end of the century, however, did some artisans commission portraits of themselves, and only

106 Lavin (1977–1978: 38).

107 Van der Velden (1998); Wilson (1999).

108 Smith (2010: 40). See also Long (2011).

109 *Verzameling* (1856: 112, 164, 190, 195, 247, 285, 380).

in the seventeenth century did they—in exceptional cases—have themselves depicted without any religious connotations.

Different Interplays between the Social and the Cultural

Comparing the Roman world between 100 BC and AD 200 with the Western Middle Ages between 1100 and 1500 is relevant *and* revealing from both a socio-economic and a cultural-ideological perspective. In both periods we notice that dynamic middle groups in a context of urbanization, commercialization, and growing artisanal production had opportunities to improve their material positions. (see Verboven in this volume) In both periods merchants and craftsmen managed to extend expressions of their presence in urban society beyond the economic context. On the other hand, the two periods differ considerably in the extent to which and the manner in which members of economically active middle groups were able to advertise their professional success and their occupational identity. Different interplays between the social and the cultural explain these discrepancies.

Some authors regard the myriad inscriptions and visual images relating to professional activities on Roman tombstones as manifestations of distinctive values. According to Eve d'Ambra and Guy Métraux, the tombstones of artisans indicate 'plebeian' forms of self-definition and specific voices from below.[110] Emanuel Mayer, in turn, interprets funerary depictions of occupational activities as typical cultural expressions by economically active middle groups, whose values were opposed to those of an agrarian-aristocratic elite and stresses the very pronounced work ethic of successful businessmen and craftsmen.[111] That such monuments increased considerably between 100 BC and AD 200 and reveal a highly developed sense of occupational pride undoubtedly proves that merchants and artisanal producers in that period had far more opportunities for social advancement. The work ethic manifested by these groups was, however, embedded in Greco-Roman culture: everybody was expected to make worthy efforts. Epitaphs and tombstones founded by highly diverse social groups express this shared value.[112] Members of the established elite catalogued their achievements to demonstrate that they derived their status from efforts made in politics or on the battlefield. Merchants and artisans

110 D'Ambra and Métraux (2006: xv).

111 Mayer (2012: 1–14, and *passim*).

112 Aloys Winterling is currently examining aristocratic work in late republican Rome. See http: //rework.hu-berlin.de/en/2012–2013.html (accessed 11 May 2016).

basically did the same: they proudly advertised their success, more specifically their progression to wealth or their exceptional craftsmanship. (see the chapter by Tran)

From the eleventh and twelfth centuries on, various groups of newcomers in cities west of the Elbe also developed vast economic and social dynamics, but they lacked channels to reveal publicly their earthly achievements, professional success, or occupational identity. The cultural-ideological context was radically different. No religion or school of philosophy in Classical Antiquity had ever had such an impact on public attitudes toward work and workers as did the Church of Rome in the Western Middle Ages. While in antiquity different valuation criteria concerning work could be applied, members of the medieval clergy applied only a single criterion: did the effort serve a higher, spiritual purpose? Work should be performed in the light of eternity and spiritual salvation and should therefore ideally be an expression of devotion. The ideological dominance of the Church and its compelling presence in public space withheld the laity from individually demonstrating economic success, technical ingenuity, or occupational pride. Exceptions were made only for the creators of religious works of art commissioned by and achieved with supervision from the clergy. In the case of economically active laypersons, this meant that they had to define and profile themselves primarily in relation to religious discourse, which excluded any kind of public demonstrations of self-awareness. In a Christian society, funerals and tombstones were clearly not suited to expressing a strong worldly message. Even in acts of charity or on portraits intended for family settings, only one central identity tended to be regarded by the Church as meaningful, namely that of the pious believer. In fifteenth-century portraits of merchants or goldsmiths and in the collective practices and rituals of craft guilds occupational references were subordinate to the spiritual or devotional dimension. Wherever an individual craftsman came to the fore, it was as an artist paying tribute to a subjective religious experience or as a mediator conveying a sacral message. The modest tendencies toward self-affirmation that were discernible undoubtedly heralded the future, but the cultural-ideological context would long continue to circumscribe the contours for manifesting an occupational awareness in public.

Bibliography

Abdy, R. (2012). 'Tetrarchy and the House of Constantine', in W. Metcalf (ed.), *The Oxford Handbook of Greek and Roman Coinage*. Oxford, 584–600.

Abbott, A. (2001). 'Professions, Sociology of', in N.J.S.B. Baltes (ed.), *International Encyclopedia of the Social & Behavioral Sciences*. Oxford, 12166–12169.

Abbott, A. (2005). 'Sociology of Work and Occupations', in *The Handbook of Economic Sociology*, 2nd edition. Princeton, 307–330.

Abrams, E.A. (1994). *How the Maya Built Their World: Energetics and Ancient Architecture*. Austin.

Acheson, J.M. (2002). 'Transaction Cost Economics: Accomplishments, Problems, and Possibilities', in J. Ensminger (ed.), *Theory in Economic Anthropology*. Walnut Creek, 27–58.

Adam, J.-P. (1994). *Roman Building. Materials and Techniques*. London.

Adams, C.E.P. (2007). *Land Transport in Roman Egypt. A Study of Economics and Administration in a Roman Province*. Oxford and New York.

Aldrete, G.S. and Mattingly, D.J. (1999). 'Feeding the City: the Organization, Operation, and Scale of the Supply System for Rome', in D.S. Potter and D.J. Mattingly (eds.), *Life, Death, and Entertainment in the Roman Empire*. Ann Arbor, 171–204.

Alexander, R.T. (2006). 'Mesoamerican House Lots and Archaeological Site Structure: Problems of Inference in Yaxcaba, Yucatan, Mexico, 1750–1847', in P.M. Allison (ed.), *Archaeology of Household Activities*. Oxford, 78–100.

Alföldi, A. (1952). 'La corporation des Transalpini et Cisalpini à Avenches', *Suisse Primitive Ur-Schweiz* 16: 3–9.

Alföldy, G. (1986). 'Zur Nomenklatur und Laufbahn eines römischen Ritters aus Concordia', *Zeitschrift für Papyrologie und Epigraphik* 63: 173–180.

Alicu, D. and Paki, A. (1995). *Town-Planning and Population in Ulpia Traiana Sarmizegetusa* (British Archaeological Reports. International series 605). Oxford.

Allard, G. (1982). 'Les arts mécaniques aux yeux de l'idéologie médiévale', in G.H. Allard and S. Lusignan (eds.), *Les arts mécaniques au Moyen Âge* (Cahiers d'Etudes Médiévales 7). Montréal, 13–32.

Allen, R.C. (2001). 'The Great Divergence in European Wages and Prices from the Middle Ages to the First World War', *Explorations in Economic History* 38: 411–447.

Allen, R.C. (2009). 'How Prosperous were the Romans? Evidence from Diocletian's Price Edict', in A.K. Bowman and A.I. Wilson (eds.), *Quantifying the Roman Economy. Methods and Problems* (Oxford Studies on the Roman Economy 1). Oxford, 327–345.

Allen, R.C., Bassino, J.-P., Ma, D., Moll-Murata, C., and Van Zanden, J.L. (2011). 'Wages, Prices, and Living Standards in China, 1738–1925: in Comparison with Europe, Japan, and India', *Economic History Review* 64: 8–38.

Allison, P. (1998). 'The Household in Historical Archaeology', *Australasian Historical Archaeology* 16: 16–29.

Alston, R. and Alston, R.D. (1997). 'Urbanism and the Urban Community in Roman Egypt', *Journal of Egyptian Archaeology* 83: 199–216.

Anderson, J.C. (1997). *Roman Architecture and Society*. Baltimore.

Ando, C. (2000). *Imperial Ideology and Provincial Loyalty in the Roman Empire*. Berkeley.

André, J.-M. (1966). *L'*otium *dans la vie morale et intellectuelle romaine*. Paris.

Andreau, J. (1987). *La vie financière dans le monde romain: les métiers de manieurs d'argent (IVe siècle av. J.-C.–IIIe siècle ap. J.-C.)* (Bibliothèque des Ecoles Françaises d'Athènes et de Rome 265). Rome.

Andreau, J. (2010). *L'Économie du monde romain*. Paris.

Arbesmann, R. (1973). 'The Attitude of St. Augustine Toward Labor', in D. Neiman and M. Schatkin (eds.), *The Heritage of the Early Church. Essays in Honor of the Very Reverend Georges Vasilievich Florovsky* (Orientalia Christiana Analecta 195). Rome, 245–259.

Ardevan, R. (1978). 'Le collège des fabres à Ulpia Traiana Sarmizegethusa', *Acta Musei Napocensis* 15: 167–172.

Arendt, H. (1998). *The Human Condition*. Chicago.

Arnaoutoglou, I. (2002). 'Roman Law and Collegia in Asia Minor', *Revue Internationale des droits de l'antiquité* 49: 27–44.

Arnaoutoglou, I. (2005). '*Collegia* in the Province of Egypt in the 1st Century A.D.', *Ancient Society* 35: 197–216.

Arnaoutoglou, I. (2011). 'Craftsmen Associations in Roman Lydia. A Tale of Two Cities?', *Ancient Society* 41: 257–290.

Arnaud, P. (2007). 'Le gouvernement provincial de M. Aurelius Masculus, la « *saeculi felicitas* » et la « crise » de Cemenelum', in J. Dalaison (ed.), *Espaces et pouvoirs dans l'Antiquité de l'Anatolie à la Gaule. Hommages à B. Rémy*. Grenoble, 59–69.

Arnold, D. (1985). *Ceramic Theory and Cultural Process*. Cambridge.

Ascough, R.S., Harland, P., and Kloppenborg, J.S. (2012). *Associations in the Greco-Roman World: A Sourcebook* (=*AGRW*). Waco, TX.

Ashley, K. (1998). 'Historicizing Margery: *The Book of Margery Kempe* as Social text', *Journal of Medieval and Early Modern Societies* 28: 371–388.

Ashtor, E. (1969). *Histoire des prix et des salaires dans l'orient medieval*. Paris.

Aubert, J.-J. (1994). *Business Managers in Ancient Rome: a Social and Economic Study of Institores*, 200 BC–AD 250. Leiden, New York and Köln.

Aubert, J.-J. (1999). 'La gestion des *collegia*: aspects juridiques, économiques et sociaux', *Cahiers du Centre Gustave-Glotz* 10: 49–69.

Ausbüttel, F.M. (1982). *Untersuchungen zu den Vereinen im Westen des Römischen Reiches* (Frankfurter Althistorische Studien 11). Kallmünz.

Baker, G., Gibbons, R. and Murphy, K.J. (2002). 'Relational Contracts and the Theory of the Firm', *Quarterly Journal of Economics* 117: 39–84.

Bakker, J. (1999). *The Mills-Bakeries of Ostia: Description and Interpretation*. Amsterdam.

Bakkum, G.C.L.M. (2008). *Latin Dialect of the Ager Faliscus: 150 Years of Scholarship*. Amsterdam.

Baldwin, B. (1963). 'Strikes in the Roman Empire', *Classical Journal* 59: 75–76.

Baldwin, J.W. (1970). *Masters, Princes and Merchants: The Social Views of Peter the Chanter and His Circle*. Princeton.

Balme, M. (1984). 'Attitudes to Work and Leisure in Ancient Greece', *Greece and Rome* 31: 140–152.

Balsdon, J.P.V.D. (1969). *Life and Leisure in Ancient Rome*. New York.

Banaji, J. (2011). *Theory as History: Essays on Modes of Production and Exploitation*. Chicago.

Bang, P.F. (2006). 'Imperial Bazaar: Towards a Comparative Understanding of Markets in the Roman Empire', in P.F. Bang, M. Ikeguchi, and H.G. Ziche (eds.), *Ancient Economies, Modern Methodologies: Archaeology, Comparative History, Models and Institutions*. Bari, 51–88.

Bang, P.F. (2008). *The Roman Bazaar: A Comparative Study of Trade and Markets in a Tributary Empire*. Cambridge.

Bang, P.F. (2009). 'The Ancient Economy and New Institutional Economics', *Journal of Roman Studies* 99: 194–206.

Bang, P.F. (2015). 'An Economist Approaches Roman Economic History. Peter Temin, *The Roman Market Economy*', *Journal of Roman Archaeology* 28: 637–640.

Barbieri-Low, A.J. (2007). *Artisans in Early Imperial China*. Seattle.

Barresi, P. (2003). *Province dell'Asia Minore: costo dei marmi, architettura publica e committenza*. Rome.

Baslez, M.-F. (2006). 'Entraide et mutualisme dans les associations des cités grecques à l'époque hellénistique', in M. Molin (ed.), *Les régulations sociales dans l'Antiquité (Actes colloque d'Angers, 2003)*. Rennes, 157–168.

Beard, M., North, J., and Price, S. (1998). *Religions of Rome*. Cambridge.

Bec, C. (1967). *Les marchands écrivains: affaires et humanisme à Florence, 1375–1434*. Paris and The Hague.

Becker, M.B. (1974). 'Aspects of Lay Piety in Early Renaissance Florence', in C. Trinkaus and H.O. Obermann (eds.), *The Pursuit of Holiness*. Leiden, 177–199.

Ben Moussa, M. (2007). *La production de sigillées Africaines: Recherches d'histoire et d'archéologie en Tunisie septentrionale et centrale*. Barcelona.

Bergamasco, M. (1995). 'Le διδασκαλικαί nella ricerca attuale', *Aegyptus* 75: 95–167.

Bergamini, M. (2007). 'Stato della ricerca e degli studi', in M. Bergamini (ed.), *Scoppieto I: Il Territorio e I Materiali (Lucerne,* Opus doliare, *Metali)*. Borgo San Lorenzo, 57–70.

Berlin, A. (2005). 'Pottery and Pottery Production in the Second Temple Period', in B. Arubas and H. Goldfus (eds.), *Excavations on the Site of the Jerusalem International Convention Center (Binyanei Ha'uma): The Pottery and Other Small Finds* (Journal of Roman Archaeology Supplementary Series no. 60). Portsmouth, R.I., 29–60.

Berman, C.H. (2000). *The Cistercian Evolution: The Invention of a Religious Order in Twelfth-Century Europe*. Philadelphia.

Bermejo Tirado, J. (2010). 'Domus and Household Production. Towards a New Model for the Study of Roman Economy: the Case of the House of Bachus and Ariadne (Thuburbo Maius)', in M. Milanese, P. Ruggeri, and C. Vismara (eds.), *L'Africa Romana. I Luoghi e le Forme dei Mestieri e della Produzione nelle Province Africane*, vol. 2. Roma, 851–862.

Bernard, S.G. (2013). 'The Transport of Heavy Loads in Antiquity: Lifting, Moving, and Building in Ancient Rome', in S. Altekamp, C. Marcks-Jacobs, and P. Seiler (eds.), *Perspektiven der Spolienforschung 1. Spolierung und Transposition*. Berlin, 99–122.

Bernard, S.G. (2016) 'Food Distributions and Immigration in Imperial Rome', in L. de Ligt and L.E. Tacoma (eds.), *Migration and Mobility in the Early Roman Empire*. Leiden, 50–71.

Bevis, E. (2015). 'Looking between Loom and Laundry. Vision and Communication in Ostian Fulling Workshops' in M. Harlow and M.-L. Nosch (eds.), *Greek and Roman Textiles and Dress: An Interdisciplinary Anthology*. Oxford, 306–322.

Biegert, S. (2010). *Congressus Vicesimus Quintus Rei Cretariæ Romanæ Fautorum Dyrrhachii Habitus MMVI*. Bonn.

Binding, G. (ed.) (2004). *Meister der Baukunst. Geschichte des Architekten- und Ingenieursberufes*. Darmstadt.

Bisconti, F. (2004). 'V. Il programma decorativo dell'ipogeo di Trebio Giusto tra attitudine e autorappresentazione', in R. Rea (ed.). *L'ipogeo di Trebio Giusto sulla Via Latina: scavi e restauri*. Vatican, 133–147.

Biscottini, M.V. (1966). 'L'archivio di Tryphon, tessitore di Oxyrhynchos', *Aegyptus* 46: 60–90, 186–292.

Bodei Giglioni, G. (1974). *Lavori pubblici e occupazione nell'antichità classica*. Bologna.

Böhnke, H. (1994). 'Ist Diokletian's Geldpolitik gescheitert?', *Zeitschrift für Papyrologie und Epigraphik* 100: 473–483.

Bollmann, B. (1998). *Römische Vereinshäuser: Untersuchungen zu den* Scholae *der römischen Berufs-, Kult- und Augustalen-Kollegien in Italien*. Mainz.

Bon, S.E. and Jones, R. (1997). *Sequence and Space in Pompeii*. Oxford.

Borgard, Ph., Brun, J.-P., Leguilloux, M., and Tuffreau-Libre, M. (2003). 'Le produzioni artigianali a Pompei. Richerche condotte dal Centre Jean Bérard'. *Rivista di Studi Pompeiani* 14: 9–29.

Bouet, A. (2001). 'Les collèges dans la ville antique: le cas des « *subaediani* »', *Revue Archéologique* 32: 227–278.

Bourdieu, P. (1980). 'Le capital social: Notes provisoires', *Actes de la Recherche en Sciences Sociales*: 31: 2–3.

Bourdieu, P. (1985). 'The Forms of Social Capital', in J.G. Richardson (ed.), *Handbook of Theory and Research for the Sociology of Education*. New York, 241–258.

Bowman, A.K. (1983). *The Oxyrhynchus Papyri. Volume L, [Nos 3522–3600]*. London.

Bradley, K.R. (1987). *Slaves and Masters in the Roman Empire: a Study in Social Control*. New York.

Bradley, K.R. (1991). *Discovering the Roman Family: Studies in Roman Social History*. New York.

Bradley, K.R. (1994). *Slavery and Society at Rome*. Cambridge.

Branca, V. (1986). *Mercanti Scrittori: Ricordi nella Firenze tra Medioevo e Rinascimento*. Milan.

Brautbar, M. and Kearns, M. (2011). 'A Clustering Coefficient Network Formation Game', in G. Persiano (ed.). *Algorithmic Game Theory: 4th International Symposium, SAGT 2011, Amalfi, Italy, October 17–19, 2011: Proceedings* (Lecture Notes in Computer Science 6982). Heidelberg, 224–235.

Brennan, G. and Pettit, P. (2004). *The Economy of Esteem: An Essay on Civil and Political Society*. Oxford.

Brewster, E.H. (1927). 'A Weaver of Oxyrhynchus: Sketch of a Humble Life in Roman Egypt', *Transactions of the American Philological Association* 58: 132–164.

Brewster, E.H. (1931). 'A Weaver's Life in Oxyrhynchus, His Status in the Community', in G.D. Hadzsits (ed.), *Classical Studies in Honour of John C. Rolfe*. Philadelphia, 19–45.

Broekaert, W. (2008). '«*Creatio ex Nihilo* »?: the Origin of the « *Corpora Nauiculariorum* » Reconsidered', *Latomus* 67: 692–706.

Broekaert, W. (2009). 'Tied Down, Wings Cut? The Relation Between the State and the *Navicularii* During the Later Roman Empire', in B. Antela-Bernárdez and A. Ñaco del Hoyo (eds.), *Transforming Historical Landscapes in the Ancient Empires* (British Archaeological Reports. International series 1986). Oxford, 169–173.

Broekaert, W. (2011). 'Partners in Business. Roman Merchants and the Advantages of Being a *Collegiatus*', *Ancient Society* 41: 219–254.

Broekaert, W. (2012). 'Joining Forces. Commercial Partnerships or *Societates* in the Early Roman Empire', *Historia* 61: 221–253.

Broekaert, W. (2012a). 'Vertical Integration in the Roman Economy', *Ancient Society* 42: 109–125.

Broekaert, W. (2012b). 'Welcome to the Family! Marriage as Business Strategy in the Roman Economy', *Marburger Beiträge zur Antiken Handels-, Wirtschafts- und Sozialgeschichte* 30: 41–65.

Broekaert, W. (2012c). 'Joining Forces: Commercial Partnerships or Societates in the Early Roman Empire', *Historia* 61: 221–253.

Broughton, T.R.S. (1938). 'A Greek Inscription from Tarsus', *American Journal of Archaeology* 42.1: 55–57.

Broughton, T.R.S. (1938). 'Roman Asia Minor', in T. Frank (ed.). *An Economic Survey of Ancient Rome*. Vol. 4. Baltimore, 499–918.

Brown, E.A.R. (1986). 'Georges Duby and the Three Orders', *Viator* 17: 51–64.

Brown, P. (1992). *Power and Persuasion in Late Antiquity: Towards a Christian Empire*. Madison.

Brown, P. (2012). *Through the Eye of the Needle: Wealth, the Fall of Rome, and the Making of Christianity in the West, 350–550 AD*. Princeton.

Brumfiel, E. and Earle, T. (1987). 'Specialization, Exchange, and Complex Societies: an Introduction', in E. Brumfiel and T. Earle (eds.), *Specialization, Exchange, and Complex Societies*. Cambridge, 1–9.

Brun, J.-P. (2016). 'The Archaeology of Ancient Urban Workshops in Southern Italy: a French Approach?' in A. Wilson and M. Flohr (eds.), *Urban Craftsmen and Traders in the Roman World*. Oxford, 77–94.

Brunt, P.A. (1966). 'The Roman Mob', *Past and Present* 35: 3–27.

Brunt, P.A. (1973). 'Aspects of the Social Thought of Dio Chrysostom and the Stoics', *Proceedings of the Cambridge Philological Society* 19: 9–34.

Brunt, P.A. (1980). 'Free Labour and Public Works at Rome', *Journal of Roman Studies* 70: 81–100.

Bruun, C. (1991). *The Water Supply of Ancient Rome: A Study of Roman Imperial Administration*. Helsinki.

Bryan, J. (2008). *Devotional Reading and the Private Self in Late Medieval England*. Philadelphia.

Buckler, W.H. (1923). 'Labour Disputes in the Province of Asia Minor', in W.H. Buckler and W.M. Calder (eds.), *Anatolian Studies Presented to Sir William Ramsay*. Manchester, 27–50.

Bülow-Jacobsen, A. (1989). 'Two Greek Papyri Carlsberg from Tebtunis: *P. Carlsberg* 53 and 57', *Zeitschrift für Papyrologie und Epigraphik* 78: 125–131.

Bülow-Jacobsen, A. (2009). *Mons Claudianus. Ostraca graeca et latina IV: The Quarry Texts, O.Claud. 632–896*. Cairo.

Bultot, R. (1990). 'Les sources philosophiques païennes de l'opposition entre "naturel" et "artificiel" en milieu chrétien', in J. Hamesse and C. Muraille-Samaran (eds.), *Le travail au Moyen Âge. Une approche interdisciplinaire*. Louvain-la-Neuve, 101–114.

Burford, A. (1972). *Craftsmen in Greek and Roman Society*. London.

Burnett, J. (1974). *Useful Toil: Autobiographies of Working People from the 1820s to the 1920s*. London.

Burt, R. (1992). *Structural Holes: The Social Structure of Competition*. Cambridge, MA.

Burt, R.S. (2005). *Brokerage and Closure: An Introduction to Social Capital*. Oxford.

Bushart, B. (1994). *Die Fuggerkapelle bei St. Anna in Augsburg*. Munich.

Buttrey, T.V. (1993). 'Calculating Ancient Coin Production: Facts and Fantasies', *The Numismatic Chronicle* 153: 335–351.

Buttrey, T.V. (1999). 'Calculating Ancient Coin Production II: Why It Cannot Be Done', *The Numismatic Chronicle* 154: 341–352.

Cameron, A. (1939). '*Threptos* and Related Terms in the Inscriptions of Asia Minor', in W.M. Calder and J. Keil (eds.). *Anatolian Studies Presented to W.H. Buckler*. Manchester, 27–62.

Cameron, A. (1979). 'The Date of the Anonymous *De Rebus Bellicis*', in M.W.C. Hassall and R.I. Ireland (eds.), *Aspects of the De Rebus Bellicis: Papers Presented to Prof. E.A. Thompson*. Oxford, 1–10.

Camodeca, G. (2006). 'Graffito con conto di infornata di sigillata tardo-Italica da Isola di Migliarino (Pisa)', in S. Menchelli and M. Pasquinucci (eds.), *Territorio e Produzione Ceramiche Paesaggi, Economia e Società in Età Romana. Atti del Convegno Internazionale (Pisa, 20–22 Ottobre 2005)*. Pisa, 207–216.

Campbell, V.L. (2010). 'The Epitaph of Aulus Umbricius Scaurus (CIL X 1024): A Reconsideration', *Zeitschrift für Papyrologie und Epigraphik* 174: 229–237.

Capogrossi Colognesi, L., Giardina, A., and Schiavone, A. (1978). *Analisi marxista e società antiche*. Roma.

Carandini, A. (1979). *L'anatomia della scimmia: la formazione economica della società prima del capitale: con un commento alle Forme che precedono la produzione capitalistica dai Grundrisse di Marx*. Torino.

Carcopino, J. (1941). *Daily Life in Ancient Rome: the People and the City at the Height of the Empire*, (English edition with bibliography and notes by H.T. Rowell, translation by E.O. Lorimer). Harmondsworth.

Carlsen, J. (1995). *Vilici and Roman Estate Managers until AD 284*. Rome.

Carlsen, J. (2016) 'Le attività agricole e dell' allevamento', in A. Marcone (ed.), *Storia del lavoro in Italia. L'età Romana. Liberi, semiliberi e schiavi in una società moderna*. Roma, 225–264.

Carney, J.A. (1998). 'The Role of African Rice and Slaves in the History of Rice Cultivation in the Americas', *Human Ecology* 26.4: 525–545.

Carrié, J.-M. (2002). 'Les associations professionnelles à l'époque tardive: entre « *munus* » et convivialité', in J.-M. Carrié and R. Lizzi Testa (eds.), *'Humana sapit': études d'antiquités tardive offertes à Lellia Cracco Rugini*. Turnhout, 309–332.

Carroll, M. (2006). *Spirits of the Dead: Roman Funerary Commemoration in Western Europe*. Oxford.

Carroll, M.D. (1993). 'In the Name of God and Profit: Jan van Eyck's Arnolfini Portrait', *Representations* 44: 96–132.

Carson, R.A.G. (1956). 'System and Product in the Roman Mint', in R.A.G. Carson and C.H. Sutherland (eds.), *Essays in Roman Coinage Presented to Harold Mattingly*. Oxford, 229–239.

Casey, P.J. (1994). *Carausius and Allectus: The British Usurpers*. London.

Castiglione, D., Deth, J.W. van, and Wolleb, G. (2008). *The Handbook of Social Capital*. Oxford and New York.

Castrén, P. (1975). *Ordo Populusque Pompeianus. Polity and Society in Roman Pompeii* (Acta Instituti Romani Finlandiae 8). Roma.

Cels-Saint-Hilaire, J. (1976). 'Un problème controversé. L'origine d'un flamine de Narbonnaise, Sextus Fadius Secundus Musa', *Eos* 66: 107–121.

Chenu, M.-D. (1968). *Nature, Man, and Society in the Twelfth Century. Essays on New Theological Perspectives in the Latin West*. Chicago.

Choisy, A. (1873). *L'art de bâtir chez les Romains*. Paris.

Clarke, J.R. (2003). *Art in the Lives of Ordinary Romans: Visual Representation and Non-Elite Viewers in Italy, 100 B.C.–A.D. 315*. Berkeley.

Clemente, G. (1972). 'Il patronato nei collegia dell'impero romano', *Studi Classici e Orientali* 21: 142–229.

Coarelli, F. (1977). 'Public Building in Rome between the Second Punic War and Sulla', *Papers of the British School in Rome* 45: 1–23.

Coarelli, F. (1979). 'La riscoperta del sepolcro degli Haterii. Una base con dedica a Silvano', in G. Kopcke and M.B. Moore (eds.) *Studies in Classical Art and Archaeology: A Tribute to Pieter Heinrich von Blanckenhagen*. New York: 255–269.

Coarelli, F. (1994). 'Moneta. Le officine della zecca di Roma tra Repubblica e Impero', *Annali dell'Istituto Italiano di Numismatica* 38–41: 23–66.

Coarelli, F. (2000). 'Discussions, sous la presidence de J-M. Pesez', in P. Boucheron, H. Broise, and Y. Thebert (eds.), *La brique antique et medievale*. Rome, 371–381.

Coase, R.H. (1937). 'The Nature of the Firm', *Economica* 4: 386–405.

Cockle, H. (1981). 'Pottery Manufacture in Roman Egypt: a New Papyrus', *Journal of Roman Studies* 71: 87–97.

Cohn Jr., S. (1994). *The Cult of Remembrance and the Black Death: Six Renaissance Cities in Central Italy*. Baltimore.

Coleman, J.S. (1988). 'Social Capital in the Creation of Human Capital', *American Journal of Sociology* 94 (Supplement): 95–121.

Coleman, K.M. (2006). M. Valerii Martialis Liber spectaculorum. *Edited with introduction, translation, and commentary*. Oxford.

Combet Farnoux, B. (1981). 'Mercure romain, les Mercuriales et l'institution du culte impérial sous le principat augustéen', in *Aufstieg und Niedergang der römischen Welt. Principat 17.1.2*. Berlin, 457–501.

Constable, G. (1995). *Three Studies in Medieval Religious and Social Thought*. Cambridge.

Constable, G. and Smith, B.S. (eds.) (1972). *Libellus de Diversis Ordinibus et Professionibus Qui Sunt in Aecclesia*. Oxford.

Conway, C. (2006). '*Aurelian's Bellum Monetariorum*: An Examination,' *Past Imperfect* [Online Journal], 12: 1–21. https://ejournals.library.ualberta.ca/index.php/pi/article/view/1578/1104/ (accessed 7 March 2013).

Cooley, A.E., Mitchell, S., and Salway, B. (2007). 'Roman Inscriptions 2001–2005', *Journal of Roman Studies* 97: 176–263.

Cooper, T. (2012). *Citizen Portrait: Portrait Painting and the Urban Elite of Tudor and Jacobean England and Wales*. New Haven and London.

Coppola, G. (1998). 'L' Architecte et le projet de construction au bas Moyen Âge', in L. Callebat (ed.), *Histoire de l'architecte*. Paris, 49–61.

Corbellini, S. (ed.) (2013). *Cultures of Religious Reading in the Late Middle Ages*. Turnhout.

Corbier, M. (1980). 'Salaires et salariat sous le haut-empire', in S. Mrozek (ed.), *Les dévaluations à Rome: Époque républicaine et impériale*, vol. 2: *Gdansk, 19–21 octobre 1978*. Paris and Rome, 61–101.

Corbier, M. (1985). 'Dévaluations et évolution des prix (Ier–IIIe Siècles)', *Revue Numismatique* 27.6: 69–106.

Corbier, M. (2005). 'Coinage and Taxation: The State's Point of View, A.D. 193–337', in A. Bowman, P.D.A. Garnsey, and A. Cameron (eds.), *The Cambridge Ancient History: Volume 12, The Crisis of Empire, AD 193–337*. Cambridge, 327–392.

Corcoran, S. (1996). *The Empire of the Tetrarchs: Imperial Pronouncements and Government, AD 284–324*. Oxford.

Corsten, T. (2005). 'Estates in Roman Asia Minor: the Case of the Kibyratis', in S. Mitchell and C. Katsari (eds.). *Patterns in the Economy of Roman Asia Minor*. Swansea, 1–51.

Corti, M. (1983). 'Structures idéologiques et structures sémiotiques dans les *sermones ad status* du XIIIe siècle', in L. Brind'Amour and E. Vance (eds.), *Archéologie du signe* (Recueils d'Études médiévales 3). Toronto, 145–163.

Costin, C. (1991). 'Craft Specialization: Issues in Defining, Documenting, and Explaining the Organization of Production', *Archaeological Method and Theory* 3: 1–56.

Coulon, G. (1994). *L'Enfant en Gaule Romaine*. Paris.

Cracco Ruggini, L. (1971). 'Le associazioni professionali nel mondo romano-bizantino', in *Artigianato e tecnica nella società dell'alto medioevo occidentale. XVIII Settimana di studi sull'Alto Medioevo (Spoleto, 2–8 Aprile, 1970)*. Spoleto, 59–193.

Cranford, C. (2005). 'Networks of Exploitation: Immigrant Labor and the Restructuring of the Los Angeles Janitorial Industry', *Social Problems* 52: 379–397.

Crawford, M.H. (1966). 'Control-Marks and the Organization of the Roman Republican Mint', *Papers of the British School at Rome* 34: 18–23.

Crawford, M.H. (2002). 'Discovery, Autopsy and Progress: Diocletian's Jigsaw Puzzles', in T.P. Wiseman (ed.), *Classics in Progress. Essays on Greece and Rome*. New York, 145–163.

Crawford, M.H. (2010). 'From Alcibiades to Diocletian: Slavery and the Economy in the Longue Durée', in U. Roth (ed.), *By the Sweat of Your Brow. Roman Slavery in Its Socio-Economic Setting*. London, 61–74.

Crawford, M.H. (ed.) (1996). *Roman Statutes. I–II* (BICS Supplement 64). London.

Crawford, M.H. and González, J. (1986). 'The *Lex Irnitana*: A New Copy of the Flavian Municipal Law', *Journal of Roman Studies* 76: 147–243.

Crook, J.A. (1983). 'The Class Struggle in the Ancient World', *Classical Review* 33: 71–72.

Cristofori, A. (2016). 'Lavoro e identità sociale', in A. Marcone (ed.), *Storia del lavoro in Italia. L'età Romana. Liberi, semiliberi e schiavi in una società moderna*. Roma, 149–174.

Csapo, E. (2005). *Theories of Mythology*. Oxford.

Cubelli, V. (2002). *Aureliano Imperatore: la rivolta dei moneteriere e la cosidetta riforma monetaria*. Florence.

Cull, N.J., Culbert, D.H., and Welch, D. (2003). *Propaganda and Mass Persuasion: A Historical Encyclopedia, 1500 to the Present*. Santa Barbara.

Cuomo di Caprio, N. (1992). *Fornaci e Officine da Vasaio Tardo-Ellenistiche*. Princeton.

Cuomo, S. (2007). *Technology and Culture in Greek and Roman Antiquity*. Cambridge.

Curtis, R.I. (1984). 'A Personalized Floor Mosaic from Pompeii', *American Journal of Archaeology* 88: 557–566.

Cuvigny, H. (1996). 'The Amount of Wages Paid to the Quarry Workers at Mons Claudianus', *Journal of Roman Studies* 86: 139–145.

D'Aloja, C. (2016). 'Il lavoro femminile', in A. Marcone (ed.), *Storia del lavoro in Italia. L'età Romana. Liberi, semiliberi e schiavi in una società moderna*. Roma, 639–662.

D'Ambra, E. and Métraux, G.P.R. (2006). 'Introduction', in E. D'Ambra and G.P.R. Métraux (eds.), *The Art of Citizens, Soldiers and Freedmen in the Roman World*. Oxford, i–xvii.

D'Arms, J. (1970). *Romans on the Bay of Naples. A Social and Cultural Study of the Villas and Their Owners from 150 B.C. to A.D. 400*. Cambridge, MA.

D'Arms, J.H. (2000). 'Memory, Money, and Status at Misenum: Three New Inscriptions from the « *Collegium* » of the Augustales', *Journal of Roman Studies* 90: 126–144.

Daly, M. and Silver, H. (2008). 'Social Exclusion and Social Capital: A Comparison and Critique', *Theory and Society* 37: 537–566.

Dannell, G.B. (2002). 'Law and Practice: Further Thoughts on the Organization of the Potteries at La Graufesenque', in M. Genin and A. Vernhet (eds.), *Céramiques de La Graufesenque et Autres Productions d'Époque Romaine*. Montagnac, 214–215.

Dark, K.R. (1996). 'Proto-Industrialisation and the End of the Roman Economy', in K.R. Dark, (ed.), *External Contacts and the Economy of Late Roman and Post-Roman Britain*, Woodbridge, 1–21.

Davies, J.K. (2007). 'Classical Greece: Production', in W. Scheidel, I. Morris, and R. Saller (eds.), *The Cambridge Economic History of the Greco-Roman World*. Cambridge, 333–361.

Davis, J. (2012). *Medieval Market Morality: Life, Law and Ethics in the English Marketplace, 1200–1500*. Cambridge.

De Benedittis, G., Gaggiotti, M., and Matteini Chiari, M. (1993). *Saepinum. Sepino*. Campobasso.

De Blois, L. (1976). *The Policy of the Emperor Gallienus*. Leiden.

De Caro, S. (1991). 'Una Conceria a Saepinum', in *Samnium, Archeologia del Molise. Catalogo della mostra*. Rome, 250–253.

de Ligt, L. (2008). 'The Population of Cisalpine Gaul in the Time of Augustus', in L. de Ligt and S.J. Northwood (eds.), *People, Land, and Politics. Demographic Developments and the Transformation of Roman Italy, 300 BC–AD 14*. Leiden and Boston, 139–183.

De Martino, F. (1979). *Storia economica di Roma antica*. Firenze.

De Munck, B., Kaplan, S.L., and Soly, H. (2007). *Learning on the Shop Floor: Historical Perspectives on Apprenticeship*. New York.

De Nardis, M. (2016a). 'Terminologia e concetto di "lavoro" in età romana', in A. Marcone (ed.), *Storia del lavoro in Italia. L'età Romana. Liberi, semiliberi e schiavi in una società moderna*. Roma, 79–90.

De Nardis, M. (2016b). 'Imparare un mestiere: apprendistato, contratti di la-voro e salari', in A. Marcone (ed.), *Storia del lavoro in Italia. L'età Romana. Liberi, semiliberi e schiavi in una società moderna*. Roma, 131–148.

de Neeve, P.W. (1984). *Colonus, Private Farm-Tenancy in Roman Italy During the Republic and the Early Principate*. Amsterdam.

De Robertis, F.M. (1946). *I rapporti di lavoro nel diritto romano*, Milan.

De Robertis, F.M. (1963). *Lavoro e lavoratori nel mondo romano*. Bari.

De Roover, R. (1948). *Money, Banking and Credit in Mediaeval Bruges; Italian Merchant Bankers, Lombards and Money-Changers*. Cambridge, MA.

De Roover, R. (1967). *San Bernardino of Siena and Sant'Antonino of Florence: Two Great Economic Thinkers of the Middle Ages*. Boston.

De Ruyt, C. (2001). 'Les foulons, artisans des textiles et blanchisseurs', in J.-P. Descoeudres (ed.), *Ostia. Port et Porte de la Rome Antique*. Genève, 186–191.

De Salvo, L. (1987). 'Il giudizio sulla *mercatura* nel mondo Romano', *Annali della Facoltà di Lettere e Filosofia dell' Universià di Macerata* 20: 9–32.

De Salvo, L. (1992). *Economia privata e pubblici servizi nell'impero romano: i* corpora naviculariorum. Messina.

de Ste. Croix, G.E.M. (1981). *The Class Struggle in the Ancient Greek World: from the Archaic Age to the Arab Conquest*. Ithaca.

De Vries, A. (2004). *Ingelijst Werk. De verbeelding van arbeid en beroep in de vroegmoderne Nederlanden*. Hilversum.

De Vries, J. (1994). 'How Did Pre-Industrial Labour Markets Function?', in G. Grantham and M. MacKinnon (eds.), *Labour Market Evolution: the Economic History of Market Integration, Wage Flexibility and the Employment Relation*. London, 39–63.

De Vries, J. and A. Van der Woude (1997). *The First Modern Economy: Success, Failure, and Perseverance of the Dutch Economy, 1500–1815*. Cambridge.

Degrassi, A. (1937). 'Iscrizioni nuove. I magistri mercuriales di Lucca e la dea Anzotica di Aenona', *Athenaeum* 284–288.

DeLaine, J. (1997). *The Baths of Caracalla in Rome: a Study in the Design, Construction, and Economics of Large-Scale Building Projects in Imperial Rome*. Portsmouth, RI.

DeLaine, J. (2000). 'Building the Eternal City: the Building Industry of Imperial Rome', in J. Coulston and H. Dodge (eds.), *Ancient Rome: the Archaeology of the Eternal City*. Oxford, 119–141.

DeLaine, J. (2003). 'The Builders of Roman Ostia: Organisation, Status and Society', in S. Huerta Fernández (ed.), *Proceedings of the First International Congress on Construction History*. Madrid, 723–732.

Delaine, J. (2005). 'The Commercial Landscape of Ostia', in A. MacMahon and J. Price (eds.), *Roman Working Lives and Urban Living*. Oxford, 2947.

DeLaine, J. (2015) 'The Pantheon Builders—Estimating Manpower for Construction', in T. Marder and M. Wilson Jones (eds.), *The Pantheon*. Cambridge.

Delaruelle, E. (1948). 'Le travail dans les règles monastiques occidentales du quatrième au neuvième siècle', *Journal de Psychologie normale et pathologique* 4: 51–62.

Deman, A. (2002). 'Avec les utriculaires sur les sentiers muletiers de la Gaule romaine', *Cahiers du Centre Gustave Glotz* 13: 233–246.

Demougin, S. (2012). 'Des collèges en Gaule Belgique', in M. Dondin-Payre and N. Tran (eds.), *Le phénomène associatif dans l'occident romain*. Bordeaux, 155–164.

Demougin, S. and Christol, M. (1984). 'Notes de prosopographie équestre', *Zeitschrift für Papyrologie und Epigraphik* 57: 163–178.

Depeyrot, G. (2012). 'Economy and Society', in N. Lenski (ed.), *The Cambridge Companion to the Age of Constantine*. Cambridge, 226–254.

Desmond, W.D. (2006). *The Greek Praise of Poverty: Origins of Ancient Cynicism*. Notre Dame.

Destephen, S. (2010). 'Familles d'Anatolie au miroir des *MAMA*', *Epigraphica Anatolica* 43: 135–148.

Devlin, M.A. (ed. 1954). *The Sermons of Thomas Brinton, Bishop of Rochester, 1373–1389* (Camden Third Series 85 and 86). London.

Devore, G. and Ellis, S.J.R. (2008). 'The Third Season of Excavations at VIII.7.1–15 and the Porta Stabia at Pompeii: Preliminary Report', *The Journal of Fasti Online* 112: 1–15.

Díaz Ariño, B. (2004). '«*Heisce Magistreis*»: aproximación a los «*collegia*» de la Hispania republicana a través de sus paralelos italianos y delios', *Gerión* 22: 447–478.

Dickmann, J.-A. (2013). 'A "Private" Felter's Workshop in the Casa Dei Postumii at Pompeii', in M. Gleba and J. Pasztokai-Szeöke (eds.), *Making Textiles in pre-Roman and Roman Times: People, Places, Identities*. Oxford, 208–226.

Dickmann, J.-A. and Pirson, F. (2001). 'Abitare e lavorare nell'antica Pompei. L'indagine nella Casa dei Postumii tra archeologia e tutela', in F. Senatore (ed.), *Pompei tra Sorrento e Sarno: Atti del terzo e quarto ciclo di conferenze di geologia, storia e archeologia, Pompei, gennaio 1999–maggio 2000*. Roma, 63–86.

Dittmann-Schöne, I. (2001). *Die Berufsvereine in den Städten des kaiserzeitlichen Kleinasiens*. Regensburg.

Dixon, S. (2000). 'The Circulation of Children in Roman Society', in M. Corbier (ed.), *Adoption et fosterage*. Paris, 217–230.

Dodwell, C.R. (ed.) (1961). *Theophilus: The Various Arts*. London.

Donderer, M. (1996). *Die Architekten der späten römischen Republik und Kaiserzeit: epigraphische Zeugnisse*. Erlangen.

Dondin-Payre, M. and Tran, N. (2012). Collegia*: le phénomène associatif dans l'Occident romain* (*Scripta antiqua* 41). Bordeaux.

Dorcey, P.F. (1992). *The Cult of Silvanus: A Study in Roman Folk Religion*. Leiden and Boston.

Drexhage, H.-J. (1991). *Preise, Mieten/Pachten, Kosten und Löhne im römischen Ägypten, bis zum Regierungsantritt Diokletians*. Skt. Katharinen.

Drexhage, H.-J. (2004). 'Vorläufige Liste der bislang ausschliesslich literarisch belegten Berufs- bzw. Tätigkeitsbezeichnungen', *Münstersche Beiträge zur antiken Handelsgeschichte* 23: 41–65.

Dry, D.D. (2013). 'Threptoi', in R.S. Bagnall *et al.* (eds.). *The Encyclopedia of Ancient History*. Malden MA, 6732.

Du Plessis, P.J. (2012). *Letting and Hiring in Roman Legal Thought: 27 BCE–284 CE*. Leiden and Boston.

Duby, G. (1978). *Les trois ordres ou l'imaginaire du féodalisme*. Paris.

Dufaÿ, B., Barat, Y., and Raux, S. (1997). *Fabriquer de la vaisselle à l'époque romaine. Archéologie d'un centre de production céramique en Gaule la boissière-école (Yvelines–France)*. Yvelines.

Dumont, J.-C. (1987). Servus: *Rome et l'esclavage sous la République*. Rome.

Duncan-Jones, R.P. (1976). 'The Size of the *Modius Castrensis*', *Zeitschrift für Papyrologie und Epigraphik* 21: 53–62.

Duncan-Jones, R.P. (1978). 'Two Possible Indices of the Purchasing Power of Money in Greek and Roman Antiquity', in G. Vallet (ed.), *Les dévaluations à Rome: Époque républicaine et imperial*, vol. 1: *Actes du colloque de Rome (13–15 novembre 1975)*. (Publications de l'École Française de Rome 37.1). Rome, 159–68.

Duncan-Jones, R.P. (1982). *The Economy of the Roman Empire: Quantitative Studies*, 2nd edition. Cambridge.

Duncan-Jones, R.P. (1990). *Structure and Scale in the Roman Economy*. Cambridge.

Duncan-Jones, R.P. (1996). 'The Impact of the Antonine Plague', *Journal of Roman Archaeology* 9: 108–136.

Dyer, C. (1989). *Standards of Living in the Later Middle Ages: Social Change in England c. 1200–1520*. Cambridge.

Easley, D. and Kleinberg, J. (2010). *Networks, Crowds, and Markets: Reasoning about a Highly Connected World*. Cambridge.

Eck, W. (1997). 'Auf der Suche nach Architekten in der römischen Welt', *Journal of Roman Archaeology* 10: 399–404.

Edmondson, J.C. (1996). 'Dynamic Arenas: Gladitorial Presentations in the City of Rome and the Construction of Roman Society During the Early Empire', in W.J. Slater (ed.), *Roman Theater and Society. E. Togo Salmon Papers I.* Ann Arbor, 69–44.

Ehmer, J. and Lis, C. (2009). *The Idea of Work in Europe from Antiquity to Modern Times.* Farnham and Burlington, VT.

Ellis, S.P. (2000). *Roman Housing.* London.

Elsner, J. (2007). *Roman Eyes. Visuality and Subjectivity in Art and Text.* Princeton.

Epstein, S. (2008). 'Why Did Attic Building Projects Employ Free Laborers Rather Than Slaves?' *Zeitschrift für Papyrologie und Epigraphik* 166: 108–112.

Epstein, S.R. and Prak, M.R. (2008). *Guilds, Innovation, and the European Economy, 1400–1800.* Cambridge.

Erasmus, C. (1965). 'Monument Building: Some Field Experiments', *Southwestern Journal of Anthropology* 21: 277–301.

Erdkamp, P. (1999). 'Agriculture, Underemployment, and the Cost of Rural Labour in the Roman World', *Classical Quarterly* 49: 556–572.

Erdkamp, P. (ed.) (2002). *The Roman Army and the Economy.* Amsterdam.

Erdkamp, P. (2005). *The Grain Market in the Roman Empire: a Social, Political and Economic Study.* Cambridge and New York.

Erdkamp, P. (2008). 'Mobility and Migration in Italy in the Second Century B.C.': in L. de Ligt and S. Northwood (eds.), *People, Land, and Politics: Demographic Developments and the Transformation of Roman Italy 300 B.C.–A.D. 14.* Leiden and Boston, 417–450.

Erdkamp, P. (2014). 'How Modern was the Market Economy of the Roman World?', *Œconomia. History, Methodology, Philosophy* 4: 225–235.

Erdkamp, P. (2015). 'Agriculture, Division of Labour, and the Paths to Economic Growth', in P. Erdkamp, K. Verboven, and A. Zuiderhoek (eds.), *Ownership and Exploitation of Land and Natural Resources in the Roman World* (Oxford Studies on the Roman Economy). Oxford, 18–39.

Fant, J.C. (2001). 'Rome's Marble Yards', *Journal of Roman Archaeology* 14: 167–198.

Farr, J.R. (2000). *Artisans in Europe, 1300–1914.* Cambridge and New York.

Ferragina, E. (2012). *Social Capital in Europe: A Comparative Regional Analysis.* Cheltenham, UK.

Fevre, R. (1992). *The Sociology of Labour Markets.* Hemel Hempstead.

Fezzi, L. (2016). 'Forme di protesta dei lavoratori nel mondo romano', in A. Marcone (ed.), *Storia del lavoro in Italia. L'età Romana. Liberi, semiliberi e schiavi in una società moderna.* Roma, 204–224.

Fikhman, I.F. (1971). 'Die Bevölkerungszahl von Oxyrhynchos in byzantinischer Zeit', *Archiv für Papyrusforschung und Verwandte Gebiete* 21: 111–120.

Filedt Kok, J.P. (2006). *De heilige Lucas tekent en schildert de Madonna*. Amsterdam.

Finley, M.L. (1976). 'Private Farm Tenancy in Italy before Diocletian', in M.I. Finley (ed.), *Studies in Roman Property*. Cambridge, 103–121.

Finley, M.I. (1981). 'Was Greek Civilization Based on Slave Labour?', in B. Shaw and R. Saller (eds.). Finley, M. *Economy and Society in Ancient Greece*. New York, 97–115.

Finley, M.I. (1999) *The Ancient Economy*. Updated with a New Foreword by Ian Morris. Berkeley. [first edition 1973, second edition 1985]

Fiorelli, G. (1877). 'Scavi di Pompei: Settembre 1877'. *Notizie degli Scavi di Antichità*, 218–222.

Fitzsimmons, R. (2007). 'Architecture and Power in the Bronze Age Argolid', in J. Bretschneider, J.M. Driessen and K. Van Lergerghe (eds.), *Power and Architecture: Monumental Public Architecture in the Bronze Age Near East and Aegean*. Leuven, 93–116.

Flambard, J.-M. (1982). 'Observations sur la nature des magistri italiens de Délos', in F. Coarelli, D. Musti, and H. Solin (eds.), *Delo e l'Italia* (Opuscula Instituti Romani Finlandiae 2). Roma, 67–77.

Flambard, J.-M. (1983). 'Les collèges et les élites locales à l'époque républicaine d'après l'exemple de Capoue', in *Les bourgeoisies municipales italiennes aux IIe et Ier siècles av. J.C. Centre Jean-Bérard, Institut français de Naples, 7–10 décembre 1981* (Colloques internationaux du CNRS 609). Paris, 75–89.

Flohr, M. (2007). '*Nec quicquam ingenuum habere potest officina*? Spatial Contexts of Urban Production at Pompeii, AD 79', *Bulletin Antieke Beschaving. Annual Papers on Classical Archaeology* 82: 129–148.

Flohr, M. (2009). 'The Social World of Roman *Fullonicae*', in M. Driessen, S. Heeren, J. Hendriks, F. Kemmers, and R. Visser (eds.), *TRAC 2008. Proceedings of the Eighteenth Annual Theoretical Roman Archaeology Conference*. Oxford: 173–186.

Flohr, M. (2011a). 'Reconsidering the Atrium House. Domestic *Fullonicae* at Pompeii', in E. Poehler, M. Flohr, and K. Cole (eds.), *Pompeii: Art, Industry, Infrastructure*. Oxford, 88–102.

Flohr, M. (2011b). 'Exploring the Limits of Skilled Craftsmanship: The *Fullonicae* of Roman Italy', in N. Monteix and N. Tran (eds.), *Les savoirs professionnels des gens de métier. Études sur le monde du travail dans les sociétés urbaines de l'empire romain*. Naples, 87–100.

Flohr, M. (2012). 'Working and Living Under One Roof: Workshops in Pompeian Atrium Houses', in A. Anguissola (ed.), Privata Luxuria*: Towards an Archaeology of Intimacy*. München, 51–72.

Flohr, M. (2013a). *The World of the Fullo. Work, Economy and Society in Roman Italy*. Oxford.

Flohr, M. (2013b). 'The Textile Economy of Pompeii', *Journal of Roman Archaeology* 26: 53–78.

Flohr, M. (2016). '*Tabernae Publicae*. Commercie en de publieke zaak in Romeins Italië', *Lampas* 49: 67–88.

Flohr, M. and Wilson, A. (2016). 'Introduction', in A. Wilson and M. Flohr (eds.), *Urban Craftsmen and Traders in the Roman World*. Oxford, 1–21.

Fogel, R.W. (1989). *Without Consent or Contract: the Rise and Fall of American Slavery*. New York.

France, J. (2004). 'Les monuments funéraires et le "capitalisme" des élites trévires', in J. Andreau, J. France and S. Pittia (eds.), *Mentalités et choix économiques des Romains*. Paris, 149–178.

Frank, T. (1927). *An Economic History of Rome*, 2nd edition. Baltimore.

Franklin, J.L. (1980). *Pompeii. The Electoral Programmata, Campaigns, and Politics, A.D. 71–79* (Papers and Monographs of the American Academy in Rome 28). Rome.

Frederiksen, M.W. (1959). 'Republican Capua: A Social and Economic Study', *Papers of the British School at Rome* 27: 80–130.

Freedman, P. (1999). *Images of the Medieval Peasant*. Stanford.

Freu, C. (2011). 'Apprendre et exercer un métier dans l'Égypte romaine (Ier–VIe siècles ap. J.-C.)', in N. Monteix and N. Tran (eds.), *Les savoirs professionnels des gens de métier: études sur le monde du travail dans les sociétés urbaines de l'empire romain* (Collection du Centre Jean Bérard 37). Naples, 27–40.

Freu, C. (2016). '*Disciplina, patrocinium, nomen*: the Benefits of Apprenticeship in the Roman World', in A. Wilson and M. Flohr (eds.), *Urban Craftsmen and Traders in the Roman world*. Oxford, 183–199.

Freyberger, K.S. (1990). *Stadtrömische Kapitelle aus der Zeit von Domitian bis Alexander Severus: zur Arbeitsweise und Organisation stadtrömischer Werkstätten der Kaiserzeit*. Mainz.

Frézouls, E. (1977). 'Salaires, prix et niveaux de vie: quelques enseignements de l'Édit du Maximum', *Ktema* 2: 253–268.

Frézouls, E. (1978). 'Prix, salaires et niveaux de vie: quelques enseignements de l'Édit du Maximum II', *Ktema* 3: 289–300.

Frezouls, E. (1995). 'L'apport de l'épigraphie à la connaissance des métiers de la construction', in M.C. Giuliana and E. Roffia (eds.) Splendida civitas nostra. *Studi archeologici in onore di Antonio Frova*. Rome, 35–44.

Friesen, S.J. and Scheidel, W. (2009). 'The Size of the Economy and the Distribution of Income in the Roman Empire', *Journal of Roman Studies* 99: 61–91.

Frisch, T.G. (1987). *Gothic Art, 1140–c1450: Sources and Documents*. Toronto.

Fröhlich, P. and Hamon, P. (eds.) (2013). *Groupes et associations dans les cités grecques (IIIe siècle av. J.-C.–IIe siècle ap. J.-C.). Actes de la table ronde de Paris, INHA, 19–20 juin 2009* (Hautes études du monde gréco-romain 49). Genève.

Fuks, A. (1951). 'Labour Exchange in Classical Athens', *Eranos* 49: 171–173.

Fukuyama, F. (1995). *Trust: The Social Virtues and the Creation of Prosperity*. New York.

Fukuyama, F. (2002). 'Social Capital and Development: The Coming Agenda', *SAIS Review* 22.1: 23–37.

Fülle, G. (1997). 'The Internal Organization of the Arretine Terra Sigillata Industry: Problems of Evidence and Interpretation', *The Journal of Roman Studies* 87: 111–155.

Fülle, G. (2000). 'Die Organisation der Terra sigillata-Herstellung in La Graufesenque. Die Töpfergraffiti', *Münstersche Beiträge zur Antiken Handelsgeschichte* 19: 62–99.

Gabba, E. (1984). 'The *Collegia* of Numa. Problems of Method and Political Ideas', *Journal of Roman Studies* 74: 81–86.

Gabrielsen, V. (2001). 'The Rhodian Associations and Economic Activity', in Z. Archibald, J.K. Davies, V. Gabrielsen, and G. Oliver (eds.), *Hellenistic Economies*. London and New York, 163–184.

Gabrielsen, V. (2007). 'Brotherhoods of Faith and Provident Planning: The Non-public Associations of the Greek World', *Mediterranean Historical Review* 22: 183–210.

Gaggiotti, M. (1988). 'Pavimenta Poenica marmore Numidico constrata', in A. Mastino (ed.), *L'Africa Romana V*. Sassari, 215–221.

Gagos, T., Koenen, L., and McNellen, B.E. (1992). 'A First Century Archive from Oxyrhynchos or Oxyrhynchite Loan Contracts and Egyptian Marriage,' in J.H. Johnson (ed.), *Life in a Multi-Cultural Society: Egypt from Cambyses to Constantine and Beyond* (SAOC 51). Chicago, 181–205.

Garnsey, P.D.A. (ed.) (1980). *Non-Slave Labour in the Greco-Roman World*. Cambridge.

Garnsey, P.D.A. (1981). 'Independent Freedmen and the Economy of Roman Italy under the Principate', *Klio* 63: 359–371.

Garnsey, P.D.A. (1998a). *Cities, Peasants, and Food in Classical Antiquity*. Cambridge.

Garnsey, P.D.A. (1998b). 'Non-Slave Labour in the Roman World', in W. Scheidel (ed.), *Cities, Peasants, and Food in Classical Antiquity: Essays in Social and Economic History*. Cambridge, 134–150.

Garnsey, P.D.A. (1998c). 'An Association of Builders in Late Antique Sardis', in W. Scheidel (ed.), *Cities, Peasants and Food in Classical Antiquity. Essays in Social and Economy History*. Cambridge, 77–87.

Gavoille E. (2003). '*Ars* et τέχνη: étude sémantique comparée', in C. Lévy, B. Besnier, and A. Gigandet (eds.)., Ars et Ratio. *Sciences, art et métiers dans la philosophie hellénistique et romaine*. Bruxelles, 49–60.

Geoghegan, A.T. (1945). *The Attitude towards Labor in Early Christianity and Ancient Culture*. Washington, DC.

George, M. (2006). 'Social Identity and the Dignity of Work in Freedmen's Reliefs', in E. D'Ambra and G.P.R. Métraux (eds.), *The Art of Citizens, Soldiers and Freedmen in the Roman World* (BAR International Series 1526). Oxford, 19–30.

Giacchero, M. (1974). *Edictum Diocletiani de pretiis: Edictum Diocletiani et collegarum de pretiis rerum venalium. In integrum fere restitutum e Latinis Graecisque fragmentis*. 2 vols. Genova.

Giacchero, M. (1987). 'Il mondo della produzione e del lavoro nell' "*Edictum de Pretiis*", in A. Biscardi, *Studi in onore di Arnaldo Biscardi VI*. Milano, 121–132.

Gibbons, R. (2005). 'Four Formal(izable) Theories of the Firm?', *Journal of Economic Behavior & Organization* 58: 200–245.

Gibbs, M. (2008). *Professional and Trade Associations in Ptolemaic and Roman Egypt*, Dissertation DPhil, University of Oxford.

Gibbs, M. (2011). 'Trade Associations in Roman Egypt. Their "Raison d'Être"', *Ancient Society* 41: 291–315.

Gibbs, M. (2012). 'Manufacture, Trade and the Economy', in C. Riggs (ed.), *The Oxford Handbook of Roman Egypt*. Oxford, 38–56.

Goitein, S.D. (1967). *A Mediterranean Society: The Jewish Communities of the Arab World as Portrayed in the Documents of the Cairo Geniza. Volume I: Economic Foundations*. Berkeley.

Goldberg, P.J. (2000). 'Household and the Organisation of Labour in Late Medieval Towns: Some English Evidence', in M. Carlier and T. Soens (eds.), *The Household in Late Medieval Cities: Italy and NorthWestern Europe Compared: Proceedings of the International Conference, Ghent, 21st–22nd January 2000* (Studies in Urban Social, Economic and Political History of the Medieval and Modern Low Countries 12). Leuven, 59–70.

Goldthwaite, R.A. (1980). *The Building of Renaissance Florence. An Economic and Social History*. Baltimore.

Goldthwaite, R.A. (2009). *The Economy of Renaissance Florence*. Baltimore.

Golubcova, E.S. (1992). 'Sklaverei- und Abhängigkeitsformen in Kleinasien', in L.P. Marinovič *et. al.* (eds.). *Die Sklaverei in den östlichen Provinzen des Römischen Reiches im 1.–3. Jahrhundert*. Stuttgart, 77–138.

Gonzales, J. and Crawford, M. (1986). 'The *Lex Irnitana*. a New Copy of the Flavian Municipal Law', *Journal of Roman Studies* 76: 147–243.

Goody, E. (1989). 'Learning: Apprenticeship and the Division of Labor', in M.W. Coy (ed.), *Apprenticeship: From Theory to Method and Back Again*. Albany, 233–256.

Graham, S. (2005). 'Of Lumberjacks and Brick Stamps: Working with the Tiber as Infrastructure', in A. MacMahon and J. Price (eds.), *Roman Working Lives and Urban Living*. Oxford, 106–124.

Granovetter, M.S. (1973). 'The Strength of Weak Ties', *American Journal of Sociology* 78: 1360–1380.

Granovetter, M.S. (1983). 'The Strength of Weak Ties: a Network Theory Revisited', *Sociological Theory* 1: 201–233.

Granovetter, M.S. (1985). 'Economic Action and Social Structure: the Problem of Embeddedness', *American Journal of Sociology* 91: 481–493.

Granovetter, M.S. (1995). *Getting a Job. A Study of Contacts and Careers*. 2nd ed. Cambridge, MA.

Granovetter, M.S. (2005). 'The Impact of Social Structure on Economic Outcomes', *The Journal of Economic Perspectives* 19: 33–50.

Grantham, G. (1999). 'Contra Ricardo: On the Macroeconomics of Pre-Industrial Economies', *European Review of Economic History* 2: 199–232.

Grantham, George. (1994). 'Economic History and the History of Labour Markets', in G. Grantham and M. MacKinnon (eds.), *Labour Market Evolution: the Economic History of Market Integration, Wage Flexibility, and the Employment Relation*. London, 1–24.

Graser, E.R. (1940). 'A Text and Translation of the Edict of Diocletian', in T. Frank, *An Economic Survey of Ancient Rome*, vol. 5: *Rome and Italy of the Empire*. Baltimore, 305–421.

Greco, E., D'Ambrosio, I., and Theodorescu, D. (1996). *Archaeological and Historical Guide to the Excavations, the Museum and the Antiquities of Poseidonia, Paestum*. Taranto.

Greene, K. (1986). *The Archaeology of the Roman Economy*. Berkeley.

Greene, K. (2000). 'Technological Innovation and Economic Progress in the Ancient World: M.I. Finley Reconsidered', *The Economic History Review* 53: 29–59.

Greene, K. (2007). 'Perspectives on Roman Technology', *Oxford Journal of Archaeology* 9: 209–219.

Greenhalgh, M. (2009). *Marble Past, Monumental Present: Building with Antiquities in the Mediaeval Mediterranean*. Leiden.

Greif, A. (1989). 'Reputation and Coalition in Medieval Trade: Evidence on the Maghribi Traders', *Journal of Economic History* 49: 857–82.

Greif, A. (1994). 'Cultural Beliefs and the Organization of Society: A Historical and Theoretical Reflection on Collectivist and Individualist Societies', *Journal of Political Economy* 102: 912–950.

Grierson P. and Mays, M. (1992). *Catalogue of Late Roman Coins in the Dumbarton Oaks Collection and in the Whittemore Collection: From Arcadius and Honorius to the accession of Anastasius*. Dumbarton Oaks.

Grierson, P. (1956). 'The Roman Law of Counterfeiting', in R.A.G. Carson and C.H. Sutherland (eds.), *Essays in Roman Coinage Presented to Harold Mattingly*. Oxford, 240–261.

Grierson, P. and Blackburn, M. (1986). *Medieval European Coinage: Volume 1, the Early Middle Ages (5th–10th Centuries)*. Cambridge.

Grillon, G. (2011). *L'ultime message: étude des monuments funéraires de la Bourgogne ducale, XIIe–XVIe siècle*. Dijon.

Groen-Vallinga, M. and Tacoma, L. (2015). 'Contextualising Condemnation to Hard Labour in the Roman Empire', in C. De Vito and A. Lichtenstein (eds.), *Global Convict Labour*. Leiden and Boston, 49–78.

Groen-Vallinga, M.J. (2013). 'Desperate Housewives? The Adaptive Family Economy and Female Participation in the Roman Urban Labour Market', in E.A. Hemelrijk and G. Woolf (eds.), *Women and the Roman City in the Latin West* (Mnemosyne Supplements 360). Leiden, 295–312.

Groethuysen, B. (1927). *Origines de l'esprit bourgeois en France*, vol. 1: *L'Église et la Bourgeoisie*. Paris.

Gros, P. (1997). 'Maisons ou sièges de corporations?: les traces archéologiques du phénomène associatif dans la Gaule romaine méridionale', *Comptes rendus de l'Académie des Inscriptions et Belles-Lettres* 141: 213–241.

Gruen, E.S. (2002). *Diaspora: Jews Amidst Greeks and Romans*. Cambridge, MA.

Guilhembet, J.P. and Royo, M. (2008). 'L'aristocratie en ses quartiers (IIe s. avant J.-C.–IIe après J.-C.)', in M. Royo, E. Huvert, and A. Bérenger (eds.), *'Rome des quartiers': des* vici *aux rioni. Cadres institutionnels, pratiques sociales, et requalifications entre Antiquité et époque modern*. Paris, 193–227.

Gummerus, H. (1913). 'Darstellungen aus dem Handwerk auf römischen Grab- und Votivsteinen in Italien', *Jahrbuch des deutschen archaeologischen Instituts* 28: 63–126.

Haag, S., Lange, C., Metzger, C., and Schütz, K. (eds. 2011). *Dürer, Cranach, Holbein. Die Entdeckung des Menschen: Das deutsche Porträt um 1500*. Vienna and Munich.

Haas, C. (1997). *Alexandria in Late Antiquity: Topography and Social Conflict*. Baltimore.

Hales, S. (2003). *The Roman House and Social Identity*. Cambridge.

Hamilton, B. (1999). 'The Cathars and Christian Perfection', in P. Biller and B. Dobson (eds.), *The Medieval Church: Universities, Heresy, and the Religious Life. Essays in Honour of Gordon Leff* (Studies in Church History, Subsidia 11). Woodbridge, 5–23.

Hamm, B. (2011). *Religiosität im späten Mittelalter: Spannungspole, Neuaufbrüche, Normierungen*. Tübingen.

Hanawalt, B. (1993). *Growing Up in Medieval London: The Experience of Childhood in History*. New York.

Hanes, C. (1996). 'Turnover Cost and the Distribution of Slave Labor in Anglo-America'. *Journal of Economic History* 56: 307–329.

Harbach, A. (2010). *Die Wahl des Lebens in der antiken Literatur*. Heidelberg.

Harker, A. (2008). *Loyalty and Dissidence in Roman Egypt: the Case of the Acta Alexandrinorum*. New York.

Harl, K.W. (1996). *Coinage in the Roman Economy, 300 B.C. to A.D. 700*. Baltimore.

Harland, P. (2003). 'Spheres of Contention, Claims of Preeminence: Rivalries among Associations in Sardis and Smyrna', in R. Ascough (ed.), *Religious Competition and Coexistence in Sardis and Smyrna*. Waterloo, 53–63.

Harland, P. (2013). *Associations, Synagogues, and Congregations: Claiming a Place in Ancient Mediterranean Society*. 2nd revised edition with links to inscriptions. Kitchener, Ontario.

Harper, K. (2008). 'The Greek Census Inscriptions of Late Antiquity', *Journal of Roman Studies* 98: 83–119.

Harper, K. (2010). 'Slave Prices in Late Antiquity', *Historia* 59: 206–238.

Harris, J.R. and M.P. Todaro (1970). 'Migration, Unemployment, and Development: A Two-Sector Analysis', *American Economic Review* 60: 126–142.

Harris, W.V. (2007). 'The Late Republic', in W. Scheidel, R.P. Saller, and I.M. Morris (eds.) *The Cambridge Economic History of the Greco-Roman World*. Cambridge, 511–539.

Harris, W.V. (2011). 'Poverty and Destitution in the Roman Empire', in W.V. Harris (ed.), *Rome's Imperial Economy: Twelve Essays*. Oxford, 27–54.

Harvey, J. (1972). *The Medieval Architect*. London.

Hasebroek, J. (1928). *Staat und Handel im alten Griechenland. Untersuchungen zur antiken Wirtschaftsgeschichte*. Tübingen.

Hasegawa, K. (2005). *The Familia Urbana during the Early Empire: A Study of Columbaria Inscriptions*. Oxford.

Hasenohr, C. (2002). 'Les collèges de magistri et la communauté italienne de Délos', in C. Müller and C. Hasenohr (eds.), *Les Italiens dans le monde grec, IIe siècle av. J.-C.-Ier siècle après J.-C.: circulation, activités, intégration* (Bulletin de correspondance hellénique. Supplément 41). Athènes, 67–88.

Hasenohr, C. (2007). 'Italiens et Phéniciens à Délos: organisation et relations de deux groupes d'étrangers résidents (IIe–Ier siècles av. J.-C.)', in R. Compatangelo-Soussignan and C.-G. Schwentzel (eds.), *Etrangers dans la cité romaine*. Rennes, 77–90.

Haudry, J. (2002). *Juno Moneta: aux sources de la monnaie*. Milan.

Hawkins, C. (2006). *Work in the City: Roman Artisans and the Urban Economy*. Dissertation DPhil, University of Chicago.

Hawkins, C. (2012). 'Manufacturing', in W. Scheidel (ed.), *The Cambridge Companion to the Roman Economy*. Cambridge, 175–194.

Hawkins, C. (2013). 'Labour and Employment', in P. Erdkamp (ed.), *The Cambridge Companion to Ancient Rome*. Cambridge, 336–351.

Hawkins, C. (2016). *Roman Artisans and the Urban Economy*. Cambridge.

Hawkins, C. (forthcoming). 'Manumission and the Organization of Labour', in A. Bresson, F. Velde, and E. Lo Cascio (eds.), *The Oxford Handbook of Economies in the Classical World*. Oxford.

Hawthorne, J.G. and Smith, C.S. (eds.) (1963). *On Divers Arts: The Treatise of Theophilus*. Chicago.

Hechter, M. (1987). *Principles of Group Solidarity*. Berkeley.

Heck, C. (2009). 'Jan van Eyck signe le *Portrait des époux Arnolfini*: la peinture entre apparences sensibles et présence au monde', in P. Boucheron (ed.), *Histoire du monde au XVe siècle*, vol. 2: *Temps et devenirs du monde*. Paris, 156–162.

Heimbach, G.E. (1850). *Basilicorum libri LX, Volume V*. Leipzig.

Heisenberg, A. (1907). *Nikolaos Mesarites. Die Palastrevolution des Johannes Komnenos*. Würzburg.

Helms, R., Ignacio, R., Brinkkemper, S., and Zonneveld, A. (2010). 'Limitations of Network Analysis for Studying Efficiency and Effectiveness of Knowledge Sharing', *Electronic Journal of Knowledge Management* 8: 53–68.

Hendy, M.F. (1985). *Studies in the Byzantine Monetary Economy c.300–1450*. Cambridge.

Hendy, M.F. (1988). 'From Public to Private: The Western Barbarian Coinages as a Mirror of the Disintegration of Late Roman State Structures', *Viator* 19: 29–78.

Herrmann-Otto, E. (1994). Ex ancilla natus: *Untersuchungen zu den « hausgeborenen » Sklaven und Sklavinnen im Westen des römischen Kaisserreiches* (Forschungen zur antiken Sklaverei 24). Stuttgart.

Herrmann-Otto, E. (ed.) (2005). *Unfreie Arbeits- und Lebensverhältnisse von der Antike bis in die Gegenwart: eine Einführung*. Hildesheim.

Heslop, T.A. (1992). 'Eadwine and His Portrait', in M.T. Gibson, T.A. Heslop and R.W. Pfaff (eds.), *The Eadwine Psalter: Text, Image, and Monastic Culture in Twelfth Century Canterbury*. University Park, 178–185.

Hirschfeld, O. (1884). 'Der *Praefectus Vigilum* in Nemausus und die Feuerwehr in den römischen Landstädten', *Sitzungsberichte der Philosophisch-Historischen Classe der Kaiserlichen Akademie der Wissenschaft* 107: 239–257.

Hirt, A.M. (2010). *Imperial Mines and Quarries in the Roman World: Organizational Aspects, 27 BC–AD 235*. Oxford.

Hofstede, G.H. (2001). *Culture's Consequences: Comparing Values, Behaviors, Institutions, and Organizations Across Nations*. Thousand Oaks, Calif.

Hodgson, G.M. (1999). *Evolution and Institutions: on Evolutionary Economics and the Evolution of Economics*. Cheltenham, UK and Northampton, MA.

Holland, W. and Leinhardt, S. (1971). 'Transitivity in Structural Models of Small Groups', *Comparative Group Studies* 2: 107–24.

Holleran, C. (2011). 'Migration and the Urban Economy of Rome', in Holleran, C. and A. Pudsey (eds.), *Demography and the Graeco-Roman World. New Insights and Approaches*. Cambridge, 155–180.

Holleran, C. (2012). *Shopping in Ancient Rome: the Retail Trade in the Late Republic and the Principate*. Oxford.

Hopkins, K. (1978). *Conquerors and Slaves*. Cambridge.

Hopkins, K. (1980). 'Taxes and Trade in the Roman Empire (200 B.C.–A.D. 400)', *Journal of Roman Studies* 70: 101–125.

Howgego, C.J. (1992). 'The Supply and Use of Money in the Roman World 200 B.C. to A.D. 300', *Journal of Roman Studies* 82: 1–31.

Howgego, C.J. (1995). *Ancient History from Coins*. London and New York.

Huebner, S. (2013). *The Family in Roman Egypt: A Comparative Approach to Intergenerational Solidarity and Conflict*. Cambridge.

Humfress, C. (2012). 'Civil Law and Social Life', in N. Lenski (ed.), *The Cambridge Companion to the Age of Constantine*. Cambridge, 205–225.

Humpheries, J. (2003). 'English Apprenticeship: A Neglected Factor in the First Industrial Revolution', in P. David and M. Thomas (eds.), *The Economic Future in Historical Perspective*. Oxford and New York, 73–102.

Humpheries, J. (2010). *Childhood and Child Labour in the British Industrial Revolution.* Cambridge.
Husa, V. (1967). *Hommes et métiers dans l'art: du XIIe au XVIIe siècle en Europe centrale.* Paris.
Irsigler, F. (1985). 'Kaufmannsmentalität im Mittelalter', in C. Meckseper and E. Schraut (eds.), *Mentalität und Alltag im Spätmittelalter*. Göttingen, 53–75.
Irving Lavin, I. (1977–1978). 'The Sculptor's Last Will and Testament', *Allen Memorial Art Museum Bulletin. Oberlin College* 35: 4–39.
Ismard, P. (2010). *La cité des réseaux: Athènes et ses associations, VIe–Ier siècle av. J.-C.* Paris.
Jansen, G.C.M. (2011). 'Toilets and Health', in G.C.M. Jansen, A.O. Koloski-Ostrow, and E. Moormann (eds.), *Roman Toilets: Their Archaeology and Cultural History*. Leuven, 157–162.
Jaritz, G. (2009). 'The Visual Representation of Late Medieval Work: Patterns of Context, People and Action', in J. Ehmer and C. Lis (eds.), *The Idea of Work in Europe from Antiquity to Modern Times*. Aldershot, 125–148.
Johnson, A.C. (1936). *Roman Egypt to the Reign of Diocletian*. Baltimore.
Johnston, A.W. (1985). 'A Greek Graffito from Arezzo', *Oxford Journal of Archaeology* 4: 119–124.
Jones, A.H.M. (1940). *The Greek City from Alexander to Justinian*. Oxford.
Jones, A.H.M. (1964). *The Later Roman Empire, 284–602: a Social, Economic, and Administrative Survey*. Oxford. [reprinted 1973]
Jones, A.H.M. (1966). *The Decline of the Ancient World*. London.
Jones, A.H.M. (1970). 'The Caste System in the Later Roman Empire', *Eirene* 8: 79–96.
Jones, C.P. (1978). *The Roman World of Dio Chrysostom*. Cambridge, MA.
Jones, N.F. (1999). *The Associations of Classical Athens. The Response to Democracy*. New York and Oxford.
Jongman, W. (1988). *The Economy and Society of Pompeii*. Amsterdam.
Jongman, W. (2003). 'Slavery and the Growth of Rome: the Transformation of Italy in the Second and First Centuries BCE', in C. Edwards and G. Woolf (eds.), *Rome the Cosmopolis*. Cambridge, 100–122.
Joshel, S.R. (1992). *Work, Identity, and Legal Status at Rome: a Study of the Occupational Inscriptions*. (Oklahoma Series in Classical Culture 11). Norman, OK, and London.
Joshel, S.R. and Hackworth-Petersen, L. (2014). *The Material Life of Roman Slaves*. Cambridge.
Jouanique, P. (1996). 'Three Medieval Merchants: Francesco di Marco Datini, Jacques Coeur and Benedetto Cotrugli', *Accounting: Business and Financial History* 6: 261–275.
Kalleberg, A.L. and Sorensen, A.B. (1979). 'The Sociology of Labour Markets', *Annual Review of Sociology* 5: 351–379.

Kampen, N. (1981). *Image and Status: Roman Working Women in Ostia*. Berlin.

Kaufman, J. (2002). *For the Common Good? American Civic Life and the Golden Age of Fraternity*. New York.

Kay, P. (2014). *Rome's Economic Revolution*. Oxford.

Kehoe, D. (1988). *The Economics of Agriculture on Roman Imperial Estates in North Africa* (Hypomnemata 89). Göttingen.

Kehoe, D.P. (2007). *Law and the Rural Economy in the Roman Empire*. Ann Arbor.

Kehoe, D. (2012). 'Contract Labor', in W. Scheidel (ed.). *The Cambridge Companion to the Roman Economy*. Cambridge, 114–128.

Kelly, C. (2004). *Ruling the Later Roman Empire*. Cambridge.

Kent, J.P.C. (1994). *Roman Imperial Coinage, Vol. X. The Divided Empire and the Fall of the Western Parts, A.D. 395–491*. London.

Kermode, J. (1999). *Medieval Merchants: York, Beverley and Hull in the Later Middle Ages*. Cambridge.

Kessler, D. and Temin, P. (2007). 'The Organization of the Grain Trade in the Early Roman Empire', *The Economic History Review* 60: 313–332.

Kessler, D. and Temin, P. (2008). 'Money and Prices in the Early Roman Empire', in W.V. Harris (ed.), *The Monetary Systems of the Greeks and Romans*. Oxford, 137–159.

Klamt, J.-C. (1999). 'Artist and Patron: The Self-Portrait of Adam Kraft in the Sacrament-House of St. Lorenz in Nuremberg', in W. Blockmans and A. Janse (eds.), *Showing Status: Representation of Social Positions in the Late Middle Ages*. Turnhout, 415–443.

Klein, B. (1996). 'Why Hold-Ups Occur: the Self-Enforcing Range of Contractual Relationships'. *Economic Inquiry* 34: 444–463.

Kloppenborg, J.S. and Ascough. R.S. (2011). *Greco-Roman Associations Texts, Translations, and Commentary: Attica, Central Greece, Macedonia, Thrace*. Berlin.

Kloppenborg, J.S. and Wilson, S.G. (eds.), (1996). *Voluntary Associations in the Greco-Roman World*. London.

Klose, D. (2006). 'Coin Production', in H. Cancik and H. Schneider (eds.), *Brill's New Pauly*. Brill Online, http://referenceworks.brillonline.com/entries/brill-s-new-pauly/coin-production-e811050 (accessed 21 March 2014).

Kluge, A. (2007). *Die Zünfte*. Stuttgart.

Knapp, R.C. (2011). *Invisible Romans: Prostitutes, Outlaws, Slaves, Gladiators, Ordinary Men and Women ... the Romans that History Forgot*. Cambridge, MA.

Kneissl, P. (1981). 'Die *utricularii*. Ihre Rolle im gallo-römischen Transportwesen und Weinhandel', *Bonner Jahrbücher des Rheinischen Landesmuseums in Bonn und Vereins von Altertumsfreunden im Rheinlande* 181: 169–204.

Kneissl, P. (1994). 'Die *fabri, fabri tignuarii, fabri subaediani, centonarii* und *dolabrarii* als Feuerwehren in den Städten Italiens und der westlichen Provinzen', in G. Rosemarie and S. Rebenich (eds.), *E fontibus haurire. Beiträge zur römischen Geschichte und zu ihren Hilfswissenschaften* (*Festschrift H. Chantraine*). Paderborn, München, Wien and Zürich, 133–146.

Koerner, J.L. (1993). *The Moment of Self-Portraiture in German Renaissance Art*. Chicago.

Kolb, A. (1993). *Die kaiserliche Bauverwaltung in der Stadt Rom: Geschichte und Aufbau der* cura operum publicorum *unter dem Prinzipat*. Stuttgart.

Kolb, A. (2008). 'Das Bauhandwerk in den Städten der römischen Provinzen: Strukturen und Bedeutung', *Tyche* 23: 101–116.

Kolb, A. and Ott, J. (1988). 'Ein *Collegium Negotiatorum Cisalpinorum et Transalpinorum* in Augusta Rauricorum?', *Zeitschrift für Papyrologie und Epigraphik* 73: 107–110.

Kolendo, J. (1980). *L'agricoltura nell'Italia romana: tecniche agrarie e progresso economico dalla tarda repubblica al principato*. Roma.

Kolendo, J. (1981). 'La répartition des places aux spectacles et la stratification sociale dans l'empire romain. A propos des inscriptions sur les gradins des amphithéâtres et théâtres', *Ktèma* 6: 301–315.

Konstan, D. (1986). 'Slavery and Class Analysis in the Ancient World. A Review Article', *Comparative Studies in Society and History* 28: 754–766.

Kubitschek, W. (1934). 'Aus Sammlung Trau in Wien: ein *Vexillum* Aufsatz', *Jahreshefte des Österreichischen Archäologischen Instituts* 29: 44–48.

Kühn, G. (1910). *De opificum Romanorum condicione privata quaestiones*. Diss. Halle-Wittenberg.

Kunow, J. (1985). 'Die capuanischen Bronzegefäßhersteller Lucius Ansius Epaphroditus und Publius Cipius Polybius', *Bonner Jahrbücher* 185: 215–242.

La Roncière, C.-M. de (1992). 'La foi du marchand: Florence, XIVe–milieu XVe siècles', in *Le marchand au Moyen Âge*. Nantes, 237–250.

Laes, C. (2008). 'Child Slaves at Work in Roman Antiquity', *Ancient society* 38: 235–283.

Laes, C. (2011). *Children in the Roman Empire: Outsiders Within*. Cambridge.

LaFaurie, J. (1972). 'Familia monetaria', *Bulletin de la Société Française de Numismatique* 27: 267–271.

Lafer, R. (2001). Omnes collegiati, 'concurrite'!: *Brandbekämpfung im Imperium Romanum*. Frankfurt-am-Main and New York.

Lancaster, L. (2002). 'The Organization of Construction for the Superstructure of the Colosseum', *Mitteilungen des Deutschen Archaeologischen Instituts, Römische Abteilung* 109: 361–374.

Lancaster, L. (2005). *Concrete Vaulted Construction in Imperial Rome: Innovations in Context*. Cambridge.

Lancaster, L. (2008). 'Roman Engineering and Construction', in J.P. Oleson (ed.), *The Oxford Handbook of Engineering and Technology in the Classical World*. Oxford, 256–284.

Lanciani, R. (1897). *The Ruins and Excavations of Ancient Rome*. London.

Lancy, D.F. (2012). '"First You Must Master Pain": the Nature and Purpose of Apprenticeship', *Anthropology of Work Review* 33: 113–126.

Lane, J. (1996). *Apprenticeship in England, 1600–1914*. Boulder, CO.

Lasserre, J.-M. and Griffe, M. (1996). 'Le moissonneur de Mactar', *Vita Latina* 143: 2–10.

Laubenheimer, F. (1988). 'Une nécropole de nourrissons gallo-romains', *Société d'Éditions Scientifiques* 208: 402–403.

Laubenheimer, F. (2001). 'L'atelier de Sallèles d'Aude et son évolution dans le temps', in F. Laubenheimer (ed.), *20 Ans de Recherches à Sallèles d'Aude*, Paris, 11–24.

Laubry, N. (2012). '*Ob sepulturam*: associations et funérailles en Narbonnaise et dans les Trois Gaules sous le Haut-Empire', in M. Dondin-Payre and N. Tran (eds.). Collegia: *le phénomène associatif dans l'Occident romain*. Bordeaux, 103–133.

Laurence, R. (2007). *Roman Pompeii: Space and Society*. London and New York. [first edition 1994]

Laurence, R. and Wallace-Hadrill, A. (1997). *Domestic Space in the Roman World: Pompeii and Beyond* (Journal of Roman Archaeology Supplementary series, no. 22). Portsmouth.

Lavan, L., Özgenel, L., and Sarantis, A. (2007). *Housing in Late Antiquity: from Palaces to Shops*. Leiden.

Lawless, G. (1987). *Augustine of Hippo and His Monastic Rule*. Oxford.

Lawrence, C.H. (2001). *Medieval Monasticism: Forms of Religious Life in Western Europe in the Middle Ages*. Harlow. [first edition 1984]

Le Gall, J. (1971). 'Rome ville des fainéants?', *Revue des Études Latines* 49: 266–277.

Le Rider, G. (2007). *Alexander the Great: Coinage, Finances, and Policy* (translated by W.E. Higgins) (Memoirs of the American Philosophical Society 261). Philadelphia.

Leach, E.W. (2004). *The Social Life of Painting in Ancient Rome and on the Bay of Naples*. Cambridge and New York.

Lee, E. (2006). *Habitatores in Urbe: The Population of Renaissance Rome*. Rome.

Leiwo, M. (1997). 'Religion, or Other Reasons? Private Associations in Athens', in J. Frösen (ed.), *Early Hellenistic Athens: Symptoms of a Change*. Helsinki, 103–117.

Lenski, N.E. (2002). *Failure of Empire: Valens and the Roman State in the Fourth Century A.D.* Berkeley, Los Angeles.

Leroi-Gourhan, A. (1993). *Gesture and Speech*. Cambridge, M.A.

Levick, B.M. (1965). 'Two Inscriptions from Pisidian Antioch', *Anatolian studies* 15: 53–10.

Lewis, N. and Reinhold, M. (1990). *Roman Civilization: the Empire* (*Volume* 2). 3rd ed. New York.

Li, Y., Pickles A., and Savage, M. (2005). 'Social Capital and Social Trust in Britain,' *European Sociological Review* 21: 109–123.

Li, Y., Savage, M., and Pickles, A. (2003). 'Social Capital and Social Exclusion in England and Wales (1972–1999)', *The British Journal of Sociology* 54: 497–526.

Liebescheutz, W. (2007). 'Was There a Crisis of the Third Century?', in O. Hekster, G. de Kleijn, and D. Slootjes (eds.), *Crisis and the Roman Empire: Proceedings of the Seventh Workshop of the International Network Impact of Empire (Nijmegen, June 20–24, 2006)*. Leiden, 11–22.

Lin, N. (2001). 'Building a Network Theory of Social Capital', in N. Lin, K.S. Cook and R.S. Burt, *Social Capital: Theory and Research*. New York, 3–29.

Linden, M. van der and Lucassen, J. (1999). Prolegomena for a global labour history. Amsterdam.

Linden, M. van der and Lucassen, J. (2001). *Work Incentives in Historical Perspective. Preliminary Remarks* (IISH-Research Papers) Amsterdam.

Lipps, J. (2011). *Die Basilica Aemilia am Forum Romanum: der kaiserzeitliche Bau und Ornamentik*. Wiesbaden.

Lis, C. and Soly, H. (2012). *Worthy Efforts: Attitudes to Work and Workers in Pre-Industrial Europe*. Leiden.

Littlewood, R.J. (2006). *A Commentary on Ovid's Fasti, Book 6*. Oxford.

Liu, J. (2005). 'Local Governments and *Collegia*: A New Appraisal of the Evidence', in J.-J. Aubert and Z. Várhelyi (eds.), *A Tall Order: Imperialism, Law, Religion, and Society in the Ancient World (Essays in Honor of William V. Harris)* (Beiträge zur Altertumskunde 216). Munich, 279–310.

Liu, J. (2008a). 'Pompeii and *Collegia*: a New Appraisal of the Evidence', *Ancient History Bulletin* 22: 53–69.

Liu, J. (2008b). 'The Economy of Endowments: The Case of Roman Associations', in K. Verboven, K. Vandorpe, and V. Chankowski-Sable (eds.), 'Pistoi dia tèn technèn'. *Bankers, loans and archives in the Ancient World. Studies in honour of Raymond Bogaert* (Studia Hellenistica 44). Leuven, 231–256.

Liu, J. (2009). Collegia Centonariorum*: The Guild of Textile Dealers in the Roman West* (Columbia Studies in the Classical Tradition 34). Leiden and Boston.

Lo Cascio, E. (2002). 'Ancora sugli « Ostia's services to Rome »: collegi e corporazioni annonarie a Ostia', *Mélanges de l'École française de Rome. Antiquité* 114: 87–110.

Lo Cascio, E. (2007). 'The Early Roman Empire: The State and the Economy', in W. Scheidel, R.P. Saller, I.M. Morris (eds.) *The Cambridge Economic History of the Greco-Roman World*. Cambridge, 619–647.

Lo Cascio, E. (2008). '*Vici, regiones* e forme di interazione sociale nella Roman imperiale', in M. Royo, E. Huvert, and A. Bérenger (eds.), *'Rome des quartiers': des* vici *aux rioni. Cadres institutionnels, pratiques sociales, et requalifications entre Antiquité et époque modern*. Paris, 64–76.

Lo Cascio, E. (2009). '*Obaerarii* (*obaerati*): la nozione della dipendenza in Varrone', in *Crescita e declino: studi di storia dell'economia romana*. Roma, 71–89.

Lo Cascio, E. (2016). 'The Impact of Migration on the Demographic Profile of the City of Rome: A Reassessment', in L. de Ligt and L.E. Tacoma (eds.), *Migration and Mobility in the Early Roman Empire*. Leiden, 23–32.

Lo Cascio, E. and Malanima, P. (2009). 'GDP in Pre-Modern Agrarian Economies (1–1820 AD). A Revision of the Estimates', *Rivista di Storia Economica* 25: 391–419.

Loewe, M. (1968). *Everyday Life in Early Imperial China During the Han Period*. London.

Long, P.O. (2011). *Artisan/Practitioners and the Rise of the New Sciences, 1400–1600*. Corvallis.

Loomis, W.T. (1998). *Wages, Welfare Costs, and Inflation in Classical Athens*. Ann Arbor.

López Barja de Quiroga, P. (1995). 'Freedmen Social Mobility in Roman Italy', *Historia* 44: 326–348.

Lopez, R.S. (1950). 'Continuità e adattamento nel medio evo: un millennio di storia delle associazioni di monetieri nell'Europa meridionale', in *Studi in Onore di Gino Luzzatto* 2. Milan, 74–117.

Lopez, R.S. (1953). 'An Aristocracy of Money in the Early Middle Ages', *Speculum* 28: 1–43.

Lós, A. (1996). 'Les fils d'affranchis dans l'«Ordo Pompeianus»', in M. Cébeillac Gervasoni (ed.), *Les élites municipales de l'Italie péninsulaire des Gracques à Néron: actes de la table ronde de Clermont-Ferrand (28–30 novembre 1991)*. Rome, 145–152.

Lott, J.B. (2004). *The Neighbourhoods of Augustan Rome*. Cambridge.

Louis, P. (1927). *Ancient Rome at Work. An Economic History of Rome from the Origins to the Empire*. London.

Lucassen, J., de Moor, T., and van Zanden, J.L. (2008). *The Return of the Guilds*. Cambridge.

Lugli, G. (1957). *La tecnica edilizia romana: con particolare riguardo a Roma e Lazio*. 2 vols. Rome.

Lutz, C.E. (ed.) (1947). *Musonius Rufus: 'The Roman Socrates'* (Yale Classical Studies 10). New Haven.

MacCormack, S. (2001). 'The Virtue of Work: An Augustinian Transformation', *Antiquité Tardive* 9: 219–237.

MacDonald, W. (1982). *The Architecture of the Roman Empire*. New Haven.

Mackensen, M. (2005). *Simitthus III: Militärlager oder Marmorwerkstätten*. Mainz am Rhein.

MacMullen, R. (1959). 'Roman Imperial Building in the Provinces', *Harvard Studies in Classical Philology* 64: 207–35.

MacMullen, R. (1963). 'A Note on Roman Strikes', *Classical Journal* 58: 269–271.

MacMullen, R. (1966). *Enemies of the Roman Order: Treason, Unrest, and Alienation in the Empire*. Cambridge and London.

MacMullen, R. (1974). *Roman Social Relations. 50 BC to AD 284*. New Haven.

Manders, E. (2002). *Coining Images of Power: Patterns in the Representation of Roman Emperors on Imperial Coinage, A.D. 193–284*. Leiden.

Marchant, E.C. and Todd, O.J. (eds. and transl.), Henderson, J. (rev.), (2013). *Xenophon: Memorabilia and Oeconomicus* (Loeb Classical Library 168). London.

Marco, L. and Noumen, R. (eds. 2008). *Benedetto Raguso Cotrugli: Traité de la marchandise et du parfait marchand*. Saint-Denis.

Marcone, A. (ed.) (2016a). *Storia del lavoro in Italia. L'età Romana. Liberi, semiliberi e schiavi in una società moderna*. Roma.

Marcone, A. (2016b). 'La storia degli studi', in A. Marcone, *Storia del lavoro in Italia. L'età Romana. Liberi, semiliberi e schiavi in una società moderna*. Roma, 17–34.

Marcone, A. (2016c). 'La tecnologia antica: limiti ed effetti sulle attività lavorative', in A. Marcone, *Storia del lavoro in Italia. L'età Romana. Liberi, semiliberi e schiavi in una società moderna*. Roma, 131–148.

Maresch, K. (1995). *Bronze und Silber. Papyrologische Beiträge zur Geschichte der Währung im ptolemäischen und römischen Ägypten bis zum 2. Jahrhundert n. Chr.* Opladen.

Marett, V. (1989). *Immigrants Settling in the City*. Leicester.

Marichal, R. (1988). *Les Graffites de La Graufesenque* (Gallia Supplement 47). Paris.

Martin, D.B. (2003). 'Slave Families and Slaves in Families', in D.L. Balch and C. Osiek (eds.). *Early Christian families in Context: an Interdisciplinary Dialogue*. Grand Rapids, MI and Cambridge (UK), 207–230.

Martin, J.J. (2004). *Myths of Renaissance Individualism*. Basingstoke.

Martin, S.D. (1989). *The Roman Jurists and the Organization of Private Building in the Late Republic and Early Empire* (Collection Latomus 204). Brussels.

Marzano, A. (2013). *Harvesting the Sea: The Exploitation of Marine Resources in the Roman Mediterranean*, (Oxford Studies on the Roman Economy 5). Oxford.

Maschke, E. (1964). 'Das Berufsbewusstsein des mittelalterlichen Fernkaufmanns', in P. Wilpert and W.P. Eckert (eds.), *Beiträge zum Berufsbewusstsein des mittelalterlichen Menschen* (Miscellanea Medievalia 3). Berlin, 177–216.

Mayer, E. (2012). *The Ancient Middle Classes: Urban Life and Aesthetics in the Roman Empire, 100 BCE–250 CE*. Cambridge, MA.

McCormick, M. (2001). *Origins of the European Economy: Communications and Commerce, A.D. 300–900*. Cambridge.

McCrindle, J.W. (1897). *The Christian Topography of Cosmas, an Egyptian Monk*. London.

McKeown, N. (2007). *The Invention of Ancient Slavery*, London.

Meadows, A. and Williams, J. (2001). 'Moneta and Monuments: Coinage and Politics in Republican Rome', *Journal of Roman Studies* 91: 27–49.

Meier, C. (2003). 'Griechische Arbeitsauffassungen in archaischer und klassischer Zeit: Praxis, Ideologie, Philosophie, Weiterer Zusammenhang', in M. Bierwisch (ed.), *Die Rolle der Arbeit in verschiedenen Epochen und Kulturen*. Berlin, 19–76.

Meiggs, R. (1997). *Roman Ostia*. Oxford. [first edition 1960, second edition 1973]

Meijlink, B. (1999). 'Molino I, xiii, 4', in J.T. Bakker (ed.), *The Mills-Bakeries of Ostia: Description and Interpretation*. Amsterdam, 61–79.

Mellor, I. (2005). 'Space, Society and the Textile Mill', *Industrial Archaeology Review* 27: 49–56.

Mennella, G. and Apicella, G. (2000). *Le corporazioni professionali nell'Italia romana: un aggiornamento al Waltzing*. Napoli.

Merola, G.D. (2016). 'Le attività commerciali', in A. Marcone (ed.), *Storia del lavoro in Italia. L'età Romana. Liberi, semiliberi e schiavi in una società moderna*. Roma, 304–340.

Metcalf, W.E. (2006). 'Roman Imperial Numismatics', in D.S. Potter (ed.), *A Companion to the Roman Empire*. West Sussex, 35–44.

Metzger Habel, D. (2013). *When All Rome was Under Construction: The Building Process in Baroque Rome*. State College, PA.

Migheli, M. (2012). 'Assessing Trust Through Social Capital? A Possible Experimental Answer', *American Journal of Economics and Sociology* 71: 298–327.

Milis, L.J.R. (1992). *Angelic Monks and Earthly Men: Monasticism and its Meaning to Medieval Society*. Woodbridge.

Millar, F. (1983). 'Empire and City, Augustus to Julian: Obligations, Excuses and Status', *Journal of Roman Studies* 73: 76–96.

Millar, F. (1984). 'Condemnation to Hard Labour in the Roman Empire, from the Julio-Claudians to Constantine', *Papers of the British School at Rome* 54: 124–147.

Miller, J.I. and Taylor-Mitchell, L. (2010). 'To Honor God and Enrich Florence in Things Spiritual and Temporal: Piety, Commerce, and Art in the Humiliati Order', in J. Vitullo and D. Wolfthal (eds.), *Money, Morality, and Culture in Late Medieval and Early Modern Europe*. Aldershot, 129–154.

Minaud, G. (2005). *La comptabilité à Rome: Essai d'histoire économique sur la pensée comptable commerciale et privée dans le monde antique romain*. Lausanne.

Minns, C. and P. Wallis (2013). 'The Price of Human Capital in a Pre-Industrial Economy: Premiums and Apprenticeship Contracts in 18th Century England'. *Explorations in Economic History* 50: 335–350.

Mitchell, S. (1983). 'Imperial Building in the Eastern Roman Provinces', *Harvard Studies in Classical Philology* 91: 333–365.

Mitchell, S. (1993). *Anatolia: Land, Men, and Gods in Asia Minor*. Vol. 1*: the Celts and the Impact of Roman Rule*. Oxford.

Moeller, W.O. (1970). 'The Riot of A.D. 59 at Pompeii', *Historia* 19: 84–95.

Moll-Murata, C. (2008). 'Chinese Guilds from the Seventeenth to the Twentieth Centuries: An Overview', *International Review for Social History* (Supplement S16) 53: 213–247.

Mommsen, T. (1887). 'Römische Münzpächterinschriften,' *Zeitschrift für Numismatik* 14: 36–39.

Monson, A. (2005). 'Private Associations in the Ptolemaic Fayyum: the Evidence of Demotic Accounts', *Papyrologica Lupiensia* 14: 179–196.

Monson, A. (2006). 'The Ethics and Economics of Ptolemaic Religious Associations', *Ancient Society* 36: 221–238.

Monteix, N. (2011). *Les lieux de métier: boutiques et ateliers d'Herculanum*. Rome.

Monteix, N. (2013) 'Espace commercial et puissance publique à Pompéi', in A. Dardenay and E. Rosso (eds.), *Dialogues entre sphère publique et sphère privée dans l'espace de la cité romaine. Vecteurs, acteurs, significations*. Paris, 161–184.

Monteix, N. (2013). 'The Apple of Discord: Fleece-Washing in Pompeii's Textile Economy', *Journal of Roman Archaeology* 26: 79–88.

Monteix, N. (2016). 'Contextualizing the Operational Sequence: Pompeian Bakeries as a Case-Study', in A. Wilson and M. Flohr (eds.), *Urban Craftsmen and Traders in the Roman World*. Oxford, 153–180.

Monteix, N. and Tran, N. (2011). *Les savoirs professionnels des gens de métier. Etudes sur le monde du travail dans les sociétés urbaines de l'empire romain*. Naples.

Morabito, M. (1981). *Les réalités de l'esclavage d'après le* Digeste. Paris.

Morandi, M. (2010). 'Neue Wege zur Heiligkeit: Homobonus von Cremona', in A. Wieczorek, B. Schneidmüller and S. Weinfurter (eds.), *Die Staufer und Italien. Drei Innovationsregionen im Mittelalterlichen Europa*, vol. 1. Darmstadt, 367–372.

Morel, J.-P. (1989). 'L'artigiano', in A. Giardina (ed.), *L'uomo romano*. Rome, 233–269.

Moretti, L. (1958). 'Sulle *stationes municipiorum* del foro Romano', *Athenaeum* n.s. 36: 106–116.

Morley, N. (2011). 'Cities and Economic Development in the Roman Empire', in A.K. Bowman and A.I. Wilson (eds.), *Settlement, Urbanization, and Population* (Oxford Studies on the Roman Economy). Oxford, 143–160.

Morrisson, C. (2002). 'Byzantine Money: Its Production and Circulation,' in A.E. Laiou (ed.), *The Economic History of Byzantium: From the Seventh Through the Fifteenth Century: Volume III*. Dumbarton Oaks, 909–966.

Morrisson, C. and Cheynet, J.-C. (2002). 'Prices and Wages in the Byzantine World' in A. Laiou (ed.) *The Economic History of Byzantium: From the Seventh through the Fifteenth Century*. Washington, DC, 807–870.

Mossé, C. (1966). Le travail en Grèce et à Rome (Que sais-je? 1240). Paris.

Mouritsen, H. (1988). *Elections, Magistrates and Municipal Elite. Studies in Pompeian Epigraphy* (Analecta Romana Instituti Danici. Supplementa 15). Roma.

Mouritsen, H. (1999). 'Electoral Campaigning in Pompeii: a Reconsideration', *Athenaeum* 87: 515–523.

Mouritsen, H. (2001a). *Plebs and Politics in the Late Roman Republic*. Cambridge and New York.

Mouritsen, H. (2001b). 'Roman Freedmen and the Urban Economy: Pompeii in the First Century AD', in F. Senatore (ed.), *Pompei tra Sorrento e Sarno: Atti del terzo e quarto ciclo di conferenze di geologia, storia e archeologia, Pompei, gennaio 1999–maggio 2000*. Napoli, 1–27.

Mouritsen, H. (2005). 'Freedmen and Decurions: Epitaphs and Social History in Imperial Italy', *Journal of Roman Studies* 95: 38–63.

Mouritsen, H. (2011). *The Freedman in the Roman World*. Cambridge.

Mrozek, S. (1975). *Prix et rémunération dans l'occident romain (31 av.n.è.–250 de n.è.)*. Gdańsk.

Mrozek, S. (1989). *Lohnarbeit im klassischen Altertum: ein Beitrag zur Sozial- und Wirtschaftsgeschichte*. Bonn.

Mukherjee, A. and D. Ray. (1995). 'Labor Tying', *Journal of Development Economics* 47: 207–239.

Munshi, K. (2003). 'Identification of Network Effects: Mexican Migrants in the US Labour Market', *Quarterly Journal of Economics* 118: 549–597.

Nani, T. (1943–1944). '*Threptoi*', *Epigraphica* 5–6: 45–84.

Ndoye, M. (2010). *Groupes sociaux et idéologie du travail dans les mondes homérique et hésiodique*. Besançon.

Nelson, J.K. and Zeckhauser, R.J. (eds.), (2008). *The Patron's Payoff: Conspicuous Commissions in Italian Renaissance Art*. Princeton.

Netzer, E. (1990). 'Architecture in Palestina prior to and during the days of Herod the Great', in *Akten des XIII Internationalen Kongresses für Klassische Archeologie*. Mainz, 37–50.

Newbery, J. (2013). 'Space of Discipline and Governmentality: The Singer Sewing Machine Factory, Clydebank, in the Twentieth Century', *Scottish Geographical Journal* 129: 15–35.

Nicolet, C. (1988). *Rendre à César. Economie et société dans la Rome antique*. Paris.

Noethlichs, K.L. (2007). 'Edictum [3] Edictum Diocletiani', *Brill's New Pauly Vol. 2. Dem–Ius*, Brill Online 2016, http: //referenceworks.brillonline.com/entries/brill-s-new-pauly/edictum-e326230 (accessed 01-04-2016).

Noreña, C.F. (2011). *Imperial Ideals in the Roman West: Representation, Circulation, Power*. Cambridge.

Norman, A.F. (1958). 'Gradations in Later Municipal Society', *Journal of Roman Studies* 48: 79–85.

Nörr, D. (1965). 'Zur sozialen und rechtlichen Bewertung der freien Arbeit in Rom', *Zeitschrift der Savigny-Stiftung für Rechtsgeschichte. Romanistische Abteilung* 82: 67–105.

North, D.C. (2005). *Understanding the Process of Economic Change*. Princeton.

Noy, D. (2000). *Foreigners at Rome: Citizens and Strangers*. London.

Oexle, O.G. (1994). 'Die Statik ist ein Grundzug des mittelalterlichen Bewusstseins. Die Wahrnehmung sozialen Wandels im Denken des Mittelalters und das Problem ihrer Deutung', in J. Miethke and K. Schreiner (eds.), *Sozialer Wandel im Mittelalter. Wahrnehmungsformen, Erklärungsmuster, Regelungsmechanismen*. Sigmaringen, 45–70.

Ogden, D. (2001). *Greek and Roman Necromancy*. Princeton.

Ogilvie, S. (2004). 'Guilds, Efficiency and Social Capital: Evidence from German Proto-Industry', *Economic History Review* 57: 286–333.

Ogilvie, S. (2007). '"Whatever Is, Is Right"? Economic Institutions in Pre-Industrial Europe', *Economic History Review* 60: 649–684.

Ogilvie, S. (2008). 'Rehabilitating the Guilds: A Reply', *Economic History Review* 61: 175–82.

Ogilvie, S. (2011). *Institutions and European Trade: Merchant Guilds, 1000–1800*, Cambridge.

Oleson, J.P. (2008). *Oxford Handbook of Engineering and Technology in the Classical World.* Oxford and New York.

Oliver, J.H. (1953). 'The Ruling Power: A Study of the Roman Empire in the Second Century after Christ through the Roman Oration of Aelius Aristides', *Transactions of the American Philosophical Society* 43: 871–1003.

Origo, I. (1992). *The Merchant of Prato: Francesco di Marco Datini.* London. [first edition 1957]

Osborne, R. (2006). 'Introduction: Roman Poverty in Context', in E.M. Atkins and R. Osborne (eds.), *Poverty in the Roman World.* Cambridge, 1–20.

Ovitt Jr., G. (1986). 'The Cultural Context of Western Technology: Early Christian Attitudes toward Manual Labor', *Technology and Culture* 27: 477–500.

Ovitt Jr., G. (1987). *The Restoration of Perfection: Labor and Technology in Medieval Culture.* New Brunswick and London.

Özmucur, S. and Pamuk, S. (2002). 'Real Wages and Standards of Living in the Ottoman Empire, 1489–1914', *Journal of Economic History* 62: 293–321.

Packer, J. (1971). *The Insulae of Imperial Ostia.* Rome.

Palmer, R.E.A. (1997). *Rome and Carthage at Peace.* Stuttgart.

Panciera, S. (ed.) (1987). *La collezione epigrafica dei musei capitolini. Inediti, revisioni, contributi al riordino*, Rome.

Paolini, L. (1991). 'Le Umiliate al lavoro. Appunti fra storiografa e storia', *Bollettino dell'Istituto storico italiano per il medioevo e archivio muratoriano* 97: 229–265.

Papadopoulos, S. (1995). 'L'organisation de l'espace dans deux ateliers de potiers traditionnels de Thasos', *Bulletin de Correspondance Hellénique* 119: 591–606.

Papagianni, E. (2002). 'Byzantine Legislation on Economic Activity Relative to Social Class', in A.E. Laiou (ed.), *The Economic History of Byzantium: From the Seventh through the Fifteenth Century.* Washington, DC, 1083–1094.

Parassoglou, G.M. (1987). 'A Lease of Fishing Rights', *Aegyptus* 67: 89–93.

Parkin, A. (2006). '"You Do Him no Service". An Exploration of Pagan Almsgiving', in E.M. Atkins and R. Osborne (eds.), *Poverty in the Roman World.* Cambridge, 60–82.

Patsch, C. (1909). 'Archäologisch-epigraphische Untersuchungen zur Geschichte der römischen Provinz Dalmatien. VII', *Wissenschaftliche mitteilungen aus Bosnien und der Hercegovina* 11: 104–183.

Patterson, J.R. (1992). 'Patronage, *Collegia* and Burial in Imperial Rome', in S. Bassett (ed.), *Death in Towns: Urban Responses to the Dying and the Dead, 100–1600.* Leicester, 15–27.

Patterson, J.R. (1994). 'The *Collegia* and the Transformation of the Towns of Italy in the Second Century AD', in *L'Italie d'Auguste à Dioclétien* (*Actes du colloque international de Rome* (*25–28 mars 1992*)) (Collection de l'École française de Rome 198). Rome, 227–238.

Patterson, J.R. (2006). *Landscapes and Cities: Rural Settlement and Civic Transformation in Early Imperial Italy*. Oxford and New York.

Patterson, O. (1982). *Slavery and Social Death: a Comparative Study*. Cambridge, MA.

Pavis d'Escurac, H. (1988). '*Origo* et residence dans le monde du commerce sous le Haut-Empire', *Ktema* 13: 57–68.

Peachin, M. (1983). 'Johannes Malalas and the Moneyers' Revolt', in C. Deroux (ed.), *Studies in Latin Literature and Roman History III*. Brussels, 325–335.

Peachin, M. (1986). 'Procurator Monetae', *Numismatic Chronicle* 146: 94–106.

Peachin, M. (1987). '"*Praepositus*" or "*Procurator*"?', *Historia* 36: 248–249.

Peacock, D.P.S. (1982). *Pottery in the Roman World: an Ethnoarchaeological Approach*. New York.

Pearl, O. (1985). 'Apprentice Contract', *Bulletin of the Amercian Society of Papyrologists* 22: 255–259.

Pearse, J.L.L. (1974). *The Organization of Roman Building During the Late Republic and Early Empire*, Dissertation DPhil, University of Cambridge.

Pearse, L. (1976). 'Three *Alba* of the *Collegium Fabrum Tignariorum* of Rome', *Bullettino della Commissione Archeologica Comunale di Roma* 85: 163–176.

Peña, J.T. and McCallum, M. (2009). 'The Production and Distribution of Pottery at Pompeii: a Review of the Evidence Part 1, Production', *American Journal of Archaeology* 113: 57–79.

Perring, D. (2002). *The Roman House in Britain*. New York.

Perry, J.S. (2011). 'Organized Societies: *Collegia*', in M. Peachin (ed.), *The Oxford Handbook of Social Relations in the Roman World*. Oxford, 499–515.

Peruzzi, E. (1966). 'La lamina dei cuochi falischi', *Atti de Memorie dell'Accademia toscana di Scienze Lettere e Arti "La Colombaria"* 31: 113–162.

Petersen, L.H. (2006). *The Freedman in Roman Art and Art History*. Cambridge.

Petrikovits, H. von. (1981). 'Die Spezialisierung des römischen Handwerks', in H. Jankuhn, W. Janssen, R. Schmidt-Wiegand, and H. Tiefenbach (eds.), *Das Handwerk in Vor- und Fruhgeschichtlicher Zeit*. Göttingen, 63–132.

Phelps Brown, H. and Hopkins, S.V. (1959). 'Builders' Wage-Rates, Prices, and Population: Some Further Evidence', *Economica* 26: 18–38.

Phelps Brown, H. and Hopkins, S.V. (1981). *A Perspective of Wages and Prices*. London.

Piccolo, M. (2003). 'Osservazioni ad alcuni papiri dell'archivio di Tryphon', *Aegyptus* 83: 197–213.

Pichonnaz, P. (2002). 'Quelques remarques sur la *relocatio tacita*'. *Revue Internationale des droits de l'antiquité* 49: 147–163.

Pickett, J. (forthcoming). 'Beyond Churches: Energetics and the Economics of Construction in the Byzantine World', in W. Caraher and M. Kourelis (eds.), *Byzantine Archaeology in Method and Theory*. Cambridge.

Pietrogrande, A. (1976). *Le Fulloniche*. Rome.

Pirson, F. (1999). *Mietwohnungen in Pompeji und Herculaneum*. Munich.

Pleket, H.W. (1988). 'Labour and Unemployment in the Roman Empire. Some Preliminary Remarks', in I. Weiler and H. Grassl (eds.), *Soziale Randgruppen und Aussenseiter im Altertum: Referate vom Symposion 'Soziale Randgruppen und Antike Sozialpolitik' in Graz (21. bis 23. September 1987)*. Graz, 267–276.

Pleket, H.W. (1990). 'Wirtschaft und Gesellschaft des Imperium Romanum. 2. Wirtschaft', in W. Fischer, J.A. van Houtte, and H. Kellenbenz (eds.), *Handbuch der europäischen Wirtschafts- und Sozialgeschichte*, vol. 1: *Europäische Wirtschafts- und Sozialgeschichte in der Römischen Kaiserzeit*. Stuttgart, 25–160.

Pleket, H.W. (2008). 'Berufsvereine im kaiserzeitlichen Kleinasien: Geselligkeit oder Zünfte?', in P. Mauritsch, W. Petermandl, R. Rollinger, and C. Ulf (eds.), *Antike Lebenswelten. Konstanz—Wandel—Wirkungsmacht. Feschrift für Ingomar Weiler zum 70. Geburtstag*. Wiesbaden, 533–544.

Poblome, J. (2004). 'Comparing Ordinary Craft Production: Textile and Pottery Production in Roman Asia Minor', *Journal of the Economic and Social History of the Orient* 47: 491–506.

Poblome, J., Bournegru, O., Degryse, P., Viaene, W., Waelkens, M., and Erdemgil, S. (2001). 'The Sigillata Manufactories of Pergamon and Sagalassos', *Journal of Roman Archaeology* 14: 143–165.

Poland, F. (1909). *Geschichte des griechischen Vereinswesens*. Leipzig.

Porena, P. (2016). 'Il lavoro infantile', in A. Marcone, *Storia del lavoro in Italia. L'età Romana. Liberi, semiliberi e schiavi in una società moderna*. Roma, 663–685.

Pomeranz, K. (2000). *The Great Divergence: China, Europe, and the Making of the Modern World Economy*. Princeton.

Polichetti, A. (2002). 'Costo del lavoro e potere d'acquisto nell'editto dei prezzi', in L. De Blois, and J. Rich (eds.), *The Transformation of Economic Life under the Roman Empire: Proceedings of the Second Workshop of the International Network Impact of Empire (Roman Empire, c. 200 BC–AD 476), Nottingham, July 4–7, 2001*. Leiden, 218–231.

Pomeroy, A.J. (1991). 'Status and Status-Concern in the Greco-Roman Dreambooks', *Ancient Society* 22: 51–74.

Poros, M.V. (2001). 'The Role of Migrant Networks in Linking Labour Markets: the Case of Asian Indian Migration to New York and London', *Global Networks* 1.3: 243–260.

Portes, A. (1998). 'Social Capital: Its Origins and Applications in Modern Sociology', *Annual Review of Sociology* 24: 1–24.

Potter, D. (2013). *Constantine the Emperor*. Oxford.

Purcell, N. (1983). 'The *Apparitores*. a Study in Social Mobility', *Papers of the British School at Rome* 51: 125–173.

Purcell, N. (1994). 'The City of Rome and the *Plebs Urbana* in the Late Republic', in J.A. Crook, A. Lintott, and B. Rawson (eds.), *Cambridge Ancient History 2nd ed. Vol IX. The Last Age of the Republic 146–43 BC.* Cambridge, 644–688.

Purcell, N. (1995). 'Eating Fish: the Paradoxes of Seafood', in J. Wilkins, D. Harvey, M. Dobson, and A. Davidson (eds.), *Food in Antiquity*. Exeter, 132–149.

Putnam, R. (1993). *Making Democracy Work: Civic Traditions in Modern Italy*. Princeton.

Putnam, R. (1997). 'The Prosperous Community: Social Capital and Public Life', *The American Prospect* 13: 35–42.

Putnam, R. (2000). *Bowling Alone: The Collapse and Revival of American Community*. New York.

Quimby, I.M.G. (1985). *Apprenticeship in Colonial Philadelphia*. New York.

Rainer, J.M. (1990). 'Bauen und Arbeit im klassischen römischen Recht', *Zeitschrift der Savigniy-Stiftung für Rechtsgeschichte, Romanistische Abteilung* 107: 376–381.

Rakob, F. (1983). '*Opus caementicium* und die Folgen', *Mitteilungen des Deutschen Archaeologischen Instituts, Römische Abteilung* 90: 359–372.

Ramin, M.J. and Veyne, P. (1981). 'Droit romain et société. Les hommes libres qui passent pour esclaves et l'esclavage volontaire', *Historia* 30: 472–497.

Rathbone, D.W. (1990). 'Village, Land and Population in Graeco-Roman Egypt', *Proceedings of the Cambridge Philological Society* 36: 103–142.

Rathbone, D.W. (1991). *Economic Rationalism and Rural Society in Third Century A.D. Egypt*. Cambridge.

Rathbone, D.W. (1997). 'Prices and Price Formation in Roman Egypt', in J. Andreau, P. Briant, R. Descat (eds.), *Économie antique: Prix et formation des prix dans les économies antiques.* Saint Bertrand de Comminges, 183–244.

Rathbone, D.W. (2007). 'Military Finance and Supply', in P. Sabin, H. Van Wees, and M. Whitby (eds.), *The Cambridge History of Greek and Roman Warfare II*. Cambridge, 158–176.

Rathbone, D.W. (2009). 'Earnings and Costs: Living Standards and the Roman Economy' (First to Third Centuries AD), in A. Bowman and A. Wilson (eds.), *Quantifying the Roman Economy: Methods and Problems* (Oxford Studies on the Roman Economy 1). Oxford, 299–326.

Rawson, B. (2003). *Children and Childhood in Roman Italy*. Oxford.

Rawson, E. (1987). '*Discrimina Ordinum*. The *Lex Julia Theatralis*', *Papers of the British School at Rome* 55: 83–114.

Ray, D. (1998). *Development Economics*. Princeton, N.J.

Reiss, A. (2000). *The Sunday Christ: Sabbatarianism in English Medieval Wall Painting*. Oxford.

Reith, R. (2003). 'Wage Forms, Wage Systems and Wage Conflicts in German Crafts During the Eighteenth and Earlier Nineteenth Centuries', in P. Scholliers and

L.D. Schwarz (eds.), *Experiencing Wages: Social and Cultural Aspects of Wage Forms in Europe Since 1500*. Oxford, 113–138.

Remesal Rodríguez, J. (1991). 'Sextus Iulius Possessor en la Bética', in J.M. Blázquez and S. Montero (eds.), *Alimenta: estudios en homenaje al Dr. Michel Ponsich*. Madrid, 281–295.

Ricci, C. (2005). Orbis in urbe. *Fenomeni migratori nella Roma imperiale*. Rome.

Rice, P. (1981). 'Evolution of Specialized Pottery Production: a Trial Model', *Current Anthropology* 22: 219–240.

Ricl, M. (2009). 'Legal and Social Status of *Threptoi* and Related Categories in Narrative and Documentary Sources', in H. Cotton, R.G. Hoyland, J.J. Price and D.J. Wasserstein (eds.), *From Hellenism to Islam: Cultural and Linguistic Change in the Roman near East*. Cambridge, 93–114.

Riße, M. (2001). *Volubilis. Eine römische Stadt in Marokko von der Frühzeit bis in die islamische Periode*. Mainz.

Robinson, D. (2005). 'Re-Thinking the Social Organization of Trade and Industry in First Century Ad Pompeii', in A. MacMahon and J. Price (eds.), *Roman Working Lives and Urban Living*. Oxford, 88–105.

Robinson, O.F. (1992). *Ancient Rome: City Planning and Administration*. London.

Rocco, M. (2016). 'Il mestiere di soldato', in A. Marcone (ed.), *Storia del lavoro in Italia. L'età Romana. Liberi, semiliberi e schiavi in una società moderna*. Roma, 543–580.

Rodríguez Almeida, E. (1984). *Il Monte Testaccio*. Rome.

Rofel, L. (1992). 'Rethinking Modernity: Space and Factory Discipline in China', *Cultural Anthropology* 7: 93–114.

Rohde, D. (2009). 'Der Piazzale delle Corporazioni in Ostia: wirtschaftliche Funktion und soziale Bedeutung', *Marburger Beiträge zur antiken Handels-, Wirtschafts- und Sozialgeschichte* 27: 31–61.

Rohde, D. (2012). *Zwischen Individuum und Stadtgemeinde: die Integration von* Collegia *in Hafenstädten* (Studien zur alten Geschichte 15). Mainz.

Rohmann, J. (1998). *Die Kapitelle des Trajanstempels von Pergamon*. Stuttgart.

Rorabaugh, W.J. (1986). *The Craft Apprentice: From Franklin to the Machine Age in America*. New York.

Rosser, G. (1997). 'Crafts, Guilds and the Negotiation of Work in the Medieval Town', *Past and Present* 154: 3–31.

Rostovtzeff, M. (1957). *Social and Economic History of the Roman Empire*, 2nd edition, revised by P.M. Fraser. Oxford.

Rothstein, B. (2005). *Social Traps and the Problem of Trust*. Cambridge.

Roueché, C.M. (1993). *Performers and Partisans at Aphrodisias in the Roman and Late Roman Periods* (Journal of Roman Studies Monographs 6). London.

Roueché, C.M. (2004). 'Aphrodisias in Late Antiquity: The Late Roman and Byzantine Inscriptions, revised second edition', http://insaph.kcl.ac.uk/ala2004/inscription/index.html (accessed 16-02-2013).

Rowlandson, J. (1998). *Women and Society in Greek and Roman Egypt: A Sourcebook.* Cambridge.

Royden, H.L. (1988). *The Magistrates of the Roman Professional* Collegia *in Italy from the First to the Third Century A.D.* Pisa.

Rubio Rivera, R. (1993). '*Collegium dendrophorum*: corporación profesional y cofradía metróaca', *Gerión* 11: 175–183.

Ruffing, K. (2008). *Die berufliche Spezialisierung in Handel und Handwerk.* 2 vols. Rahden.

Ruschenbusch, E. (1977). 'Diokletians Währungsreform vom 1.9.301', *Zeitschrift für Papyrologie und Epgraphik* 26: 193–210.

Sabatini, F. (2009). 'The Labour Market', in G.T. Svendsen and G.L.H. Svendsen (eds.), *Handbook of Social Capital: the Troika of Sociology, Political Science, and Economics.* Cheltenham and Northampton, MA, 272–286.

Saito, O. (2009). 'Land, Labour and Market Forces in Tokugawa Japan', *Continuity and Change* (special issue 01) 24: 169–196.

Salamito, J.-M. (1987). 'Les dendrophores dans l'empire chrétien. A propos du Code Théodosien XIV,8,1 et XVI,10,20,2', *Mélanges de l'École française de Rome. Antiquité* 99: 991–1019.

Salamito, J.-M. (1990). 'Les collèges de *fabri, centonarii* et *dendrophori* dans les villes de la Regio X à l'époque impériale', in *La città nell'Italia settentrionale in età romana: morfologie, strutture e funzionamento dei centri urbani delle Regiones X e XI.* Roma, 163–177.

Salamito, J.-M. (1996). 'De l'éloge des mains au respect des travailleurs: idées gréco-romaines et christianisme antique', in *La main.* Orléans, 51–75.

Saller, R.P. (1994). *Patriarchy, Property and Death in the Roman Family* (Cambridge Studies in Population, Economy, and Society in past Time 25). Cambridge and New York.

Saller, R.P. (2007). 'Household and Gender', in W. Scheidel, I. Morris and R.P. Saller (eds.), *The Cambridge Economic History of the Greco-Roman World.* Cambridge, 87–112.

Saller, R.P. (2012). 'Human Capital and Economic Growth', in W. Scheidel (ed.), *The Cambridge Companion to the Roman Economy.* Cambridge, 71–86.

Salvaterra, C. (2006). 'Labour and Identity in the Roman World. Italian Historiography during the Last Two Decades', in B. Waaldijk (ed.), *Professions and Social Identity: New European Historical Research on Work, Gender and Society*, Pisa, 15-8.

Salway, B. (2010). 'MANCIPIUM RUSTICUM SIVE VRBANVM: The Slave Chapter of Diocletian's Edict on Maximum Prices', in U. Roth (ed.), *By the Sweat of Your Brow. Roman Slavery in Its Socio-Economic Setting.* London, 61–74.

Samuelson, P.A. (1989) 'Ricardo was Right!' *Scandinavian Journal of Economics* 91: 47–62.

Sander, E. (1962). 'Der *Praefectus Fabrum* und die Legionsfabriken', *Bonner Jahrbücher des Rheinischen Landesmuseums in Bonn und Vereins von Altertumsfreunden im Rheinlande* 162: 139–161.

Sarnowsky, J. (1999). 'Das Thorner Patriziat und der Fernhandel', in N. Jörn, D. Kattinger, and H. Wernicke (eds.), *"Kopet uns werk by tyden": Beiträge zur hansischen und preussischen Geschichte: Walter Stark zum 75. Geburtstag*. Schwerin, 223–232.

Sauer, E.W., ed. (2004). *Archaeology and Ancient History: Breaking Down the Boundaries*. London.

Schaad, D. and Vernhet, A. (2007). 'Les données archéologiques de La Graufesenque', in D. Schaad (ed.), *La Graufesenque (Millau, Aveyron): Volume 1 Condatomagos une Agglomeration de Confluent en Territoire Rutène IIe s. a.C.–IIIe s. p. C.* Bordeaux, 61–218.

Schäfer, Ch. (1998). *Spitzenmanagement in Republik und Kaiserzeit: die Prokuratoren von Privatpersonen im Imperium Romanum vom 2. Jh. v.Chr. bis zum 3. Jh. n.Chr.* St. Katharinen.

Scheidel, W. (1996). 'Reflections on the Differential Valuation of Slaves in Diocletian's Price Edict and in the United States', *Münstersche Beiträge zur antiken Handelsgeschichte* 15: 67–79.

Scheidel, W. (2002a). 'The Hireling and the Slave: a Transatlantic Perspective', in P. Cartledge, E.E. Cohen, and L. Foxhall (eds.), *Money, Labour and Land: Approaches to the Economies of Ancient Greece*. London and New York, 175–184.

Scheidel, W. (2002b). 'A Model of Demographic and Economic Change in Roman Egypt After the Antonine Plague', *Journal of Roman Archaeology* 15: 97–114.

Scheidel, W. (2004). 'Human Mobility in Roman Italy I: the Free Population', *Journal of Roman Studies* 94: 1–26.

Scheidel, W. (2005a). 'Human Mobility in Roman Italy II: the Slave Population', *Journal of Roman Studies* 95: 64–80.

Scheidel, W. (2005b). 'Real Slave Prices and the Relative Cost of Slave Labor in the Greco-Roman World', *Ancient Society* 35: 1–17.

Scheidel, W. (2006). 'Stratification, Deprivation and Quality of Life', in M.E. Atkins and R. Osborne (eds.), *Poverty in the Roman World*. Cambridge, 42–54.

Scheidel, W. (2007). 'Demography', in W. Scheidel, I. Morris, and R. Saller (eds.), *The Cambridge Economic History of the Greco-Roman World*. Cambridge, 38–86.

Scheidel, W. (2008). 'The Comparative Economics of Slavery in the Greco-Roman World', in E.D. Lago and C. Katsari (eds.), *Slave Systems: Ancient and Modern*. Cambridge, 105–126.

Scheidel, W. (2009). 'New Ways of Studying Incomes in the Roman Economy', in A.K. Bowman and A.I. Wilson (eds.) *Quantifying the Roman Economy*. Oxford, 346–352.

Scheidel, W. (2010a). 'Economy and Quality of Life', in A. Barchiesi and W. Scheidel (eds.), *The Oxford Handbook of Roman Studies*. Oxford, 593–608.

Scheidel, W. (2010b). 'Real Wages in Early Economies: Evidence for Living Standards from 1800 BCE to 1300 CE', *Journal of the Economic and Social History of the Orient* 53: 425–462.

Scheidel, W. (2011). 'The Roman Slave Supply', in K.R. Bradley and P. Cartledge (eds.), *The Cambridge World History of Slavery*. Vol. 1, Cambridge, 286–310.

Scheidel, W. (ed.) (2012a). *The Cambridge Companion to the Roman Economy*. Cambridge.

Scheidel, W. (2012b). 'Slavery', in W. Scheidel (ed.), *The Cambridge Companion to the Roman Economy*. Cambridge, 89–113.

Scheidel, W. (2013). 'Explaining the Maritime Freight Charges in Diocletian's Prices Edict', *Journal Roman Archaeology* 26: 464–468.

Scheidel, W. (2014). 'Roman Real Wages in Context', in F. de Callataÿ (ed.), *Quantifying the Greco-Roman Economy and Beyond*. Bari, 209–218.

Scheidel, W. and Friesen, S.J. (2009). 'The Size of the Economy and the Distribution of Income in the Roman Empire'. *Journal of Roman Studies* 99: 61–91.

Scheidel, W., Morris, I. and Saller, R. (eds.) (2007). *The Cambridge Economic History of the Greco-Roman World*. Cambridge.

Scheller, B. (2004). *Memoria an der Zeitenwende. Die Stiftungen Jakobs Fugger des Reichen vor und während der Reformation, ca. 1505–1555*. Berlin.

Schiffer, M.B. (1987). *Formation Processes of the Archaeological Record*. Albuquerque.

Schmidt, H.-J. (1993). 'Städtekritik und Städtelob im 12. und 13. Jahrhundert', *Historische Zeitschrift* 257: 297–354.

Schmidt, V.M. (2008). 'Painters in Late Medieval and Early Renaissance Italy as Visual Mediators', in A. de Vries (ed.), *Cultural Mediators. Artists and Writers at the Crossroads of Tradition, Innovation and Reception in the Low Countries and Italy 1450–1650* (Groningen Studies in Cultural Change 31). Leuven 53–75.

Schmitt, J.-C. (2009). 'Individuation et saisie du monde', in P. Boucheron (ed.), *Histoire du monde au XVe siècle*, vol. 2: *Temps et devenirs du monde*. Paris, 644–647.

Schneider, H. (2007). 'Technology', in W. Scheidel, I. Morris, and R.P. Saller (eds.), *The Cambridge Economic History of the Greco-Roman World*. Cambridge and New York, 144–171.

Scholten, H. (2003). 'Die Bewertung körperlicher Arbeit in der Antike', *Ancient Society* 33: 1–22.

Schuler, Ch. (1998). *Ländliche Siedlungen und Gemeinden im hellenistischen und römischen Kleinasien*. Munich.

Schulz, K. (1992). *'Denn Sie Lieben die Freiheit so sehr'. Kommunale Aufstände und Entstehung des Europäischen Bürgertums in Hochmittelalter*. Darmstadt.

Schulz, K. (2010). *Handwerk, Zünfte und Gewerbe: Mittelalter und Neuzeit*. Darmstadt.

Schulz-Falkenthal, H. (1972). 'Zur politischen Aktivität der römischen Handwerkerkollegien', *Wissenschaftliche Zeitschrift der Martin-Luther-Universität Halle-Wittenberg. Gesellschafts- und sprachwissenschaftliche Reihe* 21: 79–99.

Schwarz, L.D. (1992). *London in the Age of Industrialisation: Entrepreneurs, Labour Force, and Living Conditions, 1700–1850* (Cambridge Studies in Population, Economy, and Society in past Time 19). Cambridge and New York.

Schwinden, L. (1989). 'Gallo-römisches Textilgewerbe nach Denkmälern aus Trier und dem Trevererland', *Trierer Zeitschrift* 52: 279–318.

Seidel, L. (1999). *Legends in Limestone: Lazarus, Gislebertus, and the Cathedral of Autun*. Chicago.

Seigne, J. (2006). 'Water-Powered Stone Saws in Late Antiquity. the Precondition for Industrialisation?' in G. Wiplinger (ed.), Cura Aquarum *in Ephesos*. Leiden: 383–390.

Sekedat, B. (2010). 'No Place like Stone? Assessing Social and Material Networks of Place at Quarries in Roman Anatolia', in A. Moore, G. Taylor, E. Harris, P. Girdwood and L. Shipley (eds.), *TRAC 2009: Proceedings of the Nineteenth Annual Theoretical Roman Archaeology Conference, Michigan and Southampton 2009*. Oxford, 23–30.

Sheppard, A. (1956). *Ceramics for the Archaeologist*. Washington DC.

Sheridan, J.A. (1998). *Columbia Papyri. IX: The Vestis Militaris Codex* (American studies in papyrology 39). Atlanta.

Shirley, E. (2001). *Building a Roman Legionary Fortress*. Stroud.

Sijpestein, P. (1964). Penthemeros-*Certificates in Graeco-Roman Egypt*. Leiden.

Silver, M. (2011). 'Contractual Slavery in the Roman Economy', *Ancient History Bulletin* 25: 73–132.

Simon, H.A. (1951). 'A Formal Theory of the Employment Relationship'. *Econometrica* 19: 293–305.

Singleton, J. (1989). 'Japanese Folkcraft Pottery Apprenticeship: Cultural Patterns of an Educational Institution', in M.W. Coy (ed.), *Apprenticeship: from Theory to Method and Back Again* (SUNY series in the anthropology of work). Albany, 13–30.

Sirks, A.J.B. (1989). '*Munera Publica* and Exemptions (*Vacatio, Excusatio* and *Immunitas*)', in M.J. Pelaez (ed.), *Studies in Roman Law and Legal History in Honour of Ramon D'Abadal I De Vinyals* (Annals of the Archive of 'Ferran Valls I Taberner's Library). Barcelona and Malaga, 79–111.

Sirks, A.J.B. (1991). *Food for Rome: the Legal Structure of the Transportation and Processing of Supplies for the Imperial Distributions in Rome and Constantinople*. Amsterdam.

Sirks, B. (1999). 'On the Emperor's Service. the *Corpus Pistorum* of Ostia and *Portus Uterque* from the Juridical Perspective', in J.T. Bakker (ed.), *The Mills-Bakeries of Ostia: Description and Interpretation*. Amsterdam, 102–109.

Skydsgaard, J.E. (1976). 'The Disintegration of the Roman Labour Market and the Clientele Theory', in K. Ascani (ed.), *Studia Romana in Honorem Petri Krarup Septuagenarii*. Odense, 44–48.

Skydsgaard, J.E. (1983). 'Public Building and Society at Ancient Rome', in K. De Fine Licht (ed.) *Città e architettura nella Roma imperiale*. Odense, 223–227.

Slater, W.J. (2000). 'The *Scholae* of Roman *Collegia*', *Journal of Roman Archaeology* 13: 493–497.

Smith, A. (1795). *An Inquiry into the Nature and Causes of the Wealth of Nations*. Fifth edition with additions. Dublin.

Smith, M.E. (1992). 'Braudel's Temporal Rhythms and Chronology Theory in Archaeology', in A.B. Knapp (ed.), *Archaeology, Annales, and Ethnohistory*. Cambridge, 23–34.

Smith, P.H. (2010). 'Why Write a Book? From Lived Experience to the Written Word in Early Modern Europe', *Bulletin of the German Historical Institute* 47: 25–50.

Smits, W. and Stromback, T. (2001). *The Economics of the Apprenticeship System*. Cheltenham, UK.

Soly, H. (1976). 'The "Betrayal" of the Sixteenth-Century Bourgeoisie: A Myth? Some Considerations on the Behaviour Pattern of the Merchants of Antwerp', *Acta Historiae Neerlandicae: Studies on the History of the Netherlands* 8: 31–49.

Sonenscher, M. (1989). *Work and Wages: Natural Law, Politics, and the Eighteenth-Century French Trades*. Cambridge and New York.

Sosin, J.D. (1999). 'Tyrian "*Stationarii*" at Puteoli', *Tyche* 14: 275–284.

Spanneut, M. (1957). *Le Stoïcisme des Pères de l'Eglise. De Clément de Rome à Clément d'Alexandrie*. Paris.

Štaerman, E.M. (1969). *Die Blütezeit der Sklavenwirtschaft in der römischen Republik*. Wiesbaden.

Štaerman, E.M. (1975). *La schiavitù nell'Italia imperiale: I–III secolo*. Roma.

Stedman Jones, G. (1984). *Outcast London: a Study in the Relationship Between Classes in Victorian Society*. New York.

Stein, J. (1995). 'Time, Space and Social Discipline: Factory Life in Cornwall, Ontario, 1867–1893', *Journal of Historical Geography* 21: 278–299.

Stöger, H. (2011). 'The Spatial Organization of the Movement Economy. The Analysis of Ostia's *Scholae*', in R. Laurence and D. Newsome (eds.), *Rome, Ostia, Pompeii. Movement and Space*. Oxford: 215–242.

Stone, D.L. (1998). 'Culture and Investment in the Rural Landscape: the North African "*Bonus Agricola*"', *Antiquités Africaines* 34: 103–113.

Stovel, K. and Shaw, L. (2012). 'Brokerage', *Annual Review of Sociology* 38: 139–158.

Strocka, V.M. (1991). *Casa del Labirinto: (VI, 11, 8–10)* (Haüser in Pompeji 4). München.

Stroud, R.S. (1974). 'An Athenian Law on Silver Coinage', *Hesperia* 43: 157–188.

Sullivan, L.M. (1989). 'Workers, Policy-Makers and Labor Ideals in Cistercian Legislation, 1134–1237', *Citeaux: Commentarii Cisterciensis* 40: 175–99.

Sunderland, D. (2007). *Social Capital, Trust and the Industrial Revolution 1780–1880*. London.

Szaivert, W. and Wolters, R. (2005). *Löhne, Preise, Werte: Quellen zur Römischen Geldwirtschaft*. Darmstadt.

Szilágyi, J. (1963). 'Prices and Wages in the Western Provinces of the Roman Empire', *Acta Antiqua Academiae Scientiarum Hungaricae* 11: 325–389.

Tacoma, L.E. (2014). 'Migrant Quarters in Rome', in S. Benoist and G. de Kleijn (eds.), *Integration in Rome and in the Roman World: Proceedings of the Tenth Workshop of the International Network Impact of Empire (Lille, June 23–25, 2011)* (Impact of Empire 17–. Leiden and Boston, 127–146).

Tacoma, L.E. (forthcoming a). 'The Labour Market', in A. Claridge and C. Holleran (eds.), *A Companion to the City of Rome*. Oxford.

Tacoma, L.E. (forthcoming b). 'Networks Networks Everywhere. Migration, Community Formation, and Integration in the City of Rome under the Principate'.

Tarpin, M. (2008). 'Les *vici* de Rome, entre sociabilité de voisinage et organisation administrative', in M. Royo, E. Huvert, and A. Bérenger (eds.), *'Rome des quartiers': des* vici *aux rioni. Cadres institutionnels, pratiques sociales, et requalifications entre Antiquité et époque modern*. Paris, 35–64.

Tasser, B. (2005). 'Die Vereine der « *Cisalpini* » und « *Transalpini* »: eine alpenumspannende Handelsgesellschaft?', in K. Strobel and R. Lafer (eds.), *Die Geschichte der Antike aktuell: Methoden, Ergebnisse und Rezeption*. Klagenfurt, Ljubljana, and Wien, 187–198.

Taylor, C. (2011). 'Migration and the Demes of Attica', in C. Holleran, and A. Pudsey (eds.), *Demography and the Graeco-Roman World. New Insights and Approaches*. Cambridge, 117–134.

Taylor, R.M. (2003). *Roman Builders: A Study in Architectural Process*. Cambridge.

Temin, P. (2004). 'The Labor Market of the Early Roman Empire.' *Journal of Interdisciplinary History* 34: 513–538.

Temin, P. (2006). 'The Economy of the Early Roman Empire', *The Journal of Economic Perspectives* 20: 133–151.

Temin, P. (2013). *The Roman Market Economy*. Princeton.

Tenenti, A. (1968). 'Les marchands et la culture à Florence (1375–1434)', *Annales. Économies. Sociétés. Civilisations* 23: 1319–1329.

Terpstra, T.T. (2013). *Trading Communities in the Roman World: A Micro-Economic and Institutional Perspective*, (Columbia Studies in the Classical Tradition 37). Leiden and Boston.

Thijs, A.K.L. (2006). 'Religion and Social Structure: Religious Rituals in Pre-Industrial Trade Associations in the Low Countries', in M. Prak, C. Lis, J. Lucassen, and H. Soly (eds.), *Craft Guilds in the Early Modern Low Countries: Work, Power, and Representation*. Aldershot, 157–173.

Thomas, Y. (2002). "Le corps de l'esclave et son travail à Rome. Analyse d'une dissociation juridique", in P. Moreau (ed.), *Corps romains*. Grenoble, 225–250.

Thomas, Y. (2004). 'Le droit comme matrice des catégories économiques à Rome', in J. Andreau, J. France, and S. Pittia (eds.). *Mentalités et choix économiques des Romains* (Scripta antiqua 7). Bordeaux, 201–225.

Thonemann, P. (2012). 'Monumentae Asiae Minoris Antiqua XI', http://mama.csad.ox.ac.uk/monuments/MAMA-XI-254.html (accessed 26-7-2013).

Thüry, G.E. (2001). *Müll und Marmorsäulen. Siedlungshygiene in der römischen Antike.* Mainz.

Tilly, C. and Tilly, C. (1998). *Work under Capitalism*. Boulder, CO.

Todeschini, G. (2004). *Ricchezza francescana. Dalla povertà volontaria alla società di mercato*. Bologna.

Todeschini, G. (2008). 'Theological Roots of the Medieval/Modern Merchants' Self-Representation', in M.C. Jacob and C. Secretan (eds.), *The Self-Perception of Early Modern Capitalists*. Basingstoke, 17–46.

Todisco, E. (2007). 'Aggregazioni e dinamiche di popolamento nel mondo romano', in M.M. Olivé, G. Baratta, and A. Guzmán Almagro (eds.), *XII Congressus internationalis epigraphiae graecae et latinae*. Barcelona, 1447–1454.

Toner, J.P. (1995). *Leisure and Ancient Rome*. Cambridge.

Torelli, M. (1980). 'Innovazioni nelle tecniche eddilizie romane tra il I sec. a.C. e il I sec. d.C.' in *Tecnologia economia e società nel mondo romano*. Como, 139–161.

Tran, N. (2006). *Les membres des associations romaines: le rang social des collegiati en Italie et en Gaules sous le haut-empire* (Collection de l'École française de Rome 367). Rome.

Tran, N. (2007). 'Le « procès des foulons »: l'occupation litigieuse d'un espace vicinal par des artisans romains', *Mélanges de l'École française de Rome. Antiquité* 119: 597–611.

Tran, N. (2009) '*Tabernae Publicae*: boutiques et ateliers dans le patrimoine des cités de l'occident romain', *Cahiers du Centre Glotz* 20: 327–350.

Tran, N. (2011a). 'Les collèges professionnels romains: « clubs » ou « corporations » ? L'exemple de la vallée du Rhône et de CIL XII 1797 (Tournon-sur-Rhône. Ardèche)', *Ancient Society* 41: 197–219.

Tran, N. (2011b). 'Les gens de métier romains: savoirs professionnels et supériorités plébéiennes', in N. Monteix and N. Tran (eds.), *Les savoirs professionnels des gens de métier. Études sur le monde du travail dans les sociétés urbaines de l'empire romain*. Naples, 119–133.

Tran, N. (2013). Dominus tabernae*: le statut de travail des artisans et des commerçants de l'Occident romain (Ier siècle av. J.-C.-IIIe siècle ap. J.-C.)*. Rome.

Tran, N. and Monteix, N. (eds.) (2011). *Les savoirs professionnels des hommes de métier romains*. Naples.

Trapp, M.B. (1997). *Maximus of Tyre: The Philosophical Orations*. Oxford.

Treggiari, S. (1975a). 'Roman Social History: Recent Interpretations', *Social History / Histoire Sociale* 8: 149–164.

Treggiari, S. (1975b). 'Jobs in the Household of Livia', *Papers of the British School at Rome* 43: 48–77.

Treggiari, S. (1976). 'Jobs for Women', *American Journal of Ancient History* 1: 76–104.

Treggiari, S. (1980). 'Urban Labour in Rome: *Mercennarii* and *Tabernarii*', in P.D.A. Garnsey (ed.), *Non-Slave Labour in the Greco-Roman World*. Cambridge, 48–61.

Tsigarida, I. (2015). 'Salt in Asia Minor. An Outline of Roman Authority Interest in the Resource', in P. Erdkamp, K. Verboven, and A. Zuiderhoek (eds.), *Ownership and Exploitation of Land and Natural Resources in the Roman World* (Oxford Roman Economy Series). Oxford, 277–288.

Turcan, R. (1999). *Messages d'outre-tombe. L'iconographie des sarcophages romains*. Paris.

Vagi, D.L. (1999). *Coinage and History of the Roman Empire, c. 82 BC–AD 480. Volume 2, Coinage*. Chicago and London.

Valenzuela, A, Theodore, N., Meléndez, E., and Gonzalez, A.L. (2006). 'On the Corner: Day Labour in the United States', http://www.sscnet.ucla.edu/issr/csup/uploaded_files/Natl_DayLabor-On_the_Corner1.pdf (accessed 1 June 2016).

Valenzuela, A. (2003). 'Day Labour work', *Annual Review of Sociology* 29: 307–333.

Van Bavel, B.J.P. (2007). 'The Transition in the Low Countries: Wage Labour as an Indicator of the Rise of Capitalism in the Countryside, 1300–1700', *Past and Present* 195 Suppl. 2: 286–303.

Van Bavel, B.J.P. (2014). 'New Perspectives on Factor Markets and Ancient Middle Eastern Economies: A Survey', *Journal of the Economic and Social History of the Orient* 57: 145–172.

Van Bavel, B.J.P., Campopiano, M., and Dijkman, J. (2014). 'Factor Markets in Early Islamic Iraq, c. 600–1100 AD', *Journal of the Economic and Social History of the Orient* 57: 262–289.

Van Bavel, B.J.P., De Moor, T., and van Zanden, J.L. (2009). 'Introduction: Factor Markets in Global Economic History', *Continuity and Change* 24: 9–21.

Van den Hoven, B. (1996). *Work in Ancient and Medieval Thought: Ancient Philosophers, Medieval Monks and Theologians and Their Concept of Work, Occupations and Technology*. Leiden.

Van der Leeuw, S. (1977). 'Towards a Study of the Economics of Pottery Making', in B.L. van Beek, R.W. Brandt, and W. Groenman-van Waateringe (eds.), *Ex Horreo*. Amsterdam, 68–76.

Van der Veen, M. (1998). 'A Life of Luxury in the Desert? The Food and Fodder Supply to Mons Claudianus', *Journal of Roman Archaeology* 11: 101–116.

Van der Velden, H. (1998). 'Defrocking St Eloy: Petrus Christus's *Vocational Portrait of a Goldsmith*', *Simiolus* 26: 243–276.

Van Haeperen, F. (2010). 'Quelques réflexions sur les dendrophores de Pouzzoles, à partir de CIL X 3699', *Zeitschrift für Papyrologie und Epigraphik* 172: 259–266.

Van Haeperen, F. (2012). 'Collèges de dendrophores et autorités locales et romaines', in M. Dondin-Payre and N. Tran (eds.), Collegia. *Le phénomène associatif dans l'Occident romain* (Scripta Antiqua). Bordeaux.

van Heesch, J. (2006). 'Transport of Coins in the Later Roman Empire', *Revue Belge de Numismatique* 152: 51–61.

van Heesch, J. (2007). 'Some Aspects of Wage Payments and Coinage in Ancient Rome, First to Third Centuries CE', in J. Lucassen (ed.), *Wages and Currency: Global Comparisons from Antiquity to the Twentieth Century*. Bern, 77–96.

Van Minnen, P. (1987). 'Urban Craftsmen in Roman Egypt', *Münstersche Beiträge zur antiken Handelsgeschichte* 6: 31–88.

van Nijf, O.M. (1997). *The Civic World of Professional Associations in the Roman East* (Dutch Monographs on Ancient History and Archaeology 17). Amsterdam.

van Nijf, O.M. (2002). '*Collegia* and Civic Guards. Two Chapters in the History of Sociability', in W. Jongman and M. Kleijwegt (eds.), *After the Past: Essays in Ancient History in Honour of H.W. Pleket*. Leiden and Boston, 305–340.

Van Zanden, J.L. (2009). 'The Skill Premium and the "Great Divergence"'. *European Review of Economic History* 13.1: 121–153.

Vandenbroeck, P. (1987). *Over wilden en narren, boeren en bedelaars. Beeld van de andere, vertoog over het zelf*. Antwerp.

Vanhaegendoren, K. (2007). 'Travail et loisir en Grèce ancienne', *Ancient Society* 37: 1–35.

Vauchez, A. (1987). *Les laïcs au Moyen Âge. Pratiques et expériences religieuses*. Paris.

Venticinque, P.F. (2009). *Common Causes: Guilds, Craftsmen and Merchants in the Economy and Society of Roman and Late Roman Egypt*, Dissertation DPhil, University of Chicago.

Venticinque, P.F. (2010). 'Family Affairs: Guild Regulations and Family Relationships in Roman Egypt', *Greek, Roman, and Byzantine Studies* 50: 273–94.

Venticinque, P.F. (2013). 'Matters of Trust: Associations and Social Capital in Roman Egypt'. *CHS Research Bulletin* 1.2, http://nrs.harvard.edu/urn-3: hlnc.essay: VenticinqueP.Matters_of_Trust_Associations_and_Social_Capital.2013 (accessed 1 October 2013).

Verboven, K. (2002). *The Economy of Friends. Economic Aspects of Amicitia and Patronage in the Late Republic*. Brussels.

Verboven, K. (2004). 'Mentalité et commerce: le cas des « *negotiatores* » et de ceux « *qui negotia habent* »', in J. Andreau, J. France, and S. Pittia (eds.), *Mentalités et choix économiques des Romains* (Scripta Antiqua 7). Bordeaux, 179–197.

Verboven, K. (2007a). 'Ce que negotiari et ses dérivés veulent dire', in J. Andreau and V. Chankowski (eds.), *Vocabulaire et expression de l'économie dans le monde antique* (Études 19). Bordeaux, 89–118.

Verboven, K. (2007b). 'The Associative Order: Status and Ethos Among Roman Businessmen in Late Republic and Early Empire', *Athenaeum* 95: 861–893.

Verboven, K. (2007c). 'Good for business. The Roman Army and the Emergence of a "Business Class" in the Northwestern Provinces of the Roman Empire', in L. de Blois and E. Lo Cascio (eds.), *The Impact of the Roman Army (200 BC–AD 476): Economic, Social,*

Political, Religious and Cultural Aspects (*Proceeding of the 6th workshop of the network Impact of empire. Capri 2005*), (Impact of Empire 6). Leiden and Boston, 295–313.

Verboven, K. (2009). 'Magistrates, Patrons and Benefactors of Voluntary Associations: Status Building and Romanisation in the Spanish, Gallic and German Provinces of the Roman Empire', in I.B. Antela-Bernardez and A. Ñaco del Hoyo (eds.), *Transforming Historical Landscapes in the Ancient Empires* (*Proceedings of the First Workshop Area of Research in Studies from Antiquity, Barcelona 2007*) (British Archaeological Reports, International Series 1986). Oxford, 159–167.

Verboven, K. (2011a). 'Resident Aliens and Translocal Merchant Organizations', in O. Hekster and T. Kaizer (eds.), *Frontiers in the Roman World* (9th Workshop of the International Network Impact of Empire). Leiden and Boston, 335–348.

Verboven, K. (2011b). 'Professional *Collegia*: Guilds or Social Clubs?' *Ancient Society* 41: 187–95.

Verboven, K. (2012a). 'Les collèges et la romanisation dans les provinces occidentales', in M. Dondin-Payre and N. Tran (eds.), Collegia*: le phénomène associatif dans l'Occident romain*. Bordeaux, 13–46.

Verboven, K. (2012b). 'The Freedman Economy of Roman Italy', in S. Bell and T.R. Ramsby (eds.), *Free at last! The Impact of Freed Slaves on the Roman Empire*. London, 88–109.

Verboven, K. (2012c). 'Cité et réciprocité. Le rôle des croyances culturelles dans l'économie romaine', *Annales. Histoire, Sciences Sociales* 67: 913–942.

Verboven, K. (2014). 'Attitudes to Work and Workers in Classical Greece and Rome', *Tijdschrift voor Sociale en Economische Geschiedenis* 11: 67–87.

Verboven, K., Vandorpe, K., and Chankowski-Sable, V. (eds.), (2008). *'Pistoi dia tèn technèn'. Bankers, Loans and Archives in the Ancient World. Studies in honour of Raymond Bogaert* (Studia Hellenistica 44). Leuven.

Vernant, J.-P. (1956). 'Aspects psychologiques du travail dans la Grèce ancienne', *La pensée* 66: 80–84.

Vernant, J.-P. (1971). *Mythe et pensée chez les Grecs; études de psychologie historique*. Paris.

Verzameling (1856). *Verzameling der graf- en gedenkschriften van de provincie Antwerpen*, vol. 1: *Cathedrale Kerk*. Antwerp.

Veyne, P. (1976). *Le pain et le cirque. Sociologie historique d'un pluralisme politique*. Paris.

Veyne, P. (2000). 'La "plèbe moyenne" sous le Haut-Empire romain', *Annales. Histoire, Sciences Sociales* 55: 1187–1194.

Vignes, M. (1928). *Les doctrines économiques et morales de Saint Bernard sur la richesse et le travail*. Paris.

Virlouvet, C. (2004). 'Les naviculaires d'Arles: à propos de l'inscription provenant de Beyrouth', *Mélanges de l'École française de Rome. Antiquité* 116: 327–370.

Vivenza, G. (2013). 'Roman Economic Thought', in W. Scheidel (ed.), *The Cambridge Companion to the Roman Economy*. Cambridge, 25–44.

Volpe, R. (2002). 'Un antico giornale di cantiere delle terme di Traiano', *Mitteilungen des Deutschen Archaeologischen Instituts, Römische Abteilung* 109: 377–394.

Volpe, R. and Rossi, F.M. (2012). 'Nuovi dati sull'esedra sud-ovest delle Terme di Traiano sul Colle Oppio: percorsi, iscrizioni dipinte e tempi di costruzione', in S. Camporeale, H. Dessales, and A. Pizzo (eds.), *Arqueología de la construccíon III. Los procesos constructivos en el mundo romano: la economía de las obras*. Madrid, 69–81.

von Petrikovits, H. (1981). 'Die Spezialisierung des römischen Handwerks', in H. Jannkuhn (ed.), *Das Handwerk in vor- und frühgeschichtlicher Zeit*. Vol. I. Göttingen, 63–123.

von Reden, S. (2010). *Money in Classical Antiquity*. Cambridge.

Wall, R. (1986). 'Work, Welfare and the Family: an Illustration of the Adaptive Family Economy', in L. Bonfield, R.M. Smith, and K. Wrightson (eds.), *The World We Have Gained. Histories of Population and Social Structure: Essays presented to Peter Laslett on his Seventieth Birthday*. Oxford, 261–294.

Wallace, S.L. (1969). *Taxation in Egypt from Augustus to Diocletian*. New York.

Wallace-Hadrill, A. (1991). 'Introduction', in A. Wallace-Hadrill and J. Rich (eds.), *City and Country in the Ancient World*. London, ix–xviii.

Wallace-Hadrill, A. (1994). *Houses and Society in Pompeii and Herculaneum*. Princeton.

Wallace-Hadrill, A. (2008). *Rome's Cultural Revolution*. Cambridge.

Wallis, P. (2008). 'Apprenticeship and Training in Premodern England', *Journal of Economic History* 68: 832–861.

Walser, G. (1991). 'Corpus Mercatorum Cisalpinorum et Transalpinorum', *Museum Helveticum* 48: 169–175.

Waltzing, J.-P. (1895–1900). *Étude historique sur les corporations professionnelles chez les Romains depuis les origines jusqu'a la chute de l'Empire d'Occident*, 4 Vols. Leuven.

Ward, J.P. (1997). *Metropolitan Communities: Trade Guilds, Identity, and Change in Early Modern London*. Stanford.

Ward-Perkins, B. (1984). *From Classical Antiquity to the Middle Ages: Urban Public Building in Northern and Central Italy AD 300–850*. Oxford.

Warren, M.A. (2008). 'The Nature and Logic of Bad Social Capital', in D. Castiglione, J.W. van Deth, and G. Wolleb (eds.), *The Handbook of Social Capital*. Oxford and New York, 123–149.

Wassink, A. (1991). 'Inflation and Financial Policy Under the Roman Empire to the Price Edict of 301 AD', *Historia* 40: 465–93.

Watson, A. (1999). *Aurelian and the Third Century* (Roman Imperial Biographies). London and New York.

Watson, A.A. (2000). *The Blacksmith: Ironworker and Farrier*. New York.

Watts, D.J. and Strogatz, S.H. (1998). 'Collective Dynamics of "Small-World" Networks', *Nature* 393: 440–442.

Weaver, P.R.C. (1972). *Familia Caesaris: A Social Study of the Emperor's Freedmen and Slaves*. Cambridge.

Webb, D.M. (1987). 'A Saint and His Money: Perceptions of Urban Wealth in the Lives of Italian Saints', in W.J. Shields and D. Wood (eds.), *The Church and Wealth* (Studies in Church History 24). Oxford, 61–73.

Weber, M. (1922). *Gesammelte Aufsätze zur Religionssoziologie*. Tübingen.

Weber, M. (1925). *Wirtschaft und Gesellschaft*. Tübingen.

Weiss, A. (2004). *Sklave der Stadt: Untersuchungen zur öffentlichen Sklaverei in den Städten des Römische Reiches* (Historia Einzelschriften 173). Stuttgart.

West, L.C. (1939). 'Notes on Diocletian's Edict', *Classical Philology* 34: 239–245.

Westermann, W.L. (1914). 'Apprentice Contracts and the Apprentice System in Roman Egypt'. *Classical Philology* 9: 295–315.

Westermann, W.L. (1948). 'The *Paramone* as General Service Contract'. *The Journal of Juristic Papyrology* 2: 9–50.

White, K.D. (1984). *Greek and Roman Technology*. Ithaca, N.Y.

Whitman, T.S. (1997). *The Price of Freedom: Slavery and Manumission in Baltimore and Early National Maryland*. Lexington, KY.

Whittaker, C.R. (1978). 'Land and Labour in North Africa', *Klio* 60: 331–362.

Whittaker, C.R. (1980). 'Rural Labour in Three Roman Provinces', in P.D.A. Garnsey (ed.), *Non-slave labour in the Greco-Roman world*. Cambridge, 73–99.

Wierschowski, L. (1984). *Heer und Wirtschaft: das römische Heer der Prinzipatszeit als Wirtschaftsfaktor*. Bonn.

Wierschowski, L. (2001) *Fremde in Gallien "gallier" in Der Fremde: Die Epigraphisch Bezeugte Mobilität in, von und nach Gallien vom 1. bis 3. Jh. n. Chr.*, (Historia. Einzelschriften 159). Stuttgart.

Williams, J.W. (1993). *Bread, Wine, and Money: The Windows of the Trades at Chartres Cathedral*. Chicago and London.

Wilson, A.I. (2002a). 'Machines, Power, and the Ancient Economy', *The Journal of Roman Studies* 92: 1–32.

Wilson, A.I. (2002b). 'Urban Production in the Roman World. The View from North Africa', *Papers of the British School at Rome* 70: 231–274.

Wilson, A.I. (2006). 'The Economic Impact of Technological Advances in the Roman Construction Industry', in E. Lo Cascio (ed.), *Innovazione tecnica e progresso economico nel mondo romano*. Bari, 224–236.

Wilson, A.I. (2008). 'Large-Scale Manufacturing, Standardization, and Trade', in J.P. Oleson (ed.), *The Oxford Handbook of Engineering and Technology in the Classical World*. Oxford, 393–417.

Wilson, A.I. (2011). 'City Size and Urbanization in the Roman Empire', in A.K. Bowman and A.I. Wilson (eds.), *Settlement, Urbanization, and Population* (Oxford Studies on the Roman Economy). Oxford, 161–195.

Wilson, A.I. (2012). 'Raw Materials and Energy', in W. Scheidel (ed.), *The Cambridge Companion to the Roman Economy*. Cambridge, 133–155.

Wilson, J.C. (1999). 'Self-Representation and the Evolution of the Northern European Occupational Portrait: The Metropolitan Museum's *Man Weighing Gold*, ca. 1515', *Dutch Crossing: A Journal of Low Countries Studies* 23: 29–55.

Winter, J. (1993). *London's Teeming Streets 1830–1914*. London and New York.

Wipszycka, E. (1965). *L'industrie textile dans l'Egypte romaine*. Warsaw.

Witschel, C. (1999). *Krise—Rezession—Stagnation? Der Westen des römischen Reiches im 3. Jahrhundert n. Chr.* Frankfurt.

Wood, P. (1974). '"It Was a Negro Taught Them": a New Look at African Labor in Early South Carolina', *Journal of Asian and African Studies* 9: 160–179.

Woolf, G. (2006). 'Writing Poverty in Rome', in E.M. Atkins and R. Osborne (eds.), *Poverty in the Roman World*. Cambridge, 83–99.

Woytek, B. (2013). '*Signatores* in der römischen Münzstätte: CIL VI 44 und die numismatische Evidenz,' *Chiron* 43: 243–279.

Wright, G. (2006). *Slavery and American Economic Development*. Baton Rouge.

Wu, N. (2000). 'Hugues Libergier and His Instruments', *Nexus Network Journal* 2: 93–102.

Yakobson, A. (1999). *Elections and Electioneering in Rome: a Study in the Political System of the Late Republic* (Historia Einzelschriften 128). Stuttgart.

Yakubovich, V. (2005). 'Weak Ties, Information, and Influence: How Workers Find Jobs in a Local Russian Labor Market', *American Sociological Review* 70: 408–421.

Young, A. (1999). 'Representations of Cloth Vendors and the Cloth Trade in Funerary Reliefs in Roman Gaul and Italy', in D. Cardon and M. Feugère (eds.), *Archéologie des textiles, des origines au Ve siècle. Actes du Colloque de Lattes, octobre 1999*. Montagnac, 215–233.

Zambon, A. (1935). 'Διδασκαλικαί', *Aegyptus* 15: 3–66.

Zänker, P. (1994). 'Veränderungen im öffentlichen Raum der italischen Städte der Kaiserzeit', in *L'Italie d'Auguste à Dioclétien (Actes du colloque international de Rome (25–28 mars 1992))* (Collection de l'École française de Rome 198). Rome, 259–284.

Zenger, T.R., Felin, T. and Bigelow, L. (2011). 'Theories of the Firm-Market Boundary'. *The Academy of Management Annals* 5: 89–133.

Zevi, F. (2008). 'I collegi di Ostia e le lora sedi associative tra Antonini e Severi', in C. Berrendonner, M. Cebeillac Gervasoni, and L. Lamoine (eds.), *Le quotidien municipal dans l'occident Romain*. Clermont Ferrand, 477–506.

Ziebarth, E. (1896). *Das griechische Vereinswesen*. Leipzig.

Zimmer, G. (1982). *Römische Berufsdarstellungen* (Archäologische Forschungen 12). Berlin.

Zimmer, G. (1985). 'Römische Handwerker', in *Aufstieg und Niedergang der römischen Welt. Principat*, 2,12,3. Berlin, 205–228.

Zimmermann, C. (2002). *Handwerkervereine im griechischen Osten des Imperium Romanum*. Mainz.

Zink, S. (2008). 'Reconstructing the Palatine Temple of Apollo: a Case Study in Early Augustan Temple Design', *Journal of Roman Archaeology* 21: 47–63.

Zuiderhoek, A. (2013). 'Workers of the Ancient World: Analyzing Labour in Classical Antiquity', *Workers of the World: International Journal on Strikes and Social Conflicts* 1.3: 32–48. http: //digitalcommons.ilr.cornell.edu/wotw/3/ (accessed 10 May 2016).

Index of Subjects

Index of Places and Geographical Names

As a rule, cities and villages have been cited with their Greek or Roman names throughout the chapters. However, in the case of well known places or when the ancient name is hardly ever in use, some contributors have chosen to refer to the modern name. In these cases, we added the modern name with a reference to its ancient name.

Index of Personal Names

Latin personal names are listed according to the *nomen gentilicium*. However, kings, emperors, well known historical figures and authors appear the way they are mostly known with a larger audience. Names of authors are not listed when mentioned only as a reference to their work. Deities and mythological figures are listed in the subject index.

www.ingramcontent.com/pod-product-compliance
Lightning Source LLC
LaVergne TN
LVHW010624300926
849162LV00001B/52
* 9 7 8 9 0 0 4 3 3 1 6 5 5 *